VISUAL QUICKSTART GUIDE

MICROSOFT OFFICE

FRONTPAGE 2003

FOR WINDOWS

Nolan Hester

 Peachpit Press

Visual QuickStart Guide
Microsoft Office FrontPage 2003 for Windows
Nolan Hester

Peachpit Press
1249 Eighth Street
Berkeley, CA 94710
(800) 283-9444
(510) 524-2178
(510) 524-2221 (fax)

Find us on the World Wide Web at: www.peachpit.com
To report errors, please send a note to errata@peachpit.com

Peachpit Press is a division of Pearson Education

Editor: Nancy Davis
Production Coordinator: David Van Ness
Composition: David Van Ness
Proofreaders: Ted Waitt, Jason Silvis
Cover Design: The Visual Group
Cover Production: George Mattingly / GMD
Indexer: Julie Bess

ISBN: 0-321-19449-7

0 9 8 7 6 5 4 3 2 1

Printed and bound in the United States of America

Por Mary—viente años

Special thanks to:

Nancy Davis, my simply fabulous editor for saving me from my own mistakes time after time; David Van Ness, for being the epitome of calm professionalism and the hardest working compositor in broadband; Julie Bess, for stepping into the breach and producing an index in record time; and Nancy Aldrich-Ruenzel for making this life of at-home work possible. Home wouldn't be home, of course, without Laika, whose herding skills keep me and the yard squirrels in line.

TABLE OF CONTENTS

PART 1:	GETTING STARTED	1

Chapter 1:	**Using FrontPage 2003**	**3**

What's New 4
Important Changes 6
Using This Book 8
Updates and Feedback 10
Web Planning Tips 11
    Keep it clean 11
    Keep it lean 12
    Make it easy 13

Chapter 2:	**FrontPage Basics**	**15**

The FrontPage Main Window 17
Starting and Quitting FrontPage 18
    To launch FrontPage 18
    To quit FrontPage 18
Using Design, Split, Code, and Preview Views ... 19
    Switching views 20
    To switch views 21
    Using the task pane 22
    To use the task pane 22
    To turn the task pane off or on 23
    To move the task pane to the desktop 23
    To close the task pane 23
Using the Toolbars 24
    To turn on/off toolbars 27
    To turn on/off the status bar 27
    Rearranging the toolbars 27
    To move toolbars to the desktop 27
    To dock toolbars in the main window 28
    To resize freestanding toolbars 28
    Customizing the toolbars 29
    To add or remove toolbar buttons 29
    To customize an existing toolbar 30

To create a new toolbar 31
To delete a toolbar 32
The Menus 33
The File menu 33
The Edit menu 33
The View menu 33
The Insert menu 34
The Format menu 34
The Tools menu 34
The Table menu 35
The Data menu 35
The Frames menu 35
The Window menu 35
The Help menu 35
To use FrontPage's Help 36
Creating, Opening, Saving, and Closing
   Web Pages 37
To create a new blank Web page 37
To create a new template-based Web page ...38
To open an existing Web page 39
To save a Web page 40
To save a Web page under another name 41
To close a Web page 41
Printing Web Pages 42
To print a Web page 42
Creating, Opening, and Closing Web Sites 43
To create a new blank Web site 43
To create a template-based Web site 45
To open an existing Web site 46
To close a Web site 46
To delete a Web site 47

Chapter 3:   Creating a Web Site   49

To create pages within a Web site structure .. 50
To give a new page a title 52
To rename a Web page 53
Rearranging a Web Site's Structure 54
To rearrange a single page 54
To rearrange groups of pages 56
Adding or Excluding Pages in the
   Site Structure 57
To add an existing page to a Web
   site structure 57
To remove an existing page from a
   Web site structure 58

Controlling Your View of the Site Structure 59
  To collapse the site structure 59
  To expand the site structure 59
  To view only a subtree 60
  To expand a subtree 60
  To change the site structure view 61
  To zoom in or out on the site structure 61
Using Link Bars and Shared Borders 62
  To create a navigation-based link bar 64
  Navigation-based link bar options 66
  Changing the default labels for
    navigation-based link bars 67
  To change navigation-based link bar labels ... 67
  To exclude a single page from a
    navigation-based link bar 68
  Creating back/next and custom link bars 69
  To create a back/next link bar 69
  To create a custom link bar 73
  Changing link bar properties 75
  To edit a back/next or custom link bar 75
  To add shared borders 77
  To turn off shared borders for a single page .. 78
Using Templates and Themes 79
  To create a page from a template 80
  To create a Web site from a template 81
  To create a dynamic Web site template page . 83
  To add an editable region to a dynamic
    template 84
  To remove an editable region from a
    dynamic template 86
  To attach a dynamic template to other pages 87
  To detach pages from a dynamic template ... 88
  To apply a theme to a page or Web site 89
  To modify a theme 91
  Theme options 93

PART 2:   CREATING BASIC WEB PAGES   95

Chapter 4:   Creating and Formatting Text   97
  Entering and Editing Text 98
  To enter text on a Web page 98
  To move the text cursor 99
  To select text 100
  To delete text 100

To move text 101
To undo an action 102
To redo an action 102
To add a line break to text 103
To add a paragraph 104
Showing line break and paragraph marks . . . 104
To show/hide line break and
    paragraph marks 104
Finding and Replacing Text and Code 105
To find text on a single page 105
To find text across a Web site 106
To search the site's HTML code 108
To replace text or HTML on a single page . . . 109
To replace text or HTML across a Web site . 111
Checking Spelling 113
To check spelling on a single page 113
To check spelling across a Web site 114
To check spelling as you type 116
To change the dictionary language 116
Formatting Text 117
To change the font face 118
To change the font size 119
To change the font style 120
To change the font color . . . . . . : 121
To change text alignment 122
Font options 123
To change character spacing 124
To change character positioning 124
To remove text formatting 125
Using Symbols and Special Characters 126
To add a symbol or special character 126

Chapter 5:   **Formatting Paragraphs, Lists,
             and Headings   127**
Using Paragraphs 128
To align a paragraph 128
Indenting paragraphs 129
To indent a paragraph 129
To customize paragraph indents 130
Paragraph styling 131
To modify the Normal paragraph style 131
To apply the Formatted paragraph style 132
Using Lists 133
Creating unordered lists 133
To create a bulleted list 133

Creating definition lists 134
To create a definition list 134
Creating ordered lists 135
To create a numbered list 135
Customizing lists 136
To customize lists 136
List options 137
Nested lists 139
To create a nested list 139
Using Headings 141
To add headings 141
To change a heading size 142

Chapter 6: Adding Hyperlinks 143

Absolute and Relative Links 144
To link to an external Web page 145
Insert Hyperlink options 146
To link to a page in your Web site 148
To create an email link 149
Linking to pages not yet created 150
To create a new page and link to it 150
Changing links 151
To edit a link 151
To delete a link 152
To update links 152
Using Bookmarks 153
To create a bookmark 153
To link to a bookmark in the current page .. 154
To link to a bookmark in another page 155
To find bookmarks 156
To clear a bookmark 157
Setting Link Colors 158
To change a link's color 158
Creating Image Links 160
To link an entire image to a file 160
To create an image hotspot 161
Finding image hotspots 163
To find image hotspots 163
To delete a hotspot 163
To change a hotspot link 163
Using Interactive Buttons 164
To add an interactive button 164
To edit an interactive button 166

Using the Hyperlinks View 167
   To switch to hyperlinks view 167
   To inspect links on another page 167

Chapter 7: **Adding and Editing Images**   **169**

Web Image Formats 170
   Let's get small 170
Adding Images 172
   To insert an image 172
   Clip Art options 174
   Converting image formats 176
   To convert image formats 176
   Creating alternates for images 178
   To create alternate text 178
   To create low-resolution alternate images .. 180
   Aligning images 182
   To align images 182
   To add an image border 183
   To add space around an image 183
   Adding horizontal lines 184
   To insert a horizontal line 184
   To edit a horizontal line 184
   Horizontal line options 185
Editing Images 186
   To undo image editing 186
   Resizing images 187
   To resize images 187
   Resampling images 188
   To resample an image 188
   To add text to images 189
   To wash out an image 190
   Creating auto thumbnails and
      photo galleries 191
   To create auto thumbnail images 191
   To set auto thumbnail properties 192
   To create a thumbnail photo gallery 193
   To change a photo gallery 196
   To rotate or flip images 197
   To change image contrast 198
   To change image brightness 198
   To crop images 199
   To make a GIF color transparent 199
   To remove image color 200
   To add a bevel to an image 200

Positioning Images Absolutely 201
   To position images absolutely 202
   To move absolutely positioned images
      forward and backward 204

Chapter 8:   **Adding and Editing Drawings**   **207**
   To turn on the Drawing toolbar 209
   To draw a simple shape 209
   To add an AutoShape 210
   To draw a curved line 211
   To draw a freeform shape 212
   Using the scribble tool 213
   To draw a scribble shape 213
   Using WordArt 216
   To turn on the WordArt toolbar 216
   To add WordArt 216
   To change WordArt 217
Changing Drawn Objects 219
   To resize a drawn object 219
   To move a drawn object 220
   To rotate a drawn object 220
   To flip a drawn object 220
   To change other drawn object properties ... 221
Aligning, Arranging, and Grouping
   Drawn Objects 223
   To align or distribute drawn objects 223
   To arrange drawn objects 224
   To group drawn objects 225
Using the Drawing Canvas 226
   To turn on the Drawing Canvas toolbar 226
   To create a drawing canvas 227
   To select a drawing canvas 228
   To move a drawing canvas 228
   Resizing a drawing canvas 229
   To resize a drawing canvas by hand 229
   To expand a drawing canvas with the
      toolbar 229
   To fit a drawing canvas to its contents 230
   Rescaling a drawing canvas 231
   To preserve proportion while scaling a
      drawing canvas 231
   To change proportion while scaling
      a drawing canvas 232
   Formatting a drawing canvas 233
   To change the drawing canvas format 233

PART 3:   CREATING ADVANCED PAGES   235

Chapter 9:   Adding Multimedia and Web Components   237

Adding Videos or Animations 238
To insert a video or animation 238
To set loops for videos/animations 241
Adding Sounds 243
To add a page background sound 243
Adding Web Components 244
Turning on or off Web components 245
To turn on/off Web components 245
Adding a marquee of scrolling text 246
To add a marquee 246
Marquee options 247
To change a marquee 248
To delete a marquee 248
Adding a Web site table of contents 249
To add a table of contents 249
Changing banner ads 251
To change a banner ad 251
To delete a banner ad 252
Adding page hit counters 253
To add a page hit counter 253
To change a hit counter 254
To delete a hit counter 254
Adding a Top Ten list 255
To create a Top Ten list 255

Chapter 10:   Creating and Formatting Tables   257

Creating Tables 258
To draw a table 258
To insert a table 259
To add table text 260
To add table images 260
To add table captions 261
Adding Excel spreadsheets 262
To add static Excel data 262
To add dynamic Excel data 263
Selecting Table Elements 264
To select a cell 264
To select multiple cells 264
To select a row 265

To select a column 265
To select an entire table 265
Changing Table Structure 266
To add cells 266
To add rows 267
To add columns 268
To delete any part of a table 269
Splitting and merging cells 270
To split cells 270
To merge cells 271
Evening up rows and columns 272
To make rows the same height 272
To make columns the same width 273
Formatting Tables and Cells 274
To format tables 274
To format table borders 275
To format cells 276
Making cells into headers 277
To make cells into headers 277
To keep cell text on one line 277
To color cells 278
To realign cell contents 279
Using Tables in Page Layouts 280
To add a layout table 280
To delete a cell or layout table 282
To add a layout cell to a layout table 284
To resize a layout cell or table by
    click-dragging 285
To precisely resize a layout cell or table 286
To resize a row or column using
    autostretch 287
To format layout cells 288
To convert an existing table to a
    layout table 290

Chapter 11:   **Creating Layers and Frames**   **291**

Creating Layers 292
To create a layer 292
To move a layer 294
To resize a layer 295
To add and select layers 296
To set layer stack order 298
To create nested layers 300
To set layer visibility 302

TABLE OF CONTENTS

Creating Frames 303
    To create a frames page 304
    To show a frame in a new window 307
    Setting target frames 308
    To set a link's target frame 308
    To change the target frame default 310
    Target Frame options 311
    Setting a frames page as the home page 312
    To make a frames page your home page 312
Formatting Frames 313
    To select a frame 313
    To select a frames page 313
    To delete a frame 313
    To resize a frame 314
    Splitting frames 315
    To split a frame 315
    To change frames 316
    To change spacing or borders in
        frames pages 316
    Frame Properties options 317

Chapter 12: Creating and Processing Forms 319
Creating Forms 320
    To create a form from a template 320
    To create a form from scratch 321
    To delete a field 321
    To change a field's properties 321
Adding Form Fields 322
    To add a text box 322
    Adding a text area 324
    To add a text area 324
    Text Box Validation options 326
    Adding check boxes and option buttons 327
    To add a check box 327
    To add option buttons 329
    To add a drop-down box 331
    Drop-Down Box options 333
    Using push buttons 335
    To add a push button 335
Creating Confirmation Pages 336
    To create a confirmation page 336
Saving Form Results 338
    To save form results to a file 338
    Form options 340
    To save form results as email 341
    To save form results to a database 343

Chapter 13: Adding Database Connections   **345**

Importing Databases 346
  To import databases into your Web site 346
Creating Database Connections 348
  To create a database connection 348
  To create a new database connection 353
  New Database Connection options 355
  Filtering and sorting options 356
  To filter or sort the database results 356
  Verifying a database connection 358
  To verify a database connection 358
  Changing a database connection 359
  To change a database connection 359
  To remove a database connection 360
  Changing column values 361
  To change column values in a database 361

**Chapter 14: Building Style Sheets and
Dynamic Effects**   **363**

Using Cascading Style Sheets 365
  To activate Cascading Style Sheets 366
Creating and Editing Embedded Style Sheets . . 367
  To create and apply an embedded
    style sheet 367
  To edit an embedded style sheet 370
Building External Style Sheets 372
  To create an external style sheet 372
  To build an external style sheet 374
  To edit an external style sheet 376
Specifying Multiple Fonts in External
  Style Sheets 377
  To specify multiple fonts 378
Linking to External Style Sheets 379
  To link to external style sheets 379
  To remove links to external style sheets 381
Deleting Styles 382
  To delete custom styles 382
Using Dynamic HTML Effects 383
  To apply dynamic effects 383
  To remove a dynamic effect 384
Using Page Transitions 385
  To add page transitions 385
  To remove page transitions 385
Using Behaviors 386
  To add behaviors to layers 386

TABLE OF CONTENTS

**PART 4:   MANAGING AND PUBLISHING
WEB SITES   391**

Chapter 15:   Managing Web Site Workflow   393
Creating Tasks 394
 To link files to a task 395
 To create a task not linked to a file 397
Organizing Files 398
 To create a categories master list 399
 To create a review status master list 400
 To categorize files 401
 To link a file to a review 402
 To simultaneously link multiple files
  to a review 403
Assigning Tasks 404
 To create a names master list 404
 To assign a task 405
 To reassign a task 406
 To assign a file 407
Editing Tasks 408
 To make multiple changes to a task 408
 To change a task's name or description 409
 To change a task's priority 410
 To sort tasks 410
Using the Checkout System 411
 To activate the checkout system 411
 To check out a file 412
 To check in a file 413
 To see a list of checked-out files 414
Completing Tasks 415
 To mark a task completed 415
 To delete a task 415
 To start a task 416

Chapter 16:   Checking and Publishing Web Sites 417
Checking Your Site 418
 To check and fix your site 418
 Marking pages to publish 420
 To check or change a page's
  publishing status 420
Adding Meta Tags for Search Engines 421
 To help search engines index your site 421
 To keep out search engines 423

Publishing to the Web 424
   To set the publishing destination
     and options 425
   To keep local files from being published 428
   To publish your site 429
   Publishing options 432

| **PART 5:** | **APPENDIX & INDEX** | **435** |

Appendix A: **Installing & Configuring FrontPage** **437**
   What you'll need before starting 437
Installing FrontPage 438
   To install the standard version of FrontPage 438
   To install a custom version of FrontPage 442
Setting Web Browser Compatibility 444
   To set browser compatibility 444
Setting Coding Preferences 446
   To set code preferences 446

Index   **447**

TABLE OF CONTENTS

PART 1

GETTING STARTED

Chapter 1: Using FrontPage 2003   3

Chapter 2: FrontPage Basics   15

Chapter 3: Creating a Web Site   49

USING
FRONTPAGE 2003

Welcome to Microsoft Office FrontPage 2003. FrontPage makes building a Web site easy by letting you skip the tedium of creating your Web pages directly in HTML (HyperText Markup Language), the Web's underlying language. Instead you use menus and commands similar to those you already know from Microsoft's other programs, such as Word, Excel, and PowerPoint.

Using FrontPage, you can quickly design your Web site's overall structure, create the necessary pages to flesh out the structure, add multimedia and interactive features to enliven those pages, and, finally, publish the whole thing on the Web by uploading the files to a Web server. Because Office recognizes HTML as easily as its own formats, FrontPage can insert many Office documents directly into your new Web pages.

Whether you're working for a one-person business or an international firm, FrontPage includes all the tools and functions you need to build Web sites to post on the Internet or on private intranets.

What's New

Compared with FrontPage 2002, which made a huge leap past the clunkiness of the previous editions, the changes in FrontPage 2003 may seem only incremental. But once you spend more time in the latest version, it becomes clear that it's significantly smoother and more powerful than FrontPage 2002. FrontPage 2003 also includes lots of small changes, which are highlighted throughout the book. Here's a partial list of the most important:

- **Dynamic templates** enable you to update a template and have those changes automatically reflected in any pages based on that template. FrontPage also lets you selectively lock or unlock portions of templates, a valuable feature on group sites where users may range from newbies to veteran coders. For more information, see *Creating a Web Site* on page 49.

- **Layers** allow you to create complex page designs with more flexibility than tables. Perhaps the best thing about layers is how easy they are to learn (**Figure 1.1**). For more information, see *Creating Layers and Frames* on page 291.

- **Layout tables and cells** are a welcome new feature that make building table-based page layouts a breeze. In previous versions of FrontPage, using tables to layout pages was painfully slow and seldom accurate. The difference becomes apparent when you start using the new tools in the task pane to create and format layout tables and cells. Layout cells, for example, make it easy to drop a cell into the middle of a layout table and have FrontPage take care of the messy business of creating the necessary cells to fill out the table. For more information, see *Using Tables in Page Layouts* on page 280.

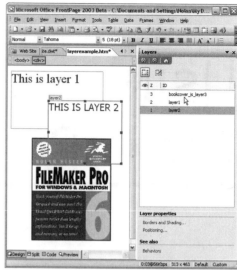

Figure 1.1 Layers let you create complex page designs with more flexibility than tables.

WHAT'S NEW

◆ **Greater XML integration and support**
means you are no longer forced to choose
between using HTML *or* XML. Instead,
you can supplement HTML with XML as
needed. FrontPage now lets you view the
XML code, format it as needed, and
ensure that the code works as intended.
For more information, see *Building Style
Sheets and Dynamic Effects* on page 363.

◆ **Support for conditional behaviors
and JavaScript-based buttons** makes
it easy to trigger interactive items, such
as cursor-driven sounds, image swaps,
popup messages, and interactive buttons.
For more information, see *Building Style
Sheets and Dynamic Effects* on page 363.

◆ **Remote Web site publishing** is now
much more intuitive with the ability to
compare your local Web site files side by
side with the files on your remote Web
site. And it's now easy to move files
between the local and remote sites, or
even synchronize them based on criteria
you select. For more information, see
Checking and Publishing Web Sites on
page 417.

Important Changes

Sometimes it's the little changes, not the flashy new features, that make the biggest difference in your daily use of a program. Here are the FrontPage changes most likely to affect your work:

- ◆ **Autostretch tables** automatically adjust to predefined widths, which makes for a lot less fussing with table layouts. For more information, see *Creating Tables* on page 258.

- ◆ **Page views** can now be split so that you can see a Web page simultaneously as it would appear in a browser and the code used to create it. What had been known as the Normal and HTML views are now called Design and Code (**Figure 1.2**). For more information, see *The FrontPage Main Window* on page 17.

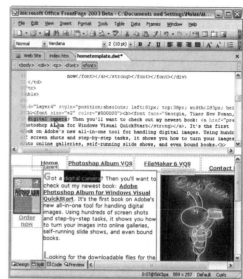

Figure 1.2 Page views can now be split so that you can see a Web page as it would appear in a browser and the code used to create it.

◆ **More graphic options** make it easier to switch between FrontPage and your favorite graphics programs. FrontPage now supports Macromedia Flash as well. You also can configure FrontPage to automatically switch from one graphics program to another based on the type of graphic selected. For more information, see *Adding and Editing Images* on page 169.

◆ **Themes** are now based on cascading style sheets (CSS) instead of HTML, which makes it simpler to apply theme changes across a Web site's pages. For more information, see *Using Templates and Themes* on page 79.

◆ **Better collaborative controls** make it easier for a group of people to work on a site through a more flexible check-in/check-out file system. For more information, see *Managing Web Site Workflow* on page 393.

IMPORTANT CHANGES

Using This Book

The key to this book, like all of Peachpit's Visual QuickStart Guides, is that word *visual*. As much as possible, I've used illustrations with succinct captions to explain how FrontPage works. Ideally, you should be able to quickly find what you need by scanning the table of contents, page tabs, illustrations, or captions. Once you find a relevant topic, the text provides the essential details and tips.

This book's written with the assumption that you're familiar with Windows' basic operation and understand the general concept of how the World Wide Web works. If you're looking for under-the-hood Web server details, this isn't your book. Instead, we take things step by step and whenever a potentially confusing step or concept arises, I'll try to steer you through any rough spots and wrong turns. As the cover says, I focus on getting you "up and running in no time."

Throughout the book, you'll find these symbols and typographic cues to speed you along in learning FrontPage:

Tips: Signified by a ✔ in the margin, tips highlight shortcuts for performing common tasks or ways you can use your new FrontPage skills to solve common problems.

Italic words: When *italicized* words appear in the book's text, you'll find the very same words on the FrontPage screen itself when you reach that step in the program. The italicized term might appear as a button or tab label, the name of a text window or an option button in a dialog box, or as one of several choices in a drop-down menu. Whatever the

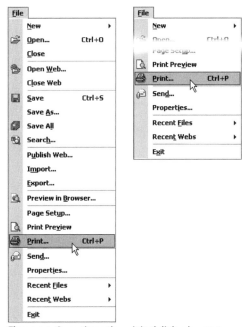

Figure 1.3 Sometimes the original dialog boxes or deep menus (left) will be faded out in the middle to save space on the page (right).

context, the italics are meant to help you quickly find the item in what can sometimes be a crowded screen. If the step includes an accompanying illustration, use it to help you find the item being discussed. Two examples: Click the *Browse* button to navigate to the file you want to use. Click the drop-down menu and select *asp* from the choices.

Code font: When a word or words appears in code font, it's used to indicate the literal text you need to type into FrontPage. Because FrontPage does its best to shield you from the tedium coding, you won't see this very much in the book. An example: After *font family:* type Verdana, Arial, Helvetica, sans serif; as the name for your connection. *Italicized code font* indicates code items where you are expected to replace the italicized word with a word related to your own files or documents. An example: Type *yourConnection* as the name for your connection.

Menu commands and keyboard shortcuts: Menu-based commands are shown as: File > New > Task. Keyboard-based shortcuts (when available) are shown in parentheses after the first step in which they can be used. For example: ([Ctrl][K]) means that to insert an image you should press the [Ctrl] and [K] keys at the same time.

Fades in figures: Sometimes a FrontPage dialog box or menu is so deep that it can be hard to fit on the page with all the other figures—and still leave it large enough to read. In those cases, I fade out the middle or end of the figure to save some space (**Figure 1.3**). Nothing critical to understanding the step is ever left out. And it sure beats running teeny, tiny figures.

Updates and Feedback

For FrontPage updates and patches, make a point of checking Microsoft's Web site from time to time: www.microsoft.com

This book also has a companion site where you'll find examples from the book, tips and tricks based on real-world tasks, and corrections for inadvertent mistakes. So drop by www.waywest.net/frontpage/ when you can.

Finally, Peachpit's editors and I have done everything possible to make this book error free and clear as glass. Please write me at frontpage@waywest.net if you spot a mistake—or have a suggestion. Readers of the previous edition offered lots of tips, which I've used throughout this new edition. With your help, the *next* edition will be even better. Like a Web site, a book's never really done.

Web Planning Tips

Despite all the hoopla about the Web being an entirely new medium, it revolves around a pretty old phenomenon: our eyeballs. Yep, we *look* at Web sites. We don't taste or smell them. And we don't test drive them. That means we depend on *visual* cues for how to use a site. By following the basic visual principles explained in the next few pages, you'll be more than halfway toward making your Web site a pleasure to use.

By the way, there are plenty of great books out there devoted solely to designing Web sites. If you want to dive deeper, here are three great jumping-off points.

The Non-Designer's Web Book: An Easy Guide to Creating, Designing, and Posting Your Own Web Site by Robin Williams and John Tollett (Peachpit Press).

Here's a pair of books that together distill lifetimes of design wisdom into timeless advice for every Web designer: *The Art and Science of Web Design* by Jeffrey Veen (New Riders); and *Web Style Guide: Basic Design Principles for Creating Web Sites* by Patrick J. Lynch and Sarah Horton (Yale University Press).

Keep it clean

Clutter kills. Sites that go a thousand directions at once leave visitors confused or, worse, irritated. Imagine if parking garages were laid out like some Web sites: We'd all still be trying to find the entrance. Make it simple, make it obvious. A rule of thumb: If you have to explain how a site works, it's not working.

Clutter comes in many guises. Everyone, for example, has encountered Web sites with what I call fake front doors. Instead of offering a home page with links to products and staff, the site's first page serves up an absolutely gorgeous graphic or layered animation. It swirls and whirls—as your hard drive churns and churns—until finally there appears the equivalent of the old "Click Here" link: "Discover the power of XYZ Widgets" or "Want to find out more?" So you click one more time and finally come to the company's *real* front door—a home page where you can start looking for the information you need.

Don't make your visitors knock twice to get in the door. And for gosh sakes, don't make them beg. If you want to orient visitors with a series of images, make them small and make them snappy to download. Most importantly, strip away every bit of clutter for the cleanest possible site.

Keep it lean

The Web's too slow. It was too slow last year; it'll still be too slow next year. Wish as we might for connections speedy enough to handle full-motion video, CD-quality sound, and Java applets galore, most folks are still using telephone modems to reach the Web. As palm-sized organizers and email-capable cell phones proliferate, more and more people will be using the Web with less rather than more bandwidth.

Even a state-of-the-art in-house intranet with fast computers and fast pipes can't entirely escape the bandwidth bogeyman. Most likely the on-the-road sales force will be tapping into that intranet via a dial-up connection for sales data or product listings. See what I mean—the Web's too slow and the speed limit will remain a problem for some years to come. Don't fight—and never ignore—such limits. Instead use them to guide you in building your site. As architect and multimedia trailblazer Charles Eames put it four decades ago: "Design largely depends on constraints."

Make it easy

Nobody has to tell you how to read a newspaper or a magazine for two reasons: You already know the "rules" and even if you didn't they're pretty obvious. Big headlines mean a story's more important than one with a small headline. Items grouped together suggest that they're related. Front page stories carry more urgency than those inside the section. Size, proximity, and placement are hallmarks of the print medium's centuries-old "interface." Because the Web's so new, there's a temptation to think that means it has no rules. But trust your eyeballs; the visual touchstones of size, proximity, and placement are fairly constant even when the medium's new.

Just as the red light is the first on a traffic signal, give visual weight to the most important item on each Web page. That, of course, means you have to decide what's most—and least—important on each page and the site overall. So before you start working on that amazing animated graphic for your home page, make sure you're clear about your site's intended message and about who will be using the site.

Just as you wouldn't put sports stories in a newspaper's food section, you shouldn't build a Web site with your tech-support advice buried in the marketing section. Obvious, you say, but lots of Web sites fail to put related items together. Save your Web visitor some work by grouping similar items.

Web Planning Tips

In planning a Web site, deciding what to put where (placement) is perhaps the hardest guideline for which to find the right balance. If a site's too "deep," visitors will have to click down layer after layer to find the information they need (**Figure 1.4**). The risk is that they'll never find what they're looking for. On the other hand, you can create a site that's too "shallow" with a home page that has so many links that it becomes a confusing mess (**Figure 1.5**).

Ideally, a visitor to your site should be able to find what they're seeking in two or three mouse clicks (**Figure 1.6**). That's easy to say, but hard to achieve. Fortunately, FrontPage's navigation view makes it easy to shuffle your pages around until you strike a happy medium where almost all the site's information can be reached in no more than four mouse clicks.

As you learn how to use FrontPage's various tools in the chapters ahead, remember: keep it clean, keep it lean, and make it easy.

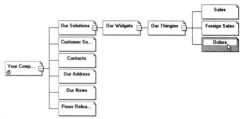

Figure 1.4 In this Web site structure, a key function—ordering products—is buried too "deep" for visitors to easily find it.

Figure 1.5 If you create a Web site structure that's too "shallow," you risk overwhelming visitors with a home page crammed with links that give equal emphasis to everything.

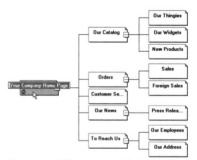

Figure 1.6 With a balanced Web site structure, the home page features only the most important links, items are grouped in logical categories, and everything can be reached in two or three clicks.

WEB PLANNING TIPS

2

FRONTPAGE BASICS

This chapter gives you a quick overview of Microsoft FrontPage's main features and the basic tasks of opening, closing, and saving Web pages and sites. Each of the items covered, whether it's FrontPage's views, menus, or toolbars, is explained in more detail later in the book. Starting here gives you an overall feel for the program's organization and functions, letting you dive in deeper when you're ready.

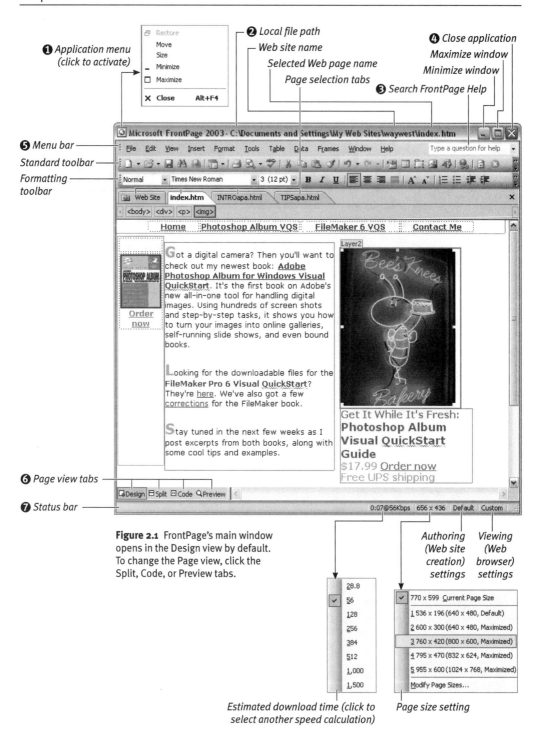

❶ *Application menu (click to activate)*

Restore
Move
Size
— Minimize
□ Maximize
✕ Close   Alt+F4

❷ *Local file path*

Web site name

Selected Web page name

Page selection tabs

❹ *Close application*

Maximize window

Minimize window

❸ *Search FrontPage Help*

❺ *Menu bar*

❺ *Standard toolbar*

Formatting toolbar

❻ *Page view tabs*

❼ *Status bar*

THE FRONTPAGE MAIN WINDOW

Figure 2.1 FrontPage's main window opens in the Design view by default. To change the Page view, click the Split, Code, or Preview tabs.

Authoring (Web site creation) settings

Viewing (Web browser) settings

28.8
✓ 56
128
256
384
512
1,000
1,500

✓ 770 x 599 Current Page Size
1 536 x 196 (640 x 480, Default)
2 600 x 300 (640 x 480, Maximized)
3 760 x 420 (800 x 600, Maximized)
4 795 x 470 (832 x 624, Maximized)
5 955 x 600 (1024 x 768, Maximized)
Modify Page Sizes...

Estimated download time (click to select another speed calculation)

Page size setting

16

The FrontPage Main Window

By default, the FrontPage 2003 main window opens in the *Design* view, (called the *Normal* view in FrontPage 2002) (**Figure 2.1**). The main window has been simplified with the removal of the Views bar that once ran down the left side (its functions remain in the View menu). For more information on the task pane, see page 22.

❶ Application menu box: Clicking the FrontPage icon triggers a pop-up box of choices for sizing the main window: Restore, Move, Size, Minimize, Maximize, and Close.

❷ Web site, selected Web page name, page selection tabs: The Web site name is set when a new site is created (see page 37). You set an individual page's name when you first create it. Click any page selection tab to select and display that Web page in the main window.

❸ Search FrontPage Help: By typing a question or keyword in the text window and pressing (Return), you'll be presented with a choice of topical answers. Click to select one and FrontPage's Help will take you directly to the answer. For more information, see *To use FrontPage's Help* on page 36.

❹ Window control buttons: Clicking the three buttons will (from left to right): collapse the window into the taskbar (minimize), expand the window to full screen (maximize), or close the application.

❺ Menu bar and toolbars: By default, FrontPage displays the Menu bar, Standard toolbar, and Formatting toolbar. To change which bars appear, choose View > Toolbars and toggle on/off your choices.

❻ Page view tabs: By default, FrontPage opens in the *Design* view, which lets you edit the open Web page. Click *Code* view to see or edit a page's coding; or click *Split* to see the Design and Code views at the same time (particularly handy for understanding how codings affect a page's appearance. Finally, you can click *Preview* to see how the page will look in a Web browser. *Preview* will not appear if you don't have Microsoft's Web browser, Internet Explorer, installed on your machine. (Internet Explorer doesn't need to be running, just installed.)

❼ Status bar: The status bar runs across the very bottom of the FrontPage window and displays four items related to the current Web page. The bar's first item shows how long it will take to download the page at various connection speeds. By default, FrontPage is set to show how many seconds the current page will take to download over a 56.6 bps modem connection. You can click to change the calculated speed at any time, but it's best to set it to reflect the average connection speed of your intended audience. If most of the viewers, for example, will be using a slow modem connection, this will help you notice when you've packed a page with fat graphics. The second item indicates the main window's current display size in pixels and lets you quickly toggle to a variety of pre-set sizes to see how your page will appear on different sized monitors. The third item indicates which settings, *Default* or *Custom*, you are using to create, or author, your Web pages. The final item, which also reads either *Default* or *Custom*, indicates which settings your Web browser is using to view pages. Double-click either label to change the settings in the dialog boxes that appear.

Starting and Quitting FrontPage

To launch FrontPage

1. Click Start in the Windows taskbar and then click the Microsoft Office FrontPage 2003 icon in the left column (top left, **Figure 2.2**), or click Start > All Programs > Microsoft Office > Microsoft Office FrontPage 2003 (bottom right, **Figure 2.2**).

2. When FrontPage launches the first time, you'll be presented with a blank Web page on the left and the Office task pane on the right, which lists common questions and tasks (**Figure 2.3**). You can either begin adding content to the blank page or use the task pane to start building a Web site.

✔ Tip

■ After you launch FrontPage the very first time, future launches will automatically open your last-viewed Web page. To turn off that default behavior, choose Tools > Options > General and uncheck *Open last Web site automatically when FrontPage starts*, which is the first checkbox in the dialog box.

To quit FrontPage

◆ After saving your work ([Ctrl][S]), choose File > Exit ([Alt][F4]) (**Figure 2.4**).

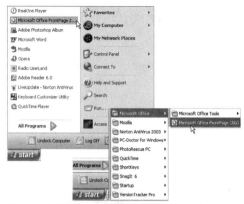

Figure 2.2 Click the Start button, and then choose Microsoft Office FrontPage 2003 (top left), or click Start > All Programs > Microsoft Office > Microsoft Office FrontPage 2003 (bottom right).

Figure 2.3 When FrontPage launches the first time, it displays a blank main window with the Office task pane on the right.

Figure 2.4 To quit FrontPage, choose File > Exit ([Alt][F4]).

Using Design, Split, Code, and Preview Views

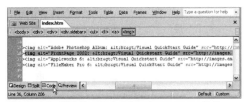

Figure 2.5 Click the *Split* tab to see the Design and Code views simultaneously.

Figure 2.6 Click the *Code* tab to inspect or edit the current page's HTML coding.

Figure 2.7 Clicking the *Preview* tab gives you a rough sense of how the current page will appear within a Web browser.

In Page view, you can choose from four different views by clicking the tabs: Design (the default), Split, Code, or Preview. The Design view lets you directly edit the current Web page—without seeing any of the underlying HTML code (**Figure 2.1**). The Split view lets you select an item in the bottom (Design) pane and see the corresponding code in the top (Code) pane, making it a great way to spot problems (and learn your codes) (**Figure 2.5**). The Code view, called the HTML view in FrontPage 2002, shows all the coding and allows you to change the code directly (**Figure 2.6**). The Preview view lets you get a better idea of how the page will look within a Web browser (**Figure 2.7**).

✔ Tips

- Instead of clicking the tabs to change your view of the page, you also can press [Ctrl][Page Up] or [Ctrl][Page Down] to cycle forward or backward from *Design* to *Split* to *Code* to *Preview*.

- In theory, the *Preview* tab should work just like the Preview in Browser command (File > Preview in Browser). In practice, some items (such as scrolling text) will appear the same with either approach. However, other effects (animation slide shows, for example) may not appear using the Preview tab but will preview correctly with the command. To be sure, always use File > Preview in Browser.

Switching views

FrontPage offers seven different ways to see and edit your Web pages or sites. This function used to be controlled by the overly busy Views bar, which ran down the left side of FrontPage 2002's main window. By default, FrontPage displays the Page view. The other choices, now accessed through the View menu, let you quickly see the folders, reports, navigation structure, hyperlinks, or tasks related to the current Web page or site. Each view displays a different set of information about your site and pages (**Figures 2.8–2.13**).

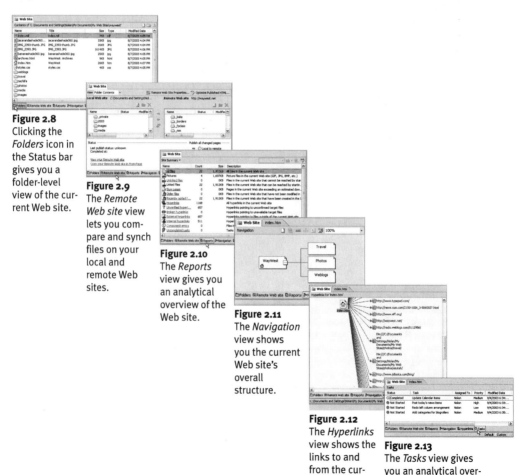

Figure 2.8
Clicking the *Folders* icon in the Status bar gives you a folder-level view of the current Web site.

Figure 2.9
The *Remote Web site* view lets you compare and synch files on your local and remote Web sites.

Figure 2.10
The *Reports* view gives you an analytical overview of the Web site.

Figure 2.11
The *Navigation* view shows you the current Web site's overall structure.

Figure 2.12
The *Hyperlinks* view shows the links to and from the current Web page.

Figure 2.13
The *Tasks* view gives you an analytical overview of the Web site.

Figure 2.14 To switch views of an open Web site, choose one of seven choices from the View menu.

Figure 2.15 Switch back to Page view by clicking the page tab at the top of the main window (left), or click the *Web Site* tab (right) to see your site's files.

Figure 2.16 To quickly see your Web site's folder structure—no matter which view you're in—click the Folder List icon in the Standard toolbar. To hide the folders, click the icon again.

Figure 2.17 Use the Folder List/Navigation tabs to quickly switch your view (left) or click the Folder List icon in the Standard toolbar (right).

To switch views

◆ Open a Web site and from the View menu, choose one of the seven choices at the top, starting with *Page* and ending with Tasks (**Figure 2.14**). FrontPage's main window will switch to reflect your choice.

✔ Tips

■ When you choose a view other than the default Page view, six view icons will appear across the bottom of the main window (**Figures 2.8-2.13**). Click any one of them to switch to another view without having to use the View menu. To switch back to Page view without using the View menu, click a page tab at the top of the main window (left, **Figure 2.15**). You can jump back to the previous view any time by clicking the *Web Site* tab (right, **Figure 2.15**), where your previous view is preserved.

■ No matter which view you're using, you can quickly see your site's folder structure by clicking the Folder List icon in the Standard toolbar (**Figure 2.16**). Click the icon again to hide the folders. Or choose View > Folder List ((Alt)(F1)) to toggle the folders on and off.

■ If the Folder List already is visible, you can quickly switch to navigation view by clicking the *Navigation* tab at the bottom of the *Folder List* pane or by clicking the Folder List icon in the Standard toolbar and selecting *Navigation Pane* (**Figure 2.17**).

Using the task pane

The task pane makes it easier to perform common tasks, such as creating new pages or using page templates. The pane clusters common tasks, such as creating a new item, working with tables, and searching. The pane automatically displays the last view used.

Despite the similar names, FrontPage's task pane has nothing to do with its Tasks view. (The task pane applies only to the current Web page, while the Tasks view works across the entire Web site.)

To use the task pane

1. Choose View > Task Pane (**Figure 2.18**).

2. When the task pane appears on the main window's right side, use the back and forward arrows, and the Home icon (left), or downward-pointing triangle (right) to choose among its views (**Figure 2.19**).

3. Once the desired pane view appears, click any icon in the pane to activate that action (**Figure 2.20**).

✔ Tip

■ The task pane's clipboard is a great place to store images, hyperlinks, or any other items you use often (left, **Figure 2.21**), while its Getting Started view displays common questions and tasks (right, **Figure 2.21**).

Figure 2.18 To display the task pane, use the View menu.

Figure 2.19 Use the arrows or triangle at the top of the task pane to choose among its views.

Figure 2.20 Click any icon in the task pane to activate that particular action.

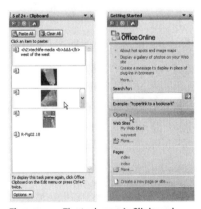

Figure 2.21 The task pane's Clipboard view (left) makes a great place to store images, hyperlinks, or other items you use often, while its Getting Started view (right) displays common questions and tasks.

Figure 2.22 To have the task pane appear by default, choose Tools > Options (left) and check Startup Task Pane in the Options dialog box (right).

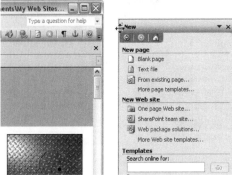

Figure 2.23 To separate the task pane from the main window, click its top bar and drag it elsewhere on your desktop.

To turn the task pane off or on

1. To change the default behavior for the task pane, which ordinarily appears when FrontPage is launched, choose Tools > Options (left, **Figure 2.22**).

2. When the Options dialog box appears, click the General tab, and check *Startup Task Pane* (right, **Figure 2.22**).

3. Click *OK* to close the dialog box. Once you restart FrontPage, the task pane will appear automatically along the main window's right side.

✔ Tip

■   You also can set FrontPage to automatically open your last-viewed Web site using a similar trick: Choose Tools > Options > General and then check or uncheck *Open last Web site automatically when FrontPage starts* (right, **Figure 2.22**).

To move the task pane to the desktop

◆   To move the task pane out of FrontPage's main window, click your cursor on the top of the pane and drag the pane to a new spot on the desktop, where it will then appear with its own title (**Figure 2.23**).

To close the task pane

◆   Choose View > Task Pane and release your cursor or click the X in the top-right corner of the task pane. The task pane will close.

USING THE TASK PANE

Using the Toolbars

By default, the Standard and Formatting toolbars (**Figures 2.24** and **2.25**) appear at the top of FrontPage's main window and the status bar appears at the bottom of the window. But depending on which Web tasks you're doing at the moment, displaying one or more of FrontPage's 11 other toolbars can be particularly handy (**Figures 2.26–2.36**). Like all of FrontPage's toolbars, they can be customized to your heart's desire. Or you can create your own custom toolbar. For details, see *To customize an existing toolbar* and *To create a new toolbar* on pages 30 and 31.

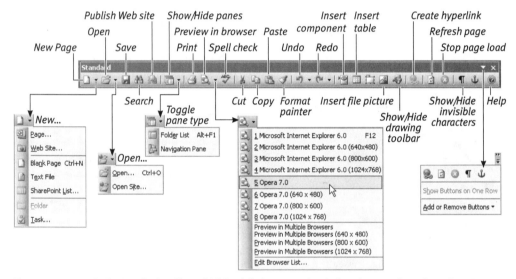

Figure 2.24 Icons in the Standard toolbar, which by default appears just below the menu bar, trigger FrontPage's most commonly used commands.

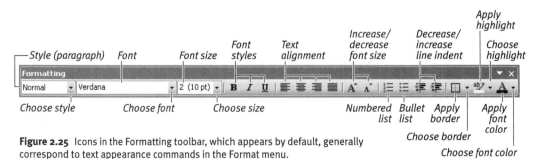

Figure 2.25 Icons in the Formatting toolbar, which appears by default, generally correspond to text appearance commands in the Format menu.

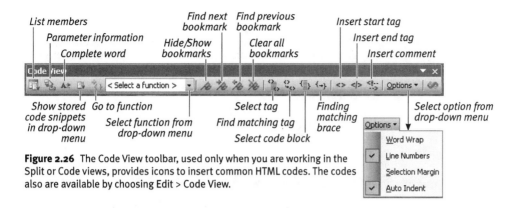

Figure 2.26 The Code View toolbar, used only when you are working in the Split or Code views, provides icons to insert common HTML codes. The codes also are available by choosing Edit > Code View.

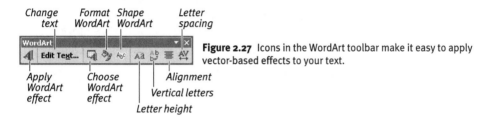

Figure 2.27 Icons in the WordArt toolbar make it easy to apply vector-based effects to your text.

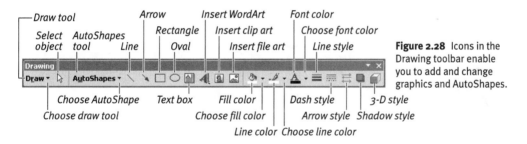

Figure 2.28 Icons in the Drawing toolbar enable you to add and change graphics and AutoShapes.

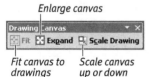

Figure 2.29 Icons in the Drawing Canvas toolbar let you control the size of the canvas when working with vector-based images.

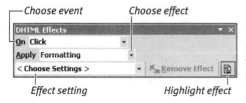

Figure 2.30 The drop-down menus in the DHTML Effects (Dynamic HTML) toolbar let you set up formatting effects that are triggered by the Web user's actions. For details, see page 383.

USING THE TOOLBARS

25

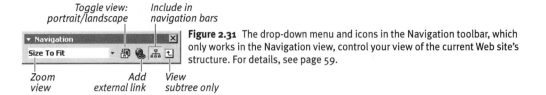

Figure 2.31 The drop-down menu and icons in the Navigation toolbar, which only works in the Navigation view, control your view of the current Web site's structure. For details, see page 59.

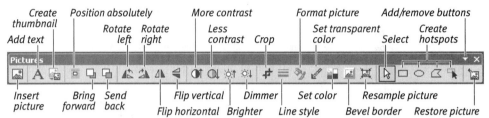

Figure 2.32 The Pictures toolbar icons help you edit aspects of any selected graphic. For details, see page 169.

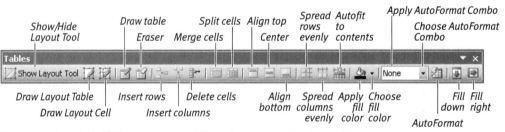

Figure 2.33 The icons and text boxes in the Positioning toolbar help you control the absolute and relative positioning of the selected page element. For details, see page 201.

Figure 2.34 Unless you're working on a Web page that already contains style sheets (top), the Style toolbar opens only a single Style button (bottom). For details, see page 363.

Figure 2.35 Icons in the Tables toolbar control the major aspects of creating and adjusting tables in your Web pages.

Figure 2.36 Use the XML View toolbar when working with XML (eXtended Markup Language) files to reformat the XML and verify that it's properly formatted.

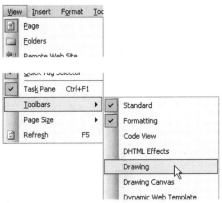

Figure 2.37 To turn on or off any toolbar, choose View > Toolbars and make a choice from the drop-down menu.

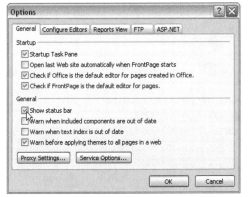

Figure 2.38 To turn on or off the status bar, choose Tools > Options and under the *General* tab check or uncheck the *Show status bar* box.

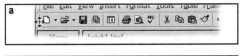

Figure 2.39 To move a docked toolbar, click anywhere in the bar (a) and drag it onto the desktop (b).

To turn on/off toolbars

1. Choose View > Toolbars and select a toolbar from the drop-down menu to turn on or off (**Figure 2.37**). Checked toolbars are already on; unchecked ones are off.

2. Release your cursor on the selected toolbar and it will appear (or disappear) above or below FrontPage's main window.

To turn on/off the status bar

1. Choose Tools > Options.

2. When the Options dialog box appears, click the *General* tab, then in the *General* section check or uncheck the *Show status bar* box (**Figure 2.38**).

Rearranging the toolbars

FrontPage lets you move any of its toolbars to where they're most convenient for your work. Sometimes it's easiest to have your activated toolbars "docked," that is, running horizontally across the top or bottom of FrontPage's main window. For some tasks, however, you may prefer to have a toolbar sitting out on the desktop itself. FrontPage also lets you resize the toolbars to fit your workspace.

To move toolbars to the desktop

◆ To move a docked toolbar (those running across FrontPage's main window), click your cursor on the toolbar and drag the toolbar to a new spot on the desktop, where it will then appear with its own title (**Figure 2.39**).

To dock toolbars in the main window

◆ To move a freestanding toolbar into a docked position, click on the toolbar and drag it to the zone just above or below FrontPage's main window. As your cursor approaches the docking area, the free-standing toolbar will snap into place (**Figure 2.40**).

To resize freestanding toolbars

◆ To shrink a *freestanding* toolbar, click its outer edge and drag the cursor toward the toolbar's center. To expand the tool-bar, drag the cursor away from the tool-bar's center (**Figure 2.41**).

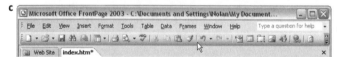

Figure 2.40 To dock a freestanding tool-bar, click and drag it to FrontPage's main window (a). As your cursor approaches the docking area (b), the freestanding toolbar will "snap" into place (c).

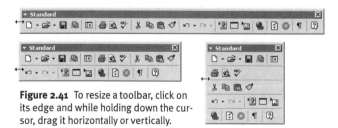

Figure 2.41 To resize a toolbar, click on its edge and while holding down the cur-sor, drag it horizontally or vertically.

Figure 2.42 To add or remove toolbar buttons, click the triangle at the end of the toolbar and the *Add or Remove Buttons* drop-down menu will appear.

Figure 2.43 Click the item you want to remove or add to the selected toolbar. When you're done, click anywhere outside the drop-down menu to trigger the change.

Figure 2.44 To reset the toolbar to its original condition, click the triangle at the end of the toolbar, move to the *Add or Remove Buttons* drop-down menu, select Standard, and click *Reset Toolbar*.

Customizing the toolbars

FrontPage lets you add or remove toolbar buttons. You also can customize toolbars by adding extra buttons to existing toolbars or by creating new, blank toolbars from scratch and adding only the buttons you need.

To add or remove toolbar buttons

1. Click the triangle at the end of the toolbar you want to customize and the *Add or Remove Buttons* drop-down menu will appear (**Figure 2.42**).

2. Move the cursor over the *Add or Remove Buttons* drop-down menu, click *Standard*, and another drop-down menu will appear showing all of the toolbar's current buttons, marked by checks. Click the item you want to remove and the check will disappear (**Figure 2.43**).

3. Continue unchecking (removing) or checking (adding) items until you're satisfied. Then click anywhere outside the drop-down menu and the toolbar will reflect your changes.

✔ Tip

■ It's all too easy to accidentally remove an entire menu. To quickly undo your button changes, you can reset a toolbar to its original condition. Just click the triangle at the end of the toolbar, and choose Add or Remove Buttons > Standard > Reset Toolbar (**Figure 2.44**). The toolbar's original buttons will reappear.

To customize an existing toolbar

1. If you want to add buttons not immediately available in a toolbar's add/remove drop-down menu, choose Add or Remove Buttons > Customize (**Figure 2.45**).

2. When the Customize dialog box appears, make sure the *Commands* tab is selected.

3. Click one of the menu categories in the left pane, then click the command in the right pane that you want to add to your toolbar (**Figure 2.46**).

4. With the command still highlighted, drag your cursor to the spot in the toolbar where you want the button to appear (**Figure 2.47**).

5. Release the cursor and the command button will be inserted into the toolbar.

Figure 2.45 To add buttons not already available in a toolbar's add/remove drop-down menu, select *Customize*.

Figure 2.46 Click a category in the left pane, then, in the right pane, click the command you want to add to your toolbar.

Figure 2.47 Once you choose a command, drag it to the toolbar you're customizing.

Figure 2.48 To create a new toolbar, choose Tools > Customize.

Figure 2.49 In the Customize dialog box, click the *Toolbars* tab, and then click *New*.

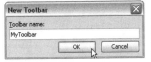

Figure 2.50 Give your new toolbar a descriptive name and click *OK*.

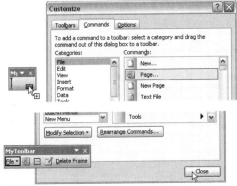

Figure 2.51 Click and drag commands from the right pane onto your new toolbar (top). When you've finished, click *Close* (bottom).

To create a new toolbar

1. Choose Tools > Customize (**Figure 2.48**).

2. When the Customize dialog box appears, click the *Toolbars* tab, and then click *New* (**Figure 2.49**).

3. When the New Toolbar dialog box appears, type in a descriptive name for your new toolbar, and click *OK* (**Figure 2.50**). The new toolbar will appear at the bottom of the Customize dialog box's list of available toolbars. The toolbar itself also will appear on the desktop, but since it doesn't have any icons yet, it'll be tiny and hard to spot.

4. To add icons to your new toolbar, click the Customize dialog box's *Commands* tab.

5. Choose a command category in the left pane, then click on a command icon in the right pane, drag it to your new toolbar, and release your cursor (top, **Figure 2.51**). The icon will be placed in your new toolbar.

6. As you continue selecting and adding icons, your new toolbar will become large enough to resize. When you have finished adding command icons, click *Close* (bottom, **Figure 2.51**). Your new toolbar will appear as a freestanding toolbar, but remember that you can always dock it in the main window. For details, see *To dock toolbars in the main window* on page 28.

✔ Tip

- By now you may realize there are three ways to get to the Customize dialog box: 1) View > Toolbars > Customize, 2) Tools > Customize, and 3) the *Add or Remove Buttons* drop-down menu that appears when you click the triangle at the right end of any toolbar. They all work identically.

To delete a toolbar

1. If you want to get rid of a toolbar (instead of just hiding it from view), choose View > Toolbars > Customize (**Figure 2.52**).

2. When the Customize dialog box appears, click in the list on the name of the toolbar you want removed, and click *Delete* (**Figure 2.53**).

3. When the alert dialog box appears, click *OK*. The toolbar will be removed from the list in the Customize dialog box.

Figure 2.52 To delete a toolbar, choose View > Toolbars > Customize.

Figure 2.53 When the Customize dialog box appears, click the toolbar you want removed, and click *Delete*.

Figure 2.54 The File menu controls application-wide actions such as creating, opening, closing, saving, publishing, and importing Web pages or sites.

Figure 2.55 Most of the Edit menu's commands are common to all programs. The fifth section lets you control file access when more than one person is working on a Web site.

Figure 2.56 The View menu lets you show or hide all seven of FrontPage's views, plus the toolbars.

The Menus

The menus that appear across the top of FrontPage's main window remain the same no matter what you're doing. However, some of the menus, such as Frames, can be used only while viewing or editing Web pages containing frames.

The File menu

Commands found in the File menu involve application-wide actions: creating, opening, closing, saving, publishing, and importing Web pages or sites (**Figure 2.54**). The File menu also lets you set up print settings, change FrontPage's general properties, and quit the program.

The Edit menu

Most of the Edit menu's commands operate just as they do in other programs—except the fifth section of the menu (**Figure 2.55**). That section lets you set up a Check In/Check Out system to avoid file version conflicts when more than one person is working on a Web site. For details, see *Managing Web Site Workflow* on page 393.

The View menu

The first section of the View menu gives you quick access to different information about your site, while the rest of the menu controls the appearance of FrontPage's main window. (**Figure 2.56**).

The Insert menu

As the name suggests, this enables you to insert into Web pages everything from line breaks, dates, and hyperlinks to Java applets and Office XP or Office 2000 components, such as charts and spreadsheets (**Figure 2.57**).

The Format menu

Commands found in the Format menu control the appearance of your text, HTML tags, and what FrontPage calls themes, which establish your Web site's overall graphic look (**Figure 2.58**).

The Tools menu

The Tools menu gives you control over many of FrontPage's overall settings (**Figure 2.59**). It also leads to FrontPage's dictionary and thesaurus.

Figure 2.57 The Insert menu lets you place into your Web pages everything from line breaks, dates, and hyperlinks to Java applets and Office components.

Figure 2.58 The Format menu controls text appearance and generally corresponds to the Formatting toolbar icons.

Figure 2.59 The Tools menu controls many of FrontPage's overall settings, plus the dictionary and thesaurus.

THE MENUS

Figure 2.60 The Table menu controls major aspects of creating and adjusting tables in your Web pages and generally corresponds to the Table toolbar icons.

Figure 2.61 The Data menu's options can only be used if your Web site is stored on a server running Windows SharePoint Services.

Figure 2.62 The Frames menu controls formatting of frame-based pages and is not accessible when viewing a non-frame page.

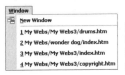

Figure 2.63 Use the Window menu to jump to any open FrontPage window.

Figure 2.64 Use the Help menu to reach the FrontPage help system.

The Table menu

Whether it's adding tables to a page or tweaking the arrangement of individual rows and columns, you'll find the most commonly used commands in the Table menu (**Figure 2.60**).

The Data menu

Commands found in the Data menu can only be used if your Web site is stored on a server running Windows SharePoint Services. (**Figure 2.61**). For that reason, we have not included coverage of the Data menu.

The Frames menu

Commands found in the Frames menu are accessible only when you're viewing a page containing HTML frames (**Figure 2.62**). Frame-based pages are created with the New Page command ([Ctrl][N]). For details, see page 303.

The Window menu

FrontPage lets you open multiple Web pages and sites simultaneously. The Window menu lets you quickly switch from one window to another (**Figure 2.63**). This also can be done by clicking the page tabs in FrontPage's main window.

The Help menu

Common to any Windows program, the Help menu gives you direct access to FrontPage's help system (**Figure 2.64**). For more information on the activation feature, see page 440.

THE MENUS

To use FrontPage's Help

1. Choose Help > Microsoft Office FrontPage Help (1) (**Figure 2.65**). The Microsoft FrontPage Help pane will appear on the right side of the main window, where the task pane normally appears.

2. Click in the *Search for* text window, type in key words for the topic you need help on, and click the green arrow or press *E* (**Figure 2.66**).

   or

   Click the *Table of Contents* link and then browse through the topics to find the one you need (**Figure 2.67**).

✔ Tips

■ To return to the task pane, click the house icon within the Help pane. You can jump back to the Help pane by either using the Help menu or clicking the task pane's drop-down menu and selecting *Help*.

■ The fastest way to use Help is to type a question into the *Type a question for help* text window, press *E*, and select an item from the list that appears (**Figure 2.68**).

Figure 2.65 To start FrontPage's Help feature, choose Help > Microsoft Office FrontPage Help.

Figure 2.66 To search all of FrontPage's help pages, click in the *Search for* text window, type in key words, and click the green arrow or press ←Enter (top). The results will be listed in an expanded list (bottom).

Figure 2.67 To browse through FrontPage's help pages, click the *Table of Contents* link (top) and click through the topic listings until you find what you need (bottom).

Figure 2.68 Get quick help by typing a question into the *Type a question for help* text window (top), pressing ←Enter, and selecting an item from the list that appears (bottom).

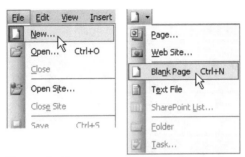

Figure 2.69 To create a new Web page, choose File > New (left) or click the New icon in the Standard toolbar and choose *Blank Page* from the drop-down menu (right) (Ctrl N).

Figure 2.70 If you chose File > New in step 1, when the New task pane appears click *Blank page* to create a new blank page.

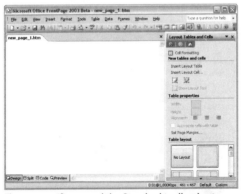

Figure 2.71 If you used the Standard toolbar in step 1, an entirely blank page will appear in FrontPage's main window and the task pane will display common new-page tasks.

Creating, Opening, Saving, and Closing Web Pages

To build a Web page, you can take three routes: Create a new page from scratch and save it. Create a new page based on a template. Or open an existing page, alter it, and then save it using the Save As command to give it a new name. For more information on templates, see *Using Templates and Themes* on page 79.

To create a new blank Web page

1. Choose File > New or click the New icon in the Standard toolbar and choose *Blank Page* from the drop-down menu (Ctrl N) (**Figure 2.69**).

2. If you chose File > New in step 1, the New task pane will appear down the right side of the main window. Click *Blank page* to create a new blank page (**Figure 2.70**).

   or

   If you used the Standard toolbar in step 1, an entirely blank page will appear in FrontPage's main window and the task pane will display common new-page tasks (**Figure 2.71**).

To create a new template-based Web page

1. Choose File > New > or click the New icon in the Standard toolbar and choose *Page* from the drop-down menu (**Figure 2.69**).

2. If you chose File > New in step 1, when the New task pane appears click either *More page templates* in the *New page* section or one of the templates listed in the *Recently used templates* section at the bottom of the pane (**Figure 2.72**). The Page Templates dialog box will appear.

   or

   If you used the Standard toolbar in step 1, the Page Templates dialog box appears immediately.

3. Within the Page Templates dialog box, click on any template icon and then click *OK* (**Figure 2.73**). A new page based on the selected template will appear, ready for your modifications (**Figure 2.74**).

✔ Tip

■ For more information on using FrontPage's templates, see *Using Templates and Themes* on page 79.

Figure 2.72 When the New task pane appears, click either *More page templates* in the *New page* section or one of the templates listed in the *Recently used templates* section.

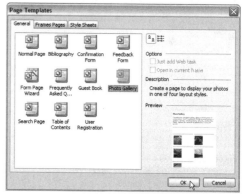

Figure 2.73 Within the Page Templates dialog box, click on any template icon and then click *OK*.

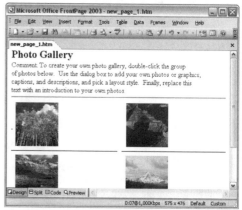

Figure 2.74 A new page based on the selected template will appear, ready for your modifications.

Figure 2.75 To open an existing Web page, choose File > Open or click the Standard tool-bar's Open icon (Ctrl O).

Figure 2.76 When the Open File dialog box appears, navigate to the file you want, and double-click it.

Figure 2.77 If you're using the task pane, click any of the choices in the *Pages* section, which also lists recently opened pages.

To open an existing Web page

1. Choose File > Open or click the Open icon (Ctrl O) in the Standard toolbar (**Figure 2.75**).

2. When the Open File dialog box appears, navigate to the file you want to open and either double-click it, or type its name into the File name box and click *Open* (**Figure 2.76**). The Web page appears in FrontPage's main window.

✔ Tips

- To narrow or widen your search for a Web page in the Open File dialog box, use the *Files of type* drop-down menu.

- If the task pane is open, you also can click any of the choices in the *Pages* section, which includes a list of recently opened Web pages (**Figure 2.77**).

To save a Web page

1. Choose File > Save (**Figure 2.78**).

2. When the Save As dialog box appears, use the folder-level icons to navigate to where you want to save the page (top, **Figure 2.79**).

3. While still in the Save As dialog box, click the *Change title* button to choose a title for your page (bottom, **Figure 2.79**). (The file name and the title need not be the same.) When the Set Page Title dialog box appears, type the name you want Web browsers to display as the Web page's title and click *OK* (**Figure 2.80**).

4. By default, FrontPage will give the file a generic name, such as *new_page_1* (top, **Figure 2.81**). If that's not what you want it called, type a distinctive name into the *File name* text box, and click *Save* (bottom, **Figure 2.81**). The file will be saved with the name you gave it.

Figure 2.78 Choose File > Save to save a Web page.

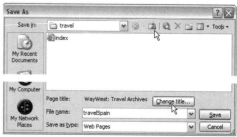

Figure 2.79 Use the folder-level icon to navigate to where you want to save the page (top), then set a title for your Web page by clicking the *Change title* button (bottom).

Figure 2.80 In the Set Page Title dialog box, enter the name you want Web browsers to display as the Web page's title, then click *OK*.

Figure 2.81 By default, FrontPage gives the file a generic name (top). Type a more distinctive name in the *File name* text box and click *Save* (bottom).

Figure 2.82 To save a Web page under another name, choose File > Save As.

Figure 2.83 To close a Web page, choose File > Close or click the X in the top-right corner of the page.

To save a Web page under another name

1. Choose File > Save As (**Figure 2.82**).

2. When the Save As dialog box opens, navigate to where you want the file saved, then click the *Change title* button to give the page a new title (**Figure 2.79**). When the Set Page Title dialog box appears, type the name you want Web browsers to display as the Web page's title and click *OK* (**Figure 2.80**).

3. Enter a distinctive name into the File name field and click *Save*. The file will be saved with the new name.

To close a Web page

◆ Assuming you have already saved the page, choose File > Close (Ctrl F4) or click the X in the top-right corner of the page (**Figure 2.83**). FrontPage remains running, leaving you free to open another Web page or move on to other tasks.

Printing Web Pages

While FrontPage doesn't let you print out an entire Web site at once, you can easily print out individual Web pages.

To print a Web page

1. If you have not already done so, check your printer's settings by choosing File > Page Setup and make any adjustments.

2. If you want to see a preview of the current Web page, choose File > Print Preview.

3. FrontPage's main window displays the preview and includes buttons to inspect each page, see two pages at a time, or zoom in and out on the pages (**Figure 2.84**). If you're satisfied with the preview, click the *Print* button. Or click *Close* and then choose File > Print (Ctrl P) (**Figure 2.85**).

Figure 2.84 FrontPage's print preview window lets you see two pages at a time or zoom in for a closer look.

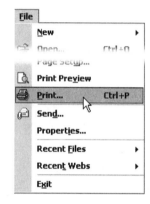

Figure 2.85 To print the current Web page, choose File > Print.

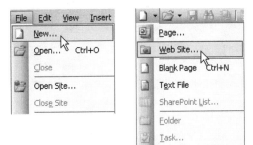

Figure 2.86 To create a new Web site, choose File > New or click the Standard toolbar's New icon and choose *Web Site* from the drop-down menu.

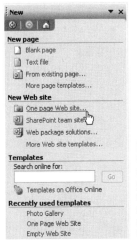

Figure 2.87 If you chose File > New in step 1, the New task pane will appear on the right side of the main window. Click any of the icons in the *New Web site* section.

Figure 2.88 When the Web Site Templates dialog box appears, the *Empty Web Site* icon will automatically be selected. If you want to store the Web site somewhere other than the folder listed in the *Specify the location of the new Web site* text window, click *Browse*.

Creating, Opening, and Closing Web Sites

Any collection of related, linked Web pages—or even a single home page—is considered a Web *site* (previous versions of FrontPage called these *Webs*, a confusing term no longer used). FrontPage automatically organizes any documents and graphics you create for your site. As long as you work within FrontPage, you can move your pages around and FrontPage will maintain the hyperlinks among the pages and files—saving you from the plague of broken links.

To create a new blank Web site

1. Choose File > New or click the New icon in the Standard toolbar and choose *Web Site* from the drop-down menu (**Figure 2.86**).

2. If you chose File > New in step 1, the New task pane will appear on the right side of the main window. Click any of the icons in the *New Web site* section (**Figure 2.87**).

3. When the Web Site Templates dialog box appears (**Figure 2.88**), the *Empty Web Site* icon will automatically be selected. If you want to store the Web site somewhere other than the folder listed in the *Specify the location of the new Web site* text window, click *Browse* and navigate to your preferred folder.

(continued)

4. When the Web Site Templates dialog box reappears, click *OK* and the Create New Web Site dialog box will appear briefly. FrontPage's main window will switch to the Folders view and display the files automatically created (**Figure 2.89**). You're ready to begin adding pages to the Web site or content to individual pages. For details on structuring your Web site, see page 50.

✔ Tips

- In step 3, you can click *OK* instead of *Browse* if you have previously created a Web site and want the new site to be stored in the same spot. Be aware, however, that FrontPage automatically bases the names of new sites on the previous site. If you're not careful, you'll wind up with *MySite1*, *MySite2*, *MySite3*. It quickly can become hard to tell which site is which, so clicking *Browse* is often the best way to keep your sanity.

- In step 4, once you have created your first Web site, FrontPage automatically highlights the icon for that same site type the next time you create a Web site.

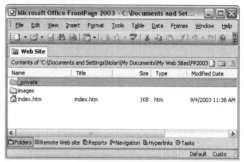

Figure 2.89 Once you create a site, FrontPage switches to the Folders view and displays the files that were automatically created.

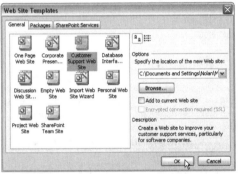

Figure 2.90 To create a template-based Web site, click the *More Web site templates* link in the task pane's *New Web site* section or any link in the *Recently used templates* section.

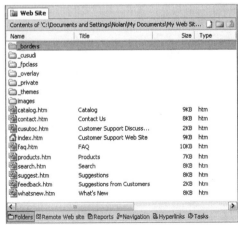

Figure 2.91 When the Web Site Templates dialog box appears, select a template or wizard, and click *OK*.

To create a template-based Web site

1. Choose File > New or click the New icon in the Standard toolbar and choose *Web Site* from the drop-down menu (**Figure 2.86**).

2. If you chose File > New in step 1, the New task pane will appear on the right side of the main window. Click the *More Web site templates* link in the task pane's *New Web site* section or any link in the *Recently used templates* section (**Figure 2.90**).

3. When the Web Site Templates dialog box appears (**Figure 2.91**), select a template or wizard icon, click *OK,* and the Create New Web dialog box will appear briefly. When the Web site opens in the *Folders* view (**Figure 2.92**) or the first page of a Web site wizard appears, you're ready to begin building the site. For details on structuring your Web site, see page 50.

Figure 2.92 When the Web site opens in the *Folders* view, you're ready to begin building the site.

To open an existing Web site

1. Choose File > Open Site or click the Standard toolbar's Open icon and choose Open Site from the drop-down menu (**Figure 2.93**).

2. When the Open Site dialog box appears, navigate to where you stored your existing Web site on your local hard drive or internal network and click *Open* (**Figure 2.94**). The Web site opens in the *Folders* view with the index (Home) page already selected (**Figure 2.95**). You're ready to begin building the site.

To close a Web site

◆ Choose File > Close Site (**Figure 2.96**). The current Web site closes.

Figure 2.93 Choose File > Open Site (left) or click the Standard toolbar's Open icon and choose Open Site from the drop-down menu (right).

Figure 2.94 When the Open Site dialog box appears, navigate to an existing Web site and click *Open*.

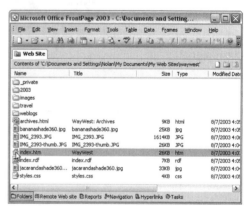

Figure 2.95 When the *Folders* view appears, you can begin adding pages and content to the new Web site.

Figure 2.96 Choose File > Close Site to close a Web site.

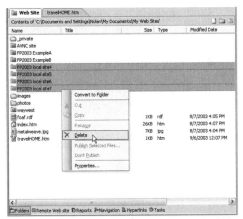

Figure 2.97 To delete a Web site, navigate to it within the Folders view, then right-click it and select Delete from the drop-down menu.

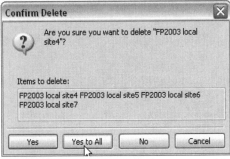

Figure 2.98 When the alert dialog box appears, click *Yes* (or *Yes to All*).

To delete a Web site

1. Using the Folders view, navigate to the Web site you want to delete and select it (Shift-click to select multiple sites in the same view), then right-click and select Delete from the drop-down menu (**Figure 2.97**).

2. When the alert dialog box appears, click *Yes* (or *Yes to All*) (**Figure 2.98**). The site(s) will be deleted.

✔ Tip

- Given how easy it is to mistakenly create new empty Web sites within existing sites, deleting sites becomes essential to keep your files in order. Just be sure you are deleting an empty site by opening the site folder and taking a look at what's inside.

DELETING A WEB SITE

CREATING
A WEB SITE

As explained in Chapter 1, giving some upfront thought to your Web site's purpose and audience will save you a lot of time and headaches once you actually begin creating your site. Assuming you've done your planning, this chapter walks you through the actual creation of your site.

FrontPage's Navigation view offers some great tools to help you quickly create a site—and restructure it if you change your mind midway through. Because FrontPage preserves the links among pages even as you restructure the site, it's easy to experiment with various options until you're satisfied.

To create pages within a Web site structure

1. Once you open a Web site (see page 46), switch to Navigation view by choosing View > Navigation (left, **Figure 3.1**) or clicking the *Web Site* tab and then clicking the Navigation view at the bottom of the main window (right, **Figure 3.1**).

2. Once in the Navigation view, click on the icon for the page to which you want to add a page. The selected page icon will change from yellow to blue.

3. Click the new page icon at the top of the navigation window (top, **Figure 3.2**) or right-click the selected page and choose *New > Page* from the shortcut menu (bottom, **Figure 3.2**). You also can add a new page by pressing ⌗Ctrl⌗⌗N⌗. The new page will appear with a generic name (**Figure 3.3**).

4. Continue adding pages until you've roughed out as much of the Web site as you want (**Figure 3.4**). You're now ready to title, rename, and rearrange your Web site's new pages.

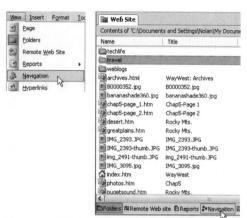

Figure 3.1 Switch to Navigation view by choosing View > Navigation (left) or clicking the *Web Site* tab and then clicking the Navigation view at the bottom of the main window (right).

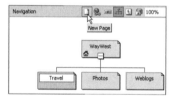

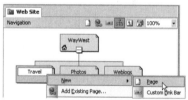

Figure 3.2 To add a new page to your Web structure, click the new page icon at the top of the navigation window (top) or right-click the selected page and choose *New > Page* from the shortcut menu (bottom).

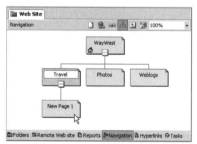

Figure 3.3 The new page, with a generic name, will appear attached to the selected page.

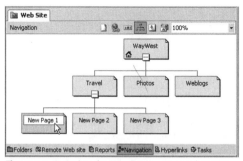

Figure 3.4 By using the New Page command repeatedly, you can quickly rough out a Web site structure.

Figure 3.5 A Web page's title (top cursor), often used as a greeting or content label, need not be the same as the actual file name (bottom cursor).

Figure 3.6 Hide site folders and files by choosing View > Folder List (left), clicking the *X* in the *Folder List* pane (middle), or clicking the Folders icon in the toolbar (right).

✔ Tips

■ The labels that appear on each page within the navigation window are the *titles* of your Web pages, which need not be identical to their actual *file names*. Since page titles appear at the very top of most Web browsers, they're often used as greetings, even when the actual file names are more mundane (**Figure 3.5**).

■ If the *Folder List* pane is visible, you may want to hide it to give yourself more screen space to work with by choosing View > Folder List ([Alt][F1]), clicking the *X* in the *Folder List* pane, or clicking the Folders icon in the toolbar (**Figure 3.6**).

■ While **Figure 3.2** shows a page being added to one level below the Home page, you can use the same steps to add a page to the Home page or *any* other page you select.

To give a new page a title

1. While in Navigation view, give each new page a distinctive title by pressing (Tab) to move to the desired page. The name of the page will become highlighted (**Figure 3.7**).

2. Type in a new name and press (Enter) or press (Tab) to apply the change and move to the next page you want to retitle (**Figure 3.8**).

✔ Tips

■ You also can retitle any page by right-clicking it and choosing *Rename* from the drop-down menu (**Figure 3.9**) and then following step 2.

■ Remember that the Navigation view displays the *titles* of pages, while the Folder List displays the *file names*. If you ever get confused, compare the Folder List names to those in the Web site's Navigation view (**Figure 3.10**). If the file name's not correct, see *To rename a Web page* on the next page. Remember, however, that you should leave your Home page named index.htm so that it's automatically presented as the Home page by your Web server.

Figure 3.7 To give each new page a distinctive title, press (Tab) to move to the desired page. When the name becomes highlighted, type in a new title, then press (Enter).

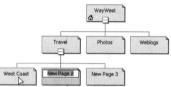

Figure 3.8 Press (Tab) or (Enter) to move from page to page and continue giving each a distinct title.

Figure 3.9 You also can retitle any page by right-clicking it and choosing *Rename* from the shortcut menu.

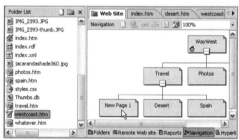

Figure 3.10 The Folder List displays the *file names* (left), while the Navigation view displays the *titles* of pages (right).

Figure 3.11 To rename a Web page, click *inside* the *Folder List* pane on the file you want to rename.

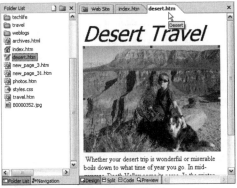

Figure 3.12 Once you rename a file, the new name appears in the *Folder List* pane and the tab at the top of the open page also will reflect the change.

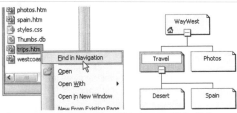

Figure 3.13 To find a file within in your Web site's structure, right-click the file in the Folder List and choose Find in Navigation in the drop-down menu (left). The page will be highlighted within the Navigation view (right).

To rename a Web page

1. Make sure that the *Folder List* is visible by choosing View > Folder List or by clicking the Folders icon (**Figure 3.6**).

2. Click inside the *Folder List* pane on the file you want to rename (**Figure 3.11**).

3. With the file highlighted, type in a new name. Make sure to end it with .htm and press (Enter). The file's name changes in the *Folder List* pane and the tab at the top of the open page also will reflect the change (**Figure 3.12**). Choose File > Save ((Ctrl)(S)).

✔ Tips

■ You also can change the name of a page file by right-clicking it in the *Folder List* and choosing *Rename* from the shortcut menu and then following step 3.

■ To quickly spot where a file is located in your Web site's structure, right-click the file in the Folder List and choose Find in Navigation in the drop-down menu (left, **Figure 3.13**). The page will be highlighted within the Navigation view (right, **Figure 3.13**).

RENAMING A WEB PAGE

Rearranging a Web Site's Structure

The ability to let you quickly restructure your Web site while preserving links between pages is one of FrontPage's best features. Such rearranging is done in the Navigation view, where FrontPage presents an easy to understand set of linked boxes, much like an organization chart. This is very handy when you're roughing out a new site and want to experiment with different structures. Move a page—or a whole group of pages—and see if you like it. If not, you can easily move it again. Most importantly, not a single hyperlink will be broken in the process.

To rearrange a single page

1. If you're not already in Navigation view, click the Navigation icon in the Views Bar.

2. Click inside the right-hand pane on the page you want to move. The page will turn from yellow to blue (**Figure 3.14**).

3. As you drag the page, FrontPage will draw a gray line to possible new destinations for the page (**Figure 3.15**). Continue dragging the page until the line connects to your intended destination (**Figure 3.16**).

4. Release the cursor and the page will move from its original position to its new place in the Web site's structure (**Figure 3.17**).

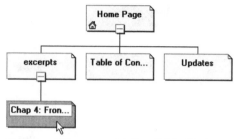

Figure 3.14 To move a page, first click inside the Navigation view and the page will change color.

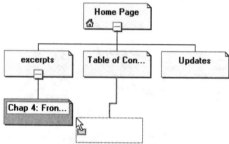

Figure 3.15 As you drag the selected page, a gray line will indicate possible new page destinations.

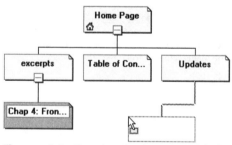

Figure 3.16 Continue dragging the page until the line connects to your intended destination.

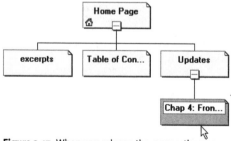

Figure 3.17 When you release the cursor, the page will move from its original position to its new place in the Web site's structure.

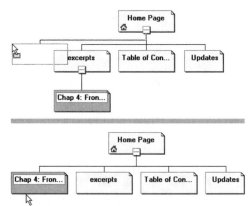

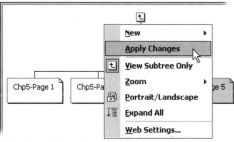

Figure 3.18 To move a page up a level, click and drag the page until a gray line connects it to the same level as its parent page (top). Release the cursor and the page will move to the new spot (bottom).

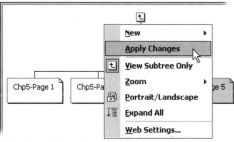

Figure 3.19 Save changes to the structure by right-clicking on a blank spot in the main window and choosing *Apply Changes*.

✔ Tips

■ To move a page up a level, click and drag the page until a gray line connects it to the same level as its parent page. Release the cursor and the page will move up a level (**Figure 3.18**).

■ To move a page to a site's top level, click and drag the page until a gray line connects it to the uppermost page. Release the cursor and the selected page will move to the top level.

■ You can save any changes to the overall navigation structure within the Navigation view by right-clicking on a blank spot in the main window and choosing *Apply Changes* from the shortcut menu (**Figure 3.19**).

To rearrange groups of pages

1. If you're not already in Navigation view, click the Navigation icon in the Views Bar.

2. Click inside the right-hand pane on the top page of the subtree of pages you want to move. The page will turn from yellow to blue.

3. Drag the top page of the subtree to a new destination. As you drag the page, FrontPage will draw a gray line to possible new destinations for the page and its subtree (**Figure 3.20**).

4. Release the cursor, and the page along with its entire subtree, will move from its original position to its new place in the Web site's structure (**Figure 3.21**).

✔ Tip

■ You can move a subtree even when it's collapsed (indicated by a ⊕ icon on the visible page) by dragging the visible page to the desired place in the site structure (**Figures 3.22** and **3.23**). For details on collapsing and expanding site subtrees, see *Controlling Your View of the Site Structure* on page 59.

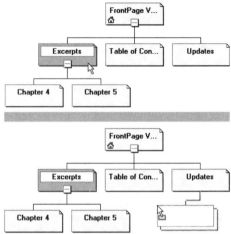

Figure 3.20 To rearrange a group of pages, click the top page of the subtree you want to move and drag it to a new destination.

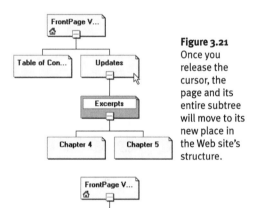

Figure 3.21 Once you release the cursor, the page and its entire subtree will move to its new place in the Web site's structure.

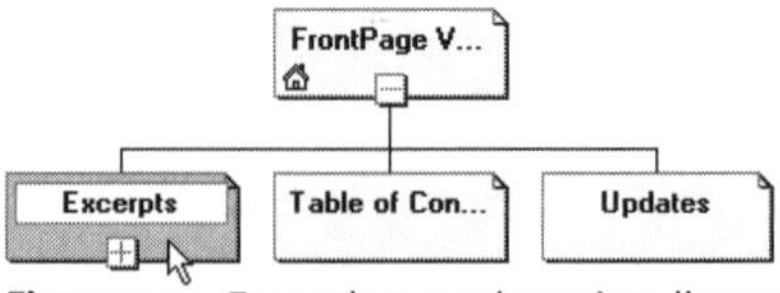

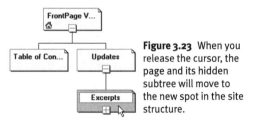

Figure 3.22 Even when a subtree is collapsed (indicated by a ⊕ icon), you can move it by clicking and dragging the visible page.

Figure 3.23 When you release the cursor, the page and its hidden subtree will move to the new spot in the site structure.

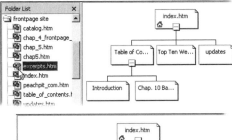

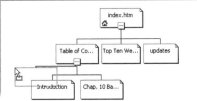

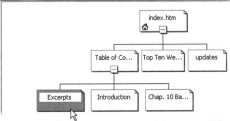

Figure 3.24 To add an existing page to the site structure, select the file in the *Folder List* (top), and drag it into place in the main window (bottom).

Figure 3.25 Release your cursor and the page will be added to the Web site structure.

Adding or Excluding Pages in the Site Structure

It may not always be practical to create new Web pages by building them within the Navigation view. Inevitably you will wind up with some freestanding Web pages that you will want to incorporate into your Web site's navigational structure. There also will be times you want to remove a page from your structure.

To add an existing page to a Web site structure

1. Switch to Navigation view, make sure the *Folder List* is visible, and select in the *Folder List* the file (Web page) you want to add to the site's structure (top, **Figure 3.24**).

2. Drag the file into the main window and, as you position it, a dotted line will connect to the nearest page (bottom, **Figure 3.24**). Without releasing the cursor, reposition the file so that the dotted line connects to the desired part of the Web site diagram.

3. Release the cursor and the page will be added to the Web site structure (**Figure 3.25**).

✔ Tip

■ Once you add a page to the structure, its position within the navigation diagram can be changed at any time.

To remove an existing page from a Web site structure

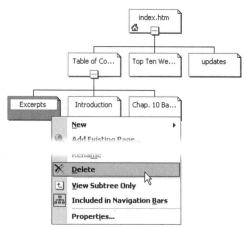

1. Make sure you are in Navigation view, right-click on the page you want to remove, and choose *Delete* from the shortcut menu (**Figure 3.26**).

2. When the Delete Page dialog box appears, make sure the option button labeled *Remove page from the navigation structure* is selected and click *OK* (**Figure 3.27**). The page will be removed from the Web site's navigation structure, while remaining in the site's *Folder List* (**Figure 3.28**).

Figure 3.26 To remove an existing page from the site structure, right-click the page and choose *Delete* from the shortcut menu.

✔ Tip

- Don't be thrown off by that word *Delete*. Fear not: The *Remove page from the navigation structure* choice is always selected by default in the Delete Page dialog box, which means the page is just removed from the navigation structure and not actually deleted. If you really do want to delete the page entirely, select *Delete this page from the Web site* and click *OK*.

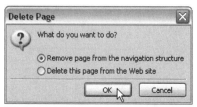

Figure 3.27 Make sure the option button labeled *Remove page from the navigation structure* is selected before you click OK.

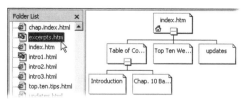

Figure 3.28 The page will be removed from the Web site's navigation structure, while remaining in the site's *Folder List*.

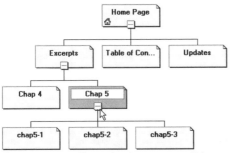

Figure 3.29 To collapse the site structure, click a page's icon to hide the pages below it.

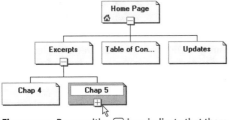

Figure 3.30 Pages with a ⊕ icon indicate that there are more pages hidden from view.

Figure 3.31 In the Navigation view, you can expand or collapse the structure by clicking the subtree icon at the top of the Web site window.

Controlling Your View of the Site Structure

When you're first setting up a Web site's structure, you'll spend a lot of time in Navigation view. For that very reason, FrontPage gives you lots of choices when using the Navigation view. You can look at the entire structure or just a portion. You can zoom in or out when viewing the site, or flip the view from vertical to horizontal. Whether you view the site vertically or horizontally simply depends on which makes more sense for you—there's no right or wrong.

To collapse the site structure

◆ While in Navigation view, click a page's icon to hide every page below it (**Figure 3.29**). All pages below the icon will disappear from view (**Figure 3.30**).

To expand the site structure

◆ While in Navigation view, click a page's ⊕ icon to show every page below it (**Figure 3.30**). Any pages hidden below the page will reappear (**Figure 3.29**).

✔ Tip

■ In the Navigation view, you can expand or collapse the structure by clicking the subtree icon at the top of the Web site window (**Figure 3.31**).

To view only a subtree

1. While in Navigation view, click the page on which you want to focus.

2. With the page still selected, right-click and choose *View Subtree Only* from the shortcut menu (**Figure 3.32**). All the pages *above* the selected page's level will be hidden (**Figure 3.33**).

To expand a subtree

◆ While in Navigation view, click the arrow extending from the subtree's top-level page (**Figure 3.34**). The entire site's structure will appear (**Figure 3.35**).

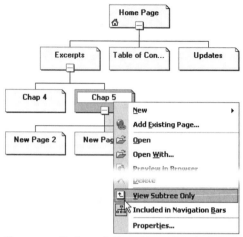

Figure 3.32 To view only the subtree of a selected page, right-click and choose *View Subtree Only* from the shortcut menu.

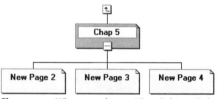

Figure 3.33 When you choose *View Subtree Only*, all the pages above the selected page will be hidden.

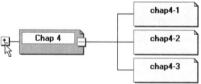

Figure 3.34 To expand a subtree, click the arrow extending from the subtree's top-level page.

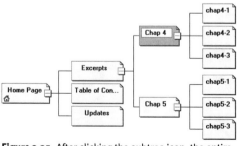

Figure 3.35 After clicking the subtree icon, the entire site's structure will appear.

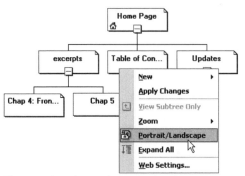

Figure 3.36 To change the Navigation view, right-click anywhere in the right pane and choose *Portrait/Landscape* from the shortcut menu.

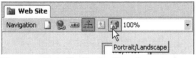

Figure 3.37 After changing the view, the structure appears in landscape mode.

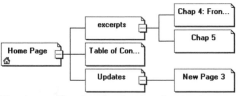

Figure 3.38 In the Navigation view, you can toggle your view of the structure by clicking the Portrait/Landscape icon.

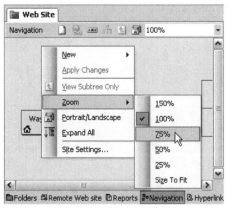

Figure 3.39 To zoom the Navigation view in or out, right-click in the Navigation view, point to *Zoom*, and choose a percentage or *Size To Fit* in the shortcut menu.

To change the site structure view

◆ While in Navigation view, right-click anywhere in the right pane and choose *Portrait/Landscape* from the shortcut menu (**Figure 3.36**). Depending on your current view, the site's structure will switch from portrait (vertical) to landscape (horizontal) or vice versa (**Figure 3.37**). To return the orientation to its original position, choose *Portrait/Landscape* again.

✔ Tip

■ In the Navigation view, you can toggle your view of the structure by clicking the Portrait/Landscape icon (**Figure 3.38**).

To zoom in or out on the site structure

◆ Right-click on a blank spot in the Navigation view, point to *Zoom*, and choose a percentage or *Size To Fit* your monitor view in the shortcut menu (**Figure 3.39**). The view will change to reflect your choice.

✔ Tip

■ In the Navigation view, you can zoom in or out using the preset percentages on the zoom drop-down menu (**Figure 3.40**).

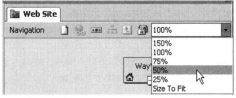

Figure 3.40 In the Navigation view, you can zoom in or out using the preset percentages on the zoom drop-down menu.

Using Link Bars and Shared Borders

Use link bars whenever you need to create a consistent set of hyperlinks for a group of pages or an entire Web site. Link bars offer several advantages over individual hyperlinks. You create them once and then apply them to any number of pages. They also offer a great way to create site-wide navigational links to let users quickly jump to your site's Home page or other main pages.

You have two choices in creating link bars: build them manually and place them on certain pages or let FrontPage generate them based on your site's navigation structure. For example, FrontPage can generate hyperlinks to any page *above* the selected page (known as a *parent* page), to all pages on the same level as the selected page, or to any page *below* its level (a *child* page). In all cases, FrontPage will update the link bars whenever you change the site's structure.

You even can put more than one link bar on a page, creating several distinct levels of navigation. For example, one bar's links could point to a site's top-level topic pages and another bar could point to previous and next pages on the same level. You also can create custom link bars for special-case links on single pages. For details, see *To create a custom link bar* on page 73.

Before you add link bars, first create your Web site's basic structure. If you haven't already roughed out that structure, see page 59. It's a matter of work style whether you create link bars as part of roughing out your Web site's structure (when the pages are still mostly empty) or after you have added content to the pages. Some folks, myself included, find that having to consider site-wide links upfront makes for a more cohesive site design. Other people find this approach completely backward and just plain frustrating. If you're one of them, skip ahead to the next few chapters and come back after you have built out your pages and want to link them together.

Shared borders offer one way to handle site-wide information that may need regular updating, such as company logos, copyright notices, or contact numbers. With shared borders, you can change that type of information in one place and it's automatically updated on every page. Dynamic web templates, new to FrontPage 2003, offer another way to automatically update layouts based on a common template layout. For more information, see *Using Templates and Themes* on page 79.

You can combine shared borders with link bars. That, however, has its own limits since the links remain relative to each page and may not be consistent enough for use in site-wide shared borders. To work around that problem you can turn *off* the shared borders for individual pages or create multiple sets of custom links. For details, see *To turn off shared borders for a single page* on page 78 and *To create a custom link bar* on page 73.

For the most benefits with the fewest headaches, however, try to avoid combining link bars and shared borders. Another way to help users find their way around large Web sites is to create a table of contents or site map. For more information, see *Adding a Web site table of contents* on page 249.

USING LINK BARS AND SHARED BORDERS

To create a navigation-based link bar

1. Assuming you've already roughed out your site's structure, make sure you are in Page view by clicking the Page icon in the Views Bar.

2. Click in the current page where you want the link bar to appear and choose Insert > Navigation (**Figure 3.41**).

3. When the Insert Web Component dialog box appears, click *Bar based on navigation structure* in the list labeled *Choose a bar type* (*Link Bars* will already be selected in the *Component type* list), and click *Next* (**Figure 3.42**).

4. Use the dialog box's scroll bar to find the bar style you want to use and click *Next* (**Figure 3.43**).

Figure 3.41 Click in the page where you want the link bar to appear and choose Insert > Navigation.

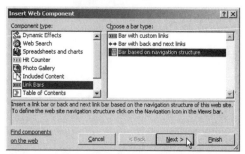

Figure 3.42 When the Insert Web Component dialog box appears, click *Bar based on navigation structure* in the right-hand list.

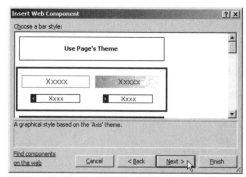

Figure 3.43 Use the scroll bar to choose one of FrontPage's many pre-built link bar styles.

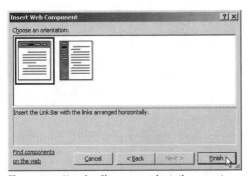

Figure 3.44 Use the *Choose an orientation* pane to have the links run across or down the page.

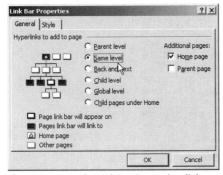

Figure 3.45 Use the Link Bar Properties dialog box's *General* tab to control which pages are included in your link bar.

Figure 3.46 A navigation-based link bar appears across the top of the page.

5. Use the *Choose an orientation* pane to have the links run across or down the page and click *Finish* (**Figure 3.44**).

6. When the Link Bar Properties dialog box appears, the *General* tab will already be activated. Choose one of the six option buttons to control which pages will be linked to the current page (**Figure 3.45**). Check one or both of the *Additional pages* boxes if you also want links to the *Home page* or *Parent page*. Based on your choices, the squares in the site diagram will change to show which pages relative to the current page will be linked. For details, see *Navigation-based link bar options* on page 66.

7. Click *OK* and the link bar will be inserted into the current page (**Figure 3.46**).

✔ Tip

- You will need to repeat these steps on every page on which you want the navigation link bar to appear.

Navigation-based link bar options

The Link Bar Properties dialog box gives you precise control over which pages are included in your link bar (**Figure 3.45**). It also lets you control the appearance of those links.

◆ **Hyperlinks to add to page:** Found under the dialog box's *General* tab, this section gives you six choices for which pages will be linked. The pages highlighted in the dialog box's site tree diagram change to reflect your choice (**Figure 3.47**). The tree doesn't actually show your particular site but simply displays which links will be activated relative to your current page. You can add two other links by clicking the *Additional pages* choices (**Figure 3.48**). In the legend below the tree, the *Page link bar will appear on* symbol refers to your current page.

◆ **Style, Orientation and appearance:** Use the dialog box's *Style* tab to further refine your link bar (**Figure 3.49**). While graphic styles dominate the top of the *Choose a style* window, if you scroll almost to the bottom, you'll find some choices for displaying the links in HTML text.

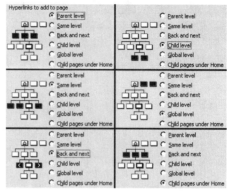

Figure 3.47 The *General* tab's *Hyperlinks to add to page* includes a diagram to show which pages will be hyperlinked to the current page.

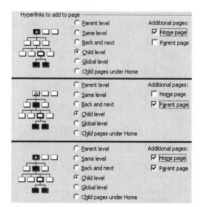

Figure 3.48 Besides the six main hyperlink choices, the Link Bar Properties dialog box also lets you include links to the site's *Home page*, your page's *Parent page*, or to both.

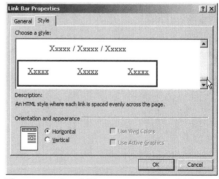

Figure 3.49 In addition to controlling which pages are linked, the Link Bar Properties dialog box's *Style* tab lets you dictate how the links look.

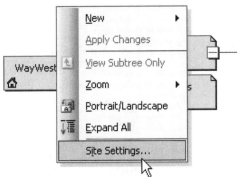

Figure 3.50 To change the default navigation labels, right-click in the main window and choose *Site Settings* from the shortcut menu.

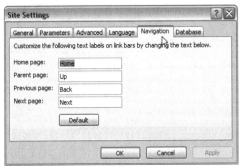

Figure 3.51 Click the *Navigation* tab in the Site Settings dialog box to reach the default navigation labels.

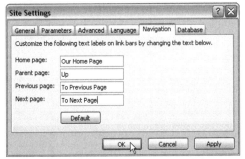

Figure 3.52 Change any of the default labels by typing your own labels into each text box and clicking *OK*. The new labels will be applied to the current Web site only.

Changing the default labels for navigation-based link bars

When you apply navigation-based link bars to pages, FrontPage uses a set of labels by default: *Home* for the *Home page*, *Up* for *Parent level* pages, and *Back* or *Next* for the previous or next page. Most times, those labels will suit your purposes. However, if you occasionally want more specific labels—*Customer Service* instead of *Home*, or *Return to last page* instead of *Back*—FrontPage lets you customize to your heart's content.

To change navigation-based link bar labels

1. Click the Navigation icon in the Views Bar to switch to the Navigation view.

2. Right-click on any blank spot in the main window and choose *Site Settings* (**Figure 3.50**).

3. When the Site Settings dialog box appears, click the *Navigation* tab (**Figure 3.51**).

4. Change any or all of the default navigation labels (*Home*, *Up*, *Back*, and *Next*) by typing your own labels into each text box (**Figure 3.52**). Click *OK* and these labels will be used when you add site-wide link bars.

✔ Tips

■ Your custom navigation labels will be used only in the current Web site, so they won't mess up custom or default labels in your other Web sites.

■ If you change your mind about using custom navigation labels, return to the *Navigation* tab in the Site Settings dialog box, click *Default*, and then *OK*. The original *Home*, *Up*, *Back*, and *Next* labels will replace the custom labels.

To exclude a single page from a navigation-based link bar

◆ In Navigation view, right-click the page you do not want included in the link bar, and choose *Included in Link Bars* from the shortcut menu (**Figure 3.53**). The action works like an on-off toggle and, so, the selected page will be *excluded* from the link bar. Its exclusion is denoted by the page turning gray in Navigation view (**Figure 3.54**).

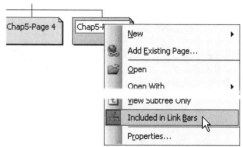

Figure 3.53 To exclude a single page from a link bar, right-click that page and choose *Included in Link Bars*.

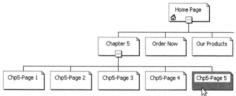

Figure 3.54 Pages excluded from a navigation-based link bar appear dark gray in Navigation view.

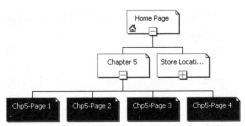

Figure 3.55 Add the same-level pages to the site's structure before creating your back/next link bar.

Figure 3.56 Click in the page where you want to insert the link bar and choose Insert > Navigation.

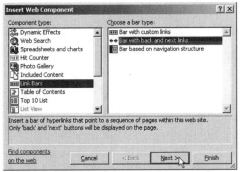

Figure 3.57 When the Insert Web Component dialog box appears, click *Bar with back and next links* in the right-hand list.

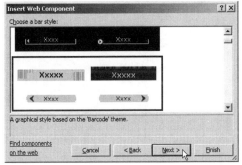

Figure 3.58 Use the scroll bar to choose a pre-built link bar style.

Creating back/next and custom link bars

You might think that a link bar that displays back and next buttons would work similarly to a navigation-based link bar since both presumably depend on the relative structure of the rest of the site. In truth, the process of creating a back/next link bar is virtually identical to how you create a custom link bar.

To create a back/next link bar

1. Assuming you've already roughed out some same-level pages on your site's structure (**Figure 3.55**), switch to Page view by clicking the Page icon in the Views Bar.

2. Click in the page where you want to insert the link bar and choose Insert > Navigation (**Figure 3.56**).

3. When the Insert Web Component dialog box appears, click *Bar with back and next links* in the list labeled *Choose a bar type* (*Link Bars* will already be selected in the *Component type* list), and click *Next* (**Figure 3.57**).

4. If your site uses a pre-built graphic theme, click *Use Page's Theme* in the *Choose a bar style* window, or scroll down and select the bar style you want to use, then click *Next* (**Figure 3.58**).

(continued)

5. Use the *Choose an orientation* pane to have the links run across or down the page and click *Finish* (**Figure 3.59**).

6. When the Create New Link Bar dialog box appears, type an easy to remember *Name* in the text window and click *OK* (top, **Figure 3.60**). That name will then appear in the *Choose existing* window of the Link Bar Properties dialog box (bottom, **Figure 3.60**).

7. Click the *Add link* button to begin building the list of pages you want to be part of the particular set of back/next links (**Figure 3.61**).

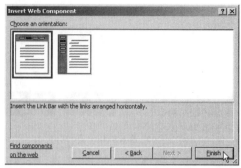

Figure 3.59 Use the *Choose an orientation* pane to have the links run across or down the page and click *Finish*.

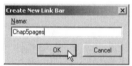

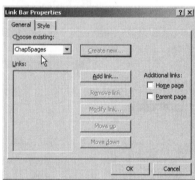

Figure 3.60 Type a *Name* in the text window (top), click *OK*, and it will appear in the *Choose existing* window of the Link Bar Properties dialog box (bottom).

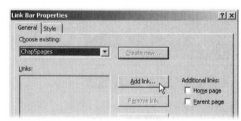

Figure 3.61 Use the *Add link* button to build a list of pages you want to be part of that set of back/next links.

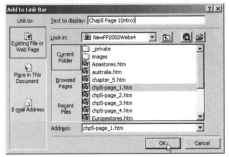

Figure 3.62 Select the current page as the first link for your link bar (top) and give it an easy to recognize label in the *Text to display* window (bottom).

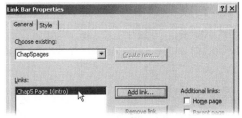

Figure 3.63 A link to this first page will be added to what will become a list of *Links*.

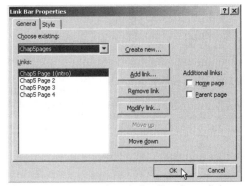

Figure 3.64 Once you have built a list of page links, click *OK*.

8. When the Add to Link Bar dialog box appears, begin by selecting the current page that's open (top, **Figure 3.62**). Type into the *Text to display* window an easy to recognize name for this page link (it doesn't have to be the page's title but that will make things simpler for you as your site grows), and click *OK* (bottom, **Figure 3.62**). A link to this first page will be added to what will become a list of *Links* in the Link Bar Properties dialog box (**Figure 3.63**).

9. Repeat step 8 for each page you want added to the list of back/next list of links for this particular link bar (**Figure 3.64**).

(continued)

USING LINK BARS AND SHARED BORDERS

10. After you finish building the list of links for this particular back/next link bar, you need to insert the link bar on every page on which you want it to appear by repeating steps 2–5. When the *General* tab of the Link Bar Properties dialog box appears, make sure that the link bar name appearing in the *Choose existing* text window is the same one you created in step 6 for the first page, then click *OK*. The *Back* and *Next* links will be inserted on each page. You'll know when you've reached the last of the pages for this back/next link bar because only the *Back* link will appear on the page (**Figure 3.65**).

11. Save the insertion of the link bar on all the pages by choosing File > Save All, and switch to your browser ([Ctrl] [Shift] [B]). Open the first page in your series, and click the *Next* link. By clicking each *Next* button, you'll be able to move through each of the pages in your series (**Figure 3.66**).

✔ Tips

■ In step 8, FrontPage by default opens the *Current Folder*, since in most cases that's where the page you want will be stored. To look elsewhere, choose another icon in the *Link to* or *Look in* columns (**Figure 3.67**).

■ In **Figure 3.65**, you'll notice that the link bar includes *+add link*. This comment text will not appear in the user's Web browser and is simply there to remind you that you can add another link to the bar at any time by right-clicking it and choosing *Link Bar Properties* from the shortcut menu. For more information, see *Changing link bar properties* on page 75.

■ Also in step 10, you can use any existing link bars by clicking the *Choose existing* drop-down menu.

Figure 3.65 The last page in a series of pages with back/next link bars will display only the *Back* link.

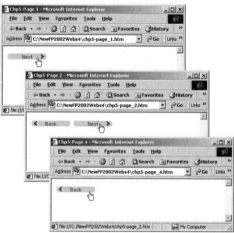

Figure 3.66 The completed back/next link enables a Web browser to move through a series of same-level pages.

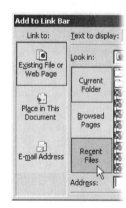

Figure 3.67 Use the *Link to* and *Look in* columns to build links to pages not in the current Web folder.

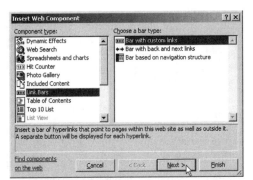

Figure 3.68 When the Insert Web Component dialog box appears, click *Bar with custom links* in the right-hand list.

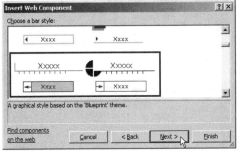

Figure 3.69 Use the scroll bar to choose a pre-built link bar style.

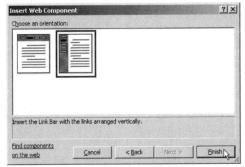

Figure 3.70 Use the *Choose an orientation* pane to have the links run across or down the page and click *Finish*.

To create a custom link bar

1. Switch to Page view by clicking the Page icon in the Views Bar, click in the page where you want to insert the link bar, and choose Insert > Navigation (**Figure 3.56**).

2. When the Insert Web Component dialog box appears, click *Bar with custom links* in the list labeled *Choose a bar type* (*Link Bars* will already be selected in the *Component type* list), and click *Next* (**Figure 3.68**).

3. If your site uses a pre-built graphic theme, click *Use Page's Theme* in the *Choose a bar style* window, or scroll down and select the bar style you want to use, and then click *Next* (**Figure 3.69**).

4. Use the *Choose an orientation* pane to have the links run across or down the page and click *Finish* (**Figure 3.70**).

5. When the Link Bar Properties dialog box appears, click *Create New* (since you're creating a new custom link bar) and give your custom link bar an easy to remember *Name* in the text window of the Create New Link Bar dialog box. Click *OK* and the Link Bar Properties dialog box will reappear displaying the name of your new link bar.

(continued)

USING LINK BARS AND SHARED BORDERS

6. Click the *Add link* button and use the Add to Link Bar dialog box to navigate to the pages you want used in building your custom link bar. Use the dialog box's *Text to display* window to create new labels for each link (**Figure 3.71**).

7. Once you have finished building the custom link list, click *OK* (**Figure 3.72**). The link bar will be displayed in the selected page (**Figure 3.73**). Save the changes to the page by choosing File > Save ([Ctrl][S]).

✔ Tip

■ Since you are building a custom set of links using pages from potentially anywhere on the Web, each page's *original* title or file name may have little to do with your list of links. For that reason, pay particular attention to giving each link a label that makes sense in its *new* context (**Figure 3.71**).

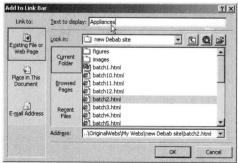

Figure 3.71 Use the Add to Link Bar dialog box's *Text to display* window to create labels for each custom link.

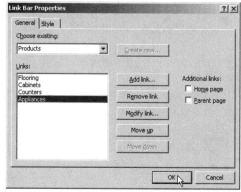

Figure 3.72 Once you finish building the custom link list, click *OK*.

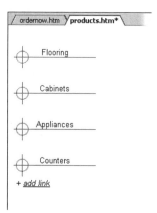

Figure 3.73 Custom link bars offer choices not found in navigation-based link bars.

Figure 3.74 To edit a back/next or custom link bar, right-click the bar and choose *Link Bar Properties*.

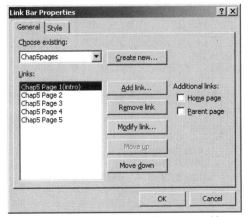

Figure 3.75 Use the *General* tab's buttons to add, remove, modify, and move up or down your links.

Changing link bar properties

FrontPage automatically updates the hyperlinks used by the link bars whenever you rearrange your Web site's structure. But you'll have to manually edit a link bar's properties if you want to change a link bar's graphics, its orientation, how and which links are labeled, or the order in which the links are listed. You can change these properties at any time. The process varies depending on whether you are changing navigation-based, back/next, or custom link bars. FrontPage also gives you the option of changing the default labels used on navigation-based and back/next link bars.

To edit a back/next or custom link bar

1. Make sure you are in Page view, then right-click the link bar you want to change and choose *Link Bar Properties* from the shortcut menu (**Figure 3.74**).

2. When the Link Bar Properties dialog box appears, the *General* tab will already be selected (**Figure 3.75**). To add another page link to the list of *Links*, click the *Add link* button; to delete a page link, click *Remove link*.

(continued)

USING LINK BARS AND SHARED BORDERS

3. To change the name of the link or the page it points to, click *Modify link* and use the Modify Link dialog box when it appears to navigate to a new page or change the link label's name, then click *OK* (**Figure 3.76**). To reorder the list of links, select a link and use the *Move up* or *Move down* buttons to change the order in the *Links* window. Check *Home page* or *Parent page* if you want those links included as well.

4. If those are all the changes you need to make, click *OK* and the Link Bar Properties dialog box will close and the changes will be applied. To change the link bar's appearance, click the *Style* tab in the Link Bar Properties dialog box (**Figure 3.77**). When you're done, click *OK* and the changes will be applied.

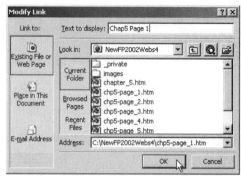

Figure 3.76 Use the Modify Link dialog box to use another page for an existing link.

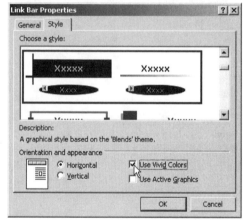

Figure 3.77 The *Style* tab lets you change a link bar's graphical style, along with its orientation or appearance.

Figure 3.78 To create site-wide link bars, first define the areas common to every page by choosing Format > Shared Borders. The same action also lets you turn off borders for single pages.

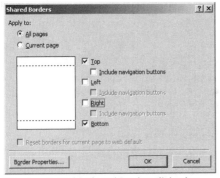

Figure 3.79 In the Shared Borders dialog box, check any or all of the four boxes: *Top*, *Left*, *Right*, and *Bottom*.

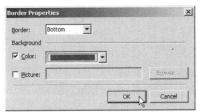

Figure 3.80 Use the Border Properties dialog box to set the shared area's *Border* or *Color*.

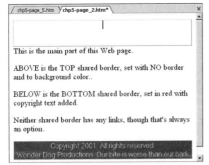

Figure 3.81 Similar to print-based headers or footers, you can use this page's top and bottom shared border areas for site-wide text or graphics.

To add shared borders

1. Make sure you've already opened the Web site for which you want to set borders, then choose Format > Shared Borders (**Figure 3.78**).

2. When the Shared Borders dialog box appears, choose the *All pages* or *Current page* radio button (**Figure 3.79**). By default, the *Top* and *Left* boxes are already checked, but you can check any or all of the four boxes: *Top*, *Left*, *Right*, and *Bottom*. (Do not check the *Include navigation buttons* boxes unless you want link bars included in the shared border areas.) A dashed line will appear within the dialog box showing where shared border areas will appear. For details on the choices, see the *Tip* below.

3. If you want to apply a border or color to the shared border, click the *Border Properties* button and use the drop-down menus in the Border Properties dialog box to set the *Border* or *Color* (**Figure 3.80**). (To use a picture for the border, you must first move it to the current Web's folder.)

4. Once you've made your choices, click *OK* to close the dialog box, then click *OK* again to close the Shared Borders dialog box. The shared borders will be added to the selected pages. You can then add text or graphics to the shared area (**Figure 3.81**).

✔ Tip

- Only the *Top, Left* and *Right* choices in the Shared Borders dialog box let you show hyperlinks to other pages—and only if you also check *Include navigation buttons*, even if you only want text links (**Figure 3.79**). The *Bottom* choice can contain text, graphics, or invisible comments but not hyperlinks. For details, see *Adding Hyperlinks* on page 143.

USING LINK BARS AND SHARED BORDERS

To turn off shared borders for a single page

1. Make sure you are in Page view, and choose Format > Shared Borders (**Figure 3.78**).

2. When the Shared Borders dialog box appears, click the *Current page* radio button and uncheck any other boxes (**Figure 3.82**). Click *OK* and the selected page appears without any shared borders (**Figure 3.83**).

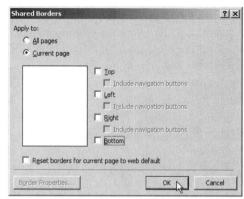

Figure 3.82 To turn off a page's shared border, choose the *Current page* button, uncheck all other boxes, and click *OK*.

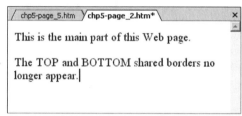

Figure 3.83 The same page as in Figure 3.81 after the shared borders have been turned off.

Using Templates and Themes

FrontPage's built-in templates and themes can save you tons of time while producing great-looking pages. Use the templates for building pages and sites, then use the themes to apply graphic touches to a single page or a whole site. To make creation of some of the more complicated templates easier, FrontPage includes program "wizards" to guide you step-by-step through the process. FrontPage 2003 also offers you the option of creating dynamic templates. When you update such templates, the changes are automatically reflected in any pages based on that template. If you have a Web site with multiple authors, FrontPage 2003 allows you to designate sections of pages as editable regions, whose content can be changed by others even while the layout remains protected from changes. By not making certain areas editable, you can protect your designs and coding from accidental changes by others also working on the site. You also can detach pages from a dynamic template at any time if, for example, you want to create a page with a layout independent of the template's.

To create a page from a template

1. Choose File > New (**Figure 3.84,** left) or click the New icon in the Standard toolbar and choose *Page* from the drop-down menu (**Figure 3.84**, right).

2. If you chose File > New in step 1, when the New task pane appears click either *More page templates* in the *New page* section. The Page Templates dialog box will appear.

   or

   If you used the Standard toolbar in step 1, the Page Templates dialog box appears immediately.

3. When the Page Templates dialog box appears with the *General* tab already selected, choose a page template and click the *OK* button (**Figure 3.85**). For help creating form pages, open the *Form Page Wizard* and follow its instructions. For more information on forms, see page 319. (For details on the *Frames Pages* and *Style Sheets* tabs, see pages 304 and 363.)

4. Once the template opens, you can select headings and text, replacing them with your own text (**Figure 3.86**). For details on creating and formatting text, see page 97.

 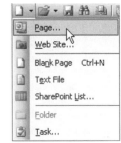

Figure 3.84 To create a page from a template, choose File > New (left) or click the New icon in the Standard toolbar and choose *Page* from the drop-down menu (right).

Figure 3.85 The Page Templates dialog box's *General* tab offers a variety of page templates. Choose one and click *OK*.

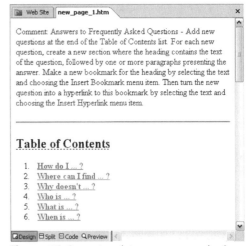

Figure 3.86 Once a template opens, you can begin replacing headings, text, and graphics with your own.

Figure 3.87 In the New task pane, click either *More page templates* in the *New page* section, *More Web site templates* in the *New Web site* section, or one of the templates listed in the *Recently used templates* section at the bottom of the pane.

Figure 3.88 Choose a Web site template in the Web Site Templates dialog box, specify where you want it saved, and click *OK*.

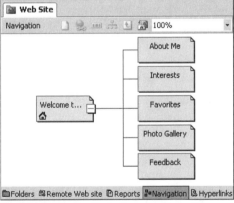

Figure 3.89 Use the Navigation view to see the overall structure and all the pages of your new template-based Web site.

To create a Web site from a template

1. Choose File > New > or click the New icon in the Standard toolbar and choose *Web Site* from the drop-down menu.

2. If you chose File > New in step 1, when the New task pane appears click either *More page templates* in the *New page* section, *More Web site templates* in the *New Web site* section, or one of the templates listed in the *Recently used templates* section at the bottom of the pane (**Figure 3.87**). The Web Site Templates dialog box will appear.

   or

   If you used the Standard toolbar in step 1, the Web Site Templates dialog box appears immediately.

3. When the Web Site Templates dialog box appears, click on one of the Web site templates (**Figure 3.88**). Be sure to specify in the pathname text box where you want the site saved, then click *OK* and the Web site will be created.

4. Switch to Navigation view to see the Web site's overall structure and all its pages (**Figure 3.89**).

(continued)

USING TEMPLATES AND THEMES

5. Double-click on any page in the site to open it and begin substituting your own copy, heads, properties, and graphics (**Figure 3.90**).

6. Save the page by choosing File > Save ((Ctrl)(S)). Continue editing other pages in your new template-based Web site until you're done, saving each in turn.

✔ Tips

■ You can add a multi-page template to an existing Web site. In the Web Site Templates dialog box (**Figure 3.88**), just be sure to choose the *Add to current Web site* checkbox. This enables you, for example, to add a customer support or discussion area to an existing corporate Web site.

■ For help creating a Web discussion board or importing an existing Web site, use the FrontPage wizards listed in the Web Site Templates dialog box (**Figure 3.88**).

■ For even more templates, use the *Search online for:* text window in the *Templates* section in **Figure 3.87** and you'll be connected to a trove of online templates.

Figure 3.90 Open a page in the template-based Web site and begin substituting your own copy, heads, properties, and graphics. Be sure to save your work with File > Save ((Ctrl)(S)).

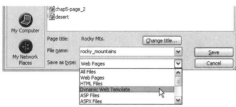

Figure 3.91 Click the *Save as type* drop-down menu and choose *Dynamic Web Template*.

Figure 3.92 The page will be saved with a .dwt suffix, indicating that it is now a dynamic Web site template page.

To create a dynamic Web site template page

1. Create a new Web page, or open an existing page, and choose File> Save As.

2. When the Save As dialog box opens, if you haven't already done so give the page a name and title. Click the *Save as type* drop-down menu and choose *Dynamic Web Template* (**Figure 3.91**).

3. The page will be saved with a .dwt suffix, indicating that it is now a dynamic Web site template page (**Figure 3.92**). You can now create the content and layout of the page. For more information on applying this template to pages, see *To attach a dynamic template to other pages* on page 87.

To add an editable region to a dynamic template

1. Open a dynamic Web page (they have a .dwt suffix) and make sure you are in Design view.

2. Select an area of the page where you want to allow others to make changes, then right-click the area and choose *Manage Editable Regions* from the drop-down menu (**Figure 3.93**).

3. When the Editable Regions dialog box appears, type a descriptive label in the *Region name* text window and click *Add* (or press [←Enter]) (**Figure 3.94**). The newly named region will appear in the *Other regions on this page* text window (**Figure 3.95**).

4. Click *Close* in the dialog box and the region selected in step 2 will be bound by an orange border and display the name you assigned it in step 3 (**Figure 3.96**). Repeat to add as many regions as you need.

Figure 3.93 Select an area where others will be allowed to make changes, right-click it, and choose *Manage Editable Regions* from the drop-down menu.

Figure 3.94 When the Editable Regions dialog box appears, type a descriptive label in the *Region name* text window and click *Add*.

Figure 3.95 The newly named region will appear in the *Other regions on this page* text window.

Figure 3.96 The selected region will be bound by an orange border and display the name you assigned it.

USING TEMPLATES AND THEMES

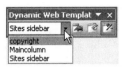

Figure 3.97 If the Dynamic Web toolbar is made visible, you can use its drop-down menu to select a particular region.

Figure 3.98 If you try to add an editable region to a regular Web page, an alert dialog box will appear asking if you'd like to save the page as a dynamic template.

✔ Tips

■ If the Dynamic Web toolbar is turned on in step 2, you can use the drop-down menu to select a particular region (**Figure 3.97**) and it will be selected immediately within the Web page.

■ If you add an editable region to a new blank page that has not been saved already, FrontPage will let you do so and automatically turn the new page into a dynamic template page by giving it a .dwt suffix when you do save it.

■ If you try to add an editable region to a regular Web page (that is ending with the .htm suffix), an alert dialog box will appear asking if you'd like to save the page as a dynamic template (**Figure 3.98**).

To remove an editable region from a dynamic template

1. Open a dynamic Web page, all of which end with the `.dwt` suffix, and make sure you are in Design view.

2. Right-click on any editable region and choose *Manage Editable Regions* from the drop-down menu (**Figure 3.99**).

3. When the Editable Regions dialog box appears, the selected region will be listed in the *Region name* text window and highlighted in the *Other regions on this page* list (**Figure 3.100**). Click *Remove* and the region name will disappear from the list. You can then select another region to remove, or click *Close* (**Figure 3.101**). The Editable Regions dialog box will close and the region selected in step 2 will no longer be editable by other group members.

✔ Tip

■ If the Dynamic Web toolbar is turned on, you can click the Manage Editable Regions icon (just right of that toolbar's drop-down menu) (**Figure 3.102**) to jump directly to the Editable Regions dialog box.

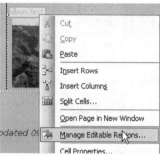

Figure 3.99 To remove an editable region from a dynamic template, right-click on any editable region and choose *Manage Editable Regions* from the drop-down menu.

Figure 3.100 The region you want removed will be listed in the *Region name* text window and highlighted in the *Other regions on this page* list.

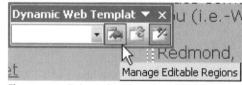

Figure 3.102 To jump directly to the Editable Regions dialog box, click the Dynamic Web toolbar's Manage Editable Regions icon.

Figure 3.101 After removing an area, you can then select another region to remove, or click *Close*.

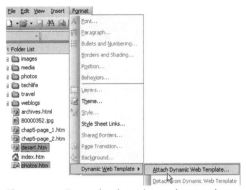

Figure 3.103 To attach a dynamic template to other pages, select the pages in the Folder list and choose Format > Dynamic Web Template > Attach Dynamic Web Template.

Figure 3.104 Select the desired template page within the existing Web site or navigate to another template and click *Open*.

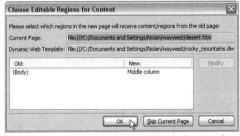

Figure 3.105 Within the Choose Editable Regions for Content dialog box two columns list what (*Old*) layout area of the selected page(s) will be replaced by a (*New*) editable region's layout from the template. Click *OK* to make the replacement or *Modify* to change the matchup.

To attach a dynamic template to other pages

1. Open the Folder List view ((Alt)(F1)) and within the list select the page ((Ctrl)(Shift) to select multiple pages) to which you want to attach a dynamic Web template. Now choose Format > Dynamic Web Template > Attach Dynamic Web Template (**Figure 3.103**).

2. When the Attach Dynamic Web Template dialog box appears, either select the desired template page within the existing web site or navigate to another template and click *Open* (**Figure 3.104**). If the selected page(s) are blank, they will be immediately attached to the template. If the pages already contain some content, the Choose Editable Regions for Content dialog box will appear.

3. When the Choose Editable Regions for Content dialog box appears (**Figure 3.105**), the selected page(s) and the template are listed at the top. The dialog box's main text window displays two columns, which list what (*Old*) layout area of the selected page(s) will be replaced by a (*New*) editable region's layout from the template. Click *OK* to start the replacement (and skip to step 5) or select the list line in the text window and click *Modify* to change the matchup.

(continued)

4. When a smaller version of the Choose Editable Regions for Content dialog box appears atop the main dialog box, use the *New Region* drop-down menu to change your choice and click *OK* (**Figure 3.106**). When the original Choose Editable Regions for Content dialog box reappears with your new choice listed, click *OK*.

5. FrontPage will display briefly an alert dialog box which tracks the matchup process and then displays a confirmation that the pages have been attached to the template (**Figure 3.107**). Click *Close* and the now-attached page will display the layout of the template's editable region (**Figure 3.108**). You or other users can now change the content of the area without changing its template-based layout.

To detach pages from a dynamic template

◆ Open the Folder List view ([Alt][F1]) and within the list select the page ([Ctrl][Shift] to select multiple pages) which you want to detach from a dynamic Web template. Now choose Format > Dynamic Web Template > Detach from Dynamic Web Template. The layout of the selected page(s) will no longer be tied to the template, meaning that changes to the template will no longer affect the page(s).

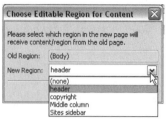

Figure 3.106 If you want to change the Old/New regions matchup, use the *New Region* drop-down menu to change your choice and click *OK*.

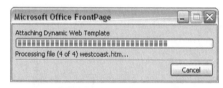

Figure 3.107 FrontPage will track the matchup process (top) and then confirm that the pages have been attached to the template (bottom).

Figure 3.108 The now-attached page will display the layout of the template's editable region.

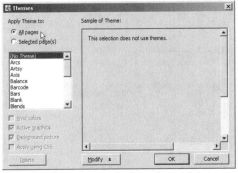

Figure 3.109 Open a page or Web site where you want to apply or change a theme and choose Format > Theme.

To apply a theme to a page or Web site

1. Open a page or Web site to which you want to apply a theme and choose Format > Theme (**Figure 3.109**).

2. If the page or site does not already have a theme, the sample area will be blank when the Themes dialog box opens (**Figure 3.110**).

3. In the dialog box's upper-left corner, choose one of the two radio buttons to apply a theme to *All pages* or to *Selected page(s)*. By default, it's set to *All pages*, which makes sense since themes mainly are used to give your site a uniform look.

4. Choose a theme by clicking on it in the left-hand list and you'll see a sample of it in the right-hand window (**Figure 3.111**).

(continued)

Figure 3.110 If a page or site doesn't already have a theme, the Themes dialog box's sample window will be blank. Choose either *All pages* or *Selected page(s)* in the upper left to control how widely a theme is applied.

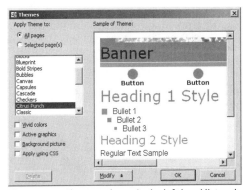

Figure 3.111 Choose a theme in the left-hand list and you'll see a sample of it in the right-hand window.

5. You can tweak the theme by choosing any of the four checkboxes in the lower-left corner: *Vivid colors*, *Active graphics*, *Background picture*, or *Apply using CSS* (if you're using Cascading Style Sheets). Each effect (except CSS) can be previewed in the right-hand sample window (**Figure 3.112**).

6. Once you've selected a theme and tweaked it to your satisfaction, click *OK* in the Themes dialog box and it will be applied to your page or site (**Figure 3.113**). If you want to change the theme even more, see *To modify a theme* on the next page.

✔ Tip

■ Even though the Themes dialog box seems to suggest that you can apply a theme to several pages at a time (**Figure 3.110**), you really only have two choices: apply a theme to the single page you have open or to the entire Web site. If you want to apply a theme to just, say, four of your site's pages, you'll have to open each page, one at a time, and then apply the theme to each in turn.

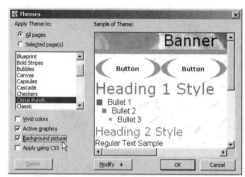

Figure 3.112 The Themes dialog box contains four checkboxes in the lower left—*Vivid colors*, *Active graphics*, *Background picture*, or *Apply using CSS*—that will punch up your pages even more.

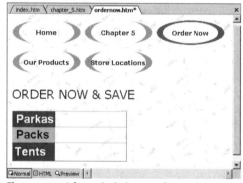

Figure 3.113 A formerly drab page after applying FrontPage's Citrus Punch theme.

Figure 3.114 Click the *Modify* button at the bottom of the Themes dialog box to customize any theme.

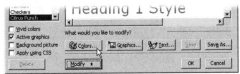

Figure 3.115 FrontPage lets you modify three aspects of a theme: its *Colors*, *Graphics*, or *Text*.

To modify a theme

1. Open a page or Web site that uses a theme you want to change, make sure you're in Page view, and choose Format > Theme (**Figure 3.109**).

2. When the Themes dialog box appears, the current theme will automatically appear in the right-hand sample window. If you want to modify it, click on it in the left-hand column, and click *Modify* at the bottom center of the dialog box (**Figure 3.114**).

3. Just above the *Modify* button, three buttons will appear: *Colors*, *Graphics*, and *Text* (**Figure 3.115**). Click one of the three (you can come back and modify the other two later if you want).

(continued)

4. Depending on your choice, the Modify Theme dialog box that appears will display options for changing your theme colors, graphics, or text (**Figures 3.116–3.118**). For details on the options, see *Theme options*. Make your changes and click *OK*.

5. When the Themes dialog box reappears, you can apply your changes to the existing theme or save them as a new theme. Click *Save* to change the existing theme; *Save As* for a new theme.

6. Finally, click *OK* and the theme modifications will be applied to the selected Web page or site.

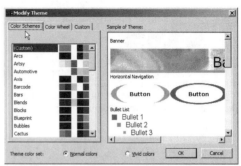

Figure 3.116 The *Color Schemes* tab in the Modify Theme dialog box lets you pick overall combinations and whether you want those colors *Normal* or *Vivid*. The other two tabs set colors for individual items.

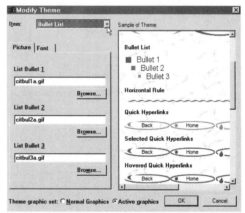

Figure 3.117 The graphics version of the Modify Theme dialog box lets you replace the graphic items used in existing themes.

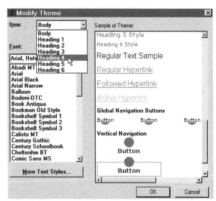

Figure 3.118 The text version of the Modify Theme dialog box lets you change the fonts associated with each HTML item.

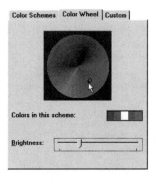

Figure 3.119
The *Color Wheel* tab in the Modify Theme dialog box lets you change the hue and brightness of a selected color combination.

Figure 3.120 The *Custom* tab in the Modify Theme dialog box lets you change the color of individual HTML items within a theme.

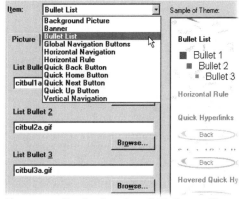

Figure 3.121 Use the drop-down list in the graphics version of the Modify Theme dialog box to change an item or category of items.

Theme options

FrontPage gives you a tremendous amount of control in customizing its built-in themes. Follow the steps in *To modify a theme* on page 91 to reach the Modify Theme dialog box and its various options (**Figures 3.116–3.118**).

◆ **Colors:** Click any of the three tabs to change aspects of a theme's color. The *Color Schemes* tab lets you apply the color combinations of another theme to the current theme (**Figure 3.116**). The *Color Wheel* tab lets you change the hue and brightness of the current color scheme (**Figure 3.119**). The *Custom* tab lets you change the color of individual HTML items, such as all your Level 1 headings or your active hyperlinks (**Figure 3.120**). Choose the *Vivid colors* radio button at the bottom of the dialog box if you want to give the color combinations a bit more punch.

◆ **Graphics:** The graphics version of the Modify Theme dialog box lets you replace various graphics in existing themes with your own graphics or other clip art (**Figure 3.117**). Use the dialog box's drop-down menu to pick an item or category of items that you want to change, such as all the bullets used in a theme (**Figure 3.121**). Then click *Browse* to navigate to the new graphic you want to use. Choose the *Active graphics* radio button at the bottom of the Modify Theme dialog box if you want to animate buttons when, for example, a user mouses over them. Preview the before, during, and after versions of the animations in the sample window. Just remember to use this option with restraint.

(continued)

USING TEMPLATES AND THEMES

◆ **Text:** As you might guess, the text version of the Modify Theme dialog box lets you change the fonts associated with each HTML item, including the text used within such graphics as buttons (**Figure 3.118**). Use the dialog box's drop-down menu to pick your body text or one of your headings. Click the *More Text Styles* button to change even more HTML items (**Figure 3.122**). The *List* drop-down menu will actually let you see all the HTML tags, but think first whether you really want to start changing fonts that widely.

✔ Tip

■ The choices available to you in the various Modify Theme dialog boxes are affected by which boxes you checked in the Themes dialog box (see step 5 in *To apply a theme to a page or Web site* on page 89). If you find yourself unable to turn on an option in one of the Modify Theme dialog boxes, go back to the Themes dialog box and change your checkbox choices.

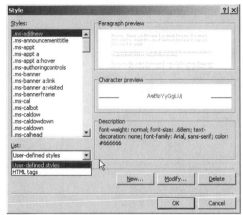

Figure 3.122 The Style dialog box—reached from the Modify Theme dialog box—lets you change the fonts used in any HTML tag.

PART 2

CREATING BASIC WEB PAGES

Chapter 4: **Creating and Formatting Text**   97

Chapter 5: **Formatting Paragraphs, Lists, and Headings**   127

Chapter 6: **Adding Hyperlinks**   143

Chapter 7: **Adding and Editing Images**   169

Chapter 8: **Adding and Editing Drawings**   207

CREATING AND FORMATTING TEXT

4

The whole point of a program like FrontPage is to spare you the tedium of coding in HTML. For that reason, creating and formatting text with FrontPage is very much like using any word processing program: You type away and the formatting is handled behind the scenes. Likewise, most of the standard techniques you use in word processing programs—selecting, moving, cutting, and copying text—work similarly in FrontPage.

Entering and Editing Text

Entering text in FrontPage works almost identically to typing in a word processing program. When your typing reaches the right edge of the document window, the text automatically wraps to the next line. Similarly, you use the cursor to select text, which then can be moved, copied, or pasted elsewhere.

To enter text on a Web page

1. If you're not already in Page view, choose View > Page (**Figure 4.1**). Also, make sure the *Design* tab at the bottom of the page is active (**Figure 4.2**).

2. Make sure the Folder List is visible by choosing View > Folder List or by clicking the Folder icon (**Figure 4.3**).

3. Select the page on which you want to enter text by double-clicking its listing in the Folder List pane.

4. Within the right pane, click your cursor where you want to enter text on the page. A blinking vertical bar will mark the text insertion spot (**Figure 4.4**).

5. Start typing and the text will appear on the page at the insertion spot (**Figure 4.5**).

Figure 4.1 Before working with text, choose View > Page.

Figure 4.2 Whenever you're working with text, make sure the *Design* tab is active.

Figure 4.3 It's easier to jump from file to file with the Folder List visible. Choose View > Folder List (left) or click the Folder icon (right).

Figure 4.4 Click inside the right pane to begin adding text to a Web page.

Figure 4.5 Because the HTML code is hidden, entering text in FrontPage is quite similar to using a standard word processor.

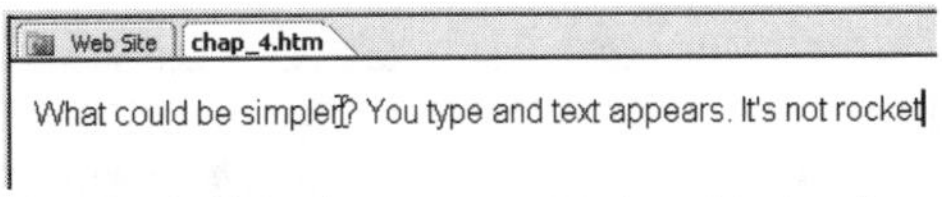

Figure 4.6 Click where you want to insert text and a blinking vertical bar will appear.

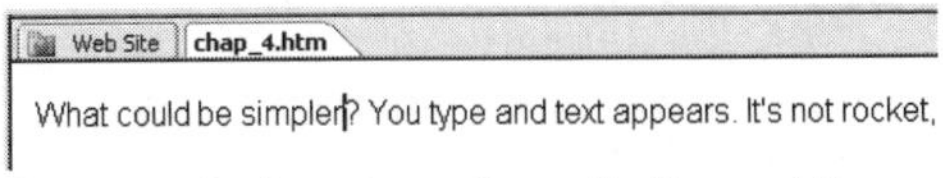

Figure 4.7 Begin typing at the vertical bar and the text will be inserted.

To move the text cursor

1. Use your mouse or the arrow keys to move the cursor to where you want to insert text. An I-beam will mark the cursor's screen location (**Figure 4.6**).

2. Click at the insertion point and the blinking vertical bar will move to that spot (**Figure 4.7**). You're ready to begin typing at the new spot.

✔ Tips

- To jump from word to word, press Ctrl S or Ctrl A.

- To jump from paragraph to paragraph, press Ctrl Z or Ctrl W.

MOVING THE TEXT CURSOR

To select text

1. Position your cursor at the beginning or end of the text you want to select (see **Table 4.1** for keyboard shortcuts).

2. Click and drag your cursor to select the text, which will become highlighted (**Figure 4.8**).

3. You now can copy the selected text (Ctrl C) or cut it to the clipboard (Ctrl X) for pasting elsewhere (Ctrl V).

To delete text

1. Position your cursor at the beginning or end of the text you want to select.

2. Click and drag your cursor to select the text, which will become highlighted (see **Table 4.2** for keyboard shortcuts) (**Figure 4.8**).

3. Press (←Backspace) or (Delete) and the text will be deleted (**Figure 4.9**).

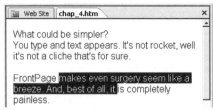

Figure 4.8 Click and drag the cursor to highlight and select text for editing.

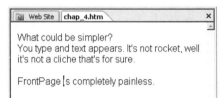

Figure 4.9 Press (←Backspace) or (Delete) and any highlighted text will be deleted.

Table 4.1

Shortcuts for selecting text	
TO SELECT	PRESS
Character to right of cursor	Delete
Character to left of cursor	←Backspace
Single word	Double-click
Word to right of cursor	Shift Ctrl →
Word to left of cursor	Shift Ctrl ←
From cursor to end of line	Shift End
From cursor to beginning of line	Shift Home
From cursor to line down	Shift ↓
From cursor to line up	Shift ↑
Entire paragraph	Alt click
To end of paragraph	Shift Ctrl ↓
To beginning of paragraph	Shift Ctrl ↑
To end of next screen	Shift Page Down
To beginning of previous screen	Shift Page Up

Table 4.2

Shortcuts for deleting text	
TO DELETE	PRESS
Character to right of cursor	Delete
Character to left of cursor	←Backspace
Word to right of cursor	Ctrl Delete
Word to left of cursor	Ctrl ←Backspace

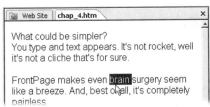

Figure 4.10 To move text, first select with your cursor.

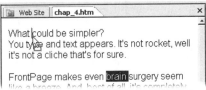

Figure 4.11 Once you've highlighted the text, drag your cursor to the text's new location.

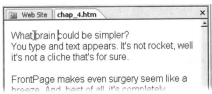

Figure 4.12 Release your cursor where you want the text inserted and it will move from its previous spot.

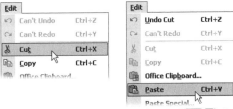

Figure 4.13 To cut text, choose Edit > Cut (Ctrl X). To paste text, choose Edit > Paste (Ctrl V).

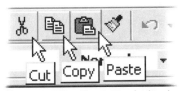

Figure 4.14 FrontPage's Standard toolbar includes icons for cutting, copying, or pasting any text you select.

To move text

1. Select the text you want to move (**Figure 4.10**).

2. Click and drag the highlighted text to its new location (**Figure 4.11**).

3. Release the cursor and the text will be moved to the new spot (**Figure 4.12**).

✔ Tips

■ You also can select the text, cut it to the clipboard ((Ctrl X)), click where you want to move it, and paste it in place ((Ctrl V)) (**Figure 4.13**).

■ If the Standard toolbar is active, you also can click the Cut, Copy, or Paste icons (**Figure 4.14**).

MOVING TEXT

To undo an action

◆ Choose Edit > Undo or press [Ctrl]-[Z]. The previous action will be undone.

To redo an action

◆ Choose Edit > Redo or press [Ctrl]-[Y]. The previous action will be reapplied.

✔ Tips

■ Both the *Undo* and *Redo* choices under the Edit menu change, depending on the previous action (**Figure 4.15**).

■ If the Standard toolbar is active, you also can click the Undo or Redo icons, which include drop-down menus listing the most recent actions (**Figure 4.16**).

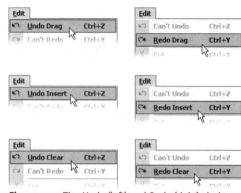

Figure 4.15 The *Undo* (left) and *Redo* (right) choices under the Edit menu change, based on the previous action.

Figure 4.16 The Standard toolbar contains Undo and Redo icons, which include drop-down menus showing the most recent actions.

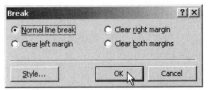

Figure 4.17 To add a line break to text, choose Insert > Break.

Figure 4.18 In the Break dialog box, *Normal line break* will be selected by default. Click *OK* and the break will be inserted.

Web Site | chap_4.htm

What could be simpler?
You type and text appears. It's not rocket, well it's not a cliche that's for sure

Figure 4.19 Once a line break is inserted, the text will break to the next line—without you having to enter the HTML code.

To add a line break to text

1. Within the right pane, click your cursor where you want the text to break to a new line.

2. Choose Insert > Break (**Figure 4.17**).

3. When the Break dialog box appears, *Normal line break* will be selected by default (**Figure 4.18**). Click *OK* (or press Enter) and a line break will be inserted (**Figure 4.19**). For details on the box's margin-related choices, see *Formatting Paragraphs, Lists, and Headings* on page 127.

✔ Tips

■ You also can insert a line break by typing Shift Enter.

■ To remove a line break, place the cursor on the beginning of the line before the break and press ←Backspace. The break will be removed.

To add a paragraph

1. Within the right pane, click your cursor where you want the paragraph to appear in the text (**Figure 4.20**).

2. Press (Enter) and a paragraph will be inserted into the text (**Figure 4.21**).

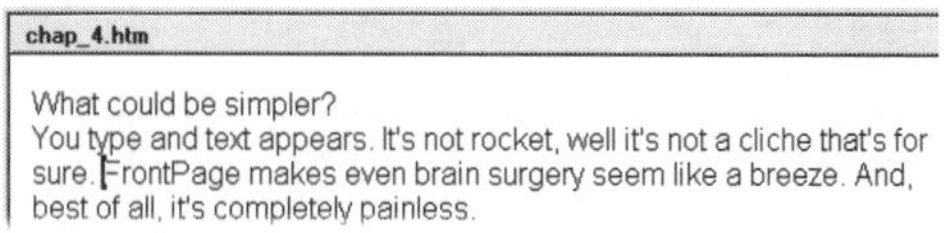

Showing line break and paragraph marks

Just as with word processing programs, you have the option of displaying normally hidden symbols that mark the location of line breaks and paragraphs within the text.

To show/hide line break and paragraph marks

◆ Click the Show All icon in the Standard toolbar (**Figure 4.22**). The text will display all line break and paragraph return marks (**Figure 4.23**). To hide the marks, click the Show All icon again.

> chap_4.htm
>
> What could be simpler?
> You type and text appears. It's not rocket, well it's not a cliche that's for sure. FrontPage makes even brain surgery seem like a breeze. And, best of all, it's completely painless.

Figure 4.20 Click your cursor where you want a paragraph to appear.

> chap_4.htm
>
> What could be simpler?
> You type and text appears. It's not rocket, well it's not a cliche that's for sure.
>
> FrontPage makes even brain surgery seem like a breeze. And, best of all, it's completely painless.

Figure 4.21 Press (Enter) and a paragraph will be inserted into the text.

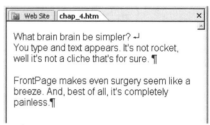

Figure 4.22 To show or hide line break and paragraph marks, click the Show All icon in the Standard toolbar.

> Web Site | chap_4.htm   ✕
>
> What brain brain be simpler? ↵
> You type and text appears. It's not rocket, well it's not a cliche that's for sure. ¶
>
> FrontPage makes even surgery seem like a breeze. And, best of all, it's completely painless.¶

Figure 4.23 The Show All icon lets you see normally hidden symbols that mark line breaks and paragraphs.

Figure 4.24 To find text on a single page or across an entire Web site, choose Edit > Find.

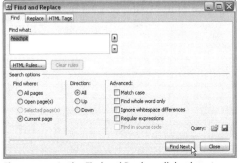

Figure 4.25 In the Find and Replace dialog box, type in the word or phrase you're seeking and choose *Current page*. Check any other search criteria and click *Find Next*.

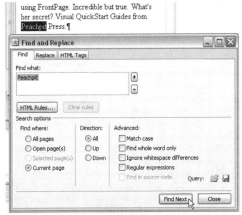

Figure 4.26 The Find and Replace dialog box remains visible even after the first instance of the word or phrase is found. Click *Find Next* again to continue searching.

Finding and Replacing Text and Code

Besides the standard find and replace functions you'd expect, FrontPage also lets you search the HTML code, which means you can find words, phrases, or even bits of code that may not be visible in the Design view. FrontPage 2003 has added some handy features for searching HTML tags, such as being able to search for a specific tag style or changing a tag's attributes across the site.

To find text on a single page

1. If you're not already in Page view, choose View > Page and make sure the *Design* tab is selected.

2. Make the Folder List visible by choosing View > Folder List or clicking the Folder icon.

3. Choose Edit > Find ($\boxed{Ctrl}$ $\boxed{F}$) (**Figure 4.24**).

4. When the *Find* tab of the Find and Replace dialog box appears, type in the word or phrase you're seeking and choose *Current page* (**Figure 4.25**).

5. By default, FrontPage will search in *All* directions, though you can use the drop-down menu to select *Up* or *Down*. Use the checkboxes if you want the search to *Match case* or *Find whole word only*. Click *Find Next* and the first instance of the word or phrase will be found (**Figure 4.26**). The *Find* tab of the Find and Replace dialog box will remain visible, allowing you to continue clicking *Find Next* until you find the instance you're looking for.

6. When you're done searching, click *Cancel* or the Close button in the dialog box's upper-right corner.

To find text across a Web site

1. If you're not already in Page view, choose View > Page and make sure the *Design* tab is selected.

2. Make the Folder List visible by choosing View > Folder List or clicking the Folder icon.

3. Choose Edit > Find ([Ctrl][F]) (**Figure 4.24**).

4. When the *Find* tab of the Find and Replace dialog box appears, type in the word or phrase you're seeking and choose *All pages* (**Figure 4.27**).

5. By default, FrontPage will search in *All* directions, though you can use the drop-down menu to select *Up* or *Down*. Use the checkboxes if you want the search to *Match case* or *Find whole word only*. Click *Find in Site*.

6. FrontPage will search through all the pages of the current Web site and list the pages containing the search phrase and how many times it appears on those pages (**Figure 4.28**).

7. Double-click on the page listing you'd like to search in detail, and you'll be taken to the first instance of the search phrase on that page. A basic Find and Replace dialog box also will appear in which you can click *Find Next* to continue searching the page (**Figure 4.29**).

8. The next instance of the search phrase on that page will appear. To keep searching, click *Find Next* again and the next instance will appear.

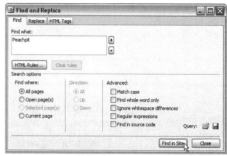

Figure 4.27 To search an entire Web site, choose *All pages*, set your other criteria, and click *Find in Site*.

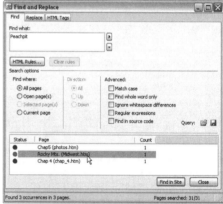

Figure 4.28 After searching the Web site, FrontPage will list every page with the phrase and how many times it appears. Double-click a page listing to search it.

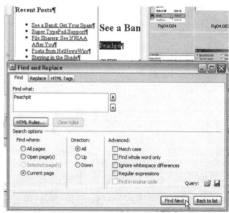

Figure 4.29 A standard Find and Replace dialog box will appear. Click *Find Next* to continue searching the individual page.

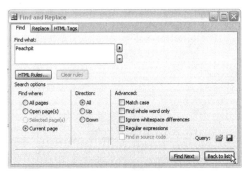

Figure 4.30 To see instances of the search phrase on one of the other pages initially listed, click the Find and Replace dialog box's *Back to list* button.

Figure 4.31 After clicking the *Back to list* button, you'll be returned to the original search results dialog box.

9. If you want to see instances of the search phrase on one of the other pages initially listed, click the Find and Replace dialog box's *Back to list* button (**Figure 4.30**). You'll be returned to the original search results dialog box (**Figure 4.31**).

10. Double-click any other page in the list and instances of the search phrase on that page will appear.

11. When you're done, click *Cancel* or the Close button in the dialog box's upper-right corner.

To search the site's HTML code

1. If you're not already in Page view, choose View > Page (see first *Tip*).

2. Choose Edit > Find ([Ctrl][F]) (**Figure 4.24**).

3. When the *Find* tab of the Find and Replace dialog box appears, type in the code you're seeking and set your other search criteria. Then check the *Find in source code* box and click *Find in Site* (**Figure 4.32**). FrontPage will list every page where the code appears (**Figure 4.33**).

4. Double-click an individual page listing and you'll be taken in *Code* view to the first instance of the code—even if it's normally not visible (**Figure 4.34**).

5. Continue to search that page by clicking *Find Next* or return to other page listings by clicking *Back to list*. When you're done, click *Cancel* or the Close button in the Find and Replace dialog box's upper-right corner.

✔ Tips

- In step 1, it's fine to stay with the *Design* tab since FrontPage will automatically switch to the *Code* tag when you view the results in step 4.

- If you know the basics of HTML coding, this option offers a quick way to fix or replace coding across an entire Web site. If you don't understand HTML, this option can get you into deep trouble—fast.

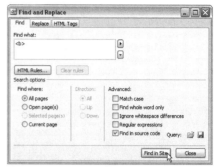

Figure 4.32 To search the Web site's HTML code, type in what you're seeking and choose *All pages*. Then check the *Find in source code* box and click *Find in Site*.

Figure 4.33 FrontPage will list every page where the search phrase exists—even pages containing invisible HTML coding.

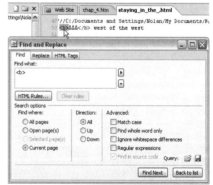

Figure 4.34 FrontPage will display in *Code* view the first instance of HTML code—even if it's normally not visible.

Figure 4.35 To replace text or HTML on a single page or the entire site, choose Edit > Replace (Ctrl H).

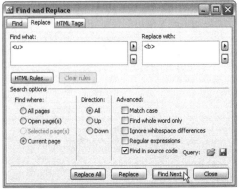

Figure 4.36 To replace text or HTML on a single page, type in the word, phrase, or code you're seeking, the replacement text or HTML, choose *Current page* and click *Find Next*.

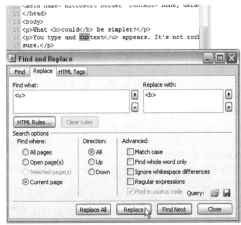

Figure 4.37 Once you begin the search, FrontPage will display the first instance of the text or code. Click *Replace*.

To replace text or HTML on a single page

1. If you're not already in Page view, choose View > Page and make sure the *Split* or *Code* tab is selected.

2. Make the Folder List visible by choosing View > Folder List or clicking the Folder icon.

3. Choose Edit > Replace (Ctrl H) (**Figure 4.35**).

4. When the *Replace* tab of the Find and Replace dialog box appears, type in the word, phrase, or code you're seeking in the *Find what* window, the text or code you want to replace it with in the *Replace with* window, choose *Current page*, and set your other search criteria, such as *Find in source code* (**Figure 4.36**).

5. Click *Find Next* and the first instance of the text or code will be found (**Figure 4.37**).

6. Click *Replace* and FrontPage will make the fix and immediately move to the next instance of the text or code.

(continued)

7. Continue clicking the *Find Next* and *Replace* buttons until an alert dialog box tells you that FrontPage has finished searching the page. Click *OK* (**Figure 4.38**).

8. When the Find and Replace dialog box reappears, click *Cancel* or the Close button in its upper-right corner.

✔ Tip

- If you're absolutely sure you want to replace every instance of a search phrase, click *Replace All* in the *Replace* tab of the Find and Replace dialog box and the search-and-replace process for the entire page will occur automatically (**Figure 4.39**).

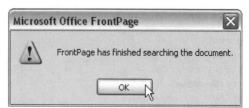

Figure 4.38 An alert dialog box appears once FrontPage has finished searching the page.

Figure 4.39 To automatically replace every instance of the search phrase, click *Replace All* in the Find and Replace dialog box.

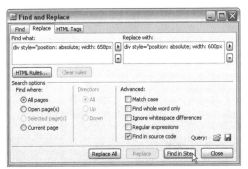

Figure 4.40 To search and replace across an entire Web site, type in the text or code you're seeking, the replacement text or HTML, choose *All pages,* and click *Find in Site.*

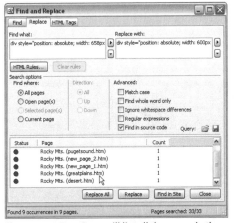

Figure 4.41 FrontPage will list all the pages in the Web site containing the search phrase and how many times it appears in each page. To see any page, double-click its listing.

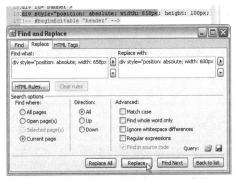

Figure 4.42 Once you double-click a page listing, FrontPage jumps to the page and displays the first instance of the search phrase. To fix it, click *Replace.*

To replace text or HTML across a Web site

1. If you're not already in Page view, choose View > Page and make sure the *Split* or *Code* tab is selected.

2. Make the Folder List visible by choosing View > Folder List or clicking the Folder icon.

3. Choose Edit > Replace ([Ctrl][H]) (**Figure 4.35**).

4. When the *Replace* tab of the Find and Replace dialog box appears, type in the text or code you're seeking in the *Find what* window, the text or code you want to replace it with in the *Replace with* window, choose *All pages,* and set your other search criteria, such as *Find in source code.* Click *Find in site* (**Figure 4.40**).

5. FrontPage will search through all the pages of the current Web site and list the pages containing the search phrase and how many times it appears in those pages (**Figure 4.41**).

6. Double-click any of the pages listed and you'll be taken to that page's first instance of the text or code you'd like to replace (**Figure 4.42**).

(continued)

7. Click *Replace* and FrontPage will fix the search phrase and immediately move to the next instance of the phrase in the same page.

8. After it replaces every instance on the selected page, FrontPage asks if you want to search the *Next Page* or go *Back To List* (**Figure 4.43**). Click *Back To List* to save and close the page and you'll be returned to the original search results dialog box. The *Replace* tab of the Find and Replace dialog box marks the page you just searched and replaced as *Edited* (**Figure 4.44**).

9. Double-click any other page in the list and that page's instances of the search phrase will appear. Repeat steps 7–9.

10. When you're done, click *Cancel* or the Close button in the dialog box's upper-right corner.

✔ Tips

■ FrontPage 2003 offers you the option of using regular expressions, such as *Zero or more* and *Beginning of line*, in your searches. In step 4, choose either the *Find* or *Replace* tab, click the first arrow next to the *Find what* or *Replace with* text windows and make a choice from the drop-down menu (**Figure 4.45**).

■ The Find and Replace dialog box now also includes an *HTML Tags* tab, which gives you new options to search and replace specific HTML tags, or their attributes (**Figure 4.46**). If you're comfortable working directly with HTML tags, this option gives FrontPage some great new search powers.

Figure 4.43 After it replaces every instance on the selected page, FrontPage asks if you want to search the *Next Page* (top) or go *Back To List* (bottom).

Figure 4.44 Once the fixes on a page have been saved, the Find and Replace dialog box will mark the page as *Edited*. Double-click any other listing to search that page.

Figure 4.45 You can also search for and replace such regular expressions as *Zero or more* and *Beginning of line*.

Figure 4.46 The Find and Replace dialog box also includes an *HTML Tags* tab, which offers new options to search and replace specific HTML tags.

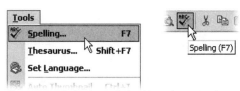

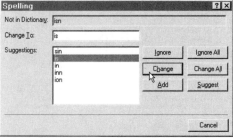

Figure 4.47 To begin spell checking, choose Tools > Spelling ([F7]) or, if the Standard toolbar is active, click the Spelling icon.

Figure 4.48 When FrontPage finds a suspected error, the Spelling dialog box will display the word and offer suggested spellings.

Figure 4.49 When FrontPage finishes checking the page, it displays an alert dialog box. Click *OK*.

Checking Spelling

FrontPage lets you check the spelling on a single page or across an entire Web site. It even lets you check spelling as you type, though that particular option drives a lot of people crazy. I prefer running the spell check after I've built a page. By the way, FrontPage lets you change the dictionary language from the default U.S. English to more than two dozen other languages.

To check spelling on a single page

1. If you're not already in Page view, choose View > Page and make sure the *Design* tab is selected.

2. Choose Tools > Spelling ([F7]) or, if the Standard toolbar is active, click the Spelling icon (**Figure 4.47**).

3. FrontPage will begin checking the current page. When it finds a suspected error, the Spelling dialog box will display the word and offer suggested spellings (**Figure 4.48**).

4. If you want to use a suggested word, click *Change* or *Change All* if you want every instance on the page fixed. If you know the word's spelled correctly— perhaps it's a trademark that FrontPage doesn't recognize—click *Ignore* or *Ignore All*. You also can add terms like trademarks to FrontPage's dictionary by clicking *Add*. If the suggested word isn't correct, you can type in your own spelling and click *Change* or *Change All*.

5. FrontPage will continue checking the page and display an alert dialog box when it's done. Click *OK* and you're done (**Figure 4.49**).

To check spelling across a Web site

1. Make sure the Folder List is visible by choosing View > Folder List or by clicking the Folder icon.

2. Choose Tools > Spelling or, if the Standard toolbar is active, click the Spelling icon.

3. When the Spelling dialog box appears, make sure that the *Entire Web site* radio button is selected (**Figure 4.50**). Click *Start* and FrontPage will begin checking the entire Web site. FrontPage will search the current Web site and list pages containing suspected misspellings and how many misspellings appear on each page (**Figure 4.51**).

4. Double-click any of the pages listed and you'll be taken to that page's first instance of the suspected misspelling. FrontPage also will show suggested spellings for the word.

5. Just as in spell checking a single page, you may click *Change* or *Change All*, *Ignore* or *Ignore All*, or you can type in your own spelling and click *Change* or *Change All*.

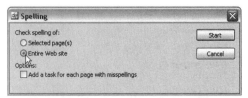

Figure 4.50 Check *Entire Web site* in the Spelling dialog box and click *Start* to spell check every page.

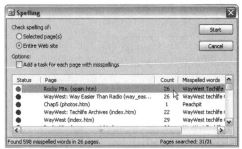

Figure 4.51 FrontPage will search the current Web site and list pages containing suspected misspellings. To see a page, double-click its listing.

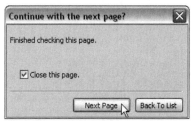

Figure 4.52 When FrontPage has fixed all the misspellings on a page, a dialog box will appear asking whether you want to continue checking the next page.

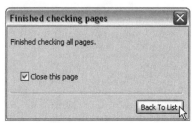

Figure 4.53 When FrontPage has fixed all the misspellings on the site, a dialog box will appear asking whether you want to close the page and return to the list. Click *Back To List*.

6. When FrontPage has fixed all the misspellings on the first page, a dialog box will appear asking whether you want to check for errors on the other pages (**Figure 4.52**). Click *Next Page* and FrontPage will automatically open and check the next page in the list. If you want to limit the spelling check to certain pages, click *Back To List* where you can jump to another page.

7. When FrontPage has fixed all the misspellings on the site, a dialog box will appear asking whether you want to close the page and return to the list (**Figure 4.53**). Click *Back To List* and you'll be returned to the list of pages with suspected misspellings. The pages you have spell checked will be marked as *Edited*.

8. When you're done, click *Cancel* or the Close button in the dialog box's upper-right corner.

To check spelling as you type

1. Choose Tools > Page Options (**Figure 4.54**).

2. When the Page Options dialog box appears, click the *General* tab and check the box marked *Check spelling as you type* (**Figure 4.55**).

3. Click *OK* and FrontPage will automatically check your spelling.

✔ Tip

■ Instead of having FrontPage check your spelling as you type, it's probably best to check *Hide spelling errors in all documents* in the Page Options dialog box. Otherwise, FrontPage will underline any word it doesn't recognize—which can make for an awful lot of red underlines (**Figure 4.56**).

To change the dictionary language

1. Choose Tools > Page Options (**Figure 4.54**).

2. When the Page Options dialog box appears, use the *Default spelling language* drop-down menu to pick a language other than U.S. English (**Figure 4.55**). When you're done, click *OK*.

Figure 4.54 To check spelling as you type, choose Tools > Page Options.

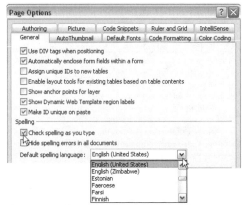

Figure 4.55 The Page Options dialog box lets you control whether FrontPage checks and shows spelling errors as you type. It also lets you set your dictionary's language.

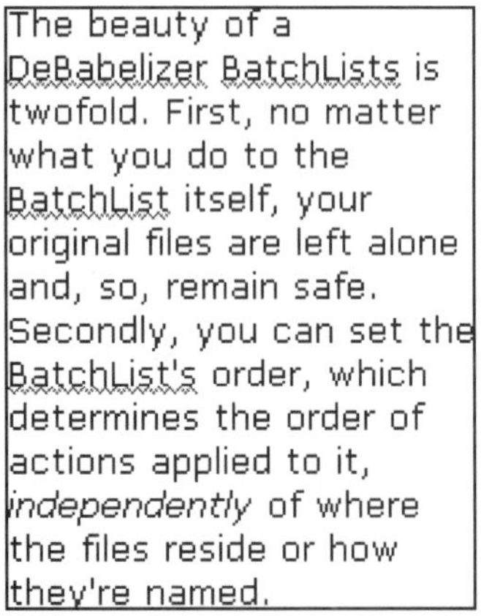

> The beauty of a DeBabelizer BatchLists is twofold. First, no matter what you do to the BatchList itself, your original files are left alone and, so, remain safe. Secondly, you can set the BatchList's order, which determines the order of actions applied to it, *independently* of where the files reside or how they're named.

Figure 4.56 The drawback of showing spelling errors as you type: Any word FrontPage doesn't recognize gets underlined, which makes for a messy page.

Formatting Text

If you're hand coding in HTML, making a word appear in bold face involves a surprising amount of rigmarole. In FrontPage, applying character styles works similarly to how it's done in word-processing programs: make a selection, click an icon, and you're done. The Formatting toolbar, which is on by default, includes everything you'll need for the most common text changes (**Figure 4.57**). Still more text formatting choices are available in the Font dialog box (details on page 123).

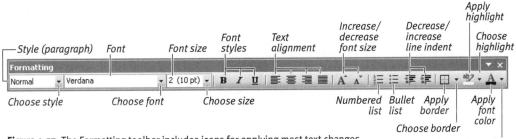

Figure 4.57 The Formatting toolbar includes icons for applying most text changes.

To change the font face

1. Make sure you're in Page view by choosing View > Page.

2. Select the text you want to change (**Figure 4.58**).

3. Click the arrow just to the right of the Formatting toolbar's font window and scroll through the drop-down menu until you find a font you want (**Figure 4.59**).

4. Click on the font you want and it will be applied to the selected text (**Figure 4.60**).

✔ Tip

■ You also can change highlighted text by right-clicking in the page and choosing *Font* (Alt Enter) from the shortcut menu (**Figure 4.61**). When the Font dialog box appears, choose the font from the scrolling Font window, then click *OK* (**Figure 4.62**). For details on the Font dialog box, see *Font options* on page 123.

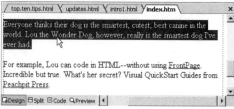

Figure 4.58 Select the text whose font you want to change.

Figure 4.59 To change the font face, click the arrow for the Formatting toolbar's font window and scroll through the drop-down menu for the font you want.

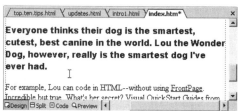

Figure 4.60 Once you click on the font, the change is applied to the selected text.

Figure 4.61 You can reach the Font dialog box any time by selecting text, right-clicking in the page, and choosing *Font* (Alt Enter) from the shortcut menu.

Figure 4.62 The Font dialog box offers extensive control over the appearance and formatting of any highlighted text.

CHANGING THE FONT FACE

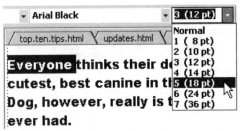

Figure 4.63 Select the text whose size you want to change, click the arrow for the Formatting toolbar's Font Size window, and scroll through the drop-down menu for the size you want.

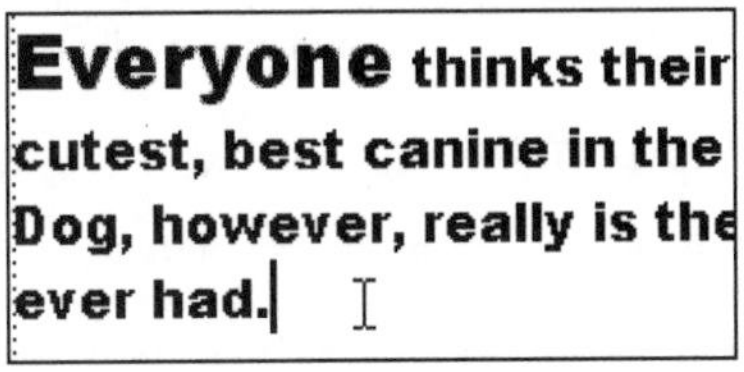

Everyone thinks their
cutest, best canine in the
Dog, however, really is the
ever had.

Figure 4.64 Once you click on the size, the change is applied to the selected text.

To change the font size

1. Make sure you're in Page view by choosing View > Page.

2. Select the text you want to change.

3. In the Formatting toolbar, click the arrow just to the right of the Font Size window and choose a size from the drop-down menu (**Figure 4.63**).

4. Release the cursor and the new size will be applied to the selected text (**Figure 4.64**).

✔ Tip

■ You also can change the text's font size by right-clicking the page and choosing *Font* (Alt Enter) from the shortcut menu (**Figure 4.61**). Within the Font dialog box, make a choice in the scrolling *Size* window, and click *OK* (**Figure 4.62**). For details, see *Font options* on page 123.

CHANGING FONT SIZE

To change the font style

1. If you're not already in Page view, choose View > Page and make sure the *Design* tab is selected.

2. Select the text you want to change (**Figure 4.65**).

3. Click one of the three style icons (*Bold*, *Italic*, or *Underline*) in the Formatting toolbar (**Figure 4.66**).

4. The style is applied to the selection (**Figure 4.67**).

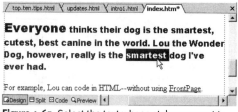

Figure 4.65 Select the text whose style you want to change.

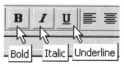

Figure 4.66 Click one of the three style icons in the Formatting toolbar.

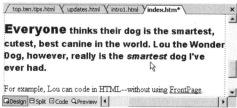

Figure 4.67 Once you click one of the style icons, the change is applied to the selected text.

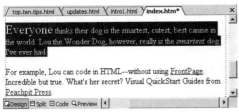

Figure 4.68 Select the text whose color you want to change.

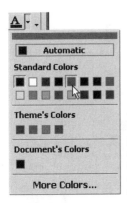

Figure 4.69 Click the arrow next to the Font Color icon and choose a color from the drop-down menu.

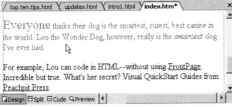

Figure 4.70 Once you release the cursor, the color change is applied to the selected text.

To change the font color

1. Make sure you're in Page view by choosing View > Page.

2. Select the text you want to change (**Figure 4.68**).

3. Click the arrow just to the right of the Font Color icon and choose a color from the drop-down menu (**Figure 4.69**).

4. Release the cursor and the color will be applied to the selected text (**Figure 4.70**).

✔ Tip

■ You also can change the text's color by right-clicking the page and choosing *Font* ([Alt][Enter]) from the shortcut menu (**Figure 4.61**). Within the Font dialog box, click the *Color* drop-down menu, make your choice, and click *OK* (**Figure 4.62**). For details see *Font options* on page 123.

To change text alignment

1. Make sure you're in Page view by choosing View > Page.

2. Select the text you want to change (**Figure 4.71**).

3. In the Formatting toolbar, click one of the four alignment icons (**Figure 4.72**).

4. Release the cursor and the text will be aligned based on which icon you clicked (**Figure 4.73**).

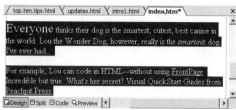

Figure 4.71 Select the text whose alignment you want to change.

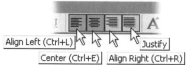

Figure 4.72 Click one of the four alignment icons in the Formatting toolbar.

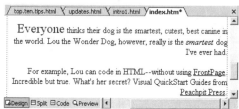

Figure 4.73 Once you click one of the alignment icons, the change is applied to the selected text.

Figure 4.74 To reach the Font dialog box, select some text, right-click, and choose *Font* from the shortcut menu.

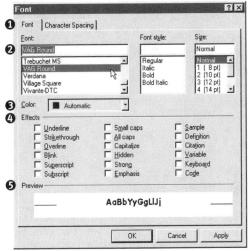

Figure 4.75 The Font dialog box's *Font* tab lets you change the selected text's font, font style, size, and text color.

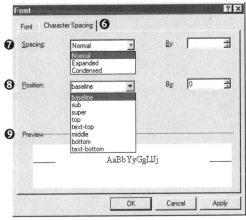

Figure 4.76 The *Character Spacing* tab lets you change the selected text's horizontal spacing and vertical positioning.

Font options

To open the Font dialog box, select some text, right-click, and choose *Font* from the shortcut menu (**Figures 4.74** and **4.75**). The dialog box's *Font* tab ❶ is active by default and lets you change the font, font style, size ❷, and text color ❸. It also lets you apply text effects ❹ not available within the Formatting toolbar. Check a box and you can see its effect within the *Preview* window ❺.

Clicking the Font dialog box's *Character Spacing* tab ❻ displays the *Spacing* ❼ and *Position* ❽ drop-down menus, which let you adjust the horizontal spacing and vertical positioning of the text you've selected (**Figure 4.76**). The *Preview* window ❾ lets you see the effects of various spacing and positioning combinations. For details on spacing and positions, see the next page.

To change character spacing

1. Make sure you're in Page view by choosing View > Page.

2. Select the text you want to change.

3. Right-click and choose *Font* from the shortcut menu (**Figure 4.74**).

4. When the Font dialog box appears (**Figure 4.76**), click the *Character Spacing* tab.

5. Use the *Spacing* drop-down menu to quickly choose whether you want the text's horizontal spacing to be *Expanded*, *Normal*, or *Condensed*. The results will be displayed in the *Preview* window. To fine tune the horizontal spacing, use the arrows of the adjacent *By* window to adjust the spacing in either direction (**Figure 4.77**).

6. When you're done, click *OK* and the spacing will be applied to the selected text.

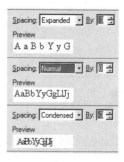

Figure 4.77 Within the Font dialog box, use the *Spacing* drop-down menu to control whether the text is *Expanded*, *Normal*, or *Condensed*. The adjacent *By* window lets you fine tune the spacing.

To change character positioning

1. Make sure you're in Page view by choosing View > Page.

2. Select the text you want to change.

3. Right-click and choose *Font* from the shortcut menu (**Figure 4.74**).

4. When the Font dialog box appears (**Figure 4.76**), click the *Character Spacing* tab.

5. Use the *Position* drop-down menu to quickly adjust the text's vertical alignment. The results will be displayed in the *Preview* window (**Figure 4.78**).

6. When you're done, click *OK* and the spacing will be applied to the selected text.

Figure 4.78 Within the Font dialog box, use the *Position* drop-down menu to control the text's vertical alignment.

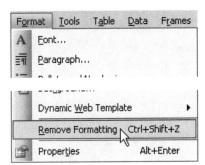

Figure 4.79 To remove all text formatting, select the text and choose Format > Remove Formatting (Ctrl Shift Z).

To remove text formatting

1. Make sure you're in Page view by choosing View > Page.

2. Select the text whose formatting you want to remove.

3. Choose Format > Remove Formatting (Ctrl Shift Z) (**Figure 4.79**). All of the text's formatting will be removed, reverting back to its default settings.

Using Symbols and Special Characters

The advantage of having FrontPage automatically handle your HTML coding becomes particularly obvious when you need to add special characters to your Web pages. Whether it's a copyright symbol, a formula operator, a Euro sign, or a Cyrillic character, FrontPage can handle it and spare you the headache of remembering the HTML equivalent.

To add a symbol or special character

1. Click in the page where you want the symbol or special character to appear.

2. Choose Insert > Symbol (**Figure 4.80**).

3. When the Symbol dialog box appears, click the *Subset* drop-down menu and choose which symbol or language subset you want to use (**Figure 4.81**). Release your cursor once you have scrolled to the desired subset and its characters will appear in the dialog box's main window.

4. Find the particular symbol you need by using the main window's scroll bar, select it, and click *Insert* (**Figure 4.82**). The character will be inserted into your Web page.

✔ Tip

■ The Symbol dialog box's *Recently used symbols* window can save you a ton of time if you use particular characters over and over (**Figure 4.81**). After you have inserted a particular character into a page once, it will be added to the *Recently used symbols* window—where it will be immediately available the next time you need it. The window can store up to 16 recent characters.

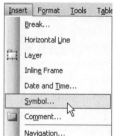

Figure 4.80 To add a symbol or special character to a page, choose Insert > Symbol.

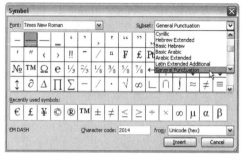

Figure 4.81 Use the Symbol dialog box's *Subset* drop-down menu to find a particular subset of characters.

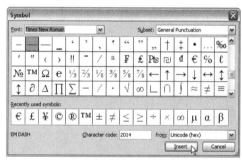

Figure 4.82 Select the desired symbol in the dialog box's main window and click *Insert*.

FORMATTING PARAGRAPHS, LISTS, AND HEADINGS

While graphics give your Web pages pizzazz, it's the paragraphs, lists, and headings that handle the real workload of setting your pages' visual hierarchy. FrontPage lets you easily set and control all three, primarily with the Formatting toolbar (**Figure 5.1**). If those controls, however, don't provide exactly what you need—or you want to create a custom style and use it repeatedly—consider using style sheets. See *Building Style Sheets and Dynamic Effects* on page 363.

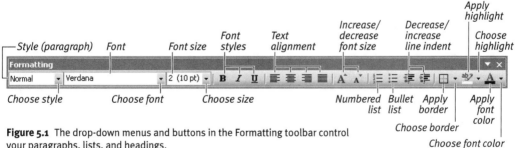

Figure 5.1 The drop-down menus and buttons in the Formatting toolbar control your paragraphs, lists, and headings.

Using Paragraphs

FrontPage lets you change the appearance of your paragraphs by adjusting the alignment, indentation, spacing above and below the paragraph, and line spacing (leading).

To align a paragraph

1. If you're not already in Page view, choose View > Page.

2. Click anywhere in the paragraph you want to change and choose one of the four alignment buttons in the Formatting toolbar (**Figure 5.2**). (By default, paragraphs are aligned to the left.) The new alignment will be applied (**Figure 5.3**).

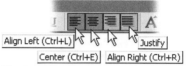

Figure 5.2 To align a paragraph, click one of the four alignment buttons in the Formatting toolbar.

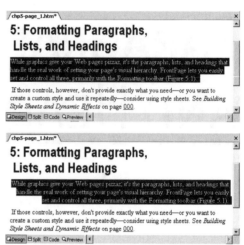

Figure 5.3 The paragraph was aligned to the left (top) until being reformatted to align on the right (bottom).

Figure 5.4 To change a paragraph's indentation, click the Increase Indent or Decrease Indent button.

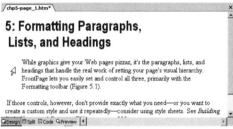

5: Formatting Paragraphs, Lists, and Headings

While graphics give your Web pages pizzaz, it's the paragraphs, lists, and headings that handle the real work of setting your page's visual hierarchy. FrontPage lets you easily set and control all three, primarily with the Formatting toolbar (Figure 5.1).

If those controls, however, don't provide exactly what you need—or you want to create a custom style and use it repeatedly—consider using style sheets. See *Building*

Figure 5.5 After applying the indent, the paragraph will shift to reflect your choice.

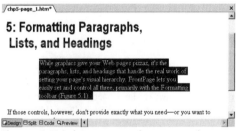

5: Formatting Paragraphs, Lists, and Headings

While graphics give your Web pages pizzaz, it's the paragraphs, lists, and headings that handle the real work of setting your page's visual hierarchy. FrontPage lets you easily set and control all three, primarily with the Formatting toolbar (Figure 5.1).

If those controls, however, don't provide exactly what you need—or you want to

Figure 5.6 To indent a paragraph even more, keep clicking the Increase Indent button.

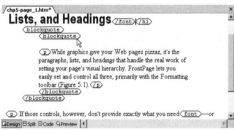

Figure 5.7 You can see the normally hidden HTML tags as you work by choosing View > Reveal Tags. Repeat the command to hide them again.

Indenting paragraphs

FrontPage gives you several ways to indent paragraphs. The quickest way involves using the buttons in the Formatting toolbar; the more precise method requires setting custom indentations within the Paragraph dialog box.

To indent a paragraph

1. Be sure you're in Page view by choosing View > Page, then click anywhere in the paragraph you want to indent.

2. Click the Increase Indent button or the Decrease Indent button in the Formatting toolbar (**Figure 5.4**). The indenting will be applied (**Figure 5.5**).

3. If you want to indent the paragraph even more, continue clicking the Increase Indent button until you're satisfied with the result (**Figure 5.6**).

✔ Tips

- The indent buttons affect both margins of the selected text *equally* (**Figure 5.6**). To set *different* indents for each margin, see *To customize paragraph indents* on the next page.

- As with all Web editors, FrontPage uses HTML tags to format your text. But to keep the document from getting cluttered, FrontPage ordinarily hides the coding from sight. To see the tags at any point, choose View > Reveal Tags (Ctrl I) (**Figure 5.7**). Repeat the command to hide the tags again.

To customize paragraph indents

1. Be sure you're in Page view, then choose Format > Paragraph (**Figure 5.8**).

2. When the Paragraph dialog box appears, use the *Indentation* section's arrows to set the indentation (in points) *Before text* and *After text* (**Figure 5.9**).

3. Click *OK* and your custom indentation will be applied (**Figure 5.10**).

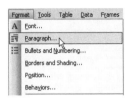

Figure 5.8 To modify the Normal paragraph style, choose Format > Paragraph.

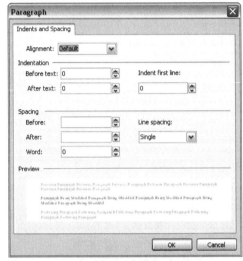

Figure 5.9 Use the Paragraph dialog box's pop-up menus and arrows to simultaneously change multiple aspects of a paragraph. The *Preview* area at the bottom shows how the changes will look.

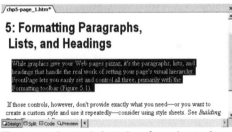

Figure 5.10 Custom indentation of 15 points to the left and 60 points to the right applied to the highlighted paragraph.

Paragraph styling

The easiest way to change several aspects of a paragraph at once is to modify FrontPage's *Normal* style. Normal style by default uses the Times New Roman font with single line spacing, left-aligned, with no indentations. Or you can use the built-in *Formatted* style, which uses Courier monospaced in a typewriter-like style that requires you to manually enter any line returns. It looks clunky, but before fancy HTML came along, it was often the only way to make text wrap exactly.

To modify the Normal paragraph style

1. Be sure you're in Page view. Click anywhere in the paragraph whose style you want to change and choose Format > Paragraph (**Figure 5.8**).

2. When the Paragraph dialog box appears, use the pop-up menus and arrows to set your paragraph's alignment, indentation, indentation for the paragraph's first line only, the amount of blank space you want before and after the paragraph, and the line spacing within the paragraph (**Figure 5.9**). The *Preview* area at the bottom of the dialog box lets you see how the indents and spacing will be applied.

3. Once you're satisfied with the changes, click *OK* and the styling will be applied to the selected paragraph.

✔ Tip

- The Paragraph dialog box includes the option to change the spacing between words (**Figure 5.9**). Unfortunately, FrontPage can't show how the word spacing will appear. You'll have to switch to your Web browser to see the effect—and most browsers don't support the feature. You're better off skipping the word spacing feature entirely.

To apply the Formatted paragraph style

1. Be sure you're in Page view and click where you want the Formatted style to begin.

2. Use the Style drop-down list in the Formatting toolbar to choose *Formatted* (**Figure 5.11**).

3. Begin typing, using the spacebar to align and wrap the text (**Figure 5.12**).

4. When you're ready to switch back to the Normal format, use the Style drop-down list in the Formatting toolbar to choose *Normal* (**Figure 5.13**).

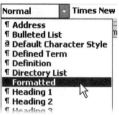

Figure 5.11 To apply the *Formatted* paragraph style, use the Style drop-down list.

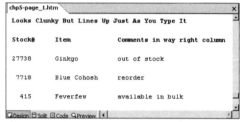

Figure 5.12 The Formatted style looks terrible, but lets you align these inventory numbers.

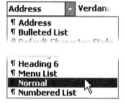

Figure 5.13 Use the Style drop-down list to switch back to the Normal format.

USING PARAGRAPHS

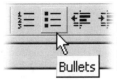

Figure 5.14 To quickly create a bulleted list, click the Bullets button in the Formatting toolbar.

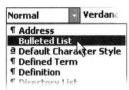

Figure 5.15 You also can create a bulleted list using the Style drop-down menu.

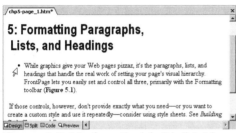

Figure 5.16 Nothing fancy: the default bullet style.

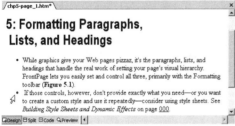

Figure 5.17 To apply bullets to several paragraphs at once, just select them and click the Bullets button.

Using Lists

FrontPage lets you create a variety of list styles, which can be broken into two general groups: unordered lists and ordered lists. Unordered lists, also known as unnumbered or bulleted lists, are great for presenting a series of items that have no particular order, such as a list of supplies. Use ordered or numbered lists whenever you want to present a list of items in sequence. While FrontPage will create directory and menu lists, they're not supported by most browsers, so it's best to avoid using them.

Creating unordered lists

By default, FrontPage uses solid, round bullets. However, you can use any of the bullets within FrontPage's built-in themes—or create custom bullets. For details, see *Customizing lists* on page 136.

To create a bulleted list

1. Be sure you're in Page view. Click anywhere in the line or paragraph that you want to begin with a bullet.

2. Click the Bullets button in the Formatting toolbar (**Figure 5.14**). Or use the Style drop-down list in the Formatting toolbar to choose *Bulleted List* (**Figure 5.15**). A bullet will be added to the line or paragraph (**Figure 5.16**).

3. To continue adding bullets to the list, press (Enter). Once you're done building the list, press (Enter) twice and FrontPage will switch back to the regular body type.

✔ Tips

- To apply bullets to several paragraphs at once, just select them and click the Bullets button (**Figure 5.17**).

- To remove bullets, click anywhere in the bulleted line or paragraph and click the Bullets button once more.

Creating definition lists

Definition lists are handy for glossaries and other dictionary-style information because the format puts a word or term on a single line with the definition indented immediately below it. Though you can type in all the terms and definitions and then format them, it's generally easier to switch to the Defined Term format and begin typing since all the formatting will be handled automatically.

To create a definition list

1. Place your cursor where you want the first definition to appear.

2. Use the Style drop-down list in the Formatting toolbar to choose *Defined Term* (**Figure 5.18**).

3. Release the cursor and type in your first term. Then press [Enter] and the cursor will jump to the next line, automatically add an indent, and switch to the Definition format (**Figure 5.19**).

4. Type in your definition. If you want to add more terms, press [Enter] again and FrontPage will jump to a new line and switch back to the Defined Term format.

5. Once you're done adding terms, press [Enter] twice and FrontPage will switch back to the normal body text (**Figure 5.20**).

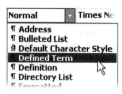

Figure 5.18 To create a definition list, place your cursor where the first definition should appear and choose *Defined Term* from the Style drop-down list.

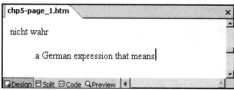

Figure 5.19 After you type in your first term and press [Enter], the cursor will jump to the next line, automatically add an indent, and switch to the Definition format.

Figure 5.20 Once you're done adding terms, press [Enter] twice and FrontPage will switch back to the normal body text.

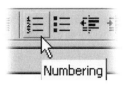

Figure 5.21 To create a numbered list, select your text and click the Numbering button in the Formatting toolbar.

Figure 5.22 You also can number text by using the Style drop-down list and choosing *Numbered List*.

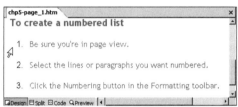

Figure 5.23 Once numbering is applied, press Enter to continue adding items to the list.

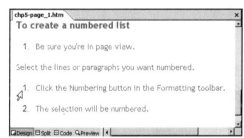

Figure 5.24 If you reformat a previously numbered item to regular text, FrontPage automatically renumbers the remaining text into *two* sequences.

Creating ordered lists

Use ordered lists whenever you want to present a list of items in sequence. Though ordered lists usually are numbered, FrontPage also lets you use letters (A, B, C,...). For details, see *Customizing lists* on the next page.

To create a numbered list

1. Be sure you're in Page view. Select the lines or paragraphs you want numbered.

2. Click the Numbering button in the Formatting toolbar (**Figure 5.21**). Or use the Style drop-down list in the Formatting toolbar to choose *Numbered List* (**Figure 5.22**). In either case, the selected lines or paragraphs will be numbered in sequence (**Figure 5.23**).

3. To continue adding numbered items to the list, press Enter. Once you're done building the list, press Enter twice and FrontPage will switch back to the regular body type.

✔ Tips

■ To remove numbers, click anywhere in the numbered line or paragraph and click the Numbering button once more. The remaining items will be renumbered and even broken into two sequences if necessary (**Figure 5.24**).

■ Instead of numbering items after you've written them, you can number them as you type. Just place your cursor where you want the first item in the list to appear, click the Numbering button, and the number 1 will appear. Begin typing, pressing Enter whenever you want the next number to begin.

USING LISTS

Customizing lists

As usual, FrontPage offers several choices for customizing your lists. Your sources of bullets for unordered lists are particularly wide: You can use FrontPage's built-in themes, the clip art that comes with FrontPage, or any graphic of your own. To use the bullets built into FrontPage's themes, see *To apply a theme to a page or Web site* on page 89.

To customize lists

1. Click anywhere in the page and choose Format > Bullets and Numbering (**Figure 5.25**). If you are changing an existing list, just right-click in the list and choose *List Properties* from the shortcut menu (**Figure 5.26**).

2. Depending on what you clicked in step 1, either the Bullets and Numbering or List Properties dialog box will appear (**Figures 5.27** and **5.28**). Choose one of the tabs, which can include *Picture Bullets*, *Plain Bullets*, *Numbers*, and *Other*.

3. Make your choices and click *OK* to apply the change to your page. For details, see *List options* on the next page.

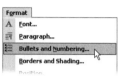

Figure 5.25 To customize your bullets or numbers, click anywhere in the page and choose Format > Bullets and Numbering.

Figure 5.26 To customize an existing list, right-click in the list and choose *List Properties* from the shortcut menu.

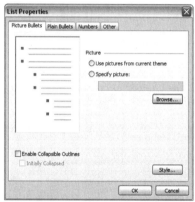

Figure 5.27 The Bullets and Numbering dialog box lets you insert your own pictures as graphical bullets.

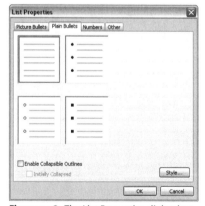

Figure 5.28 The List Properties dialog box gives you complete control over customizing bullets, numbers, and lists.

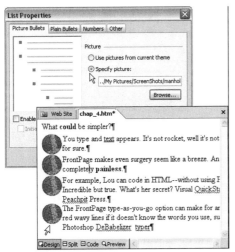

Figure 5.29 To use your own graphic as a bullet, navigate to the file and click *OK* (top). The selected graphic will be used for your bullets (bottom).

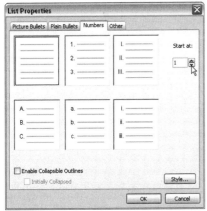

Figure 5.30 The *Numbers* tab of the List Properties dialog box gives you five numbering/lettering styles plus a blank option.

List options

Follow the steps in *To customize lists* to reach the Bullets and Numbering or List Properties dialog box (**Figures 5.27** and **5.28**). Both boxes offer the Picture Bullets, Plain Bullets, and Numbers tabs; the Other tab appears only in the List Properties box.

◆ **Picture Bullets:** This tab lets you use your own graphics as bullets—even if you're also using one of FrontPage's built-in themes. To turn off the theme's bullets, click *Specify picture*, then click *Browse* and navigate to the graphic file you want to use (top, **Figure 5.29**). Click *OK* and the selected graphic will be used for your bullets (bottom, **Figure 5.29**).

◆ **Plain Bullets:** This tab lets you choose one of three plain bullet styles (**Figure 5.28**). The fourth, upper-left choice offers a somewhat roundabout option for canceling the bullets entirely. Once you've made your choice, click *OK* to apply the plain bullet style.

◆ **Numbers:** This tab lets you choose one of five numbering/lettering styles (**Figure 5.30**). Again, the upper-left choice lets you cancel numbering. Use the *Start at* arrows if you want to start the numbering at, say, 4 or the fifth letter, E. Once you've made your choice, click *OK* to apply.

(continued)

◆ **Other:** This tab lets you quickly switch
the style of an entire list to any of the
other styles in the text window (**Figure
5.31**). Once you've made your choice,
click *OK* to apply.

✔ Tip

■ Every tab of the List Properties dialog box
includes checkboxes for *Enable Collapsible
Outlines* and *Initially Collapsed*. These fea-
tures are available only if you're using
Dynamic HTML (DHTML) and are recog-
nized only by version 4 or later browsers.
For details, see *Building Style Sheets and
Dynamic Effects* on page 363.

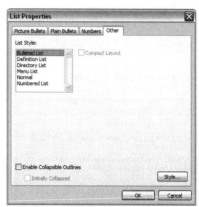

Figure 5.31 The *Other* tab of the List
Properties dialog box lets you change an
entire list to another style.

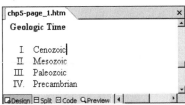

Figure 5.32 To create a nested list, click in a bulleted or numbered list just before where you want the subdivision to start.

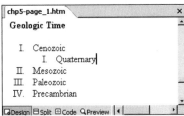

Figure 5.33 By default, the nested subdivision's numbering or lettering matches the level above it.

Figure 5.34 To change a subdivision's numbering or lettering scheme, right-click and choose List Item Properties.

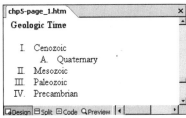

Figure 5.35 The nested item, *Quaternary*, now has a letter instead of a number.

Nested lists

Nested lists, sometimes called multilevel lists, enable you to create subdivisions within an overall list. They also lend themselves to customizing, such as using numbers at one level and letters at another.

To create a nested list

1. First create a bulleted or numbered list, then click in that list just before the place you want to insert a nested subdivision (**Figure 5.32**).

2. Press Enter and click the Increase Indent button *twice* (**Figure 5.4**).

3. When a new, blank line is inserted into the list, begin typing your first nested item. By default, it will be numbered or lettered just like the level above it (**Figure 5.33**).

4. If you want to change the *subdivision's* numbering or lettering scheme, right-click and choose *List Item Properties* from the shortcut menu (**Figure 5.34**).

5. When the List Item Properties dialog box appears, choose a numbering or lettering style, click *OK*, and the style will be applied to the nested item only (**Figure 5.35**).

(continued)

USING LISTS

6. To add another item at this same nested level, press (Enter) and it will be numbered or lettered in the same style you chose in step 5. Continue adding items at that level until you're done.

7. If you want to nest still another level in the list, repeat steps 1–6 (**Figure 5.36**).

8. When you're done building the nested list, press (Enter) twice to switch back to regular body type.

✔ Tip

■ In step 4, be sure to choose *List Item Properties*, not *List Properties* (**Figure 5.34**). *List Item Properties* controls the nested list items; *List Properties* controls the overall list in which the items nest.

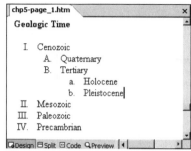

Figure 5.36 FrontPage lets you nest items within already nested items, changing the numbering or lettering style at each level.

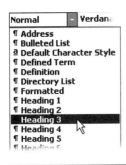

Figure 5.37 To convert text to a heading, use the Style drop-down menu to select the heading size you want.

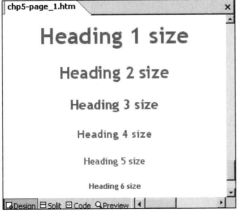

Figure 5.38 Sizes range from Heading 1, the largest, to Heading 6, the smallest.

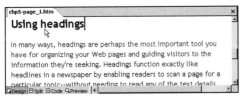

Figure 5.39 Once you release the cursor, the heading will be applied to the selected text.

Using Headings

In some ways, headings are your most important tool for guiding visitors through your Web pages. Headings function exactly like headlines in a newspaper by enabling readers to scan a page for a particular topic—without needing to read any of the text details. As with a newspaper, big headings should be used for your most important topics and smaller headings for less important items. It's simple—but vital—in bringing visual order to your pages. While this section just deals with heading sizes, remember you also can change heading font, color, and style. For details, see *Formatting Text* on page 117.

To add headings

1. Click anywhere in the line of text you want to make into a heading.

2. Click on the Style drop-down menu in the Formatting toolbar and select the heading size you want to apply (**Figure 5.37**). Heading 1 is the largest; Heading 6 is the smallest (**Figure 5.38**).

3. Release your cursor and the heading will be applied (**Figure 5.39**).

✔ Tip

■ While you can apply a heading to as much as a full paragraph of text, generally it's easier to read a heading if you use no more than two short lines of text. In fact, the fewer words the better.

To change a heading size

1. Click anywhere in the heading to select it.

2. Click on the Style drop-down menu in the Formatting toolbar and select a new heading size.

3. Release your cursor and the new heading size will be applied.

USING HEADINGS

ADDING HYPERLINKS

The Web's essential beauty springs from the user's ability to jump from file to file anywhere in the world. Hyperlinks make that possible. Hyperlinks, or simply links, come in several varieties: links to other files around the globe, links to other spots within the document already on your screen, links to send email, and links embedded in pictures. Microsoft FrontPage makes it easy to create them all.

Text links are explained on the next page; image links are covered separately on page 160. It's also worth remembering that *Creating a Web Site* on page 49 discusses how to automatically link entire pages as you build or reorganize your site.

Absolute and Relative Links

Fundamental to using links is understanding the difference between what are called absolute and relative hyperlinks. An absolute link shows a file's full Web address (`http://www.waywest.net/frontpage/index.htm`) while a relative link just includes the file name and the folder it's stored in (`/My Webs2/formatting.htm`). You *must* use an absolute link any time you create a link to a Web page or file *not* on your own Web site, sometimes called an external link. Relative links *should* be used to link to files within your own Web site.

The advantage of relative links is that you can rearrange your Web site and files without breaking any links, which stymies Web browsers. Precisely because your home page has an absolute address, a Web browser can bounce from relative link to relative link within your Web site even if you move `expensivepart.htm` from `www.yoursite.com/parts/` to `www.yoursite.com/supplies/`. Rearranging your site is inevitable. You'll outgrow the original structure, find a better way to do it, or whatever. Follow the steps in *To link to a page in your Web site* and FrontPage will automatically create relative links—saving you the work of *manually* updating all those links later on.

Figure 6.1 Switch to Page view by choosing View > Page.

Figure 6.2 To create a link, choose Insert > Hyperlink (left) or click the Insert Hyperlink button in the Standard toolbar (right).

Figure 6.3 To quickly create a link, right-click your selection and choose *Hyperlink* from the shortcut menu.

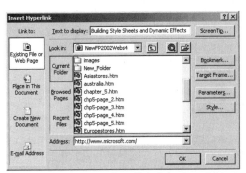

Figure 6.4 In the Insert Hyperlink dialog box, the text you selected in step 2 appears in the *Text to display* window.

Figure 6.5 To link to an external Web page, first choose the *Existing File or Web Page* button in the *Link to* column.

Figure 6.6 If you don't know a site's URL, find it by clicking the Web browser button to navigate to the desired Web page.

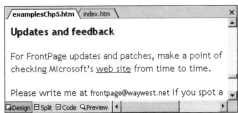

Figure 6.7 FrontPage marks linked text with an underline.

To link to an external Web page

1. Make sure you're in Page view by choosing View > Page (**Figure 6.1**).

2. Select the text you want to link.

3. Choose Insert > Hyperlink or click the Insert Hyperlink button in the Standard toolbar (**Figure 6.2**). You also can right-click in the page and choose *Hyperlink* from the shortcut menu ([Ctrl][K]) (**Figure 6.3**).

4. When the Insert Hyperlink dialog box appears (**Figure 6.4**), the text you selected in step 2 will appear in the *Text to display* window, where you can change it if you like.

5. Choose the first *Link to* button, *Existing File or Web Page* (**Figure 6.5**). For details on the *Link to* choices, see *Insert Hyperlink options* on page 146.

6. If you know the site's URL, type it directly into the *Address* text window and skip to step 9. If you don't know the URL, click the Web browser button to navigate to the desired Web page (**Figure 6.6**). For details, see *Insert Hyperlink options* on page 146.

7. When your default Web browser launches, use it to navigate to the external Web page to which you want to link.

8. Once you reach the external Web page you're seeking, switch back to the Insert Hyperlink dialog box and the URL will be automatically pasted into the *Address* text window.

9. Click *OK* to close the dialog box and your selection will be linked—indicated by the underline in the Web page (**Figure 6.7**).

ADDING EXTERNAL LINKS

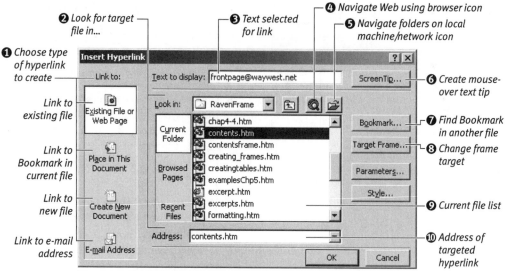

❷ *Look for target file in...*

❸ *Text selected for link*

❹ *Navigate Web using browser icon*

❺ *Navigate folders on local machine/network icon*

❶ *Choose type of hyperlink to create*

Link to existing file

Link to Bookmark in current file

Link to new file

Link to e-mail address

❻ *Create mouse-over text tip*

❼ *Find Bookmark in another file*

❽ *Change frame target*

❾ *Current file list*

❿ *Address of targeted hyperlink*

Figure 6.8 The Insert Hyperlink dialog box offers total control over FrontPage's hyperlinks.

Insert Hyperlink options

The Insert Hyperlink dialog box offers total control over FrontPage's hyperlinks (**Figure 6.8**). To reach the dialog box, choose Insert > Hyperlink ($\boxed{\text{Ctrl}}\boxed{\text{K}}$). By default, the dialog box initially displays the Web site you're working on.

❶ Choose type of hyperlink to create: Click one of the four buttons in the *Link to* column, based on the type of link you need to create.

◆ **Link to existing file:** Click the *Existing File or Web Page* button to link to a file on your local computer, local network, or the Web. Use in tandem with the dialog box's *Look in* buttons and icons to navigate to the file. (For details, see *Look for target file in* on the next page).

◆ **Link to Bookmark in current file:** Click the *Place in This Document* button to link to a bookmark (FrontPage's term for anchor links) that already exists in the page you're working on. To create a bookmark from scratch, see page 153.

◆ **Link to new file:** Click the *Create New Document* button if you want to create a link to a page on your Web site that you've not yet created (see page 150). The New dialog box will open, allowing you to create a normal page or one based on FrontPage's templates.

◆ **Link to e-mail address:** Click the *E-mail Address* button to link your selected text or image to an email address. For details, see *To create an email link* on page 149.

❷ Look for target file in: Use the three buttons (*Current Folder, Browsed Pages,* and *Recent Files*) and the two navigation icons (*Navigate Web using browser* and *Navigate folders on local machine/network*) to select a target file for the hyperlink. By default, the *Current Folder* button is selected and its contents will be displayed in the Current file list. Clicking *Browsed Pages* will display the URLs for Web pages you've browsed in Microsoft Internet Explorer. The number of pages listed reflects the content of Internet Explorer's History folder (cache). Clicking *Recent Files* will list all the files recently opened within FrontPage—no matter which Web site they are stored in.

❸ Text selected for link: By default, the *Text to display* window contains the text you initially selected for the hyperlink. In most cases, you won't want to change this, but you can type new text into the window and it will replace the original linked text after you click *OK*.

❹ Navigate Web using browser icon: Click to launch your Web browser and hunt down an external page out on the Web. Once you reach the page, switch back to FrontPage and the address is pasted automatically into the *Address* window.

❺ Navigate folders on local machine/network icon: Click to navigate to any file on your hard drive or your local network. The file location will be pasted automatically into the *Address* window.

❻ Create mouseover text tip: Based on Windows' own screen tip feature, the ScreenTip button lets you create a small text message that appears when a browser's cursor moves over the link. The text will appear only if the Web visitor is using the Windows version of Internet Explorer 4 or later.

❼ Find Bookmark in another file: By selecting a file in the Current file list, you can use the *Bookmark* button to link to a bookmark (anchor) in a file other than the current page. (To use a bookmark in the current page, click the *Place in This Document* button instead.) For more information, see *Using Bookmarks* on page 153.

❽ Change frame target: Click *Target Frame* only if your Web site contains frames (see *Creating Frames* on page 303).

❾ Current file list: By default, the list shows the current Web site's files but it will change if you click the *Browsed Pages* or *Recent Files* buttons. Use the far-right scroll bar to see all the files and folders in your site.

❿ Address of targeted hyperlink: FrontPage automatically fills in the address for your targeted hyperlink based on your choices in the *Link to* and *Look in* columns. You also can type directly in the window if you already know a file's URL (Uniform Resource Locator). FrontPage automatically begins the URL with an `http://` but just type `ftp://` to replace it if you're creating a File Transfer Protocol link for visitors to download a file.

HYPERLINK OPTIONS

To link to a page in your Web site

1. Make sure you're in Page view by choosing View > Page (**Figure 6.1**).

2. Select the text you want to link, right-click, and choose *Hyperlink* from the shortcut menu (Ctrl K) (**Figure 6.3**).

3. When the Insert Hyperlink dialog box appears, the *Link to* column's *Existing File or Web Page* button will be selected by default. Use the *Look in* buttons and folder icons to find the desired file in your Web site. If the file is in the *Current Folder*, use the dialog box's scroll bar to find the file, click it, and the name will be pasted into the *Address* text box (**Figure 6.9**). If the file is elsewhere on your computer, navigate to it and then use the Link to File dialog box to reach the desired file (**Figures 6.10** and **6.11**).

4. Click *OK* in either the Insert Hyperlink or Link to File dialog box, depending on your choice in step 3. The dialog box will close and your selected text will be linked to the file—as indicated by an underline in the Web page.

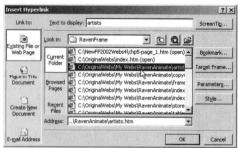

Figure 6.9 If a file's already part of your Web site, select it in the scrolling list and its name will be pasted into the *Address* text box.

Figure 6.10 To link to a file on your computer, navigate to the folder using the Insert Hyperlink dialog box.

Figure 6.11 Once you track down a local file, click *OK* in the Link to File dialog box.

Figure 6.12 To add an email link, click the *Link to* column's *E-mail Address* button.

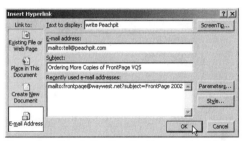

Figure 6.13 Type in the *E-mail address*, add a *Subject*, and click *OK*.

 To create an email link

1. Select the text you want linked to an email address, right-click, and choose *Hyperlink* from the shortcut menu ($\boxed{\text{Ctrl}}\boxed{\text{K}}$) (**Figure 6.3**).

2. When the Insert Hyperlink dialog box appears, click the *Link to* column's *E-mail Address* button (**Figure 6.12**). The right side of the Insert Hyperlink dialog box will change and display email-related fields (**Figure 6.13**). The text selected in step 1 will appear in the *Text to display* window, which you can change if you need to.

3. Fill in the *E-mail address* window, but don't type the *mailto:* portion of the address since it will be inserted automatically. You also may want to fill in the *Subject* window, although not all email programs will display it when receiving the message. Click *OK* and the address will be applied to the selected text in the Web page.

✔ Tip

- By clicking any item in the *Recently used e-mail addresses* list, you can quickly fill out the fields—including the *Subject*. Over time, the list will grow longer, which can save you lots of time addressing frequent contacts.

LINKING TO EMAIL

Linking to pages not yet created

On the face of it, this sounds weird: Why would you link to a non-existent page? In truth, it's common as you're creating links to realize you've forgotten to create a necessary page. This option lets you quickly make the new page and link to it from the page you're already working on.

To create a new page and link to it

1. Select the text you want linked to a not-yet-created page, right-click, and choose *Hyperlink* from the shortcut menu (Ctrl K) (**Figure 6.3**).

2. When the Insert Hyperlink dialog box appears, click the *Create New Document* button and the right side of the Insert Hyperlink dialog box will change to reflect your choice (**Figure 6.14**). The text selected in step 1 will appear in the *Text to display* window, which you can change if you need to. Also by default, the *Edit the new document now* button will be selected.

3. Unless you want to drop everything and immediately build the page, however, select the *Edit the new document later* button (**Figure 6.15**). (See *Tip* if you want to create the page right now.) Use the *Name of new document* window to create a name for the page that will jog your memory when you do return later to edit it.

4. Click *OK* and the link will be applied to the selected text in the Web page. If you open the Folder List, you'll see that the selected text now links to the newly created (blank) page (**Figure 6.16**).

✔ Tip

■ If you want to create the new page immediately, click the *Change* button in the Insert Hyperlink dialog box (**Figure 6.14**). FrontPage will open the Create New Document dialog box.

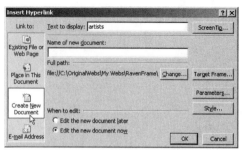

Figure 6.14 To link to a not-yet-created page, click the *Create New Document* button and the right side of the Insert Hyperlink dialog box will change to reflect your choice.

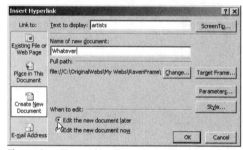

Figure 6.15 To avoid having to immediately build the page, select the *Edit the new document later* button and then fill in the *Name of new document* window.

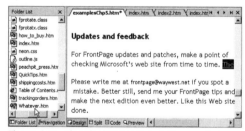

Figure 6.16 After the link is created, the new, but blank, page appears in the Folder List.

Figure 6.17 To change a link, right-click it and choose *Hyperlink Properties* from the shortcut menu.

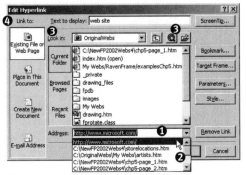

Figure 6.18 Use the Edit Hyperlink dialog box to change a link's *Address*.

Changing links

FrontPage automatically updates links as you move pages around on your Web site. But if you want to completely change a link address, or delete a link, it's easy. If you've deleted entire pages—especially without using FrontPage in the first place—running an update will guard against broken links (see *To update links* on the next page).

To edit a link

1. Right-click on any link you want to change and choose *Hyperlink Properties* from the shortcut menu (**Figure 6.17**). Or type [Alt][Enter].

2. When the Edit Hyperlink dialog box opens, the link's present *Address* will be highlighted (**Figure 6.18**). You can:

   ❶ Type a *new* URL directly into the text window.

   ❷ Click the *Address* text window's right-side arrow to choose from a drop-down menu of recent URLs.

   ❸ Click any of the *Look in* buttons or icons to navigate to a new file.

   ❹ Click one of the three other *Link to* buttons to change the type of hyperlink entirely.

3. When you've changed the *Address*, click *OK* and the link will be updated to reflect the new address.

CHANGING LINKS

To delete a link

1. Right-click on any link you want to change and choose *Hyperlink Properties* from the shortcut menu (**Figure 6.17**). Or type Alt Enter.

2. When the Edit Hyperlink dialog box opens, click the *Remove Link* button (**Figure 6.19**). The dialog box will close and the Web page text will no longer be linked.

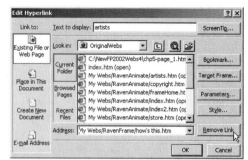

Figure 6.19 To delete a link, click the *Remove Link* button in the Edit Hyperlink dialog box.

To update links

1. Choose Tools > Recalculate Hyperlinks (**Figure 6.20**).

2. FrontPage will warn you that this might take a few minutes, depending on the size of your Web site. It rarely takes that long, so click *Yes*. FrontPage will repair any links broken when site pages were rearranged, but it can't fix a link if you entered the wrong URL in the first place.

Figure 6.20 If you delete pages without using FrontPage, update their links by choosing Tools > Recalculate Hyperlinks.

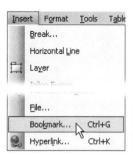

Figure 6.21 To create a bookmark, select the target text, then choose Insert > Bookmark.

4. When you're
use the Style drop
choose Normal (**Fi**

Using lists

FrontPage lets you
broken into two g
lists. Unordered, c
series of items tha
supplies. Use orde

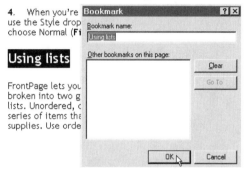

Figure 6.22 By default, the bookmark (right) assumes the name of the selected text (left). Type in another name if you prefer.

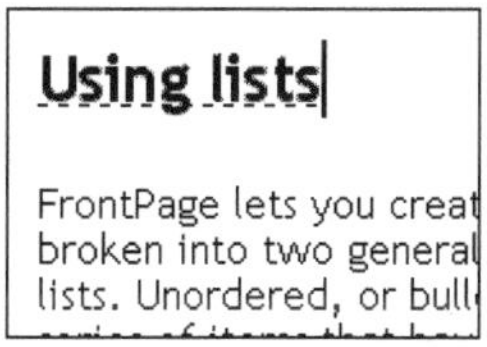

Using lists|

FrontPage lets you creat
broken into two general
lists. Unordered, or bull

Figure 6.23
FrontPage places a dashed line beneath bookmarked text.

1 Create a bookmark
2 Then Create a Hyperlink to that bookmark.

Using Bookmarks

Bookmarks, often called anchor links, let visitors jump to specific spots, such as section headings, within a long Web page. Creating anchors is a two-step process: first you create the bookmark itself (the anchor), then you create hyperlinks (the anchor links) that point to the bookmark. The bookmark can be in the current page or FrontPage lets you browse to another page containing bookmarks.

Insert anchor links into your Web pages to let readers jump ahead or back without scrolling through the whole document. Anchors aren't limited to headings. Feel free to link to a citation, word, image, or single character.

If you ever want to update or remove some bookmarks in a lengthy Web page and don't want to search for them one by one, FrontPage makes it easy to find them.

To create a bookmark

1. Select the text you want the reader to jump to, that is, the target or destination.

2. Choose Insert > Bookmark (Ctrl G) (**Figure 6.21**).

3. When the Bookmark dialog box opens, it automatically uses the selected text as the name of the bookmark (**Figure 6.22**). However, you can type in another name if that suits your purposes.

4. When you're done naming the bookmark, click *OK* and the selected text will be bookmarked, as indicated by a dashed underline (**Figure 6.23**). See the next page to complete the process.

To link to a bookmark in the current page

1. Select the text you want linked to a bookmark, right-click, and choose *Hyperlink* from the shortcut menu (Ctrl K) (**Figure 6.3**). The Insert Hyperlink dialog box will open.

Insert /

2. Click the *Link to* column's *Place in This Document* button and the right side of the Insert Hyperlink dialog box will change to reflect your choice (**Figure 6.24**).

3. Pick a bookmark in the *Select a place in this document* list, click *OK*, and your selected text will be linked to the bookmark.

Figure 6.24 To link to a bookmark in the current page, click the *Link to* column's *Place in This Document* button, choose a bookmark, and click *OK*.

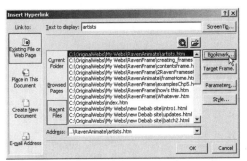

Figure 6.25 To link to a bookmark in another page, navigate to the file, select it in the folder list, and click the *Bookmark* button.

Figure 6.26
When the Select Place in Document dialog box appears, choose one of the bookmarks you've already created in the page, and click *OK*.

Figure 6.27 When the Insert Hyperlink dialog box reappears, the location of the bookmark will appear in the *Address* window. Click *OK*.

To link to a bookmark in another page

1. Select the text you want linked to a bookmark, right-click, and choose *Hyperlink* from the shortcut menu (Ctrl K) (**Figure 6.3**). The Insert Hyperlink dialog box will open.

2. Navigate to the other page containing the bookmark you want using the *Current Folder*, *Browsed Pages*, or *Recent Files* buttons, the Web browser, or the open folder icons. Select the page in the scrolling list of files and click the *Bookmark* button (**Figure 6.25**).

3. When the Select Place in Document dialog box appears, choose one of the bookmarks you've already created in the page, and click *OK* (**Figure 6.26**).

4. When the Insert Hyperlink dialog box reappears, the location of the bookmark will appear in the *Address* window (**Figure 6.27**). Click *OK* and your selected text will be linked to the bookmark.

✔ Tips

- The Select Place in Document dialog box will display the bookmarks for only one page at a time, not the entire site. To reach bookmarks in another page, you must first select the file in the Insert Hyperlink dialog box.

- Revising the link to a bookmark follows the same steps, except that in step 2, the Edit Hyperlink dialog box will appear. For details, see *To edit a link* on page 151.

To find bookmarks

1. Start by finding any bookmark in a page (marked by a dashed underline). Right-click it and choose *Bookmark Properties* from the shortcut menu (Alt Enter) (**Figure 6.28**).

2. The Bookmark dialog box will appear with the selected bookmark highlighted in the top text window. Highlight any other bookmark by clicking it within the list, then click *Go To* (**Figure 6.29**).

3. The Bookmark dialog box will remain open, but your Web page will jump to the chosen bookmark (**Figure 6.30**). Once you find the bookmark, click *OK*, and you'll be returned to the Web page. To clear the bookmark, see the next page.

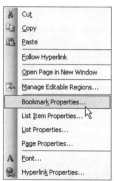

Figure 6.28 To find any bookmarks in a page, right-click any bookmark and choose *Bookmark Properties* from the short-cut menu.

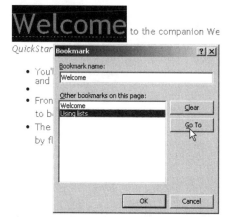

Figure 6.29 Choose the bookmark you're looking for in the *Other bookmarks on this page* list, then click *Go To*.

Figure 6.30 After clicking *Go To*, the Bookmark dialog box remains open but your Web page jumps to the chosen bookmark.

USING BOOKMARKS

Figure 6.31 To clear a bookmark after you've found it, click *Clear*.

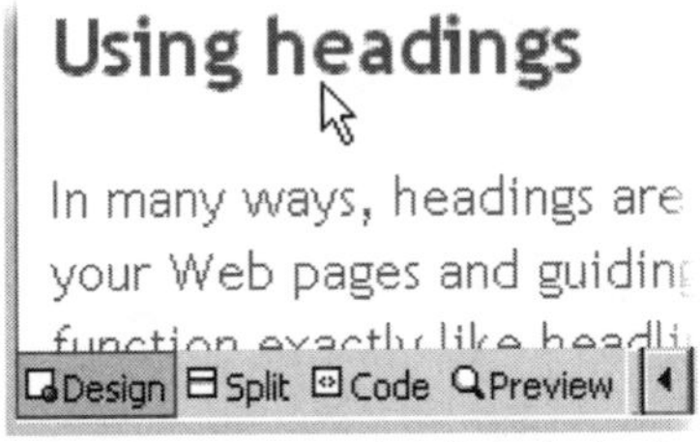

Using headings

In many ways, headings are
your Web pages and guiding
function exactly like headli

Design ☐ Split ⊡ Code ⚲ Preview ◀

Figure 6.32 Once you've cleared a bookmark, the text remains highlighted but without a dashed underline.

To clear a bookmark

1. To find a bookmark you want to clear, first follow the steps in *To find bookmarks* on the previous page.

2. Once you find the bookmark, click *Clear* in the Bookmark dialog box (**Figure 6.31**). The Bookmark dialog box will close, returning you to the Web page, where the text remains highlighted but without the dashed underline of a bookmark (**Figure 6.32**).

Setting Link Colors

By default, FrontPage follows the Web convention of showing unvisited links as blue and visited ones as dark purple. However, you can assign any Web-safe color you want to your hyperlinks. FrontPage also lets you set colors for active links (the instant you click them) and rollover links (when your cursor moves over them).

To change a link's color

1. Make sure you're in Page view by choosing View > Page.

2. Right-click anywhere in the page and choose *Page Properties* from the shortcut menu (**Figure 6.33**).

3. When the Page Properties dialog box opens, click the *Formatting* tab (**Figure 6.34**).

4. To change the color for any of a link's three states, in the *Colors* section click the far-right arrows and pick a new color from the pop-up box. If you want to create a custom color, choose *More Colors* in the pop-up box (**Figure 6.35**). When the More Colors dialog box appears, click the *Select* button, use the eye-dropper-shaped cursor to pick a color, and click *OK* (**Figure 6.36**).

5. When the Page Properties dialog box reappears, click *OK,* and the links *for that page only* will be changed (**Figure 6.37**).

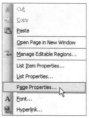

Figure 6.33 To change a link's color, right-click in the page and choose *Page Properties* from the shortcut menu.

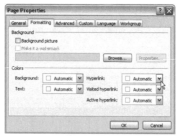

Figure 6.34 To reach the color section, click the *Formatting* tab in the Page Properties dialog box.

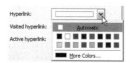

Figure 6.35 Use the pop-up box to change the color of your hyperlinks. To pick a custom color, click *More Colors*.

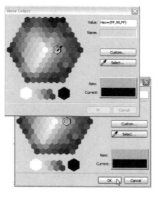

Figure 6.36 Click the *Select* button in the More Colors dialog box, use the eye-dropper–shaped cursor to pick a color, and click *OK*.

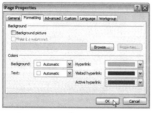

Figure 6.37 When the Page Properties dialog box reappears, click *OK,* and the links *for that page only* will be changed.

Figure 6.38 To trigger a color change when a cursor moves over a link, choose the *Advanced* tab's *Enable hyperlink rollover effects* checkbox and click *Rollover style*.

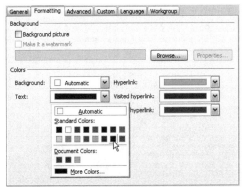

Figure 6.39 The *Formatting* tab also lets you change the page's background color and the text color.

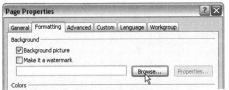

Figure 6.40 Check *Background picture*, then click *Browse* to add a tiled background graphic to a page.

✔ Tips

- Make sure your custom color stands out against the background and that unvisited and visited link colors are not so similar that it's unclear which is which.

- If you ever change your mind and want to use the default link colors, just choose *Automatic* within each link's pop-up box in step 4.

- The Page Properties dialog box's *Advanced* tab includes an option to have your links change color whenever a visitor's cursor moves over the link. Just check *Enable hyperlink rollover effects*, then click the *Rollover style* button (**Figure 6.38**). When the Font dialog box opens, use the *Color* pop-up menu to make your choice.

- The *Formatting* tab also lets you change the page's background color and the text color (**Figure 6.39**). Click the arrows to make your choices, then click *OK* to apply them to the current page.

- If you absolutely must add a background (tiled) picture to the page, the *Formatting* tab includes a checkbox to do just that (**Figure 6.40**). Check the *Background picture* box, click *Browse* to find your image, then click *OK* to apply the picture to the current page. Tiled images plagued the Web early on—with headache inducing results. It's best to use a simple, light-toned image that doesn't obliterate your text.

- To change the link colors in a *theme*, see *To modify a theme* on page 91.

Creating Image Links

Obviously the Web isn't limited to text-only links and FrontPage makes it easy to insert links into any image. You can link an entire image to a file or you can create what's called a hotspot, which links a defined area of the image to another file. By putting multiple hotspots in an image, you can create links to multiple files.

To link an entire image to a file

1. Make sure the Pictures toolbar is visible by choosing View > Toolbars > Pictures (**Figures 6.41** and **6.42**).

2. Open the page containing the image you want linked and click the image to select it (**Figure 6.43**). Square black "handles" will appear on the image's corners, indicating it's selected.

3. With the image still selected, right-click, and choose *Hyperlink* from the shortcut menu ([Ctrl][K]) (**Figure 6.44**).

4. When the Insert Hyperlink dialog box opens, you have all the choices already explained in *Insert Hyperlink options* on page 146. To link the image to another page in your current Web site, choose a file in the center window and click *OK*. The image will be linked to the selected page—as indicated by the status bar and the cursor pop-up (**Figure 6.45**).

Figure 6.41
Before working with images, choose View > Toolbars > Pictures.

Figure 6.42 The Pictures toolbar includes tools for adding links and hotspots to images.

Figure 6.43 Once an image is selected, square black handles will appear on the image's corners.

Figure 6.44 To link a selected image, right-click it and choose *Hyperlink* from the shortcut menu.

Two
Raven
Trading

Use Ctrl+Click to follow a hyperlink

Native American Crafts on the Web

Figure 6.45 Once linked, an image displays pop-up instructions whenever FrontPage's cursor moves over it. The link address appears in the bottom status bar.

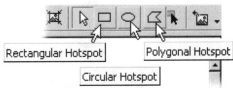

Figure 6.46 To create a hotspot, first select the entire image.

Rectangular Hotspot

Polygonal Hotspot

Circular Hotspot

Figure 6.47 Click a shape for your hotspot—rectangle, circle, or polygon—in the Pictures toolbar.

■ **Figure 6.48** Once you choose a shape tool, the cursor becomes a pencil, allowing you to draw a hotspot boundary around the image. Don't worry if it's not exact—you can
■ adjust it later.

To create an image hotspot

1. Make sure the Pictures toolbar is visible by choosing View > Toolbars > Pictures (**Figure 6.41**).

2. Open the page containing the image you want linked and click the image to select it (**Figure 6.46**).

3. Decide what shape your hotspot will be (rectangle, circle, or freeform polygon) and click the appropriate symbol in the Pictures toolbar (**Figure 6.47**).

4. Once you choose a shape tool, the cursor will turn into a pencil, allowing you to draw the hotspot's boundary in the image (**Figure 6.48**). Don't worry about getting the boundary exactly right—you can fix it in a moment.

5. The Insert Hyperlink dialog box will open, allowing you to choose which file to link to the hotspot. Choose the file, click *OK*, and you'll be returned to the image.

(continued)

CREATING IMAGE LINKS, HOTSPOTS

6. Now you can click *inside* the hotspot and move it exactly where you want it (left, **Figure 6.49**).

7. If you need to resize the hotspot—and you'll want it big enough for visitors to click on it easily—use your cursor to grab the hotspot's black rectangular "handles" to enlarge or shrink the hotspot (right, **Figure 6.49**). If you need to reposition the hotspot, repeat step 6.

8. Repeat steps 3–7 if you want to add more hotspots to the image and link them to separate files. When you're done, the image will contain multiple hotspots, each with its own link (**Figure 6.50**).

✔ Tips

- Your hotspots cannot overlap, nor extend beyond the edge of the selected image. For both reasons, you may realize the image itself needs to be enlarged. Just grab one of the *image's* handles and drag it to give your hotspots more room, then reposition and resize the hotspots as needed. If you wind up enlarging the image by more than about 10 percent, however, go back and create a larger original. Otherwise, the image will wind up looking fuzzy.

- Hotspots don't have to link to *another* file. You also can use them with anchors to link to text somewhere else in the *same* file.

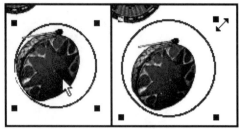

Figure 6.49 Once you've linked the image, click *inside* the hotspot and move it exactly where you want (left). To resize the hotspot, drag any image handle (right).

Figure 6.50 By adding several hotspots, a single image can link to multiple files.

CREATING IMAGE LINKS, HOTSPOTS

Figure 6.51 If an image obscures your view of its hotspots, click the Pictures toolbar's Highlight Hotspots button.

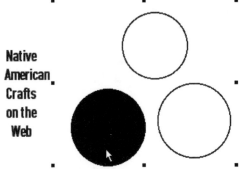

Figure 6.52 With highlighting applied, an image's hotspots are clearly outlined with the active hotspot in black.

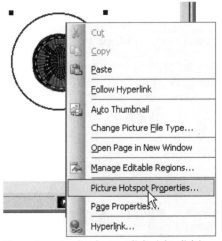

Figure 6.53 To edit a hotspot link, right-click it and choose *Picture Hotspot Properties* from the shortcut menu.

Finding image hotspots

Sometimes your image can keep you from easily seeing your hotspot boundaries. FrontPage includes a feature that lets you see the hotspots—without the images.

To find image hotspots

1. While in Page view, select the image you want to inspect by clicking on it.

2. Click the Highlight Hotspots button in the Pictures toolbar (**Figure 6.51**). The image's hotspots will be outlined against a clean background. When a hotspot is selected, it will turn black (**Figure 6.52**).

3. To see the image again, click anywhere outside the image.

To delete a hotspot

◆ Click on the hotspot you want removed and press ⌫Backspace or Delete.

To change a hotspot link

1. Right-click on the hotspot you want to edit and choose *Picture Hotspot Properties* (Alt Enter) from the shortcut menu (**Figure 6.53**).

2. When the Edit Hyperlink dialog box appears, use the buttons and arrows to navigate to the new link. For details, see *To edit a link* on page 151.

Using Interactive Buttons

Through the use of interactive buttons (previous versions of FrontPage called them hover buttons), it's incredibly easy to add button effects activated by your visitors' mouse actions. You can have a button change appearance or even trigger sounds when the mouse moves over the button.

Figure 6.54 To add an interactive button, choose Insert > Interactive Button.

To add an interactive button

1. Make sure you're in Page view by choosing View > Page. Also be sure the *Design* tab is clicked at the bottom of the page window.

2. Click where you want to add an interactive button and choose Insert > Interactive Button (**Figure 6.54**).

3. When the Interactive Buttons dialog box appears, the *Button* tab will be selected by default (**Figure 6.55**). Scroll through and make a style selection from the *Buttons* list, create a label in the *Text* text window, and add a link by clicking *Browse* and navigating to the desired file.

4. If you want to change the button's default font properties, click the dialog box's *Font* tab and use the drop-down menus to change the font, style, size, colors, and alignment (**Figure 6.56**). Use the *Preview* area to see the effects of your selections.

Figure 6.55 When the Interactive Buttons dialog box appears, use the *Button* tab to set the button's style, label, and link.

Figure 6.56 Use the *Font* tab in the Interactive Buttons dialog box to set the label's font, size, and alignment.

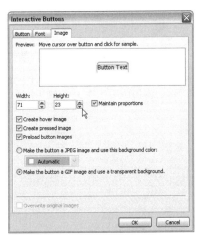

Figure 6.57 Use the *Image* tab in the Interactive Buttons dialog box to fine-tune the overall size and background for the button.

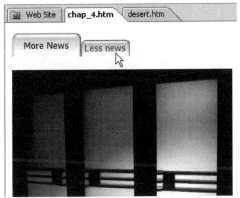

Figure 6.58 After you've closed the dialog box, the interactive button will appear where you inserted it in the Web page.

5. Use the dialog box's *Image* tab to customize the *Width, Height,* and *proportions* of your button (**Figure 6.57**). By default, FrontPage automatically creates images for when a cursor hovers over the button or clicks it. Also by default, FrontPage creates a GIF image with a transparent background, but you can create a colored background by choosing *Make the button a JPEG image.*

6. Once you've made your choices, click *OK* to close the dialog box. The interactive button will appear where you inserted it in the Web page (**Figure 6.58**).

✔ Tips

■ You may to need click the main window's *Preview* tab to see all the visual effects applied to the button.

■ The *Image* tab's *Width* and *Height* settings are a great help when you're trying to squeeze in a row of labeled buttons onto a page.

To edit an interactive button

1. Make sure the *Design* tab is clicked at the bottom of the page window.

2. Right-click the button and choose *Button Properties* from the shortcut menu (Alt Enter) (**Figure 6.59**). Or just double-click the button.

3. When the Interactive Buttons dialog box appears, use it to change your button's characteristics (**Figure 6.55**). Click *OK* when you're done and the changes will be applied.

✔ Tip

■ If your site has hover buttons created with a previous version of FrontPage, they'll still work. If you need to modify them, right-click the link and you'll still be able to choose Hover Button Properties from the drop-down menu and make changes in the dialog box that appears.

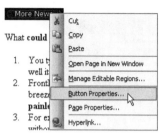

Figure 6.59
To edit an interactive button, right-click it and choose *Button Properties* from the shortcut menu.

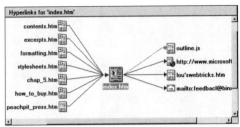

Figure 6.60 The hyperlinks view shows links *into* your page on the left and links *out from* the page on the right. The ⊕ marks indicate pages with links of their own.

Figure 6.61 In hyperlinks view, external and internal links are marked by an Internet Explorer icon (top and middle), while an envelope marks email links (bottom).

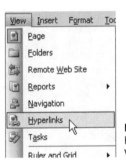

Figure 6.62 To switch to hyperlinks view, choose View > Hyperlinks.

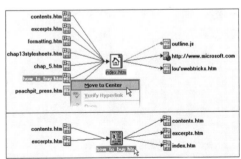

Figure 6.63 In hyperlinks view, a peripheral page (top) can be inspected by right-clicking it and choosing *Move to Center*. The peripheral page will jump to the center with its links showing (bottom).

Using the Hyperlinks View

Sometimes the easiest way to spot a missing link, or to analyze the links you already have is to use FrontPage's hyperlinks view (**Figure 6.60**). Each page's link type is marked by a distinct icon, which makes for easy reviewing (**Figure 6.61**). Want to quickly look at links for one of the peripheral pages appearing in the hyperlink view? For details, see *To inspect links on another page* below.

To switch to hyperlinks view

◆ Choose View > Hyperlinks or click the Hyperlinks icon in the Views Bar (**Figure 6.62**). The hyperlinks view will appear in the right pane with the current page in the center (**Figure 6.60**).

To inspect links on another page

◆ If you want to see the links for a page sitting on the periphery of a hyperlinks view, right-click it and choose *Move to Center* from the shortcut menu. The peripheral page will jump to the center of the view, showing all its links (**Figure 6.63**).

ADDING AND EDITING IMAGES

7

Putting pictures on the Web requires using images in the right formats, as discussed in *Web Image Formats*, this chapter's first section. The second section, *Adding Images*, covers adding images to a Web page and setting such basic aspects of the image as its size, alignment, and whether it should have borders. *Editing Images* covers tricks built right into FrontPage's Pictures toolbar (**Figure 7.1**). The final section, *Positioning Images Absolutely*, explains how images can escape the confines of grid-like layouts. To add images, links, or hotspots, see *Creating Image Links* on page 160. To use built-in graphic themes, see *Using Templates and Themes* on page 79. To add videos to Web pages, see *Adding Multimedia and Web Components* on page 237.

Right Click on Image /

Show Pictures Toolbar

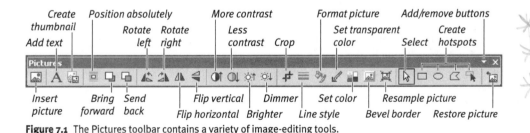

Create thumbnail · Position absolutely · Rotate left · Rotate right · More contrast · Less contrast · Crop · Format picture · Set transparent color · Add/remove buttons · Select · Create hotspots · Add text · Insert picture · Bring forward · Send back · Flip vertical · Flip horizontal · Dimmer · Brighter · Line style · Set color · Resample picture · Bevel border · Restore picture

Figure 7.1 The Pictures toolbar contains a variety of image-editing tools.

169

Web Image Formats

The world's awash with a virtual alphabet soup of image formats: BMPs, TIFFs, TGAs, EPSs, RASs—the list goes on and on. Fortunately when it comes to the World Wide Web, it really boils down to just two formats—GIFs and JPEGs. GIFs (CompuServe's Graphical Interchange Format) are used for everything but medium to large photographs, which are best formatted as JPEGs (developed by the Joint Photographic Experts Group) (**Table 7.1**).

Another file format, PNG (Portable Network Graphics) has been touted for several years now because it compresses images nicely without losing as much information as a JPEG and sidesteps an ongoing dispute over GIF rights. While version 4 and later browsers support PNG, the inability of earlier browsers to display the format has hampered its growth and acceptance. GIFs and JPEGs remain your best bets. For details, see *Converting image formats* on page 176.

Let's get small

Before you start adding images to a Web page, make sure the files are as small—no, make that as *tiny*—as possible. Bloated images can slow the downloading of your pages so much that visitors simply click on rather than wait. Take the time on your end to shave those files to save the viewer's time.

With the exception of cropping, most of this graphical liposuction should be done in a Web-savvy graphics program, such as Photoshop, DeBabelizer, or Fireworks. Start by cropping the image's width and height to remove everything but the visual gist of the picture. Who needs that blurry background or that parking lot foreground?

The real key to small files, however, is how well you compress the images. For GIFs, that means reducing the number of colors in the

Table 7.1

GIF vs JPEG: What's best?	
WEB PAGE ITEM	BEST FORMAT
buttons, arrows	GIF
illustrations	GIF
animations	GIF
blocks of solid color	GIF
button-size photographs	GIF
all but tiny photographs	JPEG

Table 7.2

Bit depth, number of colors, & file size		
NON-INDEXED ORIGINAL IMAGE		
24 bits	17 million colors	1.1 MB (original size)
15 bits	32,768 colors	816K
INDEXED AS A GIF		
8 bits	256 colors	417K
7 bits	128 colors	111K
6 bits	64 colors	94K
5 bits	32 colors	77K
4 bits	16 colors	60K
3 bits	8 colors	43K
2 bits	4 colors	17K
1 bit	2 colors	9K

image. For JPEGs, it's a matter of how much compression you can apply to the photograph while keeping it from looking artificial.

The number of colors in an image, commonly called the bit depth, has a big influence on the file's size (**Table 7.2**). Many Web surfers still use 8-bit monitors, which can only render 256 colors anyway. And since up to 40 of those colors wind up being reserved for the computer's operating system, most GIFs use just 216 colors in what's called a Web- or browser-safe palette. Converting a high-resolution image to one with a Web-safe palette is sometimes called *indexing* or *mapping* the image. That's because the color information for every pixel in the image is stored as a grid-like index.

While taking a graphic containing millions of colors and indexing it down to a few hundred may seem crazy, the whole point of the Web is that it works no matter which operating system and monitor are used. To find that balance between a minimum bit depth and decent image quality, experiment in your graphics program with saving images at various bit depths to see just how low you can go.

Photographs don't lend themselves to bit depth reduction—skin tones especially end up looking just terrible in GIFs. That's where JPEGs come in, which use an entirely different compression method. With JPEGs, you can use FrontPage to control the file size by experimenting with the level of compression. For details, see *To convert image formats* on page 176. One limitation to JPEGs is that they don't work well for one-color transparency (they wind up looking termite damaged).

Finally, if you've trimmed and slimmed an image down to a willowy minimum and it's still big, consider using FrontPage's auto thumbnail feature. For details, see *Creating auto thumbnails and photo galleries* on page 191.

Adding Images

Once you've done the sometimes tedious work within a graphics program of slimming your image files down to the smallest possible size, adding them to a FrontPage Web page is a breeze.

To insert an image

1. Make sure you're in Page view by choosing View > Page, click the *Design* tab in the main window, and then click where you want the image placed within a page.

2. Choose Insert > Picture, then choose *Clip Art* or *From File* from the submenu (**Figure 7.2**).

3. If you chose *Clip Art*, the Clip Art task pane will appear on the main window's right side. Use the *Search for* window and *Go* button to find an image (**Figure 7.3**). Click the image in the task pane and it will be added to the Web page. For details on using clip art, see *Clip Art options* on page 174.

   or

   If you chose *From File*, the Picture dialog box will appear (**Figure 7.4**). Use the *Look in* drop-down menu or navigation icons to find a picture and click *Insert* to add the image to the Web page.

4. Save the page and its new image (Ctrl S). If the image didn't come from your current Web site, the Save Embedded Files dialog box will appear (**Figure 7.5**).

5. Click *Rename* if you want to change the file name and *Change Folder* if you want to save the file in another location. When you're done, click *OK* and the image will be saved.

6. Once the image is inserted and saved, you can edit it, if necessary. See *Editing Images* on page 186.

Figure 7.2 To insert an image, choose Insert > Picture, then choose *Clip Art* or *From File* from the submenu.

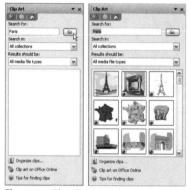

Figure 7.3 The Clip Art task pane provides a central access point for royalty free art.

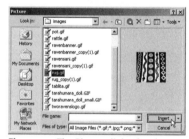

Figure 7.4 The Picture dialog box lets you choose images from your computer or the Web itself.

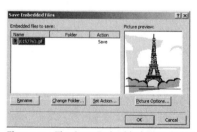

Figure 7.5 The Save Embedded Files dialog box lets you rename images added to your Web site and choose where they're stored.

Figure 7.6 If the Picture dialog box does not show a preview of the picture, click the Views drop-down menu and choose Preview.

Figure 7.7 If the Pictures toolbar is active, you can insert an image from your computer's hard drive.

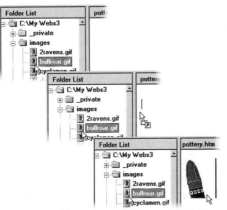

Figure 7.8 If the Folder List is visible, you can click and drag an image into a page from your Web site pane.

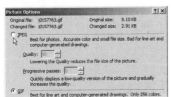

Figure 7.9 To change the picture's format, click *Picture Options* and choose *JPEG* or *GIF* in the Picture Options dialog box.

✔ Tips

■ Three of the four choices at the bottom of the submenu in step 2 (**Figure 7.2**) (*New Drawing*, *AutoShapes*, and *WordArt*) are covered in *Adding and Editing Drawings* on page 207. For more information on the last choice (*Video*), see *Adding Videos or Animations* on page 237. For more information on the *New Photo Gallery* choice, see *To create a thumbnail photo gallery* on page 193.

■ If the Picture dialog box does not show a preview of the picture, click the Views drop-down menu and choose Preview (**Figure 7.6**).

■ If the Pictures toolbar is active, you also can insert a picture by clicking the first icon (**Figure 7.7**).

■ If the Folder List is visible and you're inserting an image already in your Web site folder, just click and drag the file into the page pane (**Figure 7.8**).

■ Every FrontPage Web site automatically includes an Images folder, but imported images don't always get saved to it. To keep your images together, use the *Change Folder* button to select the folder as you add images to your site (**Figure 7.5**).

■ In step 6, if you want to change the picture's format, say from a GIF to a JPEG, click *Picture Options* and make your choice in the dialog box that appears (**Figure 7.9**). (For more information, see *Converting image formats* on page 176.)

ADDING IMAGES

Clip Art options

FrontPage 2003 comes with a bunch of clip art. If you've installed Office 2000 or Office XP, FrontPage can use the ample clip art that comes with those programs as well. The Clip Art task pane provides a central access point for clips, whether they're on your hard drive or online (**Figure 7.10**). To reach the Clip Art task pane, choose Insert > Picture > Clip Art.

❶ **Search for:** Type in the text window one or more keywords that describe the clip's subject. Use with the *Search in* drop-down menu to expand or narrow which files are searched. The trick is to not define your search so narrowly that you find nothing nor so broadly that you get hundreds of results.

❷ **Go:** Click to start the clip search after entering your search terms.

❸ **Search in:** By default, the drop-down menu is set to search *All collections*, which comprises all the clip collections that come with FrontPage or Office, plus your own clips. Use the drop-down menu to expand or narrow the search by checking or unchecking individual item boxes. Click the ⊞ or ⊟ symbols to expand or collapse a category's listings (left, **Figure 7.11**).

❹ **Results should be:** By default, the drop-down menu is set to search *All media file types*. Use the drop-down menus to expand/narrow the search by checking or unchecking the item boxes (right, **Figure 7.11**).

Figure 7.10 The Clip Art task pane provides a central access point for clips, whether they're on your hard drive or online.

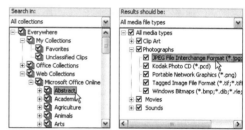

Figure 7.11 Use the drop-down menus and check-boxes to expand or narrow your clip art search.

Figure 7.12 The Clip Organizer covers the same clips as the Go button but lets you browse by category.

Figure 7.13 The first time you use the Clip Organizer, you'll be asked if you want to build an index of all your existing clips.

Figure 7.14 Microsoft's online trove of searchable clip art offers royalty-free items for use in your Web pages.

❺ **Organize clips:** The organizer covers the same clips as the Go button but lets you browse by category instead of zeroing in on particular keyword-based clips (**Figure 7.12**). When you first launch the organizer, it will ask if you want to create a catalog of your existing images (**Figure 7.13**). This can take some time, so you may want to use the *Later* option. Items found in the Clip Organizer can be dragged directly into your Web page.

❻ **Clip art on Office Online:** Click to search Microsoft's online collection of clips. Be sure to connect to the Internet before clicking this button. After accepting Microsoft's end user agreement, you'll be linked to Design Gallery Live, where you can search for still more clips (**Figure 7.14**).

❼ **Tips for finding clips:** Click to launch FrontPage's Help system for more details on using clip art.

Converting image formats

By default, FrontPage saves images created in any other format as GIFs or JPEGs. If the image's color depth is 8 bits or less, it's saved as a GIF; anything over 8 bits is saved as a JPEG. FrontPage also makes it easy to convert a GIF to a JPEG, a JPEG to a GIF, or either to a PNG.

To convert image formats

1. Right-click the image you want to convert and choose *Picture Properties* from the shortcut menu (Alt Enter) (**Figure 7.15**).

2. When the Picture Properties dialog box appears, click the *General* tab. The file name, with the suffix to indicate its format, appears within the *Picture* text window. To change the format, click the *Picture File Type* button (**Figure 7.16**).

3. When the Picture File Type dialog box appears, select one of the three other picture formats (**Figure 7.17**). If you choose *JPEG*, use the *Settings* section to fine-tune how it will be converted (for details, see *Tips* below). Once you've made your choice, click *OK* to close the dialog box.

Figure 7.15 To change an image, right-click it and choose *Picture Properties* from the shortcut menu.

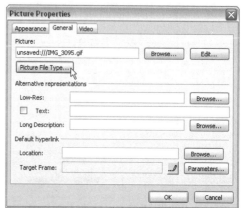

Figure 7.16 To convert an image's format, click the *General* tab in the Picture Properties dialog box and then click the *Picture File Type* button.

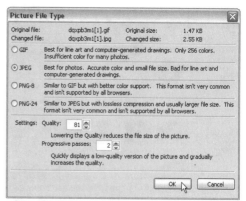

Figure 7.17 When the Picture File Type dialog box appears, select one of the three other picture formats. If you choose *JPEG*, use the *Settings* section to fine-tune how it will be converted.

Figure 7.18 When the Save Embedded Files dialog box appears, click *OK* to save the newly formatted picture.

4. When the Picture Properties dialog box reappears, click *OK* and the image changes will be applied. Save your change to the page (Ctrl S), and the image format change will trigger the appearance of the Save Embedded Files dialog box, which will reflect the formatting change with the appropriate file suffix (**Figure 7.18**). Click *OK* and the change will be saved and your Web page will reappear with the new picture in place.

✔ Tips

■ In setting the quality of a JPEG, the higher the *Quality* number, the more accurate—but less compressed—the image will be. The default is 75 for moderate compression; 100 is the maximum, which would leave the image uncompressed. The *Progressive passes* number controls how many passes it takes a Web browser to completely download the picture. As you change the settings, you can compare the image's *Changed size* with its *Original size* (upper right, **Figure 7.17**).

■ If you choose *GIF* as the file type, you can make the image *Interlaced*, which will cause the image to download in several increasingly detailed passes. The full image downloads no faster this way, but interlacing gives the viewer a quick sense of its content.

CONVERTING IMAGE FORMATS

Creating alternates for images

It's common for folks using a slow dial-up Web connection to set their browsers to not download images. By creating alternate text for each image on your site, you can give those visitors at least some sense of a page's images before they finish downloading. The text will download almost immediately—enabling visitors to judge whether they even want to wait for the images to download (top, **Figure 7.19**). If viewers use Internet Explorer, their cursor will even display the alternate text as a pop-up label, giving you an easy way to add a caption (bottom, **Figure 7.19**). Finally, visually impaired Web users depend on special programs that read aloud what's on the page. With alternate text, those users get dealt in—not left out.

FrontPage also offers another tool for dealing with slow-to-download images: low-resolution images that act as quick-to-appear placeholders. See *To create low-resolution alternate images* on page 180.

To create alternate text

1. Right-click the image and choose *Picture Properties* from the shortcut menu ((Alt)(Enter)) (**Figure 7.15**).

2. When the Picture Properties dialog box appears, click the *General* tab (**Figure 7.16**).

3. Within the *Alternative representations* section type a label or brief description in the *Text* window (**Figure 7.20**).

4. When you're done, click *OK* and the alternate text will become part of the image's HTML coding.

Figure 7.19 By creating alternate text for images (top), visitors can get a sense of an image's content before it completely downloads (bottom). In Internet Explorer, alternate text appears as pop-up text.

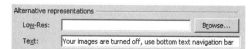

Figure 7.20 Use the *General* tab's *Alternative representations* section to enter a brief description of an image—or instructions for users who have images turned off.

Figure 7.21 To see how alternate text looks in Web browsers without images on, use Internet Explorer's Tools menu to reach the *Multimedia* settings.

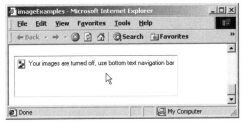

Figure 7.22 Web browsers with images turned off will display the alternate text instead.

✔ Tip

■ To check that the ordinarily invisible alternate text will appear in Web browsers where images have been turned off, launch Internet Explorer. Choose Tools > Internet Options, click the dialog box's *Advanced* tab and uncheck *Show pictures* under *Multimedia* (**Figure 7.21**). Click *OK* to close the dialog box, switch back to FrontPage, and click the Standard toolbar's Preview in browser icon (**Figure 7.22**).

CREATING ALTERNATE TEXT/IMAGES

To create low-resolution alternate images

1. Right-click the regular-resolution image within its Web page and choose *Picture Properties* from the shortcut menu (Alt Enter) (**Figure 7.15**).

2. When the Picture Properties dialog box appears, click the *Appearance* tab. Within the *Size* section, note the image's *Width* and *Height* (**Figure 7.23**). Click *Cancel* to close the dialog box.

3. Now switch to whatever graphics program you use to create images and make a duplicate of your original image. When you save the duplicate, however, save it at 18 dpi instead of the usual 96 dpi. Be sure to give the duplicate the same physical dimensions as the original (75 by 75 pixels in our example)—otherwise at 18 dpi it's going to be a tiny, tiny picture.

4. Switch back to FrontPage, right-click your *regular-resolution* image and once more choose *Picture Properties* from the shortcut menu (Alt Enter) (**Figure 7.15**).

5. When the Picture Properties dialog box appears, click the *General* tab.

6. Within the dialog box's *Alternative representations* section, click *Browse* to navigate to your low-resolution version of the image.

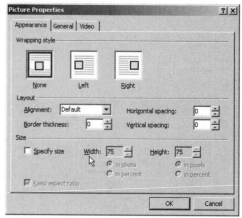

Figure 7.23 Before creating a low-resolution alternate image, note the original image's *Width* and *Height* in the Picture Properties dialog box.

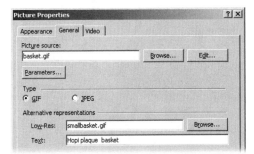

Figure 7.24 Use the *Alternative representations* section of the Picture Properties dialog box to pair low-resolution and regular-resolution versions of an image.

7. When you return to the Picture Properties dialog box, the name of the low-resolution image will appear in the text window (**Figure 7.24**). Click *OK*, and the low-resolution version will be paired with the regular-resolution image. That way, when Web browsers download the page, the low-resolution version will download almost immediately to hold the page space until the regular-resolution image takes its place.

Aligning images

Sometimes the trickiest thing about creating a Web page is getting the text to align and wrap correctly around your images.

To align images

1. Right-click the image within its Web page and choose *Picture Properties* from the shortcut menu ((Alt)(Enter)) (**Figure 7.15**).

2. When the Picture Properties dialog box appears, click the *Appearance* tab (**Figure 7.23**).

3. To quickly set how text flows around the picture, click *None*, *Left*, or *Right* in the *Wrapping style* section. To fine-tune how the picture aligns with adjacent text or pictures, use the *Layout* section's *Alignment* drop-down menu (**Figure 7.25**). (The *Alignment* drop-down menu's *Left* and *Right* choices do the same thing as *Left* and *Right* in *Wrapping style*.)

4. Click *OK* and the alignment will be applied to the image (**Figure 7.26**). To see the effect, however, you'll have to click the *Preview* tab. **Figure 7.27** shows how each alignment choice affects the layout of the image.

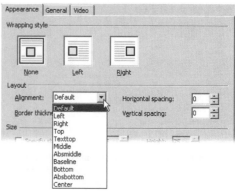

Figure 7.25 Use the *Appearance* tab's *Layout* section to set how an image aligns with adjacent text. It also controls borders and spacing around the image.

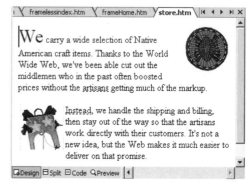

Figure 7.26 The top image is aligned right, the bottom image aligned left.

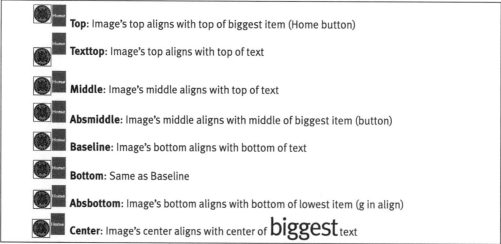

Top: Image's top aligns with top of biggest item (Home button)

Texttop: Image's top aligns with top of text

Middle: Image's middle aligns with top of text

Absmiddle: Image's middle aligns with middle of biggest item (button)

Baseline: Image's bottom aligns with bottom of text

Bottom: Same as Baseline

Absbottom: Image's bottom aligns with bottom of lowest item (g in align)

Center: Image's center aligns with center of biggest text

Figure 7.27 FrontPage's alignment choices control how the image lines up with same-line text and graphics.

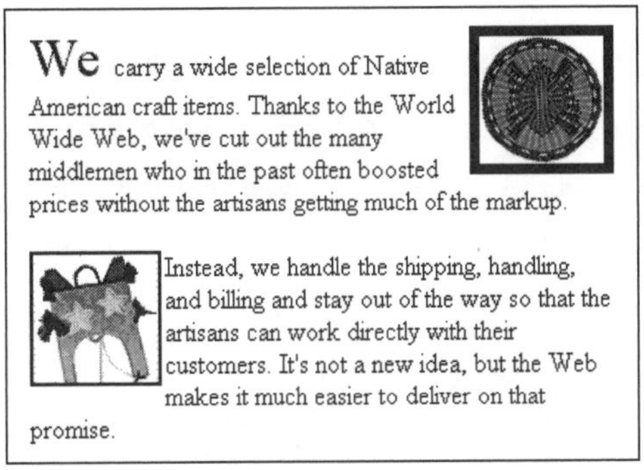

We carry a wide selection of Native American craft items. Thanks to the World Wide Web, we've cut out the many middlemen who in the past often boosted prices without the artisans getting much of the markup.

 Instead, we handle the shipping, handling, and billing and stay out of the way so that the artisans can work directly with their customers. It's not a new idea, but the Web makes it much easier to deliver on that promise.

Figure 7.28 A 6-pixel border has been applied to the top image, a 2-pixel border to the bottom image.

We carry a wide selection of Native American craft items. Thanks to the World Wide Web, we've cut out the many middlemen who in the past often boosted prices without the artisans getting much of the markup.

Instead, we handle the shipping, handling, and billing and stay out of the way so that the artisans can work directly with their customers. It's not a new idea, but the Web makes it much easier to deliver on that promise.

Figure 7.29 A horizontal spacing of 30 has been applied to the top image, a vertical spacing of 15 to the bottom one.

To add an image border

1. Right-click the image within its Web page and choose *Picture Properties* from the shortcut menu ((Alt)(Enter)) (**Figure 7.15**).

2. When the Picture Properties dialog box appears, click the *Appearance* tab (**Figure 7.23**).

3. Within the *Layout* section, you can type a number directly into the *Border thickness* text window or use the arrows just to the right to choose a number. (The numbers represent pixels.) Click *OK* and the border will be applied to the image (**Figure 7.28**).

To add space around an image

1. Right-click the image within its Web page and choose *Picture Properties* from the shortcut menu ((Alt)(Enter)) (**Figure 7.15**).

2. When the Picture Properties dialog box appears, click the *Appearance* tab (**Figure 7.23**).

3. Within the *Layout* section, you can type a number directly into the *Horizontal spacing* and *Vertical spacing* text windows or use the arrows to set how many pixels of blank space should be placed around the image. Click *OK* and the space will be added to the page (**Figure 7.29**).

ADDING BORDERS/SPACE TO IMAGES

Adding horizontal lines

OK, OK, it's not exactly an image. But a horizontal line is a basic *graphic* element for Web pages. A couple of other graphic-based approaches for dressing up pages—changing the page color and adding a background image—are covered in the tips on page 159.

To insert a horizontal line

1. Make sure you're in Page view by choosing View > Page, click the *Design* tab in the main window, and then click where you want the line placed within a page (**Figure 7.30**).

2. Choose Insert > Horizontal Line (**Figure 7.31**). The line will be inserted into the page (**Figure 7.32**).

To edit a horizontal line

1. Right-click on the line and choose *Horizontal Line Properties* from the shortcut menu (Alt Enter) (**Figure 7.33**).

2. When the Horizontal Line Properties dialog box appears, you can adjust the line's size, alignment, and color (**Figure 7.34**). For details, see *Horizontal line options* on the next page.

3. When you're done editing the line, click *OK* and the changes will be applied.

Figure 7.30 Click where you want to insert a horizontal line.

Figure 7.31 To add a line, choose Insert > Horizontal Line.

Figure 7.32 The horizontal line inserted into the document.

Figure 7.33 To edit a horizontal line, right-click it and choose *Horizontal Line Properties* from the shortcut menu.

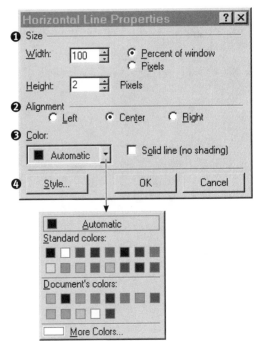

Figure 7.34 Use the Horizontal Line Properties dialog box to adjust a line's size, alignment, and color.

Horizontal line options

Use the Horizontal Line Properties dialog box to adjust a line's size, alignment, and color (**Figure 7.34**).

➊ **Size:** By default, FrontPage sets the line width as a percentage of the browser window's width. Choose *Pixels* if you want to set an absolute width. The *Height* is always set in pixels. Use the arrows to adjust the numbers or enter numbers directly in the text windows.

➋ **Alignment:** By default, FrontPage centers the line. Choose *Left* or *Right* to have the line align to either side of the page.

➌ **Color:** Click the arrow just to the right of *Automatic* (the default color) and a pop-up menu lets you pick from *Standard colors* (HTML's 16 predefined colors), the *Document's colors* (very handy for maintaining the color scheme of a page or site), or *More Colors*, which displays FrontPage's standard color wheel of all 216 Web-safe colors. By default, FrontPage adds a shadowed effect to the line. Check *Solid line (no shading)* to cancel the effect.

➍ **Style:** This button can only be used if you've created style sheets for your Web site. See *Building Style Sheets and Dynamic Effects* on page 363.

ADDING HORIZONTAL LINES

Editing Images

For major image editing, it's best to use a dedicated graphics program, but FrontPage's Pictures toolbar can easily handle a lot of basic editing (**Figure 7.1**). Remember that when using FrontPage to edit images all changes are applied to the actual image. To be safe, always keep a duplicate of the original stored outside your Web site. The Restore button, explained below, also will become one of your best friends.

To undo image editing

◆ Select the image, then click the Restore button in the Pictures toolbar (**Figure 7.35**). The image will revert to the last saved version.

Figure 7.35 To undo an image change, click the Restore button.

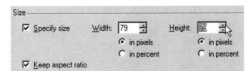

Figure 7.36 Use the *Appearance* tab's *Size* section to set an image's width and height.

Resizing images

The simplest way to resize an image is to grab one of its square black handles with the cursor and drag it. If you're looking for more precision with *minor* resizing, the following method will do it. Also see *Resampling images* on the next page.

To resize images

1. Right-click the image within its Web page and choose *Picture Properties* from the shortcut menu ((Alt)(Enter)) (**Figure 7.15**).

2. When the Picture Properties dialog box appears, click the *Appearance* tab (**Figure 7.23**).

3. Within the *Size* section, check *Specify size* and either type numbers into the *Width* and *Height* text windows or use the arrows just to the right of them (**Figure 7.36**). By default, the numbers represent pixels, unless you choose *in percent*.

4. Check *Keep aspect ratio* if you want to preserve the image's overall proportions even as you shrink or enlarge it.

5. Click *OK* and the image will be resized.

✔ Tip

- If you're making anything other than minor size adjustments (10 percent or less), you should go back to your image editing program, create a new image, and insert it into your Web page.

Resampling images

If you want to significantly enlarge or shrink an image, you'll get better looking results resizing it with a separate graphics program. But resampling, which involves FrontPage making its best guess at adding or deleting image pixels, is fine for minor size changes. In general, using resampling to shrink an image creates less distortion than enlarging it.

To resample an image

1. Make sure you're in Page view by choosing View > Page, click the *Design* tab in the main window, and then select your image by clicking on it.

2. Drag any of the image's square black handles to shrink or enlarge it (**Figure 7.37**). Use a corner handle if you want to maintain the image's original proportions.

3. Once you've shrunk or enlarged the image, click the Resample button in the Pictures toolbar to apply the resampling (**Figure 7.38**).

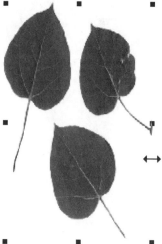

Figure 7.37 To resample an image, first drag any of the image's square black handles to shrink or enlarge it.

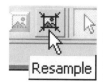

Figure 7.38 Once you've shrunk or enlarged the image, click the Resample button to apply the change.

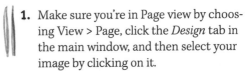

Figure 7.39 To add text to images, first click the Text button and a text box will appear centered within the image.

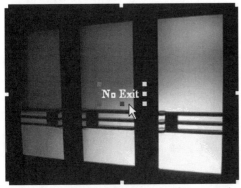

Figure 7.40 Type into the box, resizing if necessary by clicking and dragging its handles.

Figure 7.41 Once you've adjusted the text's position, size, font and color, the changes are applied.

To add text to images

1. Make sure you're in Page view by choosing View > Page, click the *Design* tab in the main window, and then select your image by clicking on it.

2. Click the Text button (**Figure 7.39)** and a text box will appear centered within the image. Type in your text (**Figure 7.40**). You may need to enlarge the text box by clicking and dragging its handles for all your text to show, though the box cannot extend beyond the image's edges.

3. To move the text box, select it and drag any of its square black handles. To set other properties for the text, select the text box, and use the Formatting toolbar (**Figure 7.41**).

✔ Tips

- Text can only be applied directly to GIF images. If you try to apply text to a JPEG image, FrontPage will offer to convert the image first.

- Make sure the text is readable against the image. Change the text's color or size by right-clicking it and choosing *Font* from the shortcut menu. Or use the Pictures toolbar's Wash Out button. See the next page.

- To delete an image's text, select the text box and press (←Backspace) or (Delete).

- A great thing about the Text button is that you can go back and change the text or move the box even after you've saved it.

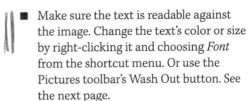

ADDING TEXT TO IMAGES

189

To wash out an image

1. Make sure you're in Page view by choosing View > Page, click the *Design* tab in the main window, and then select your image by clicking on it (**Figure 7.42**).

2. Click the Pictures toolbar's Color button and choose Wash Out from the dropdown menu (**Figure 7.43**). The image will be brightened in a single step, making it easier to use the image as a backdrop for text or another image (**Figure 7.44**).

Figure 7.42 Click to select the image you want to wash out.

Figure 7.43 Use the Color button's Wash Out choice to reduce the image's contrast.

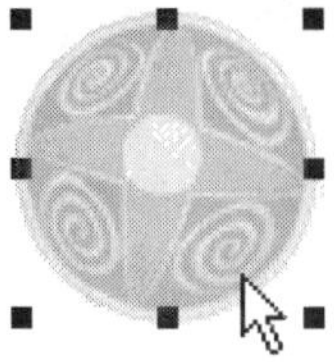

Figure 7.44 Once an image has been washed out, it will be easier to see objects placed atop it.

WASHING OUT IMAGES

Figure 7.45
Downloading the large original image would test the patience of uninterested viewers.

Figure 7.46 To create a thumbnail of a large image, click the Auto Thumbnail button or choose Tools > Auto Thumbnail ([Ctrl][T]).

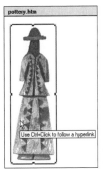

Figure 7.47 The thumbnail image includes a hyperlink to the larger image for viewers wanting a detailed look.

Creating auto thumbnails and photo galleries

Thumbnails let visitors get the gist of an image without waiting for the detailed, slow-to-download original. If they want to see the larger file version, clicking the thumbnail automatically takes them to it. Thumbnails are particularly useful for quickly presenting a catalog-style page of products. FrontPage also gives you control over thumbnail properties, so you can set the default size, border, and beveling.

What FrontPage calls auto thumbnails in fact involve manually creating thumbnails one at a time. Photo galleries overcome this drawback by letting you convert an entire folder of images into a hyperlinked set of thumbnails.

To create auto thumbnail images

1. Make sure you're in Page view by choosing View > Page, click the *Design* tab in the main window, and then select your image by clicking on it (**Figure 7.45**).

2. Click the Pictures toolbar's Auto Thumbnail button or choose Tools > Auto Thumbnail ([Ctrl][T]) (**Figure 7.46**). (If the image is already fairly small, the button will be dimmed.) A smaller version of the image will be created and automatically linked to the large original image (**Figure 7.47**).

To set auto thumbnail properties

1. Choose Tools > Page Options (**Figure 7.48**).

2. When the Page Options dialog box appears, the *Auto Thumbnail* tab will be selected by default (**Figure 7.49**). Use the *Set* drop-down menu to pick any of the four settings, then use the *Pixels* text window to change the default. If you want, check *Border thickness* and use the *Pixels* text window to set its width. You also can add a *Beveled edge*.

3. Click *OK* and the settings will be applied to all new thumbnails created.

Figure 7.48 To set thumbnail properties, choose Tools > Page Options.

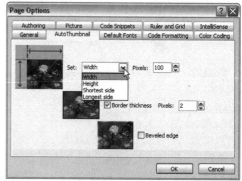

Figure 7.49 The Auto Thumbnail tab lets you set the size, border, and bevels applied to thumbnails.

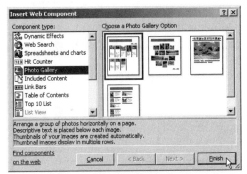

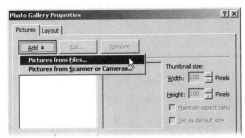

To create a thumbnail photo gallery

1. Click on the Web page where you want the photo gallery to appear and choose Insert > Web Component (**Figure 7.50**).

2. When the Insert Web Component dialog box appears, choose *Photo Gallery* in the *Component type* list, then choose a layout in the right-hand pane, and click *Finish* (**Figure 7.51**).

3. When the Photo Gallery Properties dialog box appears, the *Pictures* tab will be chosen by default. Click the *Add* button and choose *Pictures from Files* from the drop-down menu (**Figure 7.52**).

(continued)

Figure 7.50 To create a thumbnail photo gallery, choose Insert > Web Component.

Figure 7.51 Choose *Photo Gallery* in the *Component type* list, then choose a layout in the right-hand pane.

Figure 7.52 To compile the gallery, click the *Add* button and choose either *Pictures from Files* or *Pictures from Scanner or Cameras*.

4. When the File Open dialog box appears, navigate to the images you want to use, select one or more (Ctrl–click to select multiple images), and click *Open* (**Figure 7.53**). The selected images will be added to the list in the Photo Gallery Properties dialog box (**Figure 7.54**).

5. The list of files reflects the order images will be displayed in the gallery, so if necessary, select a listing and use the *Move Up* or *Move Down* buttons to change the order. Use *Remove* to drop a file from the gallery only; the file itself will not be deleted from your hard drive.

6. If you prefer, select an image in the list and use the *Width* and *Height* windows to change the *Thumbnail size*. By default, each image's horizontal-to-vertical ratio is preserved, unless you uncheck *Maintain aspect ratio*. If you check *Set as default size*, the currently selected image's *Width* and *Height* will be applied to all the images in the list—overriding each image's original aspect ratio.

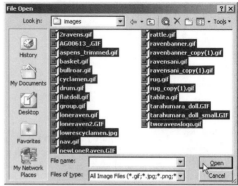

Figure 7.53 Use the File Open dialog box to navigate to the images you want to use in the photo gallery.

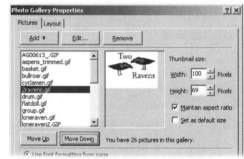

Figure 7.54 The selected images are added to the Photo Gallery Properties dialog box's list. Use the *Move Up* or *Move Down* buttons to change the order.

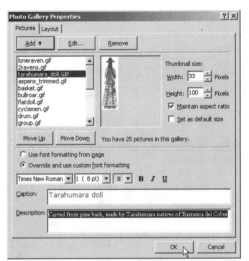

Figure 7.55 Use the *Caption* or *Description* text window to add information about a selected image.

Figure 7.56 The photo gallery as it appears in the Web page.

7. To add information about a particular image, select it in the list and type in the *Caption* or *Description* text window (**Figure 7.55**). By default, the text will *Use font formatting from page*. To apply particular fonts or styles, choose *Override and use custom font formatting* and use the formatting drop-down menus and icons to set the *Caption* or *Description*. Repeat for each image needing text description.

8. Click *OK* and the gallery will be generated and added to your Web page (**Figure 7.56**). Each thumbnail image can be clicked to reach the original image.

✔ Tip

■ If you choose *Pictures from Scanner or Cameras* when you click *Add* in step 3, FrontPage will import images directly from either connected device without having to first copy them to your hard drive (**Figure 7.52**).

To change a photo gallery

1. Open the Web page containing the gallery, right-click the gallery, and choose *Photo Gallery Properties* from the shortcut menu (**Figure 7.57**).

2. When the Photo Gallery Properties dialog box appears, the *Pictures* tab is selected by default, enabling you to reorder the list, change the size of the thumbnails, or edit the text information as described in *To create a thumbnail photo gallery*.

3. To change the gallery's basic arrangement, click the dialog box's *Layout* tab and select a new setting in the *Choose a layout* list (**Figure 7.58**). Set the *Number of pictures per row* if that choice is available.

4. You also can make some basic changes to any photo in the gallery by clicking the Photo Gallery Properties dialog box's *Pictures* tab and then clicking the *Edit* button (top, **Figure 7.59**). The Edit Picture dialog box will open, where you can change the size of the original picture itself, instead of just its thumbnail (bottom, **Figure 7.59**). You also can rotate or crop the picture and even use the *Previous* and *Next* buttons to move through the rest of the gallery list. Click *OK* to apply the changes and return to the Photo Gallery Properties dialog box.

5. Once you have finished making all your changes, click *OK* in the Photo Gallery Properties dialog box and the changes will be applied to the photo gallery.

Figure 7.57 To change a photo gallery, right-click the gallery and choose *Photo Gallery Properties*.

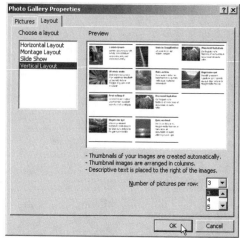

Figure 7.58 To change the gallery's basic arrangement, click the *Layout* tab and select a new setting in the *Choose a layout* list.

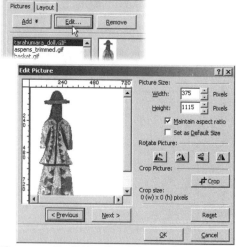

Figure 7.59 By clicking the *Edit* button (top), you can make basic changes to any photo in the gallery (bottom).

Figure 7.60 The original image before being flipped or rotated.

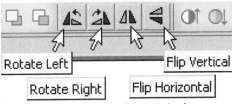

Figure 7.61 The Pictures toolbar includes four rotate/flip buttons.

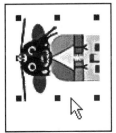 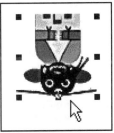

Figure 7.62 Left: The image after being rotated to the left. Right: The image after being flipped vertically.

To rotate or flip images

1. Make sure you're in Page view by choosing View > Page, click the *Design* tab in the main window, and then select your image by clicking on it (**Figure 7.60**).

2. Click one of the four rotate/flip buttons in the Pictures toolbar (**Figure 7.61**). The image will be rotated or flipped, depending on your choice (**Figure 7.62**).

✔ Tip

■ To undo any rotate or flip action, click the same button again and the image will be restored to its original position.

ROTATING, FLIPPING IMAGES

197

To change image contrast

1. Make sure you're in Page view by choosing View > Page, click the *Design* tab in the main window, and then select your image by clicking on it (**Figure 7.63**).

2. Click the More Contrast or Less Contrast button as many times as you need to boost or reduce the image's contrast (**Figures 7.64** and **7.65**). If the image gets too contrasty or too flat, use the other button of the pair to rebalance its appearance. You also can undo each incremental change by pressing Ctrl Z.

To change image brightness

1. Make sure you're in Page view by choosing View > Page, click the *Design* tab in the main window, and then select your image by clicking on it (**Figure 7.66**).

2. Click either the More Brightness or Less Brightness button as many times as you need to lighten or darken the image (**Figures 7.67** and **7.68**).

Figure 7.63 The original image before changing its contrast.

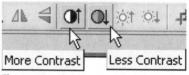

Figure 7.64 Click the More Contrast or Less Contrast button to boost or reduce the image's contrast.

Figure 7.65 Left: Image contrast boosted to maximum. Right: Image contrast reduced to a minimum.

Figure 7.66 The original image before adjusting the brightness.

Figure 7.67 Click either the More Brightness or Less Brightness button to lighten or darken the image.

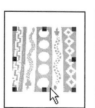

Figure 7.68 Left: Image brightened. Right: Image darkened.

Figure 7.69 To trim an image, select it and click the Crop button.

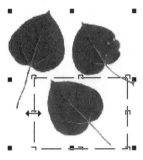

Figure 7.70 Click and drag any of the black handles to shape the cropping boundary.

Figure 7.71 After you press (Enter) or click the Crop button again, the image is trimmed.

Figure 7.72 To make a color transparent in a GIF image, click the Set Transparent Color button.

Figure 7.73 Move your cursor back over the selected image and click the eraser-like icon on the color you want made transparent.

Figure 7.74 After making the image's white background transparent, the underlying image shows through.

To crop images

1. Make sure you're in Page view by choosing View > Page, click the *Design* tab in the main window, and then select your image by clicking on it.

2. Click the Crop button (**Figure 7.69**).

3. When a dashed line surrounds the image, click and drag any of the black handles to shape the cropping boundary (**Figure 7.70**).

4. Press (Enter) or click the Crop button again and the image will be trimmed (**Figure 7.71**).

To make a GIF color transparent

1. Make sure you're in Page view by choosing View > Page, click the *Design* tab in the main window, and then select your image by clicking on it.

2. Click the Set Transparent Color button in the Pictures toolbar (**Figure 7.72**). Move your cursor back over the selected image and it will turn into an eraser-like icon (**Figure 7.73**).

3. Click the tip of the icon on the color in the image that you want to be transparent. The change will be applied, though you may not detect the change until you drag the image over another image (**Figure 7.74**).

To remove image color

1. Make sure you're in Page view by choosing View > Page, click the *Design* tab in the main window, and then select your image by clicking on it.

2. Click the Color button in the Pictures toolbar, choose Grayscale from the drop-down menu (**Figure 7.75**), and the previously full-color image will turn into a grayscale image.

✔ Tip

- The drop-down menu's Black & White choice is only available when working with vector-based images. For more information, see *Adding and Editing Drawings* on page 207.

To add a bevel to an image

1. Make sure you're in Page view by choosing View > Page, click the *Design* tab in the main window, and then select your image by clicking on it.

2. Click the Bevel button in the Pictures toolbar and a button-like beveled edge will be added to the image (**Figure 7.76**).

Figure 7.75 To remove color from an image, click the Color button and choose *Grayscale* from the drop-down menu.

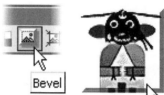

Figure 7.76 To add a bevel to an image, click the Bevel button (left) and the effect is applied (right).

Positioning Images Absolutely

FrontPage uses Cascading Style Sheets (CSS) and Dynamic Hypertext Markup Language (DHTML) to give you the ability to overlap images on your Web pages. Without CSS or DHTML, images and other objects can only be positioned in sequence, that is, one after another across and down the Web page. Thanks to FrontPage's CSS-DHTML combination—plus its new layers feature—it is now easier to place images so that they overlap. This is what's called positioning images absolutely, based on their stacking order. Since absolute positioning also makes use of FrontPage 2003's new layers feature, you may want to read *Creating Layers* on page 292.

To position images absolutely

1. Make sure you're in Page view by choosing View > Page, and click the *Design* tab in the main window. If you have more than one image on the page already, make sure they are separated by at least one paragraph return by clicking the Show All icon (Ctrl *) in the Standard toolbar (**Figure 7.77**).

2. Select your image by clicking on it, then choose Format > Position (**Figure 7.78**).

3. When the Position dialog box appears, click the *Absolute* button (**Figure 7.79**). Click *OK* to close the dialog box and the selected image will now be bound by a blue border with a *<No ID>* tag in the upper-left corner (**Figure 7.80**). This border marks the image's bounding box, which is actually a layer. (For more information on layers, see page 292.)

Figure 7.77 If you have more than one image on the page already, make sure they are separated by at least one paragraph return by clicking the Show All icon (Ctrl *) in the Standard toolbar.

Figure 7.78 Select your image by clicking on it, then choose Format > Position.

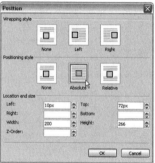

Figure 7.79 When the Position dialog box appears, click the *Absolute* button.

Figure 7.80 Once the image has been positioned absolutely, the image will be bound by a blue border with a *<No ID>* tag in the upper-left corner.

POSITIONING IMAGES ABSOLUTELY

Figure 7.81
A four-arrow icon will appear as you grab the image's bounding box and begin dragging it to a new position.

Figure 7.82
Release the cursor and the image with its bounding box will jump to the new location.

Figure 7.83 Repeat steps 2–4 for each image on the page that you want to position absolutely.

Figure 7.84 Once you absolutely position each image, you can easily reposition them anywhere on the page with a simple click-drag.

4. Click the blue border surrounding the image and your cursor will become a four-arrow icon (top left, **Figure 7.81**). (If the regular arrow-shaped cursor appears instead of the four-arrow icon, you've selected the image rather than the bounding box.) Drag the bounding box to where you want to place the image using the dashed line that appears to guide your placement (bottom right, **Figure 7.81**). Release the cursor and the image with its bounding box will jump to the new location (**Figure 7.82**).

5. Once you've positioned the image, click anywhere outside the image to deselect it. Repeat steps 2-4 for each image on the page that you want to position absolutely (**Figure 7.83**). At that point, you can click and drag each bounding box to reposition it anywhere on the page (**Figure 7.84**). For information on how to control the stacking order of the images, see *To move absolutely positioned images forward and backward* on the next page.

✔ Tips

- If you don't separate multiple images on the page by at least one paragraph return, FrontPage will place all the images in the same bounding box.

- The click-and-drag method may not be precise enough if you're working with a design requiring that images be positioned at predetermined x, y coordinates. For pixel-based precision, use the *Location and size* section of the Position dialog box (**Figure 7.79**). Use the number-entry windows to set the image's pixel coordinates.

To move absolutely positioned images forward and backward

1. Choose Help > Microsoft Office FrontPage Help (1) and when the Help pane appears, choose *Layers* in the drop-down menu (**Figure 7.85**). Make sure the Positioning toolbar is visible (View > Toolbars > Positioning).

2. Select the bounding box of one of your absolutely positioned images by clicking on its border. Be sure the cursor appears as a four-arrow icon; otherwise you've only selected the image and not its bounding box (**Figure 7.86**). In the Positioning toolbar, the *Z-Index* text window will be blank, while the highlighted layer in the *Layers* pane will have a *0* in the *Z* column.

3. Depending on whether you want to place the selected image in front of or behind the other page items, click the Bring Forward or Send Backward button in the Positioning toolbar (**Figure 7.87**). The stack order of the selected image will change, as reflected by the toolbar's *Z-Index* text window and the *Layers* pane's *Z* column (the higher the number, the closer to the top of the stack order) (**Figure 7.88**).

Figure 7.85
When the Help pane appears, choose *Layers* in the drop-down menu.

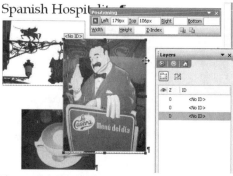

Figure 7.86 Be sure the cursor appears as a four-arrow icon; otherwise you've only selected the image and not its bounding box.

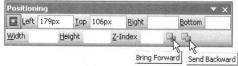

Figure 7.87 Use the Bring Forward or Send Backward button in the Positioning toolbar to set the stack order for the selected image.

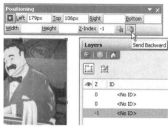

Figure 7.88 The changed stack order of the selected image will be reflected by the toolbar's *Z-Index* text window and the *Layers* pane's *Z* column.

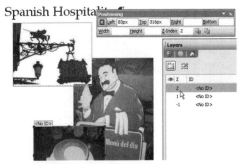

Figure 7.89 After you set the stack order, each image has its own *Z*-number in the *Layers* pane.

Figure 7.90 By making the white areas transparent in the upper-left image, the stacking arrangement can be more flexible.

4. Select another image on the page for which you want to set the stack order and repeat steps 2 and 3. Once you are done, each image will have its own *Z*-number in the *Layers* pane (**Figure 7.89**).

✔ Tips

- Any time you select the bounding box for an image, it will appear as the topmost image on the page. This is just to help you see the image. It does not indicate its actual place in the stack order. Use the *Layers* pane's *Z* column or the main window's *Preview* tab to check the image's actual position in the stack order.

- For more flexibility when stacking images, remember the option of making the background color transparent by converting an image to the GIF format. In **Figure 7.90,** shown with the *Preview* tab selected, the white background color in the top-left photo was made transparent.

Adding and Editing Drawings

8

If you have ever used Microsoft PowerPoint to create an organization chart, you have created vector-based drawings. As bit-mapped images, GIFs and JPEGs are made of differently colored pixels. Drawings, however, are vector-based images. As mathematically generated objects, vector-based images create much smaller files than their GIF or JPEG equivalents. That means they download more quickly over the Web. Just remember that only version 5 or later Web browsers can read the Vector Markup Language coding used to generate vector-based drawings.

Microsoft FrontPage includes a partial solution for earlier Web browsers by also creating a GIF version of any drawing. Web browsers that cannot handle the VML code will, instead, display the substitute GIF. The GIF file will be larger and somewhat slower to download than the original vector-based image. As with so many things Web, using drawings involves a trade off. Unless you're publishing Web pages for an audience where *everyone* uses Internet Explorer 5 or 6, for example, you may want to think twice before packing your pages with drawings.

Virtually all of FrontPage's drawings can be created using the Drawing toolbar (**Figure 8.1**) or the WordArt toolbar (**Figure 8.2**). FrontPage's drawings fall into three broad categories: simple shapes such as lines, arrows, squares, and circles; AutoShapes; and WordArt. The AutoShapes feature offers a variety of pre-drawn shapes at the click of your cursor. You'll also find the tools for drawing freeform shapes tucked away in the AutoShapes menu. For more information, see *To draw a freeform shape* on page 212. WordArt makes it easy to create fancy text and banner effects. For more information, see *Using WordArt* on page 216.

FrontPage's drawing tools also allow you to create a drawing canvas, which has advantages when creating more complicated drawings containing multiple shapes. For more information, see *Using the Drawing Canvas* on page 226. For creating complex layouts, the old vector-based text boxes have been replaced by FrontPage's new layers capability. For more information, see *Creating Layers* on page 292. You can still add text areas (which FrontPage sometimes refers to as text boxes) to Web forms. For more information, see *Adding a text area* on page 324.

ADDING AND EDITING DRAWINGS

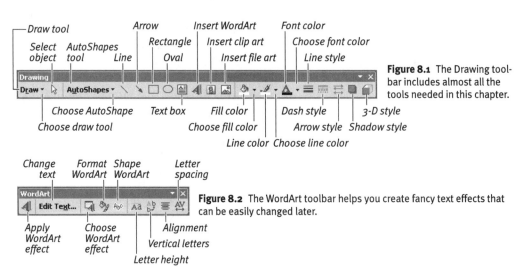

Figure 8.1 The Drawing toolbar includes almost all the tools needed in this chapter.

Draw tool
Select object
AutoShapes tool
Line
Arrow
Rectangle
Oval
Insert WordArt
Insert clip art
Insert file art
Font color
Choose font color
Line style
Choose AutoShape
Choose draw tool
Text box
Fill color
Choose fill color
Line color
Choose line color
Dash style
Arrow style
3-D style
Shadow style

Figure 8.2 The WordArt toolbar helps you create fancy text effects that can be easily changed later.

Change text
Format WordArt
Shape WordArt
Letter spacing
Apply WordArt effect
Choose WordArt effect
Letter height
Vertical letters
Alignment

Figure 8.3 To draw a simple shape, click the toolbar's line, arrow, rectangle, or oval icon.

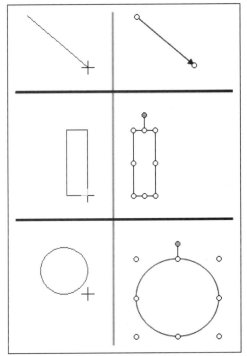

Figure 8.4 Whether you add an arrow, rectangle, or circle, the click-and-drag basics of drawing the shape remain the same.

To turn on the Drawing toolbar

◆ To view the Drawing toolbar, choose View > Toolbars > Drawing.

To draw a simple shape

1. Turn on the Drawing toolbar, then click one of the toolbar's four simple shapes (line, arrow, rectangle, or oval) (**Figure 8.3**).

2. Click and drag in the page where you want the shape to appear (left, **Figure 8.4**). Release the cursor when the shape reaches the desired size (you can adjust its location and size later). The shape will appear on the page, with small circles marking its boundary (right, **Figure 8.4**). For more information on moving or adjusting a shape, see *Changing Drawn Objects* on page 219.

To add an AutoShape

1. Turn on the Drawing toolbar, click AutoShapes in the toolbar, choose a shape category, then choose a specific shape from the drop-down menu (**Figure 8.5**).

2. Click and drag in the page where you want the shape to appear (left, **Figure 8.6**). Release the cursor when the shape reaches the desired size (you can adjust its location and size later). The shape will appear on the page, with a series of small circles marking its boundary (right, **Figure 8.6**). For more information on moving or adjusting AutoShapes, see *Changing Drawn Objects* on page 219.

✔ Tips

■ You also can add AutoShapes to a page by choosing Insert > Picture > AutoShapes and then choosing a shape from the AutoShapes toolbar (**Figure 8.7**).

■ If you plan on creating a bunch of AutoShapes all at once, you may find it easier to have a separate AutoShapes toolbar on your desktop. Just click the Drawing toolbar's AutoShapes icon and move your cursor over the top of the drop-down menu until it becomes a four-headed arrow. You can then drag the AutoShapes toolbar to the desktop (**Figure 8.8**).

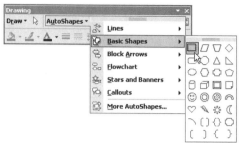

Figure 8.5 To add an AutoShape, choose a shape category, then choose a specific shape from the drop-down menu.

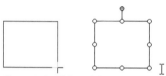

Figure 8.6 Click and drag in the page where you want the shape to appear (left), and release the cursor when the shape reaches the desired size (right).

Figure 8.7 You also can add AutoShapes to a page by choosing Insert > Picture > AutoShapes (left), and then choosing a shape from the AutoShapes toolbar (right).

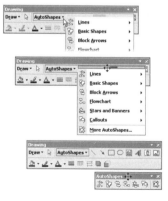

Figure 8.8 To put a separate AutoShapes toolbar on your desktop, click the AutoShapes icon and drag the drop-down menu to the desktop.

ADDING AN AUTOSHAPE

Figure 8.9 To reach the Curve tool, choose AutoShapes > Lines and click the icon in the drop-down menu.

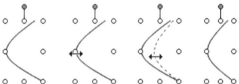

Figure 8.10 Left: To draw a curve, click where the line should begin, draw to the curve's midpoint, and click again. Middle: Continue drawing to the end of the line and the first click point becomes the curve's middle flex point. Right: When you're done drawing, double-click to select your new curved line.

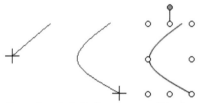

Figure 8.11 To adjust a curve's arc, move your cursor over the mid-point and drag the hollow-circle handle.

Figure 8.12 Create a separate Lines toolbar by clicking and dragging the top of the Lines drop-down menu onto your desktop.

To draw a curved line

1. Turn on the Drawing toolbar, then choose AutoShapes > Lines and click the Curve tool (**Figure 8.9**).

2. Click in your page where the line should begin, draw a line to the approximate midpoint of your curve, and click again (left, **Figure 8.10**). Continue drawing the line until you reach where you want the line to end and you'll notice that the previous cursor click created a flex point for the curve (middle, **Figure 8.10**). Double-click and the curved line will appear as a selected object on the page, denoted by its hollow-circle handles (right, **Figure 8.10**).

3. To adjust the curve's arc, move your cursor over any handle until the cursor becomes a double-headed arrow, at which point you can click and drag the handle (**Figure 8.11**).

4. Deselect the curved line by clicking elsewhere on your Web page and the line's handles will disappear.

✔ Tip

■ Because curves, freeform, and scribble shapes often require a bit of adjustment, put the Lines toolbar on your desktop where you can reach its tools in a single click. Choose AutoShapes > Lines and then click and drag the top of the Lines drop-down menu onto your desktop (top, **Figure 8.12**). Release the cursor and the tiny Lines toolbar will detach itself from the main Drawing toolbar (bottom, **Figure 8.12**).

To draw a freeform shape

1. Turn on the Drawing toolbar, then choose AutoShapes > Lines and click the Freeform tool (**Figure 8.13**).

2. Click in your page where the line should start and begin drawing, clicking at each spot where you want the line to change direction (left, **Figure 8.14**).

3. Double-click when you are done drawing the shape and it will appear as a selected object on the page, denoted by its hollow-circle handles (right, **Figure 8.14**).

4. To adjust the shape, right-click it and choose Edit Points from the shortcut menu (**Figure 8.15**).

5. When the shape's handles change to solid-black squares, click and drag any handle to adjust its position (**Figure 8.16**).

6. Repeat with any other handles you want to adjust. When you are done, deselect the freeform shape by clicking elsewhere on your Web page and the handles will disappear.

Figure 8.13 To reach the Freeform tool, choose AutoShapes > Lines and click the icon in the drop-down menu.

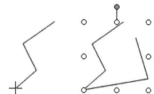

Figure 8.14 Left: Click where the freeform line should start, and begin drawing, clicking when you want to change direction. Right: Double-click when you are done to select the freeform shape.

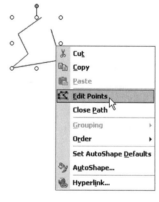

Figure 8.15 To adjust the freeform shape, right-click it and choose Edit Points from the shortcut menu.

Figure 8.16 Once the black handles appear, click and drag any handle to a new position.

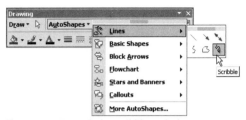

Figure 8.17 To reach the scribble tool, choose AutoShapes > Lines and click the icon in the drop-down menu.

Figure 8.18 To draw a scribble shape, click where the line should begin and draw in a continuous motion (left and middle). Double-click when you're done to select the shape (right).

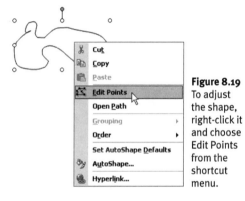

Figure 8.19 To adjust the shape, right-click it and choose Edit Points from the shortcut menu.

Using the scribble tool

Despite its unassuming name, the scribble tool is a powerful—and tricky—tool to use. More commonly known as a Bezier tool in such programs as Adobe Illustrator or Macromedia FreeHand, this tool lets you create shapes with a combination of straight and curved lines. You can then adjust the curves by clicking-and-dragging their handles. Be prepared to practice getting the hang of it.

To draw a scribble shape

1. Turn on the Drawing toolbar, then choose AutoShapes > Lines and click the Scribble tool icon (**Figure 8.17**).

2. Click in your page where the line should begin, then draw your shape without clicking (left, middle, **Figure 8.18**).

3. Double-click and the shape will appear as a selected object on the page, denoted by its hollow-circle handles (right, **Figure 8.18**).

4. To adjust the shape, right-click it and choose Edit Points from the shortcut menu (**Figure 8.19**).

(continued)

USING THE SCRIBBLE TOOL

5. When the shape's handles change to solid-black squares, click and drag any handle to adjust its position (**Figure 8.20**). You can change how a particular handle responds to adjustments by right-clicking that handle and choosing one of the four point types listed in the shortcut menu (*Auto*, *Smooth*, *Straight*, or *Corner*) (**Figure 8.21**). While the handle will not change its appearance, the line segments on each side of the point (shown as dashed lines) will respond quite differently based on the point type chosen (**Figure 8.22**).

6. Once you are finished adjusting the shape, deselect the freeform shape by clicking elsewhere on your Web page and the handles will disappear.

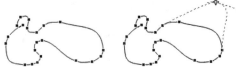

Figure 8.20 Once the black handles appear, click and drag any handle to a new position.

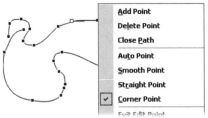

Figure 8.21 To change how a handle responds to adjustments, right-click it and choose one of the four point types listed in the shortcut menu.

Figure 8.22 Adjustments vary based on the point type. From left, the same handle as: an auto point, a smooth point, and a corner point.

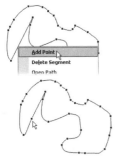

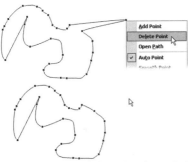

Figure 8.23 Right-click where you want another point, choose Add Point, and the point will be added.

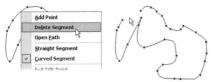

Figure 8.24 Right-click a point, choose Delete Point, and the point will be removed—along with the line segment on each side of it.

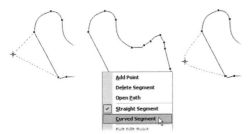

Figure 8.25 To delete a single line segment, right-click it and choose Delete Segment.

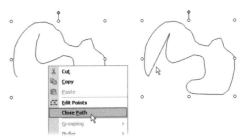

Figure 8.26 A straight line segment (left) adjusts differently than a curved line segment (right). To change one type to the other, right-click it and choose the other type in the shortcut menu (middle).

✔ Tips

- Adding handles (points) gives you finer control over a shape's outline. Right-click where you want another point, choose Add Point from the shortcut menu, and the point will be added (**Figure 8.23**).

- Deleting handles (points) simplifies a shape's outline. Right-click a point, choose Delete Point from the shortcut menu, and the point will be removed— along with the line segment on each side of it (**Figure 8.24**).

- You can delete a single line segment— without affecting any point—by right-clicking the segment and choosing Delete Segment from the shortcut menu (**Figure 8.25**).

- A shape's line segments are either straight or curved, but FrontPage lets you change one type to the other. This affects how the segment responds when adjusted (left, right, **Figure 8.26**). To change a segment's type, right-click it and choose Straight Segment or Curved Segment from the shortcut menu (middle, **Figure 8.26**).

- To close an open-ended shape, right-click it and choose Close Path from the shortcut menu (**Figure 8.27**).

Figure 8.27 To close an open-ended shape, right-click it and choose Close Path from the shortcut menu.

Using WordArt

Because it is vector based, WordArt can be changed at any time. That's especially handy for creating, and then changing, text for buttons and other navigation-related labels. For example, if you restructure your Web site, it's much quicker to change a button that uses a WordArt label than to redo a GIF-based button. While the WordArt gallery is full of wild type effects, don't overlook the usefulness of the relatively plain, but easier to read, gallery choices.

To turn on the WordArt toolbar

◆ To view the WordArt toolbar, choose View > Toolbars > WordArt or click the WordArt icon in the Drawing toolbar.

To add WordArt

1. Choose Insert > Picture > WordArt or click the Insert WordArt icon in the Drawing toolbar (**Figure 8.28**).

2. When the WordArt Gallery dialog box appears, choose one of the 30 styles and click *OK* (**Figure 8.29**).

3. When the Edit WordArt Text dialog box appears, choose your *Font*, *Size* and whether you want to use bold or italic, then type in the *Text* window (**Figure 8.30**). When you are done, click *OK* and the text will appear in the Web page (**Figure 8.31**).

Figure 8.28 To add WordArt, choose Insert > Picture > WordArt (left), or click the Insert WordArt icon in the Drawing toolbar (right).

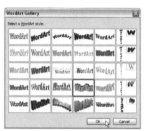

Figure 8.29 The WordArt Gallery dialog box offers you the choice of 30 type styles.

Figure 8.30 Use the Edit WordArt Text dialog box to enter your text and set its *Font*, *Size*, and whether you want to use bold or italic.

Figure 8.31 After you enter your text, it appears on the page in the chosen WordArt style.

Figure 8.32 To change the WordArt text at any time, click the WordArt toolbar's Edit Text icon.

Figure 8.33 The WordArt toolbar's shape icon offers dozens of choices.

Figure 8.34 The WordArt toolbar's horizontal/vertical icon lets you reorient your text.

To change WordArt

1. Click to select the WordArt, denoted by the appearance of small hollow circles (handles) around its boundary.

2. To change the text, click the WordArt toolbar's Edit Text icon (**Figure 8.32**), which will reopen the Edit WordArt Text dialog box, where you can then make your changes.

3. As long as the WordArt object remains selected, you can click any of the other WordArt toolbar icons and apply a second effect (**Figures 8.33–8.36**).

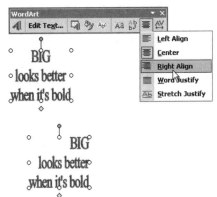

Figure 8.35 The WordArt toolbar's alignment icon offers five choices for adjusting your text.

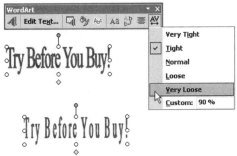

Figure 8.36 The WordArt toolbar's letter spacing icon offers five pre-set choices and a custom spacing option.

✔ Tips

- The first and third icons in the WordArt toolbar both open the WordArt Gallery.

- To quickly apply or change several WordArt effects, right-click the WordArt and choose Format WordArt or click the bucket icon in the WordArt toolbar (**Figure 8.37**). When the Format WordArt dialog box appears, use the tabs and menus to change the shape's properties (**Figure 8.38**). Click *OK* and all your changes will be applied to the selected WordArt. If you check the *Default for new objects* box, those settings will be used for any new WordArt.

- WordArt properties that can be set within the Format WordArt dialog box include: fill color and transparency; line color, style, and size; size and rotation; alignment and positioning; and alternate text.

- Some WordArt effects can only be applied using the WordArt toolbar: editing the text, making all characters the same height, reopening the WordArt Gallery, and changing the letter spacing (kerning).

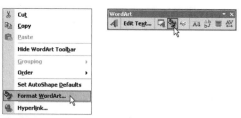

Figure 8.37 To change several WordArt effects at once, right-click the WordArt and choose Format WordArt (left) or click the WordArt toolbar's bucket icon (right).

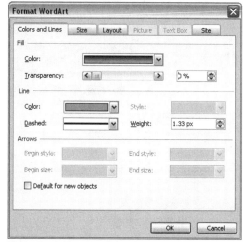

Figure 8.38 Use the tabs and menus in the Format WordArt dialog box to simultaneously change multiple WordArt properties.

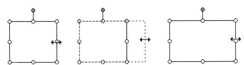

Figure 8.39 To resize an object, move the cursor over the handle you want to move, then click and drag it to a new location.

Figure 8.40 To resize lines and arrows, click and drag either point to a new location.

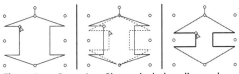

Figure 8.41 Some AutoShapes include a diamond-shaped handle, which you can use to adjust the shape's internal proportions.

Changing Drawn Objects

All three types of FrontPage drawings—simple shapes, AutoShapes, and WordArt—are generated as mathematical objects. That means you can easily resize, move, or even rotate drawings at any time. You also can change such properties as the color or style using the Drawing toolbar's icons. FrontPage also lets you group and arrange multiple objects. For more information, see *Aligning, Arranging, and Grouping Drawn Objects* on page 223.

To resize a drawn object

1. Click to select the drawn object, denoted by the appearance of small hollow circles (handles) around its boundary.

2. Move the cursor to the handle on the side that you want to expand or reduce. The cursor will become a two-headed arrow (left, **Figure 8.39**).

3. Click on the handle and drag it in the direction you want to expand or shrink. A dashed line will mark your progress (middle, **Figure 8.39**).

4. When the object reaches the desired size, release your cursor and the object will be resized (right, **Figure 8.39**).

✔ Tips

- You also can resize lines or arrows by clicking either point, dragging the point to a new spot, and releasing the cursor (**Figure 8.40**).

- Some of the more complex AutoShapes may include a diamond-shaped handle, which you can use to further adjust the shape's internal proportions (**Figure 8.41**).

CHANGING DRAWN OBJECTS

To move a drawn object

1. Click to select the drawn object and drag the object to its new destination (left, **Figure 8.42**). A dashed line will mark your progress (middle, **Figure 8.42**).

2. Release your cursor and the object will move to the new location (right, **Figure 8.42**).

To rotate a drawn object

1. Move your cursor over the object's protruding green handle until the cursor becomes a spiraling arrow (left, **Figure 8.43**).

2. Click and drag the cursor either clockwise or counter-clockwise. A dashed line will mark your progress (middle, **Figure 8.43**).

3. Release your cursor and the object will rotate to the new location (right, **Figure 8.43**).

To flip a drawn object

1. Click to select the drawn object or objects (**Figure 8.44**).

2. In the Drawing toolbar, choose Draw > Rotate or Flip and then make a choice in the drop-down menu (**Figure 8.45**). The selected object will be flipped based on your choice (**Figure 8.46**).

✔ Tip

- If you choose Rotate Left or Rotate Right, the object will be rotated exactly 90 degrees.

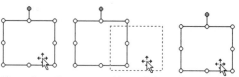

Figure 8.42 To move an object, click to select it, then drag it to a new location and release your cursor.

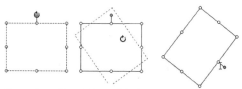

Figure 8.43 To rotate an object, move your cursor over the protruding green handle until the cursor becomes a spiraling arrow (left). Click and drag to rotate the object in either direction (right).

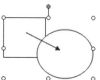

Figure 8.44 To flip an object, click to select it and its handles will become visible.

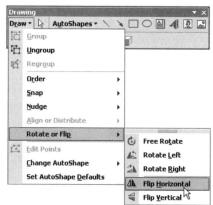

Figure 8.45 In the Drawing toolbar, choose Draw > Rotate or Flip and then make a choice in the drop-down menu.

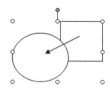

Figure 8.46 After flipping the object, it remains selected, making it easy to apply another action if necessary.

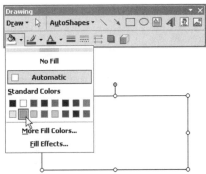

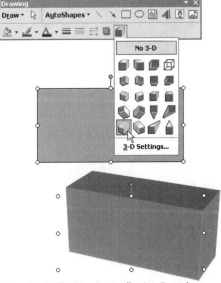

Figure 8.47 Once you select an object, you can apply any of the effects included in the Drawing toolbar's last eight icons.

Figure 8.48 The Drawing toolbar's 3-D settings can turn a rectangle (top) into a shaded box (bottom).

To change other drawn object properties

1. Click to select the drawn object, click any of the last eight icons in the Drawing toolbar, and select an effect from the icon's drop-down menu (**Figure 8.47**).

2. Release the cursor and the effect will be applied to the object.

3. As long as the object remains selected, you can click one of the other seven icons (top, **Figure 8.48**) and apply a second effect (bottom, **Figure 8.48**).

CHANGING DRAWN OBJECTS

✔ Tips

- The Drawing toolbar's icons offer a tremendous number of effects, including line shapes, shadows, and 3D shadings (**Figure 8.49**). It's worth your time to explore what's available.

- To quickly apply multiple effects, right-click an object and choose Format AutoShape (**Figure 8.50**). (This works even if the object is a simple shape and not an AutoShape.) When the Format AutoShape dialog box appears, use the tabs and menus to change the shape's properties (left, **Figure 8.51**). Click *OK* and all your changes will be applied to the selected shape (right, **Figure 8.51**). If you check the *Default for new objects* box, the settings will be used for any new shapes—a great time saver if you need to create a series of similar, custom shapes.

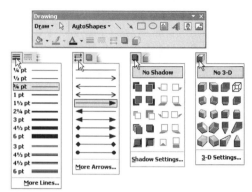

Figure 8.49 The Drawing toolbar's icons offer a tremendous number of effects.

Figure 8.50 To quickly apply multiple effects, right-click an object and choose Format AutoShape.

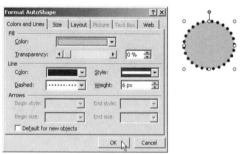

Figure 8.51 Use the tabs and menus in the Format AutoShape dialog box (left) to change multiple aspects of a shape (right).

Figure 8.52 Select several objects that you want to align by Ctrl-clicking each object.

Figure 8.53 To align or distribute the selected objects, choose Draw > Align or Distribute and then make a choice in the drop-down menu.

Figure 8.54 In this example, the two WordArt objects have been centrally aligned.

Aligning, Arranging, and Grouping Drawn Objects

FrontPage includes several options for moving and positioning drawn objects, which can be particularly helpful when working with multiple objects. Aligning lets you rearrange objects along a common axis; distributing lets you evenly space three or more objects. By default, FrontPage displays drawn objects in the order they were created with the most recent atop, that is, in front of, the earlier objects. By arranging, or ordering, the objects, you can change their so-called stack order. Finally, grouping lets you turn multiple objects into a single object, or group. This enables you to move the objects as a unit or apply property changes to all of them simultaneously. By creating groups of groups, known as subgroups, you can build fairly complex drawings, yet easily change selected sections.

To align or distribute drawn objects

1. Select several objects that you want to align by Ctrl-clicking each object (**Figure 8.52**).

2. In the Drawing toolbar, choose Draw > Align or Distribute and then make a choice in the drop-down menu (**Figure 8.53**). The previously selected objects will be aligned or distributed based on your choice (**Figure 8.54**).

✔ Tip

- If you're not sure how a particular setting will affect the objects, take a look at the icons in the *Align or Distribute* drop-down menu.

To arrange drawn objects

1. Select the object you want to move forward or backward in the stack order (**Figure 8.55**).

2. In the Drawing toolbar, choose Draw > Order and then make a choice in the drop-down menu (**Figure 8.56**). The object will change its position in the stack order.

3. Depending on the stack order, you may need to select another object and choose Draw > Order and apply a second choice in the drop-down menu (or right-click the object and use the *Order* shortcut menu) (**Figure 8.57**).

4. Keep applying the various Draw > Order choices until the stack order is arranged how you want it (**Figure 8.58**).

✔ Tip

■ If you select multiple objects by ⌃Ctrl-clicking, you can move them forward or backward simultaneously. (Right-clicking overrides the multiple selection.)

Figure 8.55
Begin by selecting the object you want to rearrange.

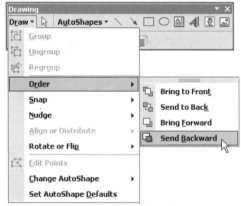

Figure 8.56 To rearrange the object, choose Draw > Order and then make a choice in the drop-down menu.

Figure 8.57 You also can right-click an object and change its order using the shortcut menu.

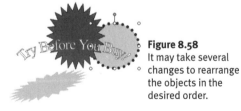

Figure 8.58
It may take several changes to rearrange the objects in the desired order.

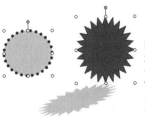

Figure 8.59
Select several
objects that you
want to group
by Ctrl-clicking
each object.

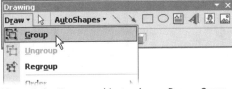

Figure 8.60 To group objects, choose Draw > Group in the Drawing toolbar.

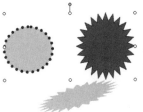

Figure 8.61
The previously
separate objects are
now grouped, as
denoted by the sin-
gle set of handles.

Figure 8.62 If you try to select an individual object in a group, its handles will be darkened to indicate that it cannot be selected.

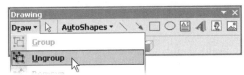

Figure 8.63 To select a single object in a group, you must first choose Draw > Ungroup to cancel the grouping.

To group drawn objects

1. Select the objects you want to group by Ctrl-clicking each object (**Figure 8.59**).

2. In the Drawing toolbar, choose Draw > Group (**Figure 8.60**). The objects will become a single group, denoted by the appearance of a single set of handles (**Figure 8.61**).

✔ Tips

- If you try to select an individual object in a group, its handles will be darkened and marked with Xs to indicate that it cannot be selected (**Figure 8.62**). To select the individual item, first choose Draw > Ungroup to cancel the grouping (**Figure 8.63**).

- In step 2, you also can right-click the selected objects and choose Grouping > Group from the shortcut menu. Similarly, you can ungroup a collection of objects by right-clicking it and choosing Grouping > Ungroup from the shortcut menu.

Using the Drawing Canvas

When adding drawings to a Web page, you can draw them directly on the page or create what FrontPage calls a drawing canvas. The canvas has several advantages over drawing individual figures directly on a Web page: you can move a canvas in a single step, instead of having to individually select all the drawings before moving them. You can easily resize the canvas and even rescale it—right along with all the drawn objects it contains. The Drawing Canvas toolbar, naturally enough, contains all the commands you need for working with the canvas (**Figure 8.64**).

To turn on the Drawing Canvas toolbar

◆ Choose View > Toolbars > Drawing Canvas or right-click an existing drawing canvas and choose Show Drawing Canvas Toolbar from the shortcut menu (**Figure 8.65**).

Enlarge canvas

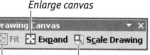

Fit canvas to drawings   *Scale canvas up or down*

Figure 8.64 The Drawing Canvas toolbar lets you resize the canvas, which can contain more complex drawings.

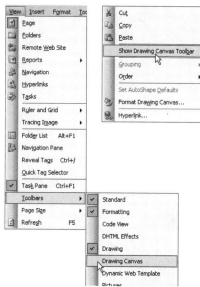

Figure 8.65 To turn on the Drawing Canvas toolbar, choose View > Toolbars > Drawing Canvas (left), or right-click an existing canvas and choose Show Drawing Canvas Toolbar from the shortcut menu (right).

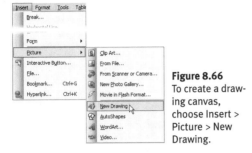

Figure 8.66
To create a drawing canvas, choose Insert > Picture > New Drawing.

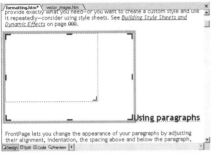

Figure 8.67 To resize a drawing canvas, click and drag the solid-black corner or side handles.

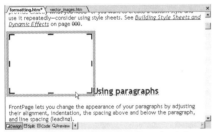

Figure 8.68 When the canvas is resized, the rest of the Web page contents will reflow to accommodate the change.

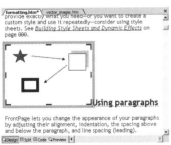

Figure 8.69 It's easy to add multiple shapes to the drawing canvas.

To create a drawing canvas

1. Click in the Web page where you want to add the drawing canvas and choose Insert > Picture > New Drawing (**Figure 8.66**).

2. When the drawing canvas appears on the page, click and drag the solid-black corner or side handles to resize it as needed (**Figure 8.67**). A dashed line will mark your progress. Release the cursor and the canvas will assume its new size (**Figure 8.68**).

3. To begin drawing, choose a shape icon in the Drawing toolbar and begin drawing inside the canvas area. If necessary, switch to other icons to add other shapes until you are done (**Figure 8.69**).

To select a drawing canvas

1. Move your cursor over the drawing until it becomes a four-headed arrow.

2. Click once and the hashed border will appear (**Figure 8.70**). At that point, you can then move, resize, or rescale the drawing canvas.

To move a drawing canvas

1. Select the drawing canvas (top, **Figure 8.71**).

2. Click and drag the cursor to where you want the drawing canvas moved (middle, **Figure 8.71**).

3. Release your cursor and the drawing canvas—along with all its contents—will move to the new destination (bottom, **Figure 8.71**).

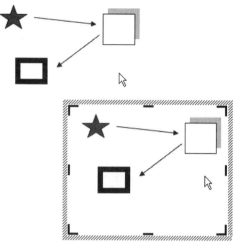

Figure 8.70 To see the sometimes hidden edges of a canvas, click your cursor on the drawing and its hashed border will appear.

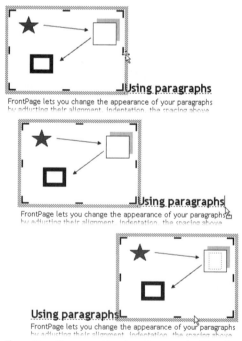

Figure 8.71 To move a drawing canvas, select it and then drag your cursor to the new location. Release the cursor and the canvas will appear in the new spot.

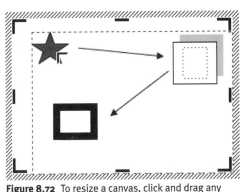

Figure 8.72 To resize a canvas, click and drag any handle.

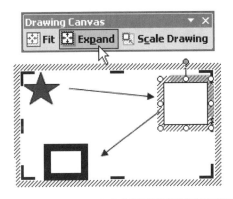

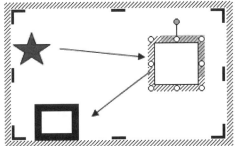

Figure 8.73 To incrementally enlarge a canvas, select it and click the *Expand* icon repeatedly until the canvas reaches the desired size.

Resizing a drawing canvas

Maybe you need space for more shapes, or now that you're done drawing you want to make the canvas a bit smaller. FrontPage offers several ways to resize the canvas while leaving the shapes within it unchanged.

To resize a drawing canvas by hand

1. Click on the hashed boundary of the drawing canvas to select it.

2. Click and drag one of the black handles on the corners or sides of the drawing canvas. Whether you enlarge or reduce the canvas, a dashed line will mark your progress (**Figure 8.72**).

3. Release the cursor and the canvas will assume its new size, without affecting the shapes within.

To expand a drawing canvas with the toolbar

1. Make sure the Drawing Canvas toolbar is visible, then select the canvas by clicking on its hashed boundary.

2. Click the *Expand* icon in the Drawing Canvas toolbar and the canvas will expand to the right and downward (**Figure 8.73**).

3. Continue clicking the *Expand* icon until the canvas reaches the desired size.

To fit a drawing canvas to its contents

1. Make sure the Drawing Canvas toolbar is visible, then select the canvas by clicking on its hashed boundary (left, **Figure 8.74**).

2. Click the Fit icon in the Drawing Canvas toolbar and the canvas will shrink to just fit around its contents (right, **Figure 8.74**).

✔ Tip

■ The Fit icon is available only when the canvas contains more than one shape. For a canvas containing a single shape, resize the canvas by clicking and dragging.

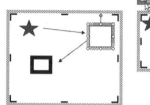
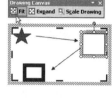

Figure 8.74 To fit a canvas to its contents, select the canvas (left), click the *Fit* icon, and the canvas will shrink to just fit around its contents (right).

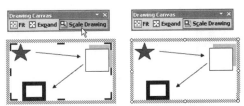

Figure 8.75 Select the canvas (left), then click the *Scale Drawing* icon in the toolbar and the previously solid-black handles will become hollow circles (right).

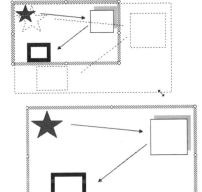

Figure 8.76 To preserve the proportions of its contents while scaling the canvas, click and drag a corner handle.

Rescaling a drawing canvas

Rescaling a canvas affects everything inside the canvas—unlike resizing a canvas, which does not change the size of its contents. When rescaling a canvas, you can choose to keep the height and width of its contents in proportion to each other or affect only one of the dimensions.

To preserve proportion while scaling a drawing canvas

1. Select the canvas by clicking on its hashed boundary, then click the *Scale Drawing* icon in the toolbar and the previously solid-black handles will become hollow circles (**Figure 8.75**).

2. Click and drag any corner handle of the canvas. You can enlarge or shrink the canvas and a dashed line will mark your progress (top, **Figure 8.76**).

3. Release your cursor and the canvas will be rescaled proportionately, along with its contents (bottom, **Figure 8.76**).

4. Once you're done scaling the canvas, click the toolbar's *Scale Drawing* icon again to turn off the scaling feature.

To change proportion while scaling a drawing canvas

1. Select the canvas by clicking on its hashed boundary, then click the *Scale Drawing* icon in the toolbar and the previously solid-black handles will become hollow circles (**Figure 8.75**).

2. Click and drag a handle on the side, top, or bottom of the canvas. Clicking a side handle will change the contents' width but not the height; clicking a top or bottom handle will change the height but not its width. You can enlarge or shrink the canvas and a dashed line will mark your progress (top, **Figure 8.77**).

3. Release your cursor and the canvas will be rescaled in only one dimension and change the proportions of its contents (bottom, **Figure 8.77**).

4. Once you're done scaling the canvas, click the toolbar's *Scale Drawing* icon again to turn off the scaling feature.

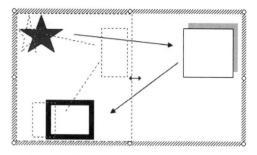

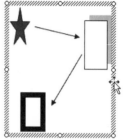

Figure 8.77 Clicking and dragging the canvas's side handle (top) will change the contents' width but not the height (bottom).

Figure 8.78 To change the drawing canvas format, right-click the canvas and choose Format Drawing Canvas from the shortcut menu.

Figure 8.79 Use the tabs in the Format Drawing Canvas dialog box to change several canvas settings simultaneously.

Figure 8.80 By default, a drawing canvas's *Positioning style* is set to *None*, which lets the page's contents flow around the canvas.

Formatting a drawing canvas

By default, the drawing canvas automatically flows the page contents around its boundary. That makes it possible to quickly drop a drawing into your Web page without having to readjust the surrounding content.

To change the drawing canvas format

1. Select the drawing canvas you want to reformat, then right-click and choose Format Drawing Canvas from the shortcut menu (**Figure 8.78**).

2. When the Format Drawing Canvas dialog box appears, use the *Colors and Lines* tab to set the canvas's background color or border (**Figure 8.79**). Use the *Size* tab to resize or rescale the canvas using pixels. Use the *Layout* tab's *Wrapping style* and *Positioning style* to control the placement of the canvas amid the page's contents (**Figure 8.80**). The *Picture* and *Text Box* tabs, used in formatting text boxes, are not available and will be dimmed. But you can use the *Site* tab to create alternate text.

3. Once you are done changing the formatting for the drawing canvas, click *OK* to close the dialog box and apply the changes to the canvas.

FORMATTING A DRAWING CANVAS

PART 3

CREATING ADVANCED PAGES

Chapter 9:   **Adding Multimedia and Web Components**   **237**

Chapter 10: **Creating and Formatting Tables**   **257**

Chapter 11: **Creating Layers and Frames**   **291**

Chapter 12: **Creating and Processing Forms**   **319**

Chapter 13: **Adding Database Connections**   **345**

Chapter 14: **Building Style Sheets and Dynamic Effects**   **363**

ADDING MULTIMEDIA AND WEB COMPONENTS

9

Used judiciously, a bit of multimedia can juice up your Web pages and grab visitor attention. As always, bear in mind that visitors won't wait around for downloads, so use FrontPage's download progress indicator to gauge how long pages with multimedia elements will take to appear on screen (see page 17).

FrontPage gives you three basic categories for turning your Web pages into a multimedia extravaganza: videos or animations; background page sounds; and Web components, which include such things as ticker-tape marquees and visitor-driven hit counters. FrontPage now includes more than 25 of these components. A few, such as Interactive buttons, you've already used. Banner ads, a component available in FrontPage 2002, can no longer be added with FrontPage 2003. However, the new version still provides a way to update existing banner ads. See *Adding Web Components* on page 244 to learn how to put them to work on your pages.

Adding Videos or Animations

Although you technically could add an hour-long training video to your Web site, there are precious few network connections fast enough to handle such a huge file. In practice, Web videos/animations are best kept small—things like logos with moving type or animated arrows. Just remember: a little motion goes a long way.

To insert a video or animation

1. Make sure you're in Page view by choosing View > Page, click the *Design* tab in the main window, and click where you want the video or animation placed within a page.

2. Choose Insert > Picture > Video (**Figure 9.1**).

3. When the Video dialog box appears, it will show all the files already in your Web site (**Figure 9.2**). To make your search easier, select *All Video Files* in the *Files of type* drop-down menu. If the video/animation you want isn't listed, use the drop-down menus, folder icons, or buttons to navigate to the desired file.

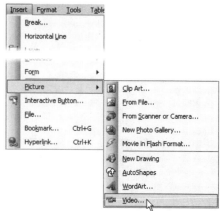

Figure 9.1 To insert a video or animation, choose Insert > Picture > Video.

Figure 9.2 When the Video dialog box appears, make your search easier by selecting *All Video Files* in the *Files of type* drop-down menu.

Figure 9.3 Depending on your computer's settings, a placeholder image may appear in the Web page instead of the usual first frame of the video or animation.

Figure 9.4 If the video/animation didn't come from your current Web site, the Save Embedded Files dialog box will give you a chance to save it.

Figure 9.5 The video or animation will appear as soon as your Web browser launches.

4. Once you find the file, click *Open* to insert the video/animation into the Web page. Depending on your computer's settings, a placeholder image may appear in the Web page instead of the usual first frame of the video or animation (**Figure 9.3**). (For more information, see *Why Can't I See the Video* on page 242.)

5. Save the page with its new video/animation (Ctrl S). If the file didn't come from your current Web site, the Save Embedded Files dialog box will appear (**Figure 9.4**).

6. Click *Rename* if you want to change the file name and *Change Folder* if you want to save the file in another location. When you're done, click *OK* and the video/animation will be saved.

7. Once the video/animation is inserted and saved, you can set how often it repeats and other aspects. See *To set loops for videos/animations* on page 241. To see the video/animation in action, click the *Preview* tab in FrontPage's main window. If nothing happens in Preview, you can still see the video by choosing File > Preview in Browser and selecting your browser from the drop-down menu. The video/animation will appear as soon as the browser launches (**Figure 9.5**).

ADDING VIDEOS OR ANIMATIONS

Chapter 9

✔ Tips

- To use a clip art video/animation in step 3, click *Open* and choose *Open From Clip Organizer* in the shortcut menu (top, **Figure 9.6**). When the Select Movie dialog box appears, search for the movie clip you need by typing terms in the *Search text* text window and clicking *Go* or by scrolling through the thumbnails window (bottom, **Figure 9.6**). For more information, see *Clip Art options* on page 174.

- FrontPage 2003 lets you insert movies created with Macromedia Flash directly into your Web pages—as long as you have installed the Flash Player on your computer. Remember, as well, that visitors to your Web site must also have the Flash Player installed to see Flash movies on your site. The process for adding Flash movies to a Web page is identical to inserting a video/animation, as described above, except in step 2 choose Insert > Picture > Movie in Flash Format.

Figure 9.6 Use the Clip Organizer to search for royalty-free movie clips.

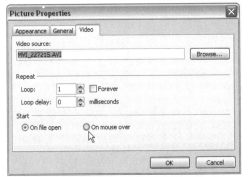

Figure 9.7
To set looping for a video or animation, right-click it and choose *Picture Properties*.

Figure 9.8 The *Video* tab in the Picture Properties dialog box lets you set how the video/animation repeats.

To set loops for videos/animations

1. Switch to Page view, right-click the video/animation and choose *Picture Properties* from the shortcut menu ([Alt][Enter]) (**Figure 9.7**).

2. When the Picture Properties dialog box appears, click the *Video* tab (**Figure 9.8**).

3. If you want to substitute another video/animation for the current one, click *Browse* to find it.

4. Use the arrows and text windows in the *Repeat* section to set how many times the video/animation will *Loop* (or check the *Forever* box) and how long the *Loop delay* should be between the loop finishing and starting again.

5. By default, the video/animation is set to start as soon as the file opens, but you can give more control to the user by selecting *On mouse over* in the *Start* section.

6. Once you've made your choices, click *OK* and the changes will be applied to the video/animation.

SETTING LOOPS FOR VIDEOS/ANIMATIONS

Why Can't I See the Video?

Multimedia programs such as RealOne Player, QuickTime Player, and Windows Media Player constantly battle to be your machine's default video player. Mistakenly click a *Yes* in one of the pop-up dialog boxes that constantly appear and, presto, one program supplants another. Unfortunately, that sometimes means that when you click FrontPage's *Preview* tab to see how a video looks in the Web page, another program, like RealOne Player, launches instead of the video running within your Web browser.

If this happens, or if in step 4 of *To insert a video or animation* FrontPage displays a place-holder image instead of the first frame of your video or animation, check what program has been assigned to open .avi files. Choose Start > Set Program Access and Defaults (Windows XP) or Start > Control Panel > Folder Options (pre-Windows XP). When the Folder Options dialog box appears, click the *File Types* tab, then scroll down the *Registered file types* window until you can select *AVI* (top, **Figure 9.9**). Look in the *Details for 'AVI' extension* pane to see what program opens those files. If it's something other than your preferred Web browser, click the *Change* button. When the Open With dialog box appears, scroll through the *Programs* window until you find your browser, select it, and click *OK* (bottom, **Figure 9.9**). Your browser will now open any .avi files. If you ever need to go back to the original .avi program default, navigate to the Folder Options dialog box and click *Restore* (**Figure 9.10**).

And, remember, even if the video's first frame doesn't appear in FrontPage's main window, you can still run the video by choosing File > Preview in Browser and selecting your browser from the drop-down menu.

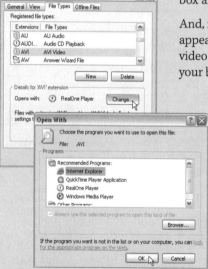

Figure 9.9 When the Folder Options dialog box appears, click the *File Types* tab and scroll down the *Registered file types* window to select *AVI*, then click *Change* (top). When the Open With dialog box appears, scroll through the *Programs* window until you find your browser (bottom).

Figure 9.10 If you ever need to go back to the original .avi program default, click *Restore* in the Folder Options dialog box.

Figure 9.11 To add a page background sound, right-click anywhere in the page and choose *Page Properties*.

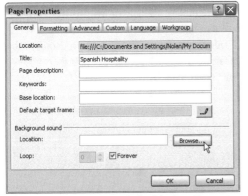

Figure 9.12 Click the *General* tab of the Page Properties dialog box to reach the *Background sound* section. Click *Browse* to find a sound file.

Adding Sounds

Short sound loops can be effective mood setters on the appropriate pages—and maddening on strictly business pages. Pick and choose your sound pages carefully.

To add a page background sound

1. Switch to Page view, right-click anywhere in the page and choose *Page Properties* from the shortcut menu (**Figure 9.11**).

2. When the Page Properties dialog box opens, click the *General* tab (**Figure 9.12**).

3. Within the *Background sound* section, click *Browse* to locate a sound file. By default, *Forever* is checked. If you want the sound to play a short time, uncheck the box and use the text window or arrows to set the number of loops.

4. Click *OK* and the sound will become part of your Web page. Click the *Preview* tab at the bottom of FrontPage's main window to hear the sound or test it with your Web browser.

✔ Tips

■ Since background sounds are linked to specific pages, you can give different pages different sounds.

■ To remove a sound from a page, right-click in the page, choose *Page Properties* from the shortcut menu, and delete the file from the *Location* window.

Adding Web Components

FrontPage includes more than two dozen other multimedia components—what it calls Web components—that can make your pages more interactive. In general, Web components fall into two categories: those without special requirements that will run on any Web server and work on any Web browser, and those that require either special software on the Web server or that only work with Microsoft Internet Explorer. Several of the components without special requirements—

link bars, interactive buttons, and photo galleries—were explained in earlier chapters. FrontPage 2003 calls some of these nothing-special-needed components *Author-time components* because they are so useful in helping you, the Web page's author, build your site. Other components, known as *Browse-time components*, however, require that special FrontPage or Microsoft extensions be installed on the hosting Web server. While these components do cool things, they often do not work for people using non-Microsoft Web browsers.

Table 9.1

Requirements for Web components by type	
RUNS ON ALL OR AUTHOR-TIME	**BROWSE-TIME OR SHARE SERVICES**
No special requirements	FrontPage extensions or SharePoint Services
Dynamic Effects	Web Search
Marquee text	
Interactive buttons	
Spreadsheets and Charts	Hit Counter
Photo Gallery	Top 10 List
	Most-visited pages
	Referring URLs, domains
	Most-common browsers
Included Content	
Page & picture swaps	
Link Bars	
Table of Contents	
Expedia Components	
MSN Components	
MSNBC Components	
Advanced Controls	

Figure 9.13 To turn on or off Web components, choose Tools > Page Options.

Figure 9.14 When the Page Options dialog box appears, click the *Authoring* tab.

Figure 9.15 Check or uncheck the *SharePoint Services*, *Browse-time Web Components*, and *Author-time Web Components* boxes.

Turning on or off Web components

FrontPage lets you turn Web components on or off, depending on whether you are using special FrontPage extensions or other Microsoft software on your Web server. In deciding which components to use, always consider the software your target audience most likely will be using. For more information on setting site-wide options, see *Installing and Configuring FrontPage* on page 437.

To turn on/off Web components

1. Open your Web site and choose Tools > Page Options (**Figure 9.13**).

2. When the Page Options dialog box appears, click the *Authoring* tab (**Figure 9.14**).

3. Depending on your decisions about who will be using your site, within the first section check or uncheck the *SharePoint Services*, *Browse-time Web Components*, and *Author-time Web Components* boxes (**Figure 9.15**). (There's no need to separately turn on or off the *Navigation* or *Shared Borders* boxes.) Once you've made your choices, click *OK* and the changes will be applied to your site.

See page 401 Reports

·View / Reports | ······

Adding a marquee of scrolling text

The marquee Web component lets you add a ticker-tape-style line of scrolling text on any page. The marquee feature does not require special Web server or browser software, so all your visitors will be able to see the scrolling text.

To add a marquee

1. Switch to Page view and click in the page where you want the marquee to appear.

2. Choose Insert > Web Component.

3. When the Insert Web Component dialog box appears, click *Dynamic Effects* in the left-hand *Component type* list, choose *Marquee* in the right-hand list, and then click *Finish* (**Figure 9.16**).

4. When the Marquee Properties dialog box appears, enter the text you want displayed in the marquee; set its direction, speed, behavior, size; how often it should repeat; and the background color (**Figure 9.17**). For details, see *Marquee options* on the next page.

5. Once you've made your choices, click *OK*, then save the page (Ctrl S). The marquee will be inserted into the Web page.

6. To see how the marquee looks and decide if it needs adjustment, click FrontPage's *Preview* tab (**Figure 9.18**). To edit the marquee, see *To change a marquee* on page 248.

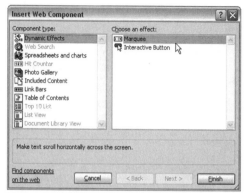

Figure 9.16 To add a marquee, choose *Dynamic Effects* in the left-hand *Component type* list and *Marquee* in the right-hand list.

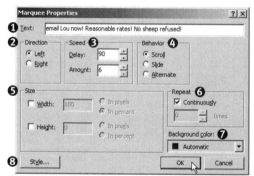

Figure 9.17 Use the Marquee Properties dialog box to enter the display text and control its motion and appearance.

Figure 9.18 Click the *Preview* tab to see if the marquee needs adjusting.

Marquee options

To reach the Marquee Properties dialog box (**Figure 9.17**), see *To add a marquee* or right-click an existing marquee and choose *Marquee Properties* from the shortcut menu.

❶ **Text:** Type in the message you want the marquee to display.

❷ **Direction:** By default, *Left* will be selected since Western languages are read left to right. Choose *Right* for languages that read right to left.

❸ **Speed:** The marquee's speed is controlled by two factors. *Delay* sets how *often* (in milliseconds) the marquee moves. *Amount* controls the *distance* (in pixels) the marquee moves each time. Experiment with both settings to find the best speed.

❹ **Behavior:** The difference between *Scroll* and *Slide* is subtle and only appears at the end of your text message (**Figure 9.19**). With *Scroll*, the message keeps moving until the marquee is *blank*, then the message repeats. With *Slide*, the marquee is never blank. *Alternate* switches from *Scroll* to *Slide* after each sequence.

❺ **Size:** Set the *Width* and *Height* of the marquee in pixels or as a percent of the browser window.

❻ **Repeat:** Set the marquee to run *Continuously* or use the text window or arrows to set a limited number of repetitions.

❼ **Background color:** Use the drop-down menu to choose a marquee color. Since the text is always black, choose a lighter color for good contrast.

❽ **Style:** This button can only be used if you've created style sheets for your Web site. See *Building Style Sheets and Dynamic Effects* on page 363.

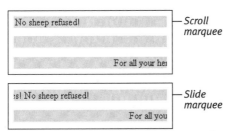

— *Scroll marquee*

— *Slide marquee*

Figure 9.19 A subtle difference: marquee *scroll* (top) leaves the marquee blank before the text begins again; marquee *slide* (bottom) does not.

To change a marquee

1. Right-click the marquee and choose *Marquee Properties* from the shortcut menu (Alt Enter) (**Figure 9.20**).

2. When the Marquee Properties dialog box appears (**Figure 9.17**), make your changes to the marquee, and click *OK*.

3. Save the page (Ctrl S) and the changes will be applied to the marquee.

4. To see the changes, click the *Preview* tab.

✔ Tip

■ If you just need to resize the marquee, don't bother with the Marquee Properties dialog box. Instead, click on the marquee while in Page view and drag any of its handles to resize the marquee's text area (**Figure 9.21**).

To delete a marquee

◆ Make sure you're in Page view, right-click the marquee, and choose *Cut* from the shortcut menu. The marquee will be deleted.

Figure 9.20 To change a marquee, right-click it and choose *Marquee Properties*.

For all your herding needs

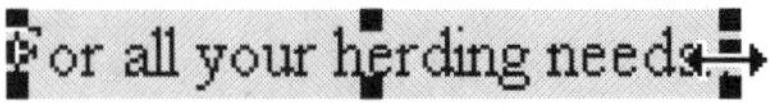

Figure 9.21 To resize a marquee, click and drag any of its handles.

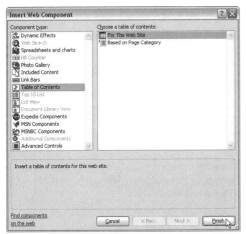

Figure 9.22 To add a table of contents, choose *Table of Contents* in the left-hand *Component type* list and *For This Web Site* in the right-hand list.

Figure 9.23 If you want another page to be the starting point for a table of contents, click *Browse* and navigate to that page.

Adding a Web site table of contents

FrontPage includes a component that makes it relatively easy to build a dynamically updated table of contents for your Web site. This acts like a map of your Web site, offering a helpful way for visitors to find what they need. Using the table of contents feature does not require special Web server or browser software, so you can use it knowing that all your visitors will be able to see the feature.

To add a table of contents

1. Create a new Web page on which to display the table of contents, then choose Insert > Web Component.

2. When the Insert Web Component dialog box appears, click *Table of Contents* in the left-hand *Component type* list, choose *For This Web Site* in the right-hand list, and then click *Finish* (**Figure 9.22**).

3. When the Table of Contents Properties dialog box appears, it will list the index page for the site by default as the *Page URL for starting point of table* (**Figure 9.23**). If you want another page to be the starting point for the table, click *Browse* and navigate to that page.

(continued)

4. Adjust the *Heading font size* if desired, then check which *Options* you want used. By default, *Show each page only once* and *Show pages with no incoming hyperlinks* are checked. If you want the table of contents automatically updated as you change the site, also check *Recompute table of contents when any other page is edited.*

5. Click *OK* and a placeholder table of contents will appear on your Web page (**Figure 9.24**). Choose File > Preview in Browser and the actual table of contents will appear (**Figure 9.25**).

✔ Tips

■ You also can build a table of contents using page categories by choosing *Based on Page Category* from the right-hand list in step 2. For more information on using categories, see *Organizing Files* on page 298.

■ To change the particular properties of a table of contents, right-click the table and choose *Table of Contents Properties* from the shortcut menu (**Figure 9.26**). Make your changes when the Table of Contents Properties dialog box appears.

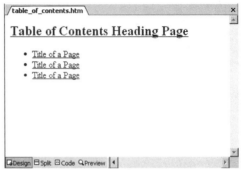

Figure 9.24 A placeholder table of contents appears on the Web page.

Figure 9.25 To see the actual table of contents, choose File > Preview in Browser.

Figure 9.26 To change a table of contents, right-click the table and choose *Table of Contents Properties* from the shortcut menu.

Figure 9.27 To change a banner ad, right-click it and choose *Banner Ad Manager Properties*.

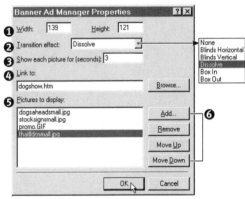

Figure 9.28 Use the Banner Ad Manager Properties dialog box to set the ad's size, transition from one image to another, and images used.

Changing banner ads

Banner ads, a component available in FrontPage 2002 that let you assign a rotating selection of images to a page area, can no longer be added with FrontPage 2003. However, the new version still provides a way to update existing banner ads created with FrontPage 2002. The replacement function, the MSWC.AdRotator object, is only available if you are using the Microsoft IIS Web server, a high-end server not covered here.

To change a banner ad

1. Right-click the banner and choose *Banner Ad Manager Properties* from the shortcut menu (**Figure 9.27**).

2. When the Banner Ad Manager Properties dialog box appears (**Figure 9.28**), set the dimensions for the banner images ❶.

3. Using the drop-down menu, select a *Transition effect* for moving from one image to another ❷.

4. Decide how long you want to *Show each picture for* and enter the number of seconds in the text window ❸.

5. Use the *Browse* button to select which Web page users will be linked to if they click the banner ad ❹.

6. Use the *Add* button ❻ to locate each of the images you want displayed by the banner ad. Use the *Move Up* and *Move Down* buttons to rearrange the display order of the images ❺.

(continued)

7. Once you've made your choices, click *OK*, then save the page (⟨Ctrl⟩⟨S⟩). The banner ad will change based on your selections.

8. FrontPage can only show the banner ad's first image, so launch your Web browser to see the images actually change.

9. When you're satisfied with the changes, click *OK*, and save the page (⟨Ctrl⟩⟨S⟩).

✔ Tips

■ By default, the Banner Ad Manager is set to show each image for five seconds but that's often a tad slow—three seconds sets a better pace. Experiment to find what's best for your particular images.

■ You can freely mix JPEGs and GIFs in your banner ad's rotation of images.

■ You cannot link each image to a separate Web page. Every image in a banner ad must link to the same page.

To delete a banner ad

◆ Right-click the banner, and choose *Cut* from the shortcut menu. The banner will be deleted.

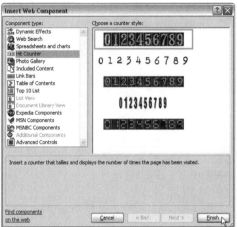

Figure 9.29 To add a page hit counter, choose *Hit Counter* in the left-hand *Component type* list and choose a counter style in the right-hand list.

Figure 9.30 Use the Hit Counter Properties dialog box to pick a *Counter Style* or *Custom Picture*.

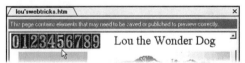

Figure 9.31 After you add a hit counter, a placeholder will appear on the page. The actual counter won't show until you publish the site.

Adding page hit counters

In early days of the Web, page hit counters were common, as if Web site builders couldn't quite believe so many folks visited their site. Frankly, they seem a bit tired these days. Remember that page hit counters require that Browse-time Web components be turned on. For more information, see *To turn on/off Web components* on page 245.

To add a page hit counter

1. Switch to Page view, and click in the page where you want the counter to appear.

2. Choose Insert > Web Component.

3. When the Insert Web Component dialog box appears, click *Hit Counter* in the left-hand *Component type* list, choose a counter style in the right-hand list, and then click *Finish* (**Figure 9.29**).

4. When the Hit Counter Properties dialog box appears (**Figure 9.30**), check *Reset counter to* and enter a number in the text window if you want the counter to start with a particular number.

5. Check *Fixed number of digits* if you want the counter to roll back to zero when it reaches 10, 100, 1,000, or whatever.

6. Once you've made your choices, click *OK*. The hit counter image will appear on your page, though the actual count won't start until you publish the site (**Figure 9.31**).

✔ Tip

■ The hit counter only works if FrontPage's extensions have been installed on your Web server. Check with the server administrator to be sure. Most Internet Service Providers, such as EarthLink, will install the extensions if asked.

To change a hit counter

1. Right-click the counter and choose *FrontPage Component Properties* from the shortcut menu (**Figure 9.32**).

2. When the Hit Counter Properties dialog box appears, change the *Counter Style*, reset the counter, or limit the number of digits (**Figure 9.30**).

3. When you're satisfied with the changes, click *OK*, and save the page ([Ctrl][S]).

To delete a hit counter

◆ Make sure you're in Page view, right-click the counter, and choose *Cut* from the shortcut menu. The counter will be deleted.

Figure 9.32 To change a hit counter, right-click it and choose *FrontPage Component Properties*.

Figure 9.33 To add a Top Ten list, choose *Top 10 List* in the left-hand *Component type* list and one of the seven choices in the right-hand list.

Figure 9.34 Use the Top 10 List Properties dialog box to choose the *List settings* and *List Style*.

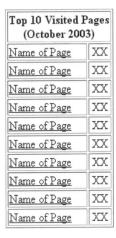

Figure 9.35 Until you actually publish the Web site, a placeholder table appears on the Web page.

Adding a Top Ten list

The Top Ten list feature lets you share information about your Web site with your visitors. You can, for example, create a continuously updated list of the ten most visited pages on your site. In contrast, FrontPage's reporting features (see page 393) are available only to members of your publishing team. Top Ten lists require that Browse-time Web components be turned on. For more information, see *To turn on/off Web components* on page 245.

To create a Top Ten list

1. Create a new Web page on which to display the list, then choose Insert > Web Component.

2. When the Insert Web Component dialog box appears, click *Top 10 List* in the left-hand *Component type* list, choose one of the seven choices in the right-hand list, and then click *Finish* (**Figure 9.33**).

3. When the Top 10 List Properties dialog box appears, type in the *Title Text* (**Figure 9.34**). Check *Include date usage processing was last run* if you want users to see just how current the list is, then choose a *List Style*.

4. Click *OK* and a placeholder list will appear on your Web page (**Figure 9.35**). To see the actual Top Ten list, you will have to publish your Web site (see page 417).

CREATING AND FORMATTING TABLES 10

Tables make it easy to present related text or images in a quick-to-scan form. With their rows and columns composed of individual cells, tables also lend themselves to clean-looking border and color treatments. A major plus of using tables is their consistent appearance no matter which browser your Web site visitors use. That's why so many commercial Web sites build their page layouts using tables. FrontPage 2003 makes that approach much easier with its new layout tables and cells. In fact, FrontPage 2003 includes predefined tables for building your own table-based Web pages. For more information, see *Using Tables in Page Layouts* on page 280. Before settling on how to lay out your pages, you may also want to take a look at *Creating Layers and Frames* on page 291, since using layers is often more flexible than using layout tables. By the way, you'll find it much quicker building tables using the Tables toolbar (**Figure 10.1**). Activate it by choosing View > Toolbars > Tables.

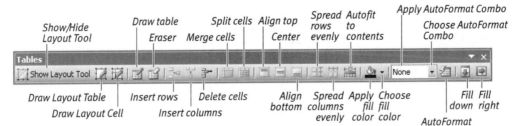

Figure 10.1 Using the Tables toolbar lets you bypass many of FrontPage's menu commands for building tables.

Creating Tables

FrontPage offers two main ways to create tables: one based on freehand drawing and one driven by dialog boxes. With the free-hand approach, you use a pencil-shaped cursor to draw directly in your Web page. It's straightforward and will quickly become your favorite way to handle tables. If you ever need absolute precision, however, the dialog box approach lets you create a table of pre-determined dimensions.

To draw a table

1. Make sure you're in Page view by choosing View > Page, click the *Design* tab in the main window, and click where you want a table placed in the page.

2. Choose Table > Draw Table or, if the Tables toolbar is active, click the Draw Table button in the Tables toolbar (**Figure 10.2**).

3. A pencil icon will appear on the page. Click and drag the pencil until the dashed box is roughly the size of the table you want, release the mouse, and a simple table will appear on the page (**Figure 10.3**).

4. To further divide the table into columns and rows, click and drag the pencil to draw in their boundaries (**Figure 10.4**).

5. To resize any part of the table, move your cursor over the cell border until the cursor becomes a two-headed arrow. Then click and drag the border until you're satisfied, release the cursor, and the table is resized (**Figure 10.5**). Double-click to switch the pencil back to an I-beam cursor.

✔ Tip

■ Unfortunately, FrontPage won't let you proportionately resize the table by grabbing one of its corners.

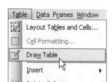

Figure 10.2 To draw a table directly, choose Table > Draw Table from the menu (left) or click the Draw Table button in the Tables toolbar (right).

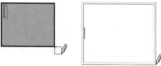

Figure 10.3 Draw a table by dragging the pencil icon across the page (left), then release the cursor (right).

Figure 10.4 To further divide a table into columns and rows, click, drag, and release the pencil cursor.

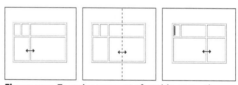

Figure 10.5 To resize any part of a table, move the cursor until it becomes a two-headed arrow. Then click, drag, and release the cursor.

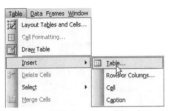

Figure 10.6 To insert a table, choose Table > Insert > Table from the menu.

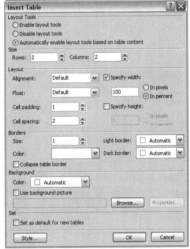

Figure 10.7 Use the Insert Table dialog box to set the table's size and layout.

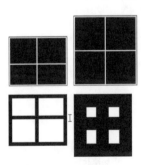

Figure 10.8 Black areas show changes in cell *padding*, which is the area *inside* the cells (top), versus changes in cell *spacing*, which is the area *between* cells (bottom).

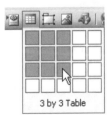

Figure 10.9 For quick tables, click the Insert Table button in the Standard toolbar and drag your cursor to choose how many rows and columns you want.

To insert a table

1. Make sure you're in Page view by choosing View > Page, click the *Design* tab in the main window, and click where you want a table placed in the page.

2. Choose Table > Insert > Table (**Figure 10.6**).

3. When the Insert Table dialog box appears (**Figure 10.7**), use the *Size* section to set the number of *Rows* and *Columns*.

4. Use the dialog box's *Layout* section to set the table's *Alignment* (left, center, or right), the *Border size* (the area around the outside of the entire table), and the *Cell padding* and *Cell spacing* (**Figure 10.8**).

5. Check *Specify width* to set the width of the entire table, and use the option buttons to choose whether the width should be absolute (*In pixels*) or relative to the width of the visitor's Web page (*In percent*).

6. Once you're done, click *OK* and the table will be inserted into your Web page.

✔ Tips

- Whatever changes you make in the Insert Table dialog box become the *default* settings for the next time you insert a table. That's great for making the same customized table, but not if you want a plain table. To avoid constant messing with the defaults, insert a plain table. Then customize it as explained in *To format tables* on page 274.

- For quick tables using the default settings, click the Insert Table button in the Standard toolbar and drag your cursor into the pop-up table to choose how many rows and columns you want (**Figure 10.9**). Release the cursor and a table of that size will be inserted into the page.

- If you want a borderless table, set *Border size* to 0 in the Insert Table dialog box.

INSERTING TABLES

To add table text

1. If your cursor doesn't have the familiar I-beam shape, first click outside the table. Then click inside any table cell (**Figure 10.10**).

2. Start typing and the cell will grow to accommodate your text (**Figure 10.11**).

To add table images

1. If your cursor doesn't have the familiar I-beam shape, first click outside the table. Then click inside any table cell (**Figure 10.10**).

2. Click the Insert Picture From File button in either the Standard or Pictures toolbar (**Figure 10.12**).

3. When the Picture dialog box appears, navigate to the image you want inserted (**Figure 10.13**). For details, see *Adding Images* on page 172.

4. Click *Insert* and the image will be inserted into the table cell, which will expand to accommodate its size (**Figure 10.14**).

✔ Tip

- FrontPage includes what it calls AutoFit to automatically fit any material inserted into a cell. First, make sure the Tables toolbar is active, then after you've inserted an item, click the AutoFit to Contents button (**Figure 10.15**).

Figure 10.10 To add table text, just click inside a table cell.

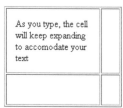

Figure 10.11 As you type, the cell grows to accommodate your text.

Figure 10.12 To add images to a table, click the Insert Picture From File button.

Figure 10.13 Use the Picture dialog box to navigate to the image you want inserted in the table.

Figure 10.14 When a picture is inserted, the table cell expands to hold it.

Figure 10.15 If material inserted into a cell doesn't fit, click the AutoFit to Contents button in the Tables toolbar.

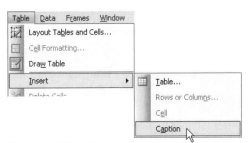

Figure 10.16 To add a caption, click inside the table and choose Table > Insert > Caption from the menu.

Figure 10.17 By default, captions are centered at the top of tables.

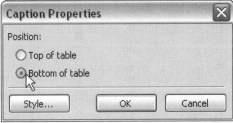

Figure 10.18 Use the Caption Properties dialog box to reposition captions beneath tables.

To add table captions

1. Click anywhere inside the table and choose Table > Insert > Caption (**Figure 10.16**).

2. When the cursor appears, it will be centered at the top of the table. Type in your caption (**Figure 10.17**).

3. Once you've entered the caption, you can change the font or size just like any other FrontPage text.

✔ Tip

- You can move the caption beneath the table by right-clicking it and choosing *Caption Properties* from the shortcut menu. When the Caption Properties dialog box appears, choose *Bottom of table* and click *OK* (**Figure 10.18**). The caption will move to the bottom.

Adding Excel spreadsheets

FrontPage offers several ways to add Excel spreadsheets to your Web pages. The first simply creates a table based on the Excel data *at the time you import it*. In other words, it's static data—not a "live" spreadsheet that's dynamically updated.

The second method actually lets you use Excel inside Web pages for entering dynamic numbers and formulas. There's a catch of course: The page's visitors must have Microsoft Office 2000 or Office XP installed on their computers, along with Microsoft's Office Web Components. Obviously, that's not much help if you're a solo worker or don't have a network administrator to handle the component installation. But if you're working in a networked office across a corporate intranet, those requirements are easily met. And the payoff is being able to share—and dynamically update—Excel spreadsheets over the Web.

To add static Excel data

1. Make sure you're in Page view, then click where you want the Excel data inserted into the Web page.

2. Choose Insert > File (**Figure 10.19**).

3. When the Select File dialog box appears, use the *Files of type* drop-down menu to select *Microsoft Excel Worksheet* (*.xls,*.xlw)* (**Figure 10.20**).

4. Navigate to the spreadsheet you need, click *Open*, and the data will be inserted into the Web page as a borderless table (denoted by the dashed outlines) (**Figure 10.21**).

✔ Tip

- You can easily reformat the borderless Excel-based table into something more "Webby" (**Figure 10.22**). For details, see *To format tables* on page 274.

Figure 10.19 To add static Excel data to a table, choose Insert > File.

Figure 10.20 To find Excel files, use the Select File dialog box's drop-down menu to select *Microsoft Excel Worksheet*.

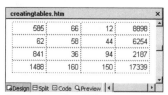

Figure 10.21 Excel files inserted into FrontPage initially appear as borderless tables, denoted by the dashed outlines.

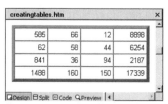

Figure 10.22 It's easy to reformat an Excel-based table into a more traditional Web-styled table.

ADDING TABLE CONTENT

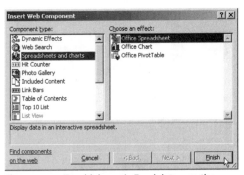

Figure 10.23 To add dynamic Excel data, use the Insert Web Component dialog box.

Figure 10.24 A blank Excel spreadsheet inserted into the Web page can be filled in with Excel-based formulas.

Figure 10.25 To import an *existing* Excel spreadsheet into a Web page, click the blank spreadsheet's *Commands and Options* button.

Figure 10.26 Use the *Import* tab in the Commands and Options dialog box to bring existing Excel data into your FrontPage table.

To add dynamic Excel data

1. Make sure you're in Page view, click where you want the Excel spreadsheet inserted into the Web page, and choose Insert > Web Component.

2. When the Insert Web Component dialog box appears, click *Spreadsheets and charts* in the left-hand *Component type* list, *Office Spreadsheet* in the right-hand list, and then click *Finish* (**Figure 10.23**). A blank Excel spreadsheet will appear inside the Web page, which can then be filled in with numbers and formulas (**Figure 10.24**).

✔ Tip

■ To import an *existing* Excel spreadsheet into the Web page you just created, click the blank spreadsheet's *Commands and Options* button (**Figure 10.25**). When the Commands and Options dialog box appears, click the *Import* tab (**Figure 10.26**). Leave the *Data type* set to *XML*, enter the spreadsheet's *URL* (or click the folder icon to browse to the file), check *Refresh data from URL at run time*, and click *Import Now*. The latest version of the data will be dumped into your blank spreadsheet.

Selecting Table Elements

Unlike many FrontPage procedures, selecting cells, rows, and columns within tables isn't always a click-and-drag affair.

To select a cell

◆ Press (Alt) and click inside any cell. The cell will be selected, denoted by its colors reversing (**Figure 10.27**).

or

◆ Click anywhere in a cell and choose Table > Select > Cell (**Figure 10.28**). The cell will be selected, denoted by its colors reversing (**Figure 10.27**).

To select multiple cells

◆ To select *adjacent* cells, click and hold your cursor in a cell, then drag the cursor to select additional cells (**Figure 10.29**).

or

◆ To select *non-adjacent* cells, press (Alt) and click inside any cell, then press (Alt)(Shift) and click another cell. Repeat until you've selected all the cells you need (**Figure 10.30**).

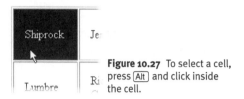

Figure 10.27 To select a cell, press (Alt) and click inside the cell.

Figure 10.28 To select any element of a table, choose Table > Select and make a choice from the submenu.

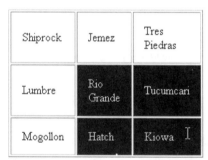

Figure 10.29 To select *adjacent* cells, click the cursor in a cell, then drag the cursor to select additional cells.

Figure 10.30 To select *non-adjacent* cells, press (Alt) and click inside any cell, then press (Alt)(Shift) as you select other cells.

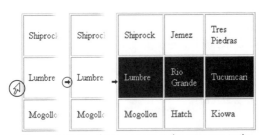

Figure 10.31 To select a row, move the cursor up to the edge of a row (left). When it becomes a black arrow (middle), click once and the row will be selected (right).

To select a row

◆ Click anywhere in a row and choose Table > Select > Row (**Figure 10.28**). The row will be selected.

or

◆ Click and hold your cursor anywhere in a row, then drag the cursor to select the rest of the cells in the row.

or

◆ Move the cursor slowly up to the left edge of a row until it becomes an arrow, then click once. The row will be selected (**Figure 10.31**).

To select a column

◆ Click anywhere in a column and choose Table > Select > Column (**Figure 10.28**). The column will be selected.

or

◆ Click and hold your cursor anywhere in a column, then drag the cursor to select the rest of the cells in the column.

or

◆ Move the cursor slowly up to the top edge of a column until it becomes an arrow, then click once. The column will be selected.

To select an entire table

◆ Click anywhere in a table and choose Table > Select > Table (**Figure 10.28**). The entire table will be selected.

or

◆ Click your cursor at the table's upper-left or lower-right corner and, while keeping the mouse pressed, drag the cursor to select the entire table.

SELECTING TABLE ELEMENTS

Changing Table Structure

With FrontPage you can go back and expand a table at any time, whether it's by adding a single cell, a row or column, or even inserting another table into the table.

To add cells

1. Click in the cell to the right of where you want to add a cell (**Figure 10.32**).
2. Choose Table > Insert > Cell (**Figure 10.33**).
3. A single cell will be inserted into the table just left of the cell selected in step 1 (**Figure 10.34**).

✔ Tip

- Adding or deleting single cells in a table can produce a strangely shaped table. So what's the point? Well, if you're using tables to design Web *pages*, this ability might give you just the shape or design you need. The moral: Experiment!

Shiprock	Jemez	Tres Piedras
Lumbre	Rio Grande	Tucumcari
Mogollon	Hatch	Kiowa

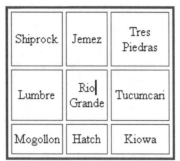

Figure 10.32 Click in the cell to the *right* of where you want to add a cell.

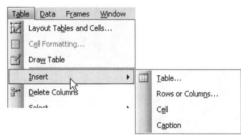

Figure 10.33 To add any element of a table, choose Table > Insert and make a choice from the submenu.

Shiprock	Jemez	Tres Piedras	
Lumbre		Rio Grande	Tucumcari
Mogollon	Hatch	Kiowa	

Figure 10.34 A single cell is inserted into the table left of the cell selected in Figure 10.32.

Figure 10.35
Select the row next to where you want to insert a new row.

Insert Rows

Figure 10.36 If the Tables toolbar is active, you also can add rows by clicking the Insert Rows button.

Figure 10.37
Use the Insert Rows or Columns dialog box to set how many rows you want added.

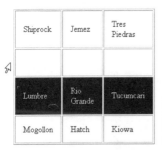

Figure 10.38
A new row inserted into the table will be blank.

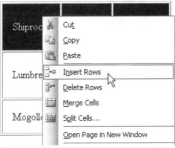

Figure 10.39 To quickly add rows, right-click and choose *Insert Rows* from the shortcut menu.

To add rows

1. Select a row next to where you want to insert a new row (**Figure 10.35**).

2. Choose Table > Insert, then choose Rows or Columns from the submenu (**Figure 10.33**). Or, if the Tables toolbar is active, click the Insert Rows button (**Figure 10.36**).

3. When the Insert Rows or Columns dialog box appears, *Rows* will already be selected (**Figure 10.37**). Use the text window or arrows to choose the *Number of rows* you want to add and decide whether to add the rows above or below the row selected in step 1.

4. Click *OK* and the row(s) will be inserted into the table (**Figure 10.38**).

✔ Tip

- You also can select a row, right-click, and choose *Insert Rows* from the shortcut menu (**Figure 10.39**). When the Insert Rows or Columns dialog box appears, follow steps 3 and 4.

To add columns

1. Select a column next to where you want to insert a new column (**Figure 10.40**).

2. Choose Table > Insert, then choose Rows or Columns from the submenu (**Figure 10.33**). Or, if the Tables toolbar is active, click the Insert Columns button (**Figure 10.41**).

3. When the Insert Rows or Columns dialog box appears, *Columns* will already be selected (**Figure 10.42**). Use the text window or arrows to choose the *Number of columns* you want to add and decide whether to add the columns to the left or right of the column selected in step 1.

4. Click *OK* and the column(s) will be inserted into the table (**Figure 10.43**).

✔ Tip

- You also can select a column, right-click, and choose *Insert Columns* from the shortcut menu (**Figure 10.44**). When the Insert Rows or Columns dialog box appears, follow steps 3 and 4.

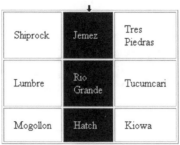

Figure 10.40 Select the column next to where you want to insert a new column.

Figure 10.41 If the Tables toolbar is active, you also can add columns by clicking the Insert Columns button.

Figure 10.42 Use the Insert Rows or Columns dialog box to set how many columns you want added.

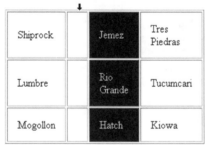

Figure 10.43 A new column inserted into the table will be blank.

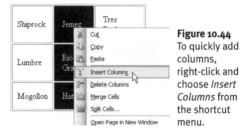

Figure 10.44 To quickly add columns, right-click and choose *Insert Columns* from the shortcut menu.

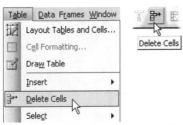

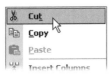

Figure 10.45 To delete any part of a table, select it and choose Table > Delete Cells from the menu (left) or click the Delete Cells button (right).

Figure 10.46 To quickly remove any table element, select it, right-click and choose *Cut*.

To delete any part of a table

1. Select the part or parts of the table you want to delete, whether it's a cell, a single row, or several rows or columns.

2. Choose Table > Delete Cells, or if the Tables toolbar is active, click the Delete Cells button (**Figure 10.45**). All the selected cells will be deleted.

✔ Tip

■ For even faster deletion, select any part of the table, right-click and choose *Cut* from the shortcut menu (**Figure 10.46**).

Splitting and merging cells

While it's easy to add or delete parts of a table, sometimes you'll want to create or delete an individual cell and not affect the overall dimensions of the rest of the table. That's where the ability to split a cell into two cells, or merge several cells into a single cell, becomes especially handy. You can, for example, create a large cell in the center of a table by merging several adjacent cells and avoid messing up anything else in the table.

To split cells

1. Click inside the cell you want to split.

2. Choose Table > Split Cells (**Figure 10.47**) or if the Tables toolbar is active, click the Split Cells button (right, **Figure 10.48**).

3. When the Split Cells dialog box appears, choose whether you want the selected cell divided horizontally into rows or vertically into columns (**Figure 10.49**).

4. Use the arrows or enter numbers directly in the text window to set the *Number of rows* or *Number of columns* you want the cell split into. When you're done, click *OK* and the cell will be split.

✔ Tip

■ The fastest way to split a cell is simply to right-click inside it, choose *Split Cells* from the shortcut menu, and follow steps 3 and 4, above.

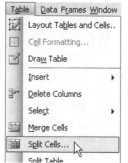

Figure 10.47
To split a cell, click inside it and choose Table > Split Cells.

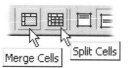

Figure 10.48 If the Tables toolbar is active, you also can combine cells with the Merge Cells button or split them with the Split Cells button.

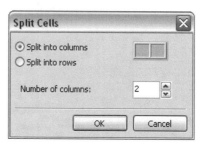

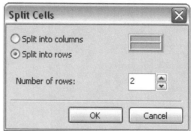

Figure 10.49 Use the Split Cells dialog box to divide a cell vertically into columns or horizontally into rows.

Figure 10.50
To merge cells, select them and choose Table > Merge Cells.

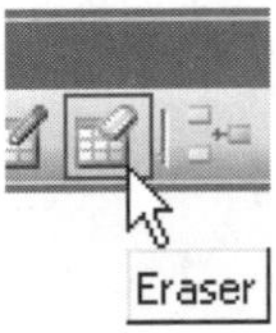

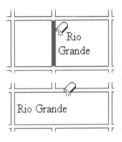

Figure 10.51 The Eraser button in the Tables toolbar offers a quick way to merge cells.

Figure 10.52 Drag the eraser-shaped cursor across a cell border until it's highlighted, release the mouse, and the border disappears.

To merge cells

1. Select the cells you want merged.

2. Choose Table > Merge Cells (**Figure 10.50**) or if the Tables toolbar is active, click the Merge Cells button (left, **Figure 10.48**). The selected cells will be combined into a single cell.

✔ Tips

■ Akin to the freehand Pencil button, the Tables toolbar's Eraser button offers a quick way to merge cells (**Figure 10.51**). Click the button, press and drag your now eraser-shaped cursor across a cell border until it's highlighted, and then release the mouse. The border will disappear (**Figure 10.52**). To deactivate the eraser, double-click anywhere outside the table.

■ You also can expand a cell by increasing its span, explained in *To format cells* on page 276.

CHANGING TABLE ELEMENTS

Evening up rows and columns

As you work on a table, things inevitably get messy. Fortunately, FrontPage offers a way to tidy things up by making all your rows the same height or all your columns the same width. The process, by the way, initially seems a bit backward because you select a *column* to even up the *row* height and select a *row* to even up the *column* width.

To make rows the same height

1. Select a *column* containing a cell from each uneven *row* (**Figure 10.53**).

2. Choose Table > Distribute Rows Evenly (left, **Figure 10.54**). If the Tables toolbar is active, you also can click the Distribute Rows Evenly button (left, **Figure 10.55**). The height of the rows will be evened up (**Figure 10.56**).

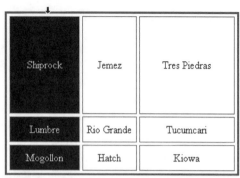

Figure 10.53 To make rows the same height, select a *column* containing a cell from each uneven row.

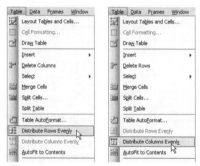

Figure 10.54 To even up a table, choose Table > Distribute Rows Evenly (left) or Table > Distribute Columns Evenly (right).

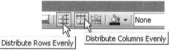

Figure 10.55 If the Tables toolbar is active, you also can even up a table with the Distribute Rows Evenly button (left) or the Distribute Columns Evenly button (right).

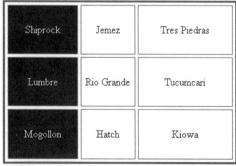

Figure 10.56 Once evened up, the rows will have the same height.

Shiprock	Jemez	Tres Piedras
Lumbre	Rio Grande	Tucumcari
Mogollon	Hatch	Kiowa

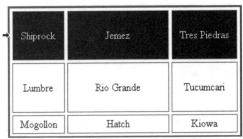

Figure 10.57 To make columns the same width, select a *row* containing a cell from each uneven column.

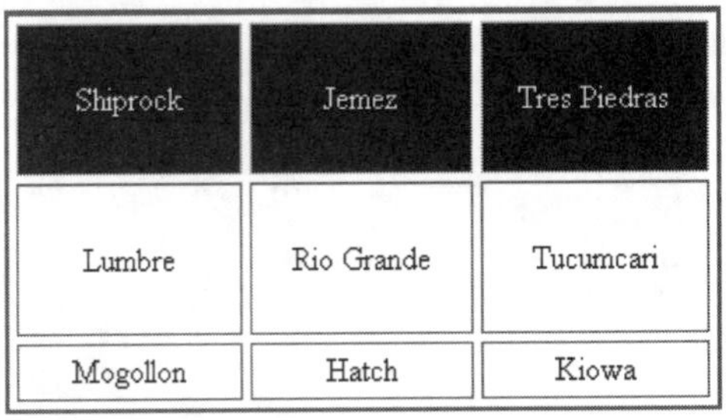

Shiprock	Jemez	Tres Piedras
Lumbre	Rio Grande	Tucumcari
Mogollon	Hatch	Kiowa

Figure 10.58 Once evened up, all the columns will have the same width.

To make columns the same width

1. Select a *row* containing a cell from each uneven *column* (**Figure 10.57**).
2. Choose Table > Distribute Columns Evenly (right, **Figure 10.54**). If the Tables toolbar is active, you also can click the Distribute Columns Evenly button (right, **Figure 10.55**). The width of the columns will be evened up (**Figure 10.58**).

✔ Tip

- If the Tables toolbar is active and you want to tidy up a whole table at once, select all of it. That will activate the Distribute Rows Evenly button *and* the Distribute Columns Evenly button, allowing you to click one button right after the other without bothering to make a second selection.

Formatting Tables and Cells

Once you've added a table to your page, put some text and images into it, and perhaps changed its structure, you're ready for the final step: formatting the full table and individual cells.

To format tables

1. Right-click the table and choose *Table Properties* from the shortcut menu (**Figure 10.59**).

2. When the Table Properties dialog box appears (**Figure 10.60**), use the *Layout* section to set the table's *Alignment*, width, and the *Cell padding* and *Cell spacing* (**Figure 10.8**). The *Float* drop-down menu lets you have the table "float" on the left or right side of text that ordinarily would appear below the table (**Figure 10.61**).

3. Use the dialog box's *Borders* section to set the table's borders. For details, see *To format table borders* on the next page.

4. If you want to apply the same color to every cell in the table, use the pop-up box in the *Background* section to choose your color. For details, see *To color cells* on page 278.

5. Once you're done, click *OK* and the changes will be applied to your table.

Figure 10.59
To format a table, right-click it and choose *Table Properties*.

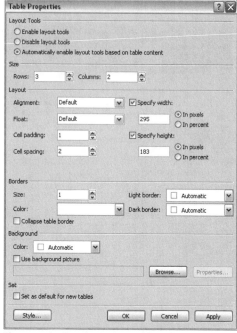

Figure 10.60 Use the *Layout* section of the Table Properties dialog box to set the table's *Alignment*, width, and the *Cell padding* and *Cell spacing*.

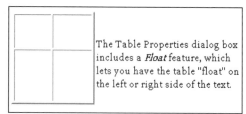

The Table Properties dialog box includes a *Float* feature, which lets you have the table "float" on the left or right side of the text.

Figure 10.61 The Table Properties dialog box *Float* drop-down menu lets you have the table "float" on the left or right side of text.

Figure 10.62 To create a single-color border, use the *Color* pop-up box and leave the *Light border* and *Dark border* pop-up boxes set to *Automatic*.

Figure 10.63 To create a two-color 3D effect, use the *Light border* and *Dark border* pop-up boxes.

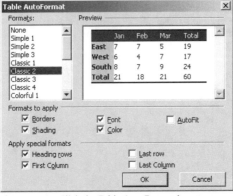

Figure 10.64 Click the Table AutoFormat icon to preview the preformatted table choices.

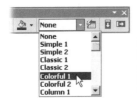

Figure 10.65
Click the drop-down menu in the Tables toolbar to quickly reach Table AutoFormats.

To format table borders

1. Select the table to which you want borders applied, then right-click and choose *Table Properties* from the shortcut menu (**Figure 10.59**).

2. When the Table Properties dialog box appears (**Figure 10.60**), use the *Borders* section to set the *Size* (width) of your border. The larger the number, the wider the border. For a borderless table, set the number at 0.

3. If you want a single-color border, use the *Color* pop-up box to pick a color and leave the *Light border* and *Dark border* pop-up boxes set to *Automatic* (top, **Figure 10.62**).

   If you want a two-color 3D effect, use the *Light border* and *Dark border* pop-up boxes to pick your colors (top, **Figure 10.63**).

4. Once you've set the width and color, click *OK* and the border will be applied (bottom, **Figures 10.62** and **10.63**).

✔ Tips

- FrontPage 2003 has changed its default setting for table borders. In FrontPage 2002, table borders were collapsed to 1 pixel by default. In the 2003 version, you need to select *Collapse table border* in the *Borders* section to achieve the same effect.

- If you use the two-color 3D effect, it will automatically appear instead of whatever single color you set.

- Use the Table AutoFormat icon in the Tables toolbar to preview and modify a variety of preformatted table settings (**Figure 10.64**). Once you learn the names of the preformatted choices, you can reach them directly by clicking the drop-down menu next to the Table AutoFormat button (**Figure 10.65**).

FORMATTING TABLES AND CELLS

To format cells

1. Select the cell or cells, then right-click and choose *Cell Properties* from the shortcut menu (**Figure 10.66**).

2. When the Cell Properties dialog box appears (**Figure 10.67**), use the *Layout* section to change the alignment and size of the selected cell(s).

3. Check *Specify width* and *Specify height* if you want to set the dimensions. Choose *In pixels* to make either dimension absolute or *In percent* to make it relative to the size of the viewer's Web browser window.

4. If you want to have the selected cell(s) span more than one row, enter a number in the *Rows spanned* window. To have the cell(s) span more than one column, enter a number in the *Columns spanned* window.

5. Click *OK* and the changes will be applied to the selected cell(s).

✔ Tips

■ While the Cell Properties dialog box offers the option of setting border colors for individual cells, it's more effective visually to adjust borders for an entire table. For details, see *To format table borders* on page 275.

■ For details on the dialog box's *Background* section, see *To color cells* on page 278.

Figure 10.66 To format cells, select them, right-click, and choose *Cell Properties*.

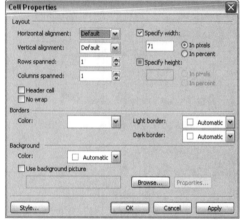

Figure 10.67 Use the Cell Properties dialog box to change a cell's alignment, size, and span.

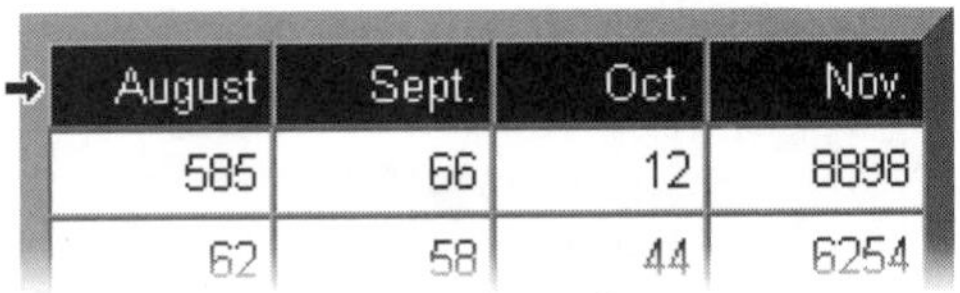

Figure 10.68 Select the cell or cells you want to turn into header cells.

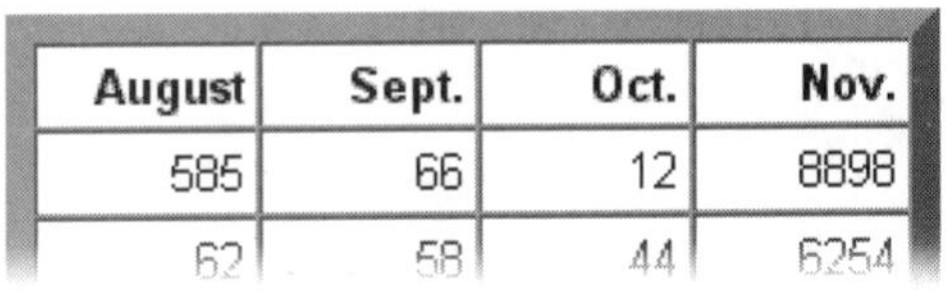

Figure 10.69 Once you've made cells into headers, the text inside will be boldfaced.

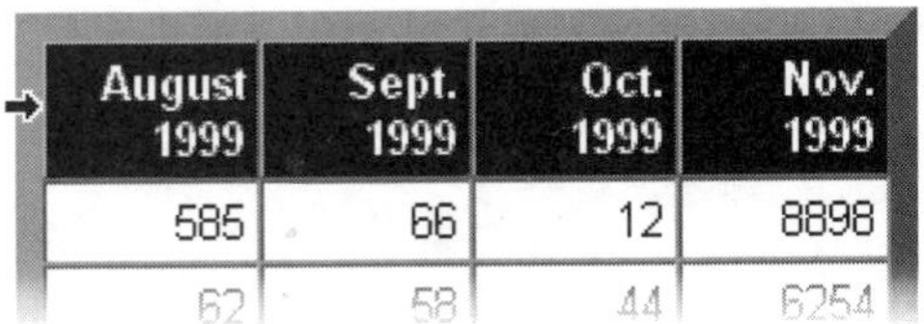

Figure 10.70 To keep cell text on one line, select the text that's wrapping to the next line.

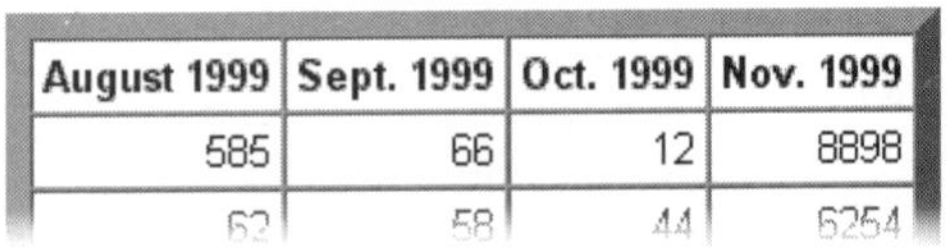

Figure 10.71 After *No wrap* is applied, the text in the selected cell(s) will rewrap to a single line.

Making cells into headers

Header cells typically act as labels for rows or columns within a table. FrontPage makes the text in header cells boldfaced.

To make cells into headers

1. Make sure you're in Page view, then select the cell or cells you want as headers (**Figure 10.68**).

2. Right-click and choose *Cell Properties* from the shortcut menu ([Alt][Enter]) (**Figure 10.66**).

3. When the Cell Properties dialog box appears (**Figure 10.67**), check *Header cell* in the *Layout* section.

4. Click *OK* and the text in the selected cell(s) will become a header, indicated by its boldfaced text (**Figure 10.69**).

To keep cell text on one line

1. Make sure you're in Page view, then select the cell or cells with text that's wrapping to the next line (**Figure 10.70**).

2. Right-click and choose *Cell Properties* from the shortcut menu ([Alt][Enter]) (**Figure 10.66**).

3. When the Cell Properties dialog box appears (**Figure 10.67**), check *No wrap* in the *Layout* section. Line wrapping is the default.

4. Click *OK* and the text in the selected cell(s) will rewrap to a single line (**Figure 10.71**).

FORMATTING TABLES AND CELLS

To color cells

1. Make sure you're in Page view and that the Tables toolbar is activated.

2. Select a cell by clicking inside the cell while pressing (Alt).

3. Click and hold the cursor on the arrow next to the paint bucket-shaped Fill Color button. When the pop-up box of colors appears, keep pressing your cursor and move to the color of your choice (left, **Figure 10.72**). Release the cursor and the fill color will be applied to the selected cell.

✔ Tips

■ If your fill color is already set to what you want—denoted by the color bar just below the Fill Color button and the pop-up tag (right, **Figure 10.72**), follow steps 1 and 2 above, and then click the button once to fill the cell.

■ You also can color a cell by right-clicking it and using the *Background* section of the Cell Properties dialog box (**Figure 10.73**). Click the *Color* arrow to reach a pop-up box of possible colors. Check *Use background picture* and click *Browse* if you want to drop a graphic into the cell. Click *OK* and the changes will be applied to the cell.

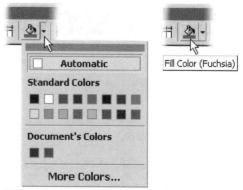

Figure 10.72 Left: To add color to a selected cell, click the arrow next to the paint bucket-shaped button and move the cursor to the color of your choice. Right: To fill with the default color—in this case, fuchsia—just click the Fill Color button.

Figure 10.73 You also can color a cell by right-clicking it and using the *Background* section of the Cell Properties dialog box.

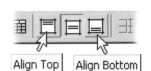

Figure 10.74 To align the contents to the top or bottom of the cell, click the respective button in the Tables toolbar.

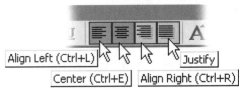

Figure 10.75 To align the contents equidistant from the cell's top and bottom, click the Center Vertically button.

Figure 10.76 To realign the cell contents *horizontally*, click any of the four alignment buttons in the Formatting toolbar.

To realign cell contents

1. Make sure the Tables and Formatting toolbars are active, then click inside the cell you want realigned.

2. If you want to realign the contents *vertically*, click any of the three alignment buttons in the Tables toolbar (**Figures 10.74** and **10.75**). The changes will be applied to the cell.

3. If you want to realign the contents *horizontally*, click any of the four alignment buttons in the Formatting toolbar (**Figure 10.76**). The changes will be applied to the cell.

✔ Tip

- You also can realign a cell's contents using the Cell Properties dialog box as explained in *To format cells* on page 276.

Top & Left.

✳

Using Tables in Page Layouts

If you've ever struggled to build a just-so table for a page layout, you will love FrontPage's new layout tables and cells. Layout tables and cells still conform to HTML-coding standards. The real difference becomes apparent when you start using the new tools in the Layout Tables and Cells task pane to create and format layout tables and cells. Layout cells, for example, make it easy to drop a cell into the middle of a layout table and have FrontPage take care of the messy business of creating the necessary cells to surround the added cell (**Figure 10.77**). In FrontPage 2002, the process was painfully slow and seldom accurate.

To add a layout table

1. Make sure you're in Page view by choosing View > Page, click the *Design* tab in the main window, and click anywhere in the page.

2. If the task pane is not active, choose Table > Layout Tables and Cells (**Figure 10.78**) and the Layout Tables and Cells task pane will appear (**Figure 10.79**). If the task pane is already active, click its drop-down menu and choose Layout Tables and Cells (**Figure 10.80**) to change your view of the task pane.

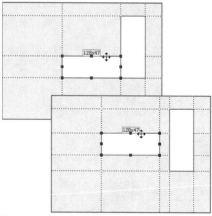

Figure 10.77 FrontPage's new layout tables and cells make it easy to adjust complicated table-based layouts.

Figure 10.78 If the task pane is not active, choose Table > Layout Tables and Cells.

Figure 10.79 The Layout Tables and Cells task pane contains a bevy of new tools for creating layouts.

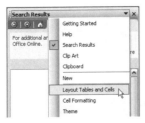

Figure 10.80
If the task pane is already active, choose Layout Tables and Cells from the drop-down menu to change your view.

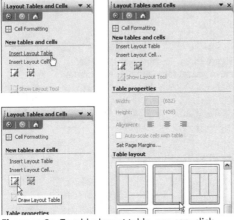

Figure 10.81 To add a layout table, you can: click *Insert Layout Table* (top left), the Draw Layout Table tool (bottom left), or the predefined layouts in the scrolling *Table layout* window (right).

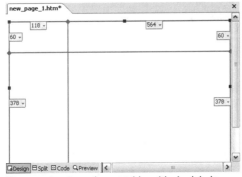

Figure 10.82 A new layout table, with size labels marking each cell, after being added to the page.

3. Within the Layout Tables and Cells task pane, you have three choices: click *Insert Layout Table*, the Draw Layout Table tool, or any one of the predefined layouts in the scrolling *Table layout* window (**Figure 10.81**).

4. Unless you chose the Draw Layout Table tool, a layout table will be added automatically to the page (**Figure 10.82**). (For more information on using the draw table option, see *To draw a table* on page 258.) You can now resize the table, add cells to it, or add content to the existing cells, as explained in the rest of this chapter.

To delete a cell or layout table

1. Make sure you're in Page view by choosing View > Page and click the *Design* tab in the main window. As explained in step 2 of *To add a layout table*, make sure the Layout Tables and Cells task pane is visible.

2. To select the cell you want to delete, move your cursor over the cell until its border turns blue, and click (**Figure 10.83**). If the cell's selected, a size label will appear at the top of the cell (**Figure 10.84**). To select the entire table, move your cursor over the table's edge until its border turns green, and click (**Figure 10.85**). If you accidentally select a cell instead of the entire table, click the Show Layout Tool twice and the table will be selected (**Figure 10.86**). (See *Tip* on the next page on selecting cells and tables.)

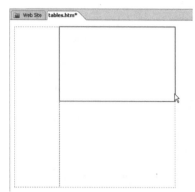

Figure 10.83 To select a cell to delete, move your cursor until the cell's border is highlighted, then click.

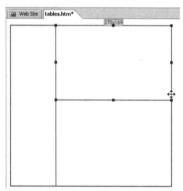

Figure 10.84 Once a cell is selected, a size label will appear at the top of the cell.

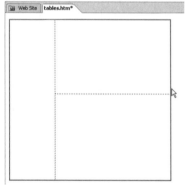

Figure 10.85 To select a table to delete, move your cursor until the table's entire border is highlighted, then click.

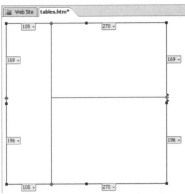

Figure 10.86 Once a table is selected, size labels will appear along each side.

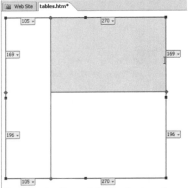

Figure 10.87 If you delete a single cell within a table, the rest of the table will remain with the missing cell marked by a dark beige.

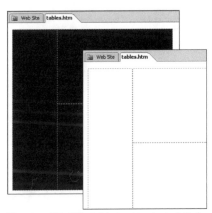

Figure 10.88 If the table is not selected, its border will be marked only by dashed lines—no matter whether the table appears black or white.

3. Press ⌐Delete⌐ and the selected cell or table will no longer appear within the page. If you delete a single cell within a table, the rest of the table will remain with the missing cell marked by a dark beige (**Figure 10.87**).

✔ Tip

■ It can be hard to tell if the Layout Tool is on or off, especially since the only difference within the Layout Tables and Cells task pane is a slightly dimmed border around the tool. Fortunately, it's easy to tell the difference just by looking at your Web page: If the table is selected, you'll see labels on all four sides of the table (**Figure 10.86**). If the table is not selected, you'll see no labels and the table's border will be marked only by dashed lines—regardless of whether the table appears black or white (**Figure 10.88**). If you've selected a single cell, instead of the entire table, a single size label will appear at the top of that cell (**Figure 10.84**).

To add a layout cell to a layout table

1. Make sure you're in Page view by choosing View > Page, click the *Design* tab in the main window, and click anywhere in the page.

2. If the task pane is not active, choose Table > Layout Tables and Cells (**Figure 10.78**) and the Layout Tables and Cells task pane will appear (**Figure 10.79**). If the task pane is already active, click its drop-down menu and choose Layout Tables and Cells (**Figure 10.80**) to change your view of the task pane.

3. Click the Show Layout Tool once or twice to select the table to which you want to add a cell. (See the previous *Tip* for help on selecting a table.)

4. Within the Layout Tables and Cells task pane, select the Draw Layout Cell tool (**Figure 10.89**).

5. Click inside the table with your cursor, which becomes an arrow-capped pencil, and then drag until you've drawn the cell to the desired size (**Figure 10.90**). Release your cursor and the cell will be added to the layout table (**Figure 10.91**). If you need to reposition the cell, select and drag it to a new spot. If you need to resize it, see the next two sections.

Figure 10.89
To add a layout cell to a layout table, select the task pane's Draw Layout Cell tool.

 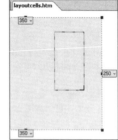

Figure 10.90 Click inside the table with your cursor (left), then drag until you've drawn the cell to the desired size (right).

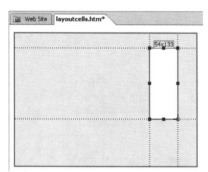

Figure 10.91 The layout cell is highlighted once it's been added to a layout table.

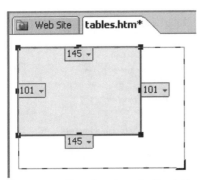

Figure 10.92 To resize a layout cell or table, press [Alt] while clicking and dragging the square handle to enlarge or shrink the cell or table.

To resize a layout cell or table by click-dragging

1. Select one of the blue squares, or "handles," on the side or corner of the layout cell or table.

2. While pressing [Alt], click and drag the blue handle to enlarge or shrink the cell or table (**Figure 10.92**). Release the cursor and the cell or table will assume its new size (**Figure 10.93**).

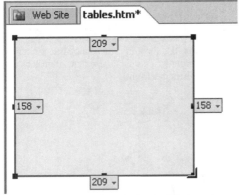

Figure 10.93 The numbers in the size labels update to reflect the new size of the cell or table.

To precisely resize a layout cell or table

1. Click on one of the size labels attached to the top or side of the layout cell or table you want to resize. Depending on which label you click, choose Change Row Height (or Change Column Width) from the drop-down menu (**Figure 10.94**).

2. Depending on your choice in step 1, either the Row Properties or Column Properties dialog box will appear (left, **Figure 10.95**). Enter a new height or width directly in the text window or use the arrows to set the number, then click *OK* or press ⌐Enter (right, **Figure 10.95**). The box will close and the cell or table will be resized and the corresponding size label will reflect the change (**Figure 10.96**).

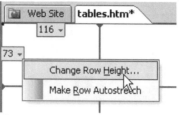

Figure 10.94 To precisely resize a layout cell or table, click a size label and choose Change Row Height (or Change Column Width) from the drop-down menu.

Figure 10.95 Use the Properties dialog box to change the *Row Height* (or *Column Width*) (left), then click *OK* to apply the change (right).

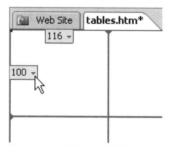

Figure 10.96 The size label numbers will change to reflect the new size.

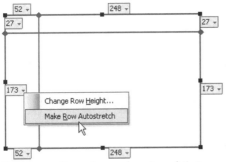

Figure 10.97 To create rows (or columns) that expand or shrink to match the Web browser window, click a size label and choose the auto-stretch feature.

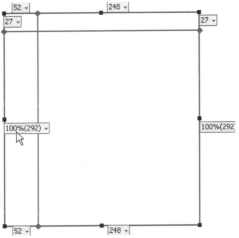

Figure 10.98 The size label for an autostretched row or column will include *100%*.

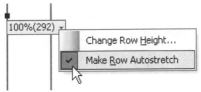

Figure 10.99 To cancel autostretch, click on the autostretched row or column and unselect that choice in the drop-down menu.

To resize a row or column using autostretch

◆ Click on one of the size labels attached to a row or column that you want to fill out the viewer's Web browser window, and choose Make Row Autostretch or Make Column Autostretch from the drop-down menu (**Figure 10.97**). The row or column will immediately expand so that the layout table fills FrontPage's Design view (**Figure 10.98**). You can test the autostretch feature by viewing the page in your Web browser, where the table will resize automatically as the size of the browser window changes.

✔ Tips

■ To cancel autostretch, click on the autostretched row or column and unselect Make Row Autostretch or Make Column Autostretch from the drop-down menu (**Figure 10.99**). The row or column will return to its original size before autostretch was applied.

■ Autostretch can be applied to only one row or column in a layout table.

USING TABLES IN PAGE LAYOUTS

To format layout cells

1. Select a layout cell whose properties you want to change (**Figure 10.100**).

2. If the task pane is not active, choose Table > Cell Formatting or right-click the cell and choose Cell Formatting from the shortcut menu (**Figure 10.101**). The Cell Formatting task pane will appear, with its Cell Properties and Borders view selected by default (**Figure 10.102**). If the Layout Tables and Cells task pane is already active, click *Cell Formatting* (**Figure 10.103**). The Cell Formatting task pane will appear.

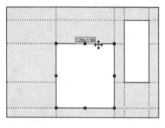

Figure 10.100 Select a layout cell whose properties you want to change.

Figure 10.101 If the task pane is not active, choose Table > Cell Formatting (left) or right-click the cell and choose Cell Formatting (right).

Figure 10.102 The Cell Properties and Borders view of the Cell Formatting task pane lets you change a cell's size, padding, alignment, color, borders, and margins.

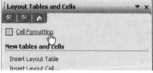

Figure 10.103 If the Layout Tables and Cells task pane is already active, click *Cell Formatting* to switch to that view.

Figure 10.104
The Cell Header and Footer view of the Cell Formatting task pane lets you control the formatting of the selected cell's header or footer.

Figure 10.105
The Cell Corners and Shadows view of the Cell Formatting task pane lets you apply fancy effects to the selected cell.

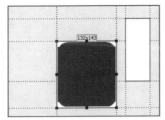

Figure 10.106
The selected cell after changes made in the Cell Formatting task pane have been applied.

3. Select the changes you want to make to the selected cell's properties and borders, or switch views by clicking *Cell Header and Footer* (**Figure 10.104**) or *Cell Corners and Shadows* (**Figure 10.105**).

4. Once you've finished making your selections, click the corresponding buttons or press ⏎Enter to apply the changes to the selected cell (**Figure 10.106**).

✔ Tips

■ The formatting buttons work like toggles, so you can turn off an effect by clicking the same button twice.

■ Resist the urge to apply too many effects to your cells. Ultimately, it's the information within the cell that's most important.

To convert an existing table to a layout table

1. Right-click an existing table and choose Table Properties from the drop-down menu.

2. When the Table Properties dialog box appears, select *Enable layout tools* (**Figure 10.107**). Click *OK* and when the dialog box closes, the regular table will now appear as a layout table.

✔ Tip

■ You can reverse the process, or turn a layout table into a regular table, by reopening the Table Properties dialog box and selecting *Disable layout tools* and clicking *OK*.

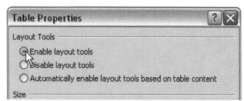

Figure 10.107 To convert an existing table to a layout table, select *Enable layout tools* in the Table Properties dialog box.

CREATING LAYERS AND FRAMES

11

One of the big advantages of creating frame-based pages is that you can have site-wide navigation links or buttons that remain visible in one frame even as visitors scroll around in the main frame. That's a great help in keeping visitors oriented while enabling them to easily jump to other parts of your Web site. Version 3 and later browsers support frames, by the way, so you can create frame-based pages without leaving too many folks in the dark.

Frames, however, do have several drawbacks. The page title remains the same even as visitors move from frame to frame, which sometimes creates confusion. It's also not possible for visitors to bookmark a particular frame in their Web browsers. Instead, they'll be sent to the site's home page. One way around these problems, while keeping the site's navigation clear, is to use link bars instead. For more information, see *Using Link Bars and Shared Borders* on page 62.

Not previously available in FrontPage, the new layers feature offers another way to create flexible, dynamic page layouts similar to those seen in glossy magazines (**Figure 11.1**). One of the advantages layers have over layout tables or frames is that you can overlap layers by setting their stack order, much as you can overlap images (see *Positioning Images Absolutely* on page 201). What's more, you can pair layers with behaviors triggered by a user's cursor actions. For more information, see *Using Dynamic HTML Effects* on page 383. By the way, the most recent surveys show that 97 percent of all Web browsers now can display layers properly—a dramatic shift from just a few years ago.

Creating Layers

If you have used FrontPage's tools for drawing tables or layout tables, you'll feel right at home using the layer-creating tools. Also, as you'll see, controlling the stack order of layers works exactly like positioning images, which is explained on page 201.

To create a layer

1. Make sure you're in Page view by choosing View > Page, then click the *Design* tab in the main window.

2. If the task pane is not active, choose Format > Layers (**Figure 11.2**) and the Layers task pane will appear. If the task pane is already active, click its drop-down menu and choose Layers (**Figure 11.3**) to change your view of the task pane.

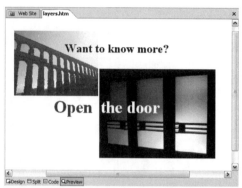

Figure 11.1 The new layers feature offers another way to create flexible, dynamic page layouts.

Figure 11.2 If the task pane is not active, choose Format > Layers.

Figure 11.3 If the task pane is already active, click its drop-down menu and choose Layers.

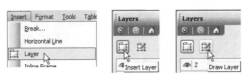

Figure 11.4 You have three choices for creating a layer: choose Insert > Layer (left), click the Insert Layer tool (middle), or click the Draw Layer tool in the Layers task pane (right).

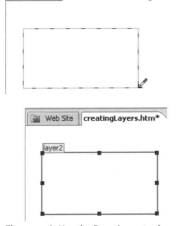

Figure 11.5 Unless you chose the Draw Layer tool, a layer will be added automatically to the page.

Figure 11.6 Use the Draw Layer tool to click and drag the cursor (top), then release and the new layer will appear (bottom).

3. You have three choices for creating a layer: choose Insert > Layer, click the Insert Layer tool, or click the Draw Layer tool in the Layers task pane (**Figure 11.4**).

4. Unless you chose the Draw Layers tool, a layer will be added automatically to the page (**Figure 11.5**). If you chose the Draw Layer tool in step 3, click inside the page with your cursor, which becomes an arrow-capped pencil, drag until you've drawn the layer to the desired size, and when you release the cursor the layer will appear (**Figure 11.6**). You can now move or resize the layer, or add more layers and then set their stack order and visibility.

CREATING LAYERS

To move a layer

1. Make sure you're in Page view by choosing View > Page, then click the *Design* tab in the main window, and choose Format > Layers to show the Layers task pane.

2. Select the layer by clicking on or inside its border, which will become highlighted in blue (**Figure 11.7**).

3. Now move the cursor toward the layer's border until it becomes a four-headed arrow, then click and drag the layer to its new position. A dashed outline will mark your progress (**Figure 11.8**). Release the cursor and the layer will move to the new position (**Figure 11.9**).

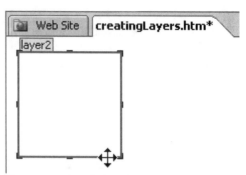

Figure 11.7 Select the layer by clicking on or inside its border, which will become highlighted.

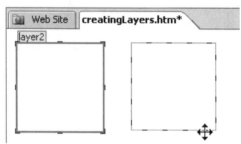

Figure 11.8 Move the cursor toward the layer's border until it becomes a four-headed arrow, then click and drag the layer to its new position.

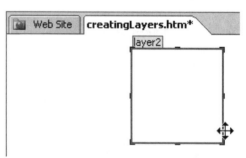

Figure 11.9 Release the cursor and the layer will move to its new position.

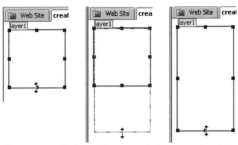

Figure 11.10 Click and drag any of the square handles (left) and a dashed outline will mark your progress (middle). Release the cursor and the layer will be resized (right).

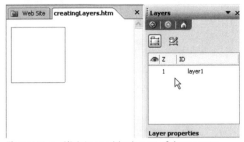

Figure 11.11 Click in any blank part of the page to ensure that no existing layer is selected (left). You can double-check that no layer is selected by looking at the list in the Layers task pane.

To resize a layer

1. Make sure you're in Page view by choosing View > Page, then click the *Design* tab in the main window, and choose Format > Layers to show the Layers task pane.

2. Select the layer by clicking on its border, which will become highlighted in blue with small squares (handles) on each side and at the corners (left, **Figure 11.10**).

3. Click on, then drag any of the handles. A dashed outline will mark your progress (middle, **Figure 11.10**). Release the cursor and the layer will be resized (right, **Figure 11.10**).

To add and select layers

1. Make sure you're in Page view by choosing View > Page, then click the *Design* tab in the main window, and choose Format > Layers to show the Layers task pane.

2. Click in a blank part of the page to ensure that no layer is selected. You also can double-check that no layer is selected by making sure nothing is highlighted in the Layers task pane (**Figure 11.11**).

3. Just as when you first created a layer, you can add a layer by choosing Insert > Layer, or clicking either the Insert Layer or Draw Layer tool in the Layers task pane.

4. Unless you chose the Draw Layer tool, the new layer will be added to the page exactly on top of the first layer (**Figure 11.12**). If you chose the Draw Layer tool in step 3, go ahead and click inside the page and drag the cursor to draw a layer, using the dashed outline as a guide. Release the cursor and the layer will be added where you've drawn it (**Figure 11.13**).

Figure 11.12 Unless you chose the Draw Layer tool, the new layer will be added automatically to the page exactly on top of the first layer.

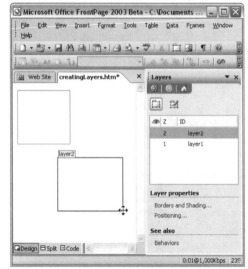

Figure 11.13 Use the Draw Layer tool to draw a new layer, which will appear wherever you release the cursor.

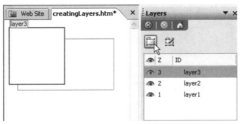

Figure 11.14 Add as many layers as you need, all of which will be listed in the Layers task pane.

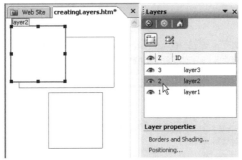

Figure 11.15 Select each layer by clicking on it directly or within the Layers task pane list, then drag it into position and resize if necessary.

5. Continue adding layers until you have as many as you need, though you can always add more later. As you add each layer, it will be listed in the Layers task pane (**Figure 11.14**).

6. Select each layer by clicking on it directly or within the Layers task pane list, then drag it into position and resize if necessary (**Figure 11.15**).

✔ Tips

■ The selected layer always will be highlighted in the Layers task pane.

■ You can select, and then move, multiple layers by Ctrl-clicking each layer in turn.

■ Whenever you add a layer, the new layer will be selected by default. When you start to create yet another layer, remember to deselect that new layer. Otherwise, you'll wind up creating a layer that's nested within the previous layer. For more information, see *Parent and Child: Controlling Nesting* on page 301.

ADDING AND SELECTING LAYERS

To set layer stack order

1. Make sure you're in Page view by choosing View > Page, then click the *Design* tab in the main window, and choose Format > Layers to show the Layers task pane.

2. If you don't remember the name/number of the layer, select it in the page, then right-click the highlighted row in the Layers task pane and choose Modify Z-Index from the drop-down menu (**Figure 11.16**). The text window for that layer's Z number will be highlighted for editing. If you already know which layer is which, double click directly on the layer's Z number in the Layers task pane and it will be highlighted for editing.

3. Type a new number into the Z text window based on where you want the layer to appear in the stack order (**Figure 11.17**). The greater the number, the closer to the top of the stack that layer will appear; smaller or negative numbers move layers down in the stack order. Press (←Enter) or (Tab) after entering a number and the Layers task pane will update to display the new stack order (**Figure 11.18**).

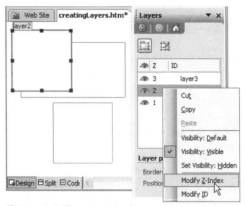

Figure 11.16 If you want to change a layer's stack order, but can't remember its name/number, select it in the page, then right-click the highlighted row in the Layers task pane and choose Modify Z-Index from the drop-down menu.

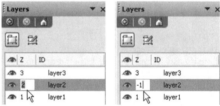

Figure 11.17 Double-click the layer's Z text window to select it (left), then enter a new number based on where you want the layer to appear in the stack order (right).

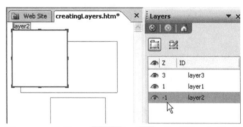

Figure 11.18 Press (←Enter) or (Tab) after filling in the Z text window and the layer will assume its new position in the stack order.

Figure 11.19 If any layer is selected, it will appear at the top of the stack order—even if it sits elsewhere in the stack order.

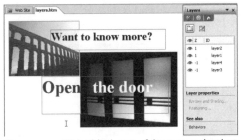

Figure 11.20 Click a blank area of the page to deselect all the layers and you'll see the layers in their actual stack order.

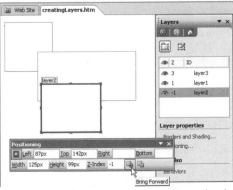

Figure 11.21 You also can use the Bring Forward and Move Backward buttons in the Positioning toolbar to set the stack order for a selected layer.

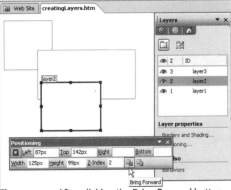

Figure 11.22 After clicking the Bring Forward button, the layer moves up in the stack order.

✔ Tips

- If any layer is selected, it will appear at the top of the stack order—even if it sits elsewhere in the stack order (**Figure 11.19**). Click in a blank area of the page to deselect all the layers and you'll see the layers in their actual stack order (**Figure 11.20**).

- If you prefer, you can use the Bring Forward and Move Backward buttons in the Positioning toolbar to set the stack order for a selected layer (**Figures 11.21** and **11.22**).

SETTING LAYER STACK ORDER

To create nested layers

1. Make sure you're in Page view by choosing View > Page, then click the *Design* tab in the main window, and choose Format > Layers to show the Layers task pane.

2. Click in the Layers task pane or the Web page itself to select the particular layer you want to make the parent, or controlling, layer, then click the Insert Layer tool (**Figure 11.23**). A new child, or nested, layer will be created in the same position as the parent layer, with its name indented beneath the parent layer in the Layers task pane (**Figure 11.24**).

3. To create another nested layer for the same parent layer, reselect the parent layer and click the Insert Layer tool again (**Figure 11.25**). Another nested layer will appear, with its name indented beneath the parent layer in the Layers task pane.

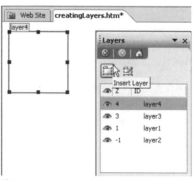

Figure 11.23 Select the particular layer you want to make the parent, or controlling, layer, then click the Insert Layer tool.

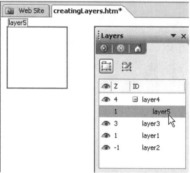

Figure 11.24 A new child, or nested, layer will be created in the same position as the parent layer, with its name indented beneath the parent layer in the Layers task pane.

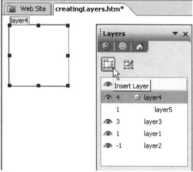

Figure 11.25 To create another nested layer for the same parent layer, reselect the parent layer and click the Insert Layer tool again.

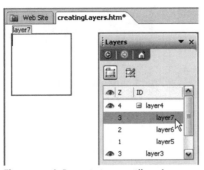

Figure 11.26 Repeat step 3 until you've created as many nested layers as you need.

4. Repeat step 3 until you've created as many nested layers as you need (**Figure 11.26**).

✔ **Tip**

■ To create a non-nested layer, make sure that no other layer is selected before creating a new layer. Such child-free layers can be moved about without disturbing any of the other layers.

Parent and Child: Controlling Nesting

If you've already used FrontPage's Group and Ungroup commands on drawn objects, you'll immediately recognize that parent and child layers work in much the same way. As with grouped objects, a child layer moves whenever a parent layer is moved (**Figures 11.27** and **11.28**). FrontPage calls this nesting one layer within another. Once you know how to control nesting, you can use parent-child layers to create design modules that can be kept and moved together as you build a page design.

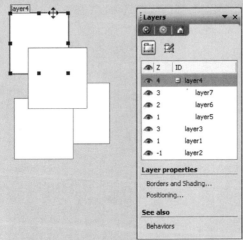

Figure 11.27 By selecting the parent, or controlling, layer, you automatically select the child layers nested within.

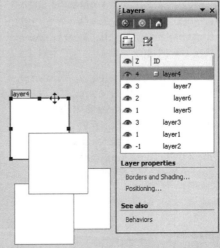

Figure 11.28 Move the parent layer and all the nested layers move with it.

To set layer visibility

1. Make sure you're in Page view by choosing View > Page, then click the *Design* tab in the main window, and choose Format > Layers to show the Layers task pane.

2. Click in the Layers task pane or the Web page itself to select the particular layer whose visibility you want to set.

3. Click in the Layers task pane's first column (the one topped with an open eye) to cycle the layer's visibility through three states: no eye (default), an open eye (visible), or a closed eye (hidden) (**Figure 11.29**). No eye means the layer will default to the visibility of the page element that contains it, which in this case is layer 4, its parent layer. An open eye means the layer will be visible, even if it's nested in an otherwise hidden parent layer. A closed eye means the layer will be hidden, even if its parent layer is visible. Once you make your choice, the layer's visibility will be set.

✔ **Tips**

■ You also can set the visibility for all the layers at once by clicking the eye atop the first column within the Layers task pane (**Figure 11.30**).

■ By combining the visibility—or invisibility—of layers with Dynamic HTML-based behaviors, you can create such things as drop-down navigation menus that change in reaction to a visitor's cursor movements. For more information, see *Using Dynamic HTML Effects* on page 383.

Figure 11.29 Click in the Layers task pane's first column (the one topped with an open eye) to cycle through the layer's three visibility states.

 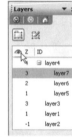 

Figure 11.30 You also can set the visibility for all layers at once by clicking the eye atop the first column within the Layers task pane.

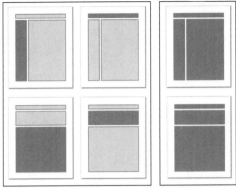

Figure 11.31 Left: Each of the four thumbnails contains one darkened *frame*. Right: Collectively, all the frames make up a *frames page*.

Creating Frames

Each frame you create can display a separate Web page. Whether you create those content pages before or after you create the frames themselves is up to you. Generally, however, it's less confusing to at least rough out the content pages first, then create the frames that will contain them. At that point, it's common to tweak the content for the frame. In creating frames and frames pages, sometimes it's helpful to see just the content without any frames. For details, see *To show a frame in a new window* on page 307.

A few terms need explaining: Individual *frames* are collectively displayed in a special page called a *frames page* (**Figure 11.31**). Frames pages used to be called *framesets*, a term you'll still come across. Finally, FrontPage lets you set a hyperlink's *target frame*, which is the frame where the link's content will be displayed.

A frames page can contain as many frames as you like. Bear in mind, however, that each page and its content must be downloaded, increasing the potential wait for your visitors. Use FrontPage's download progress indicator to gauge how long pages will take to appear on screen (see page 17).

To create a frames page

1. Make sure you're in Page view by choosing View > Page, then click the *Design* tab in the main window, then choose File > New > Page ($\boxed{Ctrl}\boxed{N}$) or click the New icon in the Standard toolbar and choose *Page* from the drop-down menu (**Figure 11.32**).

2. When the task pane appears, click *More page templates* (**Figure 11.33**).

3. When the Page Templates dialog box appears, click the *Frames Pages* tab (**Figure 11.34**). Use the dialog box's *Preview* area to choose a frames page template and click *OK*. A blank frames page, based on the template, will appear with each frame offering two choices: *Set Initial Page* and *New Page* (**Figure 11.35**).

Figure 11.32 To create a frames page, choose File > New > Page.

Figure 11.33 When the task pane appears, click *More page templates*.

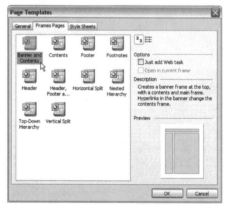

Figure 11.34 Click the *Frames Pages* tab in the Page Templates dialog box to reach a collection of frames page templates.

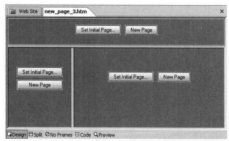

Figure 11.35 A new blank frames page offers two choices in each frame: *Set Initial Page* for linking to an existing page and *New Page* for creating a page from scratch.

Figure 11.36 To link a frame to an existing page, use the Insert Hyperlink dialog box to navigate to the page.

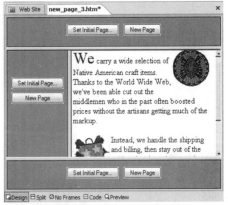

Figure 11.37 Once you link an existing page to a frame, the page will appear in the frame.

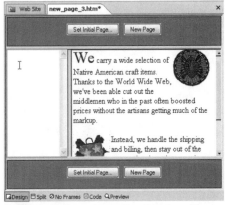

Figure 11.38 If you choose *New Page* in setting up a frame, a blank page will appear—allowing you to start creating content.

4. To link a frame to an *existing* page on your Web site, click *Set Initial Page*. When the Insert Hyperlink dialog box appears (**Figure 11.36**), navigate to the page you want to use and click *OK*. The existing page will appear in the frame (**Figure 11.37**). For details on using the Insert Hyperlink dialog box, see page 146.

To create a *new* page from scratch for the frame, click *New Page*. A blank page based on the Normal template will appear within the frame (**Figure 11.38**). You then can begin adding content to the frame.

(continued)

5. Press Ctrl S to save any new frame and the *frames page* itself. If you've created a brand new page for any of your frames, that page will be the first to appear in the Save As dialog box (**Figure 11.39**).

6. Give the new page a distinct name and title, then click *Save*. The new page will be saved and a new Save As dialog box will appear for saving the entire frames page, denoted by a heavy blue border surrounding the full page in the preview window (**Figure 11.40**).

7. Give the frames page a distinct name and title, then click *Save*. The frames page will be saved.

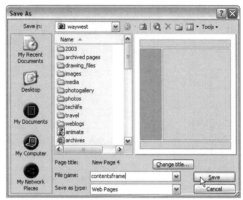

Figure 11.39 If you've created a brand new page for any frame, that page's frame will be highlighted in the Save As dialog box's preview area.

Figure 11.40 When you save a frames page, the entire page is highlighted in the Save As dialog box's preview area.

Figure 11.41 To show a frame in a full-sized window, right-click the frame and choose *Open Page in New Window* from the shortcut menu.

To show a frame in a new window

◆ Right-click in the frame and choose *Open Page in New Window* from the shortcut menu (**Figure 11.41**). The content of the frame will expand to a full-size window, replacing your view of the frames page.

✔ Tip

■ If you want to return to the frames page, make sure the Folder List is visible and double-click the frames page file. The frames page will become visible in FrontPage's main window once more.

Setting target frames

In general, FrontPage will automatically set the large, main frame as the target for links clicked in, say, a left-hand table of contents frame. FrontPage, however, gives you a way to directly set any frame as the target of a link.

You won't need to mess with changing the default target frame, because FrontPage usually gets it right based on the context of the rest of the page's frames. But if you need to, see *To change the target frame default* on page 310.

To set a link's target frame

1. Right-click the link for which you want to set a target frame and choose *Hyperlink* from the shortcut menu ([Alt][Enter]) (**Figure 11.42**).

2. When the Insert Hyperlink dialog box appears, make sure the link's *Address* is correct. If not, change it.

3. If you're happy with the link address, click the *Target Frame* button (**Figure 11.43**). When the Target Frame dialog box appears, you'll see that the *Target setting* text box says *main*, which is the main frame of the current page (**Figure 11.44**).

Figure 11.42 To set a target frame for a link, right-click it and choose *Hyperlink* from the shortcut menu.

Figure 11.43 Click the *Target Frame* button in the Insert Hyperlink dialog box to set or change the target frame.

Figure 11.44 Use the Target Frame dialog box to change your link's targeted frame.

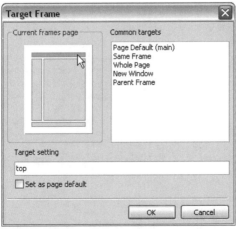

Figure 11.45 Clicking the top frame in the *Current frames page* pastes its name into the *Target setting* text window.

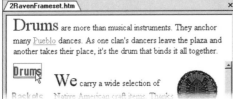

Figure 11.46 When clicked (top), the *Drums* link content replaces the Two Ravens Trading logo in the targeted frame (bottom).

Figure 11.47 You can check what's listed as the *Target Frame* at the bottom of the Insert Hyperlink dialog box.

4. To change the setting, either click a frame in the *Current frames page* thumbnail or click a listing in the *Common targets* window. The frame's name will be pasted into the *Target setting* text window (**Figure 11.45**). For details, see *Target Frame options* on page 311.

5. Click *OK* and when the Insert Hyperlink dialog box reappears, click *OK* again.

6. To check the link target, click the *Preview* tab in FrontPage's main window (top, **Figure 11.46**). When clicked, the link selected in step 1 will now display its linked page in the selected target (bottom, **Figure 11.46**).

✔ Tip

■ Much of the time, FrontPage will automatically assign the correct frame as the target. Just check which frame is listed as the *Target Frame* at the bottom of the Insert Hyperlink dialog box (**Figure 11.47**).

To change the target frame default

1. Make sure you're in Page view by choosing View > Page, then click the *Design* tab in the main window, then right-click anywhere in the page and choose *Page Properties* from the shortcut menu (**Figure 11.48**).

2. When the Page Properties dialog box appears, click the *General* tab, then click the Change Target Frame button (**Figure 11.49**).

3. When the Target Frame dialog box appears (**Figure 11.50**), either click a frame in the *Current frames page* thumbnail or click a listing in the *Common targets* window. The frame's name will be pasted into the *Target setting* text window. For details, see *Target Frame options* on the next page.

4. Click *OK*, and when the Page Properties dialog box reappears, the target frame's name will be pasted into the *Default target frame* text box.

5. Click *OK* again and that frame will become the page's default target.

Figure 11.48 To change the target frame default, right-click the page and choose *Page Properties* from the shortcut menu.

Figure 11.49 When the Page Properties dialog box appears, click the *General* tab, then click the Change Target Frame button.

SETTING TARGET FRAMES

Figure 11.50 Use the Target Frame dialog box to change your link's targeted frame.

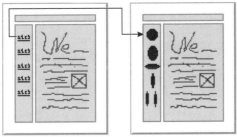

Figure 11.51 If you use *Same Frame* as your target frame, clicking the link will replace its frame with the link's content.

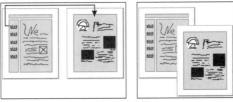

Figure 11.52 Left: If you use *Whole Page* as your target, clicking the link replaces the entire frames page. Right: Using *New Window* instead opens another window, leaving the frames page undisturbed.

Target Frame options

To reach the Target Frame dialog box (**Figure 11.50**), right-click a link in a frame, then click the *Target Frame* button in the Insert Hyperlink dialog box.

❶ Current frames page: Click any frame in the thumbnail to make it the frame where the link's content will be displayed.

❷ Common targets: Click any of these listings, which supplement those in the *Current frames page.*

Page Default (main): With this option chosen, clicking a link will display its content in the frame designated as the default page—in this example, the main frame of the current frame page.

Same Frame: With this option, clicking a link in a frame will replace *that same frame* with the linked content (**Figure 11.51**).

Whole Page: With this option, clicking a link in a frame will replace the entire frames page with a single page showing the linked content (left, **Figure 11.52**).

New Window: With this option, clicking a link in a frame will open up a new browser window to display the linked content (right, **Figure 11.52**). It's a good choice if you're linking a visitor to a page off your own site because your site will remain visible in the original browser window. That increases the chances that the visitor will remain on your site.

Parent Frame: This advanced option is used in creating discussion groups.

❸ Target setting: The text box will be filled automatically based on your choice in either the *Current frames page* or the *Common targets* list.

❹ Set as page default: Check this box to make *every* link in the selected page default to the selected target frame.

Setting a frames page as the home page

By default, FrontPage names your home page index.htm. If your site already has a frame-less home page that you'd like to replace with a frames-based home page, you simply have to replace the old index.htm with a new one containing your frames page. (On some servers, the home page is named default.htm. The steps are the same.)

To make a frames page your home page

1. Make sure the Folder List is visible, find the index.htm file, and click it so that its name becomes highlighted (left, **Figure 11.53**).

2. Type in a new name, for example framelessindex.htm, being sure to preserve the .htm suffix (right, **Figure 11.53**).

3. Again looking in the Folder List, find the frame-based file you want to use as your home page, and click it so that its name becomes highlighted (left, **Figure 11.54**).

4. Replace its name by typing in index.htm as the file's new name (right, **Figure 11.54**). Now when FrontPage looks for the home page, it will open your frames-based page.

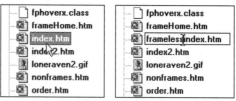

Figure 11.53 To make a frames page your home page, find the original home page in the Folder List (left) and rename it (right).

Figure 11.54 To finish making a frames page your home page, change the frames page's name (left) to index.htm (right).

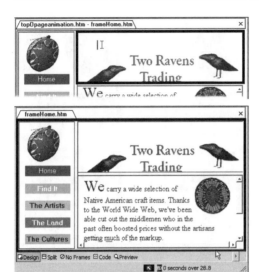

Figure 11.55 Top: To select a *frame*, click anywhere inside it. Bottom: To select an entire *frames page*, it's easiest to click its border in the lower right.

Figure 11.56 To delete a frame, click inside the frame and choose Frames > Delete Frame.

Formatting Frames

Once you've created some frames and set targets for the links inside them, you may find yourself wanting to reformat or modify some frames. FrontPage includes options for resizing, splitting, and changing basic properties of your frames. It also lets you customize a message to help visitors whose Web browsers don't support frames.

To select a frame

◆ To select a frame, click anywhere *inside* the frame. A wide gray border will highlight the selected frame (top, **Figure 11.55**).

To select a frames page

◆ To select the whole frames page, click the page's outer border. Because the outer border is so narrow, it's easiest to find it by clicking in the bottom-right corner of the status bar. Once you click the right spot, a wide gray border will surround the frames page (bottom, **Figure 11.55**).

To delete a frame

◆ Click inside the frame you want to delete and choose Frames > Delete Frame (**Figure 11.56**). The frame will be removed *from the frames page*, although the page that had been displayed in the frame will remain part of your Web site's files.

To resize a frame

1. Make sure you're in Page view by choosing View > Page, then click the *Design* tab in the main window, then select the frame you want to resize by clicking anywhere inside the frame.

2. Move your cursor over one of the wide gray frame borders where it will become a double-headed arrow (left, **Figure 11.57**). Click and drag the cursor to make the frame smaller or larger (right, **Figure 11.57**). When it reaches the size you want, release the cursor and the frame will be resized.

✔ Tip

- If you need more precision in resizing a frame, right-click it, choose *Frame Properties* from the shortcut menu, and use the dialog box's *Frame size* area to enter numerical values.

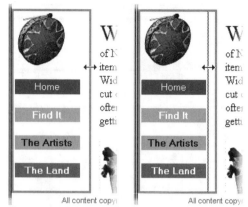

Figure 11.57 To resize a frame, move your cursor over a frame border until it becomes a double-headed arrow (left), then click and drag to make the frame smaller or larger (right).

RESIZING FRAMES

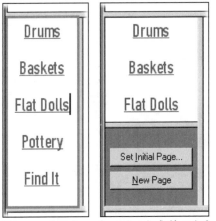

Figure 11.58 Before a frame is split (left) and afterward (right).

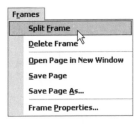

Figure 11.59 To split a frame, choose Frames > Split Frame.

Figure 11.60 The Split Frame dialog box offers the choice of dividing a frame vertically into columns or horizontally into rows.

Splitting frames

You can split frames as a quick way to add another frame to an existing frames page.

To split a frame

1. Click inside the frame you want split (left, **Figure 11.58**).

2. Choose Frames > Split Frame (**Figure 11.59**).

3. When the Split Frame dialog box appears, choose whether you want to divide the frame vertically into columns or horizontally into rows (**Figure 11.60**). Click *OK* and the frame will be split into two equal-sized frames (right, **Figure 11.58**).

✔ Tips

- An even faster way to split a frame is to click and drag its border while pressing Ctrl.

- If the frame you split didn't have a scrollbar initially, you may need to add one to see all its contents. For details, see *Frame Properties options* on page 317.

To change frames

1. Right-click the frame you want to change and choose *Frame Properties* from the shortcut menu (**Figure 11.61**).

2. When the Frame Properties dialog box appears (**Figure 11.62**), set the frame's name, size, and margins.

3. FrontPage will have assigned the frame a name based on its position (e.g., top, left, center). Type in a new *Name* if you like.

4. Use the dialog box's *Options* section to restrict the user's ability to resize the frame. You also can turn scrollbars on or off for the selected frame.

5. When you're done, click *OK* and the changes will be applied to the selected frame.

To change spacing or borders in frames pages

1. Right-click anywhere in the frames page and choose *Frame Properties* from the shortcut menu (**Figure 11.61**).

2. When the Frame Properties dialog box appears (**Figure 11.62**), click *Frames Page* in the lower-right corner.

3. When the Page Properties dialog box appears, click the *Frames* tab (**Figure 11.63**).

4. Type a number directly into the *Frame Spacing* text window or use the arrows to change the distance *between* the page's frames.

5. To hide the boundaries of the page's frames, uncheck *Show Borders*.

6. Click *OK* to return to the Frame Properties dialog box, then click *OK* again to apply the changes to the frames page.

Figure 11.61 To change a frame or frames page, right-click the frame or page and choose *Frame Properties* from the shortcut menu.

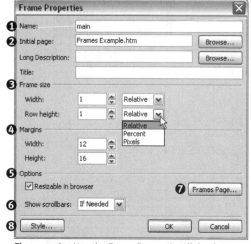

Figure 11.62 Use the Frame Properties dialog box to change a frame's name, size, and margins. Or click *Frames Page* in the lower right to change the frames page.

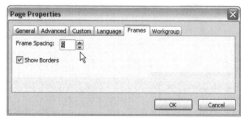

Figure 11.63 Use the Page Properties dialog box's *Frames* tab to set the spacing and borders between a page's frames.

Frame Properties options

To reach the Frame Properties dialog box (**Figure 11.62**), right-click any frame and choose *Frame Properties*.

❶ **Name:** By default, FrontPage assigns a name to the frame based on its position. Type in another name if you prefer.

❷ **Initial page:** Click *Browse* to find a new page to appear in the frame.

❸ **Frame size:** By default, the *Width* is set to *Pixels*. *Row height* is dimmed unless the current frame is part of a row of frames. Use the drop-down menus to change the settings. *Relative* sets the width relative to other frames in the frames page: If you set a value of 1 for one frame and 2 for another, the second frame will be twice as wide. *Percent* sets the frame's width as a percentage of the browser window's width.

❹ **Margins:** The *Width* and *Height* windows set the frame's margin in pixels.

❺ **Resizable in browser:** By default, this box is checked, allowing the user to resize the frame. Uncheck the box if you want the frame size fixed.

❻ **Show scrollbars:** Use the drop-down menu to choose whether you want the frame to *Always* or *Never* have a scrollbar. *If Needed* will add a scrollbar only if the frame's content extends beyond the visible area.

❼ **Frames Page:** Click the button to change properties for the entire frames page. For details, see *To change spacing or borders in frames pages* on the previous page.

❽ **Style:** This button can only be used if you've created style sheets for your Web site. See *Building Style Sheets and Dynamic Effects* on page 363.

CREATING AND PROCESSING FORMS 12

Forms enable you to collect information from your users by presenting them with questions, interactive option buttons, check boxes, and multiple-choice menus. The first step in setting up forms is creating the forms and adding the fields you need to collect information. As you add and edit fields within the form, you have the option of setting up data entry rules for the users. FrontPage calls this process validating the data. Once that's done, you can create a confirmation page, which provides crucial feedback to the user and cuts down on incorrect form entries. Finally, you set whether you want the form results saved as a file, email, database entry, or as part of a custom script.

Creating Forms

The fastest way to create a form is to use a template and customize it to meet your needs. FrontPage's form templates include a confirmation form and a feedback form, plus a form wizard that walks you through creating a custom form. Of course, you also can build a form from scratch.

Figure 12.1
To create a new form, choose File > New.

To create a form from a template

1. Choose File > New (Ctrl N) or click the New icon in the Standard toolbar and choose *Page* from the drop-down menu (**Figure 12.1**).

2. If you chose File > New in step 1, when the New task pane appears click *More page templates* in the *New page* section (**Figure 12.2**). The Page Templates dialog box will appear.

   or

   If you used the Standard toolbar in step 1, the Page Templates dialog box appears immediately.

3. Within the Page Templates dialog box, choose *Feedback Form* and click *OK* (**Figure 12.3**). When the page appears, save it (Ctrl S).

4. When the Save As dialog box appears, give the form page a distinctive name and title, then click *Save* (**Figure 12.4**). You're now ready to change and add form fields to the template-based form page (**Figure 12.5**). For details, see *Adding Form Fields* on page 322.

Figure 12.2 When the New task pane appears, click *More page templates*.

Figure 12.3
When the Page Templates dialog box appears, choose *Feedback Form* and click *OK*.

Figure 12.4
Use the Save As dialog box to give the page a distinctive name and title.

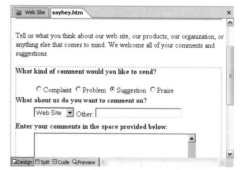

Figure 12.5 By basing your form on a FrontPage template, you can reduce the time needed to add fields.

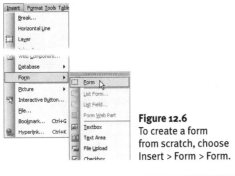

Figure 12.6
To create a form from scratch, choose Insert > Form > Form.

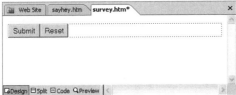

Figure 12.7 A dashed outline denotes a new form, along with a *Submit* button and a *Reset* button.

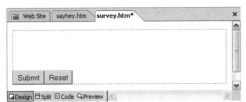

Figure 12.8 To give yourself some working space in a new form, press Enter several times.

Figure 12.9 To delete a field, right-click it and choose *Cut* from the shortcut menu.

To create a form from scratch

1. Open an existing Web page or create a new page by choosing File > New (Ctrl N) (**Figure 12.1**). If you're creating a new page, go ahead and save it (Ctrl S) and give it a distinctive name in the Save As dialog box (**Figure 12.4**).

2. Click in the page where you want the form inserted and choose Insert > Form > Form (**Figure 12.6**).

3. The form, bounded by a dashed outline, will be inserted into the page, along with a *Submit* button and a *Reset* button (**Figure 12.7**).

4. Give yourself some working space within the form by pressing Enter several times (**Figure 12.8**). You're now ready to add whatever form fields you need. For details, see *Adding Form Fields* on page 322.

To delete a field

◆ Make sure the *Design* tab is active, select the field you want to delete, and press ←Backspace or Delete. The field will be deleted.

or

◆ Right-click the field and choose *Cut* from the shortcut menu (**Figure 12.9**). The field will be deleted.

To change a field's properties

1. Make sure you're in Page view by choosing View > Page, click the *Design* tab in the main window, and then double-click the field.

2. When the field's properties dialog box opens, make your changes, click *OK,* and they will be applied to the field. For details on the dialog boxes for each field type, see *Adding Form Fields* on page 322.

Adding Form Fields

Whether you create a form from scratch or start with one of FrontPage's form templates, it's easy to add a variety of form fields to match your needs.

Figure 12.10 First create some text to identify the field for the user, then click in the form page where you want to add the field.

To add a text box

1. Click in the form page where you want to add the field, typically next to text that identifies the field for users (**Figure 12.10**).

2. Choose Insert > Form > Textbox (**Figure 12.11**).

3. When the one-line field appears in the page, right-click it and choose *Form Field Properties* from the shortcut menu ([Alt][Enter]) (**Figure 12.12**).

4. When the Text Box Properties dialog box appears, FrontPage will have assigned the field an arbitrary name, such as *T1* (**Figure 12.13**). Type in a distinctive name of your own ❶, which won't be visible to site visitors.

5. If you want some text to appear *inside* the one-line box, such as "Enter your name here," type it into the *Initial value* text box ❷.

6. Set how many characters wide you want the line to be ❸ and enter a number for the field's tab order ❹ within the form.

7. If the field will be used for a password ❺, choose *Yes*. Otherwise, leave it set to the default *No*. By the way, *Style* ❻ is used only if you're building style sheets.

8. If you want to define entry requirements for the field, click *Validate* ❼. For details, see *Text Box Validation options* on page 326.

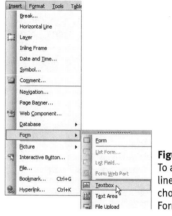

Figure 12.11
To add a single-line text field, choose Insert > Form > Textbox.

Figure 12.12
To modify any form field, right-click it and choose *Form Field Properties* from the shortcut menu.

Figure 12.13 Use the Text Box Properties dialog box to give your field a name, initial value, size, and password.

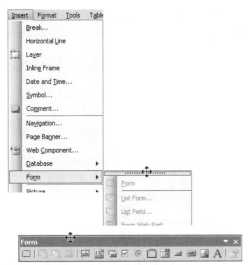

Figure 12.14 To put a separate Form toolbar on your desktop, choose Insert > Form, move your cursor to the top of the submenu, and drag it to the desktop.

9. When you're done, click *OK* and the properties will be applied to the one-line text field. To see how the field looks and decide if it needs adjustment, click FrontPage's *Preview* tab.

✔ Tips

■ If you need to resize a text box, don't bother using the Text Box Properties dialog box. Just click the box and use one of its square black handles to enlarge or shrink it.

■ If you're creating a bunch of form fields at once, you may find it easier to have a separate Form toolbar on your desktop. Just choose Insert > Form and move your cursor to the top of the submenu and drag it to the desktop (**Figure 12.14**).

Adding a text area

While a text box contains only a single line of text, a text area can be as large as you need. FrontPage will automatically add a scrollbar if the entire area is not visible on the Web page.

To add a text area

1. Click in the form page where you want to add the text area, typically next to text that identifies the field for users or asks them to enter comments in the field.

2. Choose Insert > Form > Text Area or click the Text Area icon in the Form toolbar (**Figure 12.15**).

3. When the field appears in the page, click it and use the square black handles to enlarge or shrink it (**Figure 12.16**).

4. Right-click the field and choose *Form Field Properties* from the shortcut menu ((Alt)(Enter)) (**Figure 12.12**).

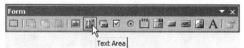

Figure 12.15 To add a text area, click the Text Area icon in the Form toolbar.

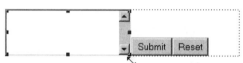

Figure 12.16 To resize a text area, click and drag the square black handles.

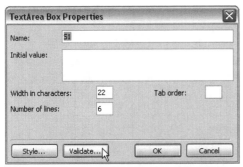

Figure 12.17 Use the TextArea Box Properties dialog box to give the field a name, initial value, and size.

5. When the TextArea Box Properties dialog box appears, FrontPage will have assigned the field an arbitrary name, such as *S1* (**Figure 12.17**). Type in a distinctive name of your own, which won't be visible to site visitors.

6. If you want some text to appear *inside* the box, such as "Enter your name here," type it into the *Initial value* text box.

7. If you aren't happy with your initial resizing, set the *Width in characters* and *Number of lines* using the text boxes. Enter a number for the field's tab order within the form.

8. If you want to define entry requirements for the field, click *Validate*. For details, see *Text Box Validation options* on the next page.

9. When you're done, click *OK* and the properties will be applied to the text area. To see how the field looks and decide if it needs adjustment, click FrontPage's *Preview* tab.

Text Box Validation options

Use the Text Box Validation dialog box to set rules for the kind of data users can enter in text boxes (**Figure 12.18**). To reach the dialog box, click the *Validate* button in the Text Box Properties or TextArea Box Properties dialog boxes (**Figure 12.19**).

❶ **Display name:** Though it sits at the top of the dialog box, this text box won't become available until after you've used the other boxes to set the data entry requirements. Once you've filled out your data requirements, you can then enter a distinctive name.

❷ **Data type:** By default, the drop-down menu is set to *No Constraints*. Use the drop-down menu to narrow the valid options for users. If you choose *Text*, use the *Text format* section to define what text will be allowed. If you choose *Integer* or *Number*, use the *Numeric format* section to define entry requirements.

❸ **Text format:** These options are available only if you choose *Text* as your *Data type*. Check which types of data you will *allow*. Check *Whitespace* to allow spaces, returns, or tabs. Check *Other* to allow such characters as punctuation marks and hyphens. Use the adjacent text box to specify which characters are allowed.

❹ **Numeric format:** These options are available only if you choose *Integer* or *Number* as your *Data type*.

❺ **Data length:** If you don't want the field left blank, check *Required*. Use *Min length* and *Max length* to ensure that users enter a number correctly (for example, a 16-digit credit card number).

❻ **Data value:** Use the check boxes, drop-down menus, and text boxes to further define what information users must enter.

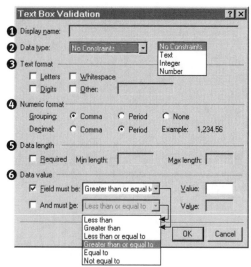

Figure 12.18 Use the Text Box Validation dialog box to set data entry rules for one-line text and scrolling text fields.

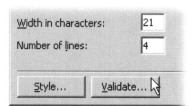

Figure 12.19 To reach the Text Box Validation dialog box, click the *Validate* button in the Text Box Properties or TextArea Box Properties dialog boxes.

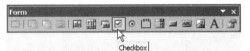

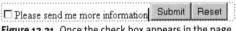

Figure 12.20 To add a check box, click the Checkbox icon in the Form toolbar.

□ Please send me more information| Submit | Reset

Figure 12.21 Once the check box appears in the page, be sure to add some explanatory text.

Figure 12.22 Right-click the field and choose *Form Field Properties* from the shortcut menu.

Adding check boxes and option buttons

Unlike text boxes in which users can enter a variety of information, check boxes and option buttons have only two states: On (checked) or Off (not checked). The main difference between check boxes and option buttons is that users can choose *several* check boxes, while option buttons force users to make *one* choice among several in a single group.

To add a check box

1. Click in the form page where you want to add the check box.

2. Choose Insert > Form > Check Box or click the Checkbox icon in the Form toolbar (**Figure 12.20**).

3. When the check box appears in the page, add text that explains the field for users (**Figure 12.21**).

4. Right-click the field and choose *Form Field Properties* from the shortcut menu (Alt Enter) (**Figure 12.22**).

(continued)

ADDING FORM FIELDS

5. When the Check Box Properties dialog box appears, FrontPage will have assigned the field an arbitrary name, such as *C1* (**Figure 12.23**). Type in a distinctive name of your own (which, by the way, won't be visible to site visitors).

6. By default, the *Value* will be *ON*. This text is not seen by the user, and you can type in any word that helps you quickly identify the user's response. In **Figure 12.23**, for example, it'd be clearer to use something like *Contact*.

7. By default, the check box's *Initial state* is *Not checked*. Choose *Checked* if you're sure most users will want the box already selected.

8. Enter a number for the field's tab order within the form and click *OK*.

9. If you want to add more check boxes, repeat steps 1–8. Once you're done, you can see how the check boxes look and decide if any need adjustment by clicking FrontPage's *Preview* tab.

Figure 12.23 Use the Check Box Properties dialog box to set the field's name and whether its default is *Checked* or *Not checked*.

CHOOSE A COLOR|

Figure 12.24 Click in the form page where you want to add one or more option buttons. Be sure to add text to prompt users to make a choice.

Option Button|

Figure 12.25 To add option buttons, click the Option Button icon in the Form toolbar.

CHOOSE A COLOR ○ Green| | Submit | Reset |

Figure 12.26 Add a label to your first option button when it appears in the form.

Figure 12.27 When the Option Button Properties dialog box appears, FrontPage will have assigned the field an arbitrary *Group name*, a *Value*, and set the *Initial state*.

Figure 12.28 Once you've typed in descriptive names for the *Group name* and the *Value*, set the button's *Initial state* and *Tab order*.

To add option buttons

1. Click in the form page where you want to add the option button, typically next to text asking users to choose among what will be several option buttons (**Figure 12.24**).

2. Choose Insert > Form > Option Button or click the Option Button icon in the Form toolbar (**Figure 12.25**).

3. When the option button appears in the form, type in some text identifying that choice (**Figure 12.26**).

4. Click where you want the next option button inserted and repeat steps 2 and 3. Continue until you've added as many option buttons as you need.

5. Right-click the first option button and choose *Form Field Properties* from the shortcut menu ((Alt)(Enter)) (**Figure 12.22**).

6. When the Option Button Properties dialog box appears, FrontPage will have assigned the field an arbitrary *Group name*, such as *R1*, a *Value* of *V1*, and set the *Initial state* as *Selected* (**Figure 12.27**).

7. Type in descriptive names of your own for the *Group name* and the *Value*. Since you want the user to pick a color, change the *Initial state* to *Not selected* (**Figure 12.28**). Click *OK* and the changes will be applied to that option button only.

(continued)

ADDING FORM FIELDS

8. Select each of the other option buttons you've created and choose *Form Field Properties* from the shortcut menu. In the Option Button Properties dialog box for each, give them the same *Group name*, a different *Value* to match the choice represented by that individual button, and choose *Not selected* as the *Initial state*. Click *OK* to close each dialog box.

9. If you want to make sure that users actually choose one of the option buttons and don't ignore them, double-click any of the option buttons. When the Option Button Properties dialog box appears, click *Validate* to reach the Option Button Validation dialog box (**Figure 12.29**). Check *Data required* and type a message in *Display name* to prompt the user. Click *OK* to close the dialog box.

10. Once you're done, you can see how the option buttons look and decide if any need adjustment by clicking FrontPage's *Preview* tab (**Figure 12.30**).

✔ Tip

■ If you create multiple option buttons and expect that most users will choose one choice over the others, set its *Initial state* to *Selected* in step 7.

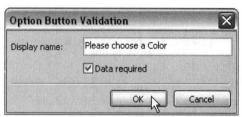

Figure 12.29 Use the Option Button Validation dialog box to enter a message to prompt users or to require a selection.

Figure 12.30 All three option buttons belong to the same group.

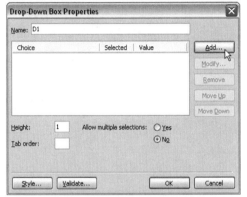

Figure 12.31 To add a drop-down box, click the Drop-Down Box icon in the Form toolbar.

Figure 12.32 When the Drop-Down Box Properties dialog box appears, click *Add* to create menu choices.

Figure 12.33 Use the Add Choice dialog box to create a menu choice, give it a value, and set an initial state.

To add a drop-down box

1. Click in the form page where you want to add the field, typically next to text that identifies the field for users or asks them to pick from the drop-down choices.

2. Choose Insert > Form > Drop-Down Box or click the Drop-Down Box icon in the Form toolbar (**Figure 12.31**).

3. When the drop-down menu appears in the page, right-click the field and choose *Form Field Properties* ((Alt)(Enter)) (**Figure 12.22**). Or double-click the field.

4. When the Drop-Down Box Properties dialog box appears, FrontPage will have assigned the field an arbitrary name, such as *D1* (**Figure 12.32**). Type in a distinctive name of your own.

5. To add choices to the drop-down menu, click *Add*. When the Add Choice dialog box appears (**Figure 12.33**), enter your first *Choice*.

6. If you want to create another name for the choice, such as a part number or shorter name, check *Specify Value* and enter it in the text box. Choose whether you want the choice's *Initial state* to be *Selected* or *Not selected*. Click *OK* and the choice will be added to the Drop-Down Box Properties dialog box.

(continued)

ADDING FORM FIELDS

7. Repeat steps 5 and 6 using the *Add* button ❷ until you have added all the choices you want (**Figure 12.34**).

8. To change, delete, or reorder choices, select each in the *Choice* ❶ list and click *Modify* ❸, *Remove* ❹, or *Move Up* or *Move Down* ❺. Set the menu's height ❻, tab order in the form ❼, and whether multiple choices are allowed ❽. For details, see *Drop-Down Box options* on the next page.

9. Once you adjust the drop-down menu, click *OK* and the changes will be applied.

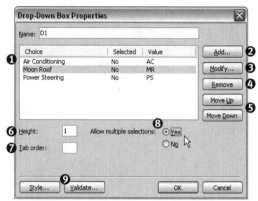

Figure 12.34 Once you've created menu choices, you can rearrange them and allow multiple selections.

Figure 12.35 The Modify Choice dialog box lets you change an item's description, value, and initial state.

Drop-Down Box options

To reach the Drop-Down Box Properties dialog box (**Figure 12.34**), right-click the field and choose *Form Field Properties* from the shortcut menu ([Alt][Enter]) (**Figure 12.22**).

❶ **Choice list:** Click any listing in the window to select it. The window displays all the drop-down menu's choices, whether they will be selected within the menu, and the shorthand value you assigned each choice.

❷ **Add:** Click to add more choices to the drop-down menu.

❸ **Modify:** To change one of your menu choices, select it in the *Choice* list and click *Modify*. The Modify Choice dialog box will appear (**Figure 12.35**), which works identically to the Add Choice dialog box (**Figure 12.33**).

❹ **Remove:** To remove an item, select it in the *Choice* list and click *Remove*. It will be deleted immediately.

❺ **Move Up/Move Down:** To rearrange your choices, select one in the *Choice* list and click *Move Up* or *Move Down*. The item will move up or down by one position.

❻ **Height:** Use the text box to set how many lines of the drop-down menu should appear in the form. If you enter a number and the list has more items than that, a scrollbar will be added to the menu.

(continued)

❼ Tab order: Enter a number in the text box to set the drop-down menu's tab order within the form.

❽ Allow multiple selections: By default, *No* is chosen. Choose *Yes* if, as in the example, you want users to be able to choose more than one item.

❾ Validate: Click to define entry requirements for the drop-down menu. When the Drop-Down Box Validation dialog box appears (**Figure 12.36**), check *Data Required* if you want users to choose at least one item from the menu. Use the *Minimum Items* and *Maximum Items* text boxes to further refine your requirements. Click *OK* and you'll be returned to the Drop-Down Box Properties dialog box.

Figure 12.36 Use the Drop-Down Box Validation dialog box to set data entry rules for the menu.

ADDING FORM FIELDS

Figure 12.37 Before you create a push button, click in the form where you want it to appear.

Figure 12.38 To add a push button, click the Push Button icon in the Form toolbar.

Figure 12.39 Use the Push Button Properties dialog box to name the button, create a label for it, and choose its type.

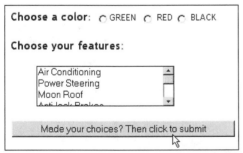

Figure 12.40 After you've created a push button, click the *Preview* tab to see how it looks.

Using push buttons

Once you've created a form using text boxes, check boxes, option buttons, or drop-down menus, you'll need to give users some way to submit their information. That's where FrontPage's push buttons, sometimes called command buttons, come in. While you can link push buttons to custom scripts, most of the time you'll be using them to have visitors submit their information or reset the form if they want to start over.

To add a push button

1. Click in the form page where you want to add the push button (**Figure 12.37**).

2. Choose Insert > Form > Push Button or click the Push Button icon in the Form toolbar (**Figure 12.38**).

3. When the button appears in the page, right-click it and choose *Form Field Properties* from the shortcut menu ([Alt][Enter]) (**Figure 12.22**).

4. When the Push Button Properties dialog box appears, FrontPage will have assigned the button an arbitrary name, such as *B1* and labeled it *Button* (**Figure 12.39**). If you like, type in a distinctive name of your own, which won't be seen by site visitors. Type in a button label, such as "Click to Submit," which will help users know what to do.

5. Choose which *Button type* you want to use. By default, the button is set to *Normal*, which is used if you plan on creating your own script that will be triggered by the button. More typically, users will be using the button to *Submit* form information or to *Reset* the form to its original, blank condition.

6. Enter a number for the field's tab order within the form and click *OK*. Your choices will be applied to the button. To see how the button looks, switch to FrontPage's *Preview* view (**Figure 12.40**).

ADDING FORM FIELDS

Creating Confirmation Pages

The idea behind a confirmation page is simple: You take some or all of the information your visitors have entered in form fields and present it back to them so they can confirm that it's correct.

While it's relatively easy to create a custom confirmation letter, FrontPage also includes a template to get you started. No matter which route you take, the confirmation pages use the *names* of your form fields to serve back to the user the values they've entered within those fields. If you get the field name wrong, the confirmation page won't work.

To create a confirmation page

1. Make sure you're in Page view by choosing View > Page, click the *Design* tab in the main window, and choose File > New > Page ([Ctrl][N]), and when the New task pane appears, click *More page templates*.

2. When the Page Templates dialog box appears, click the *General* tab, select *Confirmation Form*, and click *OK* (**Figure 12.41**).

3. When the new confirmation page appears, save it ([Ctrl][S]).

4. When the Save As dialog box appears, give the confirmation page a distinctive name and title, then click *Save*.

5. You're now ready to modify the page's text and existing confirmation fields, which are set off by [brackets] (**Figure 12.42**). You'll also notice that if you move the cursor over a pair of brackets, it turns into a hand holding a page.

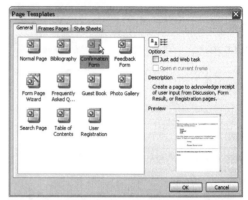

Figure 12.41 When the Page Templates dialog box appears, click the *General* tab, select *Confirmation Form*, and click *OK*.

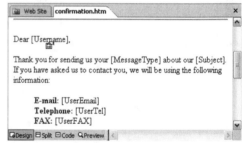

Figure 12.42 Confirmation fields are set off by [brackets] and trigger a hand-and-page icon to appear when the cursor moves over them.

Figure 12.43 To rename an *existing* confirmation field, right-click it and choose *Confirmation Field Properties* from the shortcut menu.

Figure 12.44 Use the Confirmation Field Properties dialog box to enter a field name from your form page.

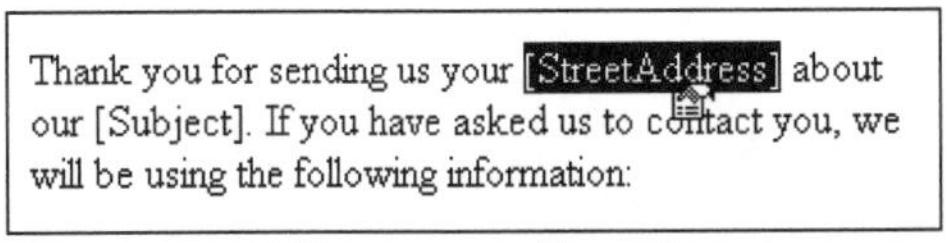

Thank you for sending us your StreetAddress about our [Subject]. If you have asked us to contact you, we will be using the following information:

Figure 12.45 Field names used in confirmation pages must exactly match those used in the form page.

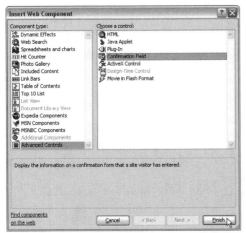

Figure 12.46 When the Insert Web Component dialog box appears, click *Advanced Controls* in the left-hand *Component type* list, *Confirmation Field* in the right-hand list, and then click *Finish*.

Figure 12.47 Give your confirmation field an easy-to-remember name in the text window and click *OK*.

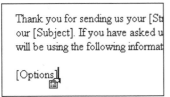

Thank you for sending us your [St our [Subject]. If you have asked u will be using the following informat

[Options]

Figure 12.48 Just like existing confirmation fields, new ones will be marked by brackets in the confirmation page.

6. To change the field name used in an *existing* confirmation field, right-click it and choose *Confirmation Field Properties* from the shortcut menu ([Alt][Enter]) (**Figure 12.43**).

7. When the Confirmation Field Properties dialog box appears (**Figure 12.44**), type in the name you assigned to a field when creating your form page. Click *OK* and the new name will appear in the brackets (**Figure 12.45**).

8. To add a *new* confirmation field, choose Insert > Web Component.

9. When the Insert Web Component dialog box appears, click *Advanced Controls* in the left-hand *Component type* list, *Confirmation Field* in the right-hand list, and then click *Finish* (**Figure 12.46**).

10. When the Confirmation Field Properties dialog box appears, type an easy-to-remember name in the text window and click *OK* (**Figure 12.47**). The confirmation field will be added to the page (**Figure 12.48**).

11. Continue adding text and confirmation fields, then save the confirmation page ([Ctrl][S]) when you're done.

✔ Tip

■ It's too bad that FrontPage does not present a drop-down menu of your form field names to jog your memory. If you can't remember a field's name, double-click it in the form page and check what's in the *Name* field.

Saving Form Results

You can save the results collected in a form as a file, email, database record, or data handled by custom scripts. Depending on your choices, FrontPage will configure what are called form handlers to save the results.

If you save the results of a form as a file, FrontPage gives you eight different formats in which to store the data. If you like, FrontPage lets you save the results as a file *and* as email, rather than forcing you to choose one or the other.

By default, FrontPage uses the Save Results Component to handle your form results. But it also includes a Discussion Form Handler and a Registration Form Handler. FrontPage also recognizes a variety of custom scripts.

To save form results to a file

1. While in Page view, right-click the form and choose *Form Properties* from the shortcut menu (**Figure 12.49**).

2. When the Form Properties dialog box appears (**Figure 12.50**), choose *Send to* ❶ in the *Where to store results* section.

3. By default, FrontPage gives the file a name and places it in your Web site's *private* folder, which can't be found by Web search engines. If you want to change the name or folder location, type a new path and name into the text box or click *Browse* if you want the results stored in an existing file.

4. Use the *Form properties* section if you want to give the form another name ❹ or if you want to set a target frame for the form ❺. For details on target frames, see *Setting target frames* on page 308.

5. Click *Options* ❻, and the *File Results* tab of the Saving Results dialog box (**Figure 12.51**) will appear with the file name already entered.

Figure 12.49
To control how form results will be saved, right-click the form and choose *Form Properties* from the shortcut menu.

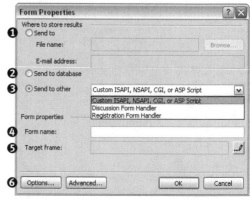

Figure 12.50 Use the Form Properties dialog box to choose whether form results are saved as a file, email, database record, or customized data.

SAVING FORM RESULTS

Figure 12.51 The *File Results* tab lets you set the file's name, format, and other details of saving the data.

Figure 12.52 The *File format* drop-down menu offers eight choices for formatting the results data.

Figure 12.53 To test and inspect a form, click the Preview in Browser button in FrontPage's Standard toolbar.

6. Use the *File format* drop-down menu ❶ to choose one of the eight text choices (**Figure 12.52**).

7. Check *Include field names* ❷ if you want to pair the values from each form field with the field's name. Unless you choose *HTML*, the *Latest results at end* ❸ box cannot be checked. By checking it, you'll put any new results at the bottom of the file.

8. If you want to create another file for the results, perhaps in another of the eight formats, use the *Optional second file* section ❹ to enter a new name or *Browse* to an existing file. The section's other choices work identically to those described in steps 6 and 7.

9. Click *OK* to return to the Form Properties dialog box. Click *OK* again and the settings will be applied to the form. To test the form, click the Preview in Browser button in FrontPage's Standard toolbar (**Figure 12.53**).

Form options

To reach the Form Properties dialog box
(**Figure 12.54**), choose Insert > Form >
Form Properties, click the Form Properties
icon in the Form toolbar (**Figure 12.55**), or
right-click the form and choose *Form
Properties* from the shortcut menu.

❶ **Send to:** Choose this option and use *File
name* to save the form results as a text or
HTML file. Use *E-mail address* and enter
an address in the text box if you want the
results saved in that form.

❷ **Send to database:** Choose this option to
save the results to a database.

❸ **Send to other:** Use the drop-down menu
to select a handler other than FrontPage's
default. Use the *Options* button to configure the custom handler you choose.

❹ **Form name:** By default, FrontPage will
assign a name to the form. If you prefer,
use the text box to type in a distinctive
name for the form.

❺ **Target frame:** Click the pencil icon to
set a target frame. For details, see *Setting
target frames* on page 308.

❻ **Options:** Click to configure the details of
how the form results will be saved.

❼ **Advanced:** Click to set Hidden fields,
which are needed only if you're using CGI
scripts to handle the form results.

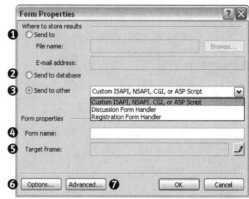

Figure 12.54 Use the Form Properties dialog box to
choose whether form results are saved as a file,
email, database record, or customized data.

Figure 12.55 To reach the Form
Properties dialog box, click the Form
Properties icon in the Form toolbar.

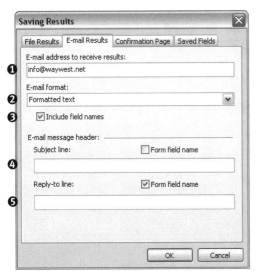

Figure 12.56 The *E-mail Results* tab lets you set the message's address, format, subject line, and reply address.

To save form results as email

1. While in Page view, right-click the form and choose *Form Properties* from the shortcut menu (**Figure 12.49**).

2. When the Form Properties dialog box appears (**Figure 12.54**), choose *Send to* ❶ in the *Where to store results* section.

3. Type into the *E-mail address* text box the address of where you want the results sent.

4. By default, FrontPage fills in the *File name* text box. If you want your results saved *only* as email, delete the name from the text box. If you want the results saved as email *and* as a file, leave the *File name* as it is.

5. Use the *Form properties* section if you want to give the form another name ❹ or if you want to set a target frame for the form ❺. For details on target frames, see *Setting target frames* on page 308.

6. Click *Options* ❻ and when the Saving Results dialog box appears, click the *E-mail Results* tab (**Figure 12.56**). The address you entered in step 3 will already be entered in the *E-mail address to receive results* text box ❶.

7. Use the *E-mail format* drop-down menu ❷ to choose one of the eight text choices (**Figure 12.52**).

8. Check *Include field names* ❸ if you want to pair the values from each form field with the field's name.

9. By default, the email's subject line ❹ would be *Form Results*. If you want something more descriptive, type it into the text box or check *Form field name* to have it appear in the subject line.

(continued)

10. Type into the *Reply-to line* text box ❺ the address you want used as the *sender* of the email. However, if your form includes a field that collects the user's email address, check *Form field name* and enter that field's name in the text box. That way the reply will go directly to the person who filled out the form in the first place.

11. Click *OK* to return to the Form Properties dialog box. Click *OK* again and the settings will be applied to the form. To test the form, click the Preview in Browser button in FrontPage's Standard toolbar (**Figure 12.53**).

Figure 12.57 The *Database Results* tab lets you port the form results to an existing or new database.

To save form results to a database

1. While in Page view, right-click the form and choose *Form Properties* from the shortcut menu (**Figure 12.49**).

2. When the Form Properties dialog box appears (**Figure 12.54**), choose *Send to database* in the *Where to store results* section.

3. Use the *Form properties* section if you want to give the form another name or if you want to set a target frame for the form. For details on target frames, see *Setting target frames* on page 308.

4. Click *Options* and when the Options for Saving Results to Database dialog box appears, click the *Database Results* tab (**Figure 12.57**).

5. Click *Add Connection* to link to your Web site's database. For details, see *Creating Database Connections* on page 348.

6. Click *OK* to return to the Form Properties dialog box. Click *OK* again and the settings will be applied to the form. To test the form, click the Preview in Browser button in FrontPage's Standard toolbar (**Figure 12.53**).

SAVING FORM RESULTS

ADDING DATABASE CONNECTIONS

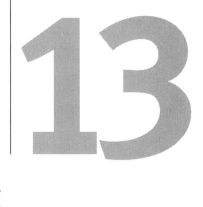

 FrontPage 2003 includes more database-related features than the previous version—but only if your Web server is running Windows SharePoint Services 2.0. If you are part of a corporate or governmental organization running SharePoint, ask your system administrators for help. For those of you working in smaller organizations, you can still connect Web pages to databases using some of FrontPage's long-standing database features. The only requirements are that your Web server include FrontPage server extensions and that it is configured to handle Active Server Pages. Most of the larger Internet service providers, such as EarthLink, offer small-business packages that include FrontPage's server extensions. Many smaller providers do so as well.

Whether your Web server is running SharePoint Services or simply using the FrontPage server extensions, the basic process is the same, and FrontPage uses the Database Results Wizard to walk you through the entire procedure. While a bit lengthy, the process involves five basic steps.

First, you create a connection, sometimes called a "view," between FrontPage and the database you want to work with. Once the connection's established, you choose the database records you want to use. The third

(continued)

step involves filtering and sorting out which fields and records will be displayed. At that point, you decide how to format the results. Finally, you have the option of displaying all the results at once or breaking them into smaller groups.

Importing Databases

Whether the database is part of your Web site or resides on a server somewhere else doesn't really matter. However, if you want to place the database on your Web site, you'll need to import it in a format compatible with FrontPage (**Table 13.1**). If the database uses some other file extension, then use your database application to export it or save it in one of the formats FrontPage supports. Once you've done that, you're ready to import the database using FrontPage.

To import databases into your Web site

1. Use Windows to navigate to the database you want to use, right-click it and choose Copy from the shortcut menu (**Figure 13.1**).

2. Switch back to your Web site in FrontPage and make sure the Folder List is visible. Right-click the Web site's folder in the Folder List and choose Paste from the shortcut menu (**Figure 13.2**). The database will be added to the Web site.

Table 13.1

Compatible Database Formats for FrontPage	
FILE EXTENSION	**FORMAT**
.MDB	Microsoft Access
.DBF	dBase, Microsoft FoxPro
.XLS	Microsoft Excel
.TXT	Tab-separated text
.CSV	Comma-separated text

Figure 13.1
To import a database to FrontPage, right-click the database and choose Copy.

Figure 13.2
Right-click your Web site folder in the Folder List and choose Paste to import a database into FrontPage.

Figure 13.3 When you add a database file to your site, FrontPage automatically asks if you want to add a database connection to the database (top) and name it (bottom).

Figure 13.4 Click *Yes* when FrontPage asks if you want to create an *fpdb* folder in your Web site.

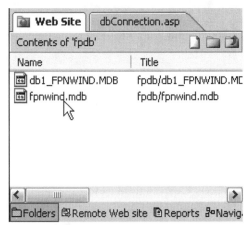

Figure 13.5 The imported database is placed inside the Web site's *fpdb* folder.

3. FrontPage will automatically ask if you want to add a database connection to the database (top, **Figure 13.3**). Give the connection an easy-to-recognize *Name* and click *Yes* (bottom, **Figure 13.3**).

4. Click *Yes* when a FrontPage alert dialog box appears asking if you want to create an *fpdb* folder in your Web site (**Figure 13.4**). The folder will be created and the imported database placed inside it (**Figure 13.5**). You can now extract information from the database through a database connection. For details, see *To create a database connection* on the next page.

IMPORTING DATABASES

347

Creating Database Connections

It's a subtle but crucial distinction: a database connection is not the same as a database. The connection acts as a view, or portal, from a Web page to the information within the database. By using FrontPage to create and configure that connection, you can control exactly which pieces of the database your Web visitors see and use. As you follow the steps detailed in the rest of the chapter, remember that you're making a *connection* with a database, not creating the database itself.

To create a database connection

1. Make sure you know the pathname or URL for the database you want to use, whether it's already part of your Web site or on a remote server.

2. Open an existing Web page and click where you want the database to appear. You also can create a new page by choosing File > New > ([Ctrl][N]) and then using the New task pane to open a blank page.

3. Once the page appears, your choice depends on which Web server setup you are using. If you're using Windows SharePoint Services 2.0 (see page 345), choose Insert > Database > Data View (left, **Figure 13.6**). If you're using the FrontPage server extensions, choose Insert > Database > Results (right, **Figure 13.6**).

4. When the first screen of the Database Results Wizard appears (**Figure 13.7**), choose the connection you want to use: a sample connection with one of FrontPage's example databases, an existing connection, connect to an external database or a new connection. For more information on creating a new connection, see page 353.

Figure 13.6 If you're using Windows SharePoint Services, choose Insert > Database > Data View (left). If you're using the FrontPage server extensions, choose Insert > Database > Results (right).

Figure 13.7 Use the first screen of the Database Results Wizard to choose a database connection.

Figure 13.8 Use the second screen of the Database Results Wizard to select a *Record source* using an existing field or to create a *Custom query*.

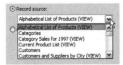

Figure 13.9 If you choose *Record source*, use the drop-down menu to select the set of records you want to use.

Figure 13.10 Use the third screen of the Database Results Wizard to edit which fields will appear. The *More Options* button lets you filter and sort the results.

Figure 13.11 The Displayed Fields dialog box lets you add, remove, or rearrange the database fields shown.

5. Once you've made your choice, click *Next* and, after a moment, the second screen of the Database Results Wizard appears (**Figure 13.8**). Decide whether you want to select a *Record source* using the existing fields listed in the drop-down list or create a *Custom query*. (Custom queries use SQL statement syntax, which falls beyond the scope of this book.) If you choose *Record source*, use the drop-down menu to select the set of records you want to use (**Figure 13.9**).

6. Once you've made your choices, click *Next* and the third screen of the Database Results Wizard appears (**Figure 13.10**). By default, all of the record source's fields will be listed for display. If you want to exclude some fields, click *Edit List*.

7. When the Displayed Fields dialog box appears, use the *Remove* button to narrow the *Displayed fields* to only those you want users to see (**Figure 13.11**). The removed fields will be listed in the *Available fields* column. Use the *Move Up* and *Move Down* buttons to rearrange the order in which the fields will be displayed on your Web page. Click *OK* when you're done and you'll return to the wizard's third screen (**Figure 13.10**). If you want to sort or filter the fields more precisely, click *More Options*. For details, see *Filtering and sorting options* on page 356.

(continued)

8. Once you've made your choices, click *Next* and the fourth screen of the Database Results Wizard appears (**Figure 13.12**). Use the first formatting drop-down menu to choose whether to display the results as a table, list, or drop-down list. Depending on your choice, the dialog box will offer additional choices for formatting the results (**Figures 13.13** and **13.14**). Use the check boxes and drop-down menus to refine the appearance of the records and click *Next*.

Figure 13.12 Use the drop-down menu in the Database Results Wizard's fourth screen to format how the results are displayed.

Figure 13.13 If you choose a list format, use the check boxes and *List options* drop-down menu to fine-tune how the results are displayed.

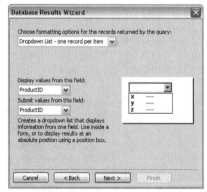

Figure 13.14 If you choose a drop-down menu format, use the dialog box's drop-down menus to fine-tune how the results are displayed.

Figure 13.15 Use the fifth screen of the Database Results Wizard to decide whether to split the results into smaller groups.

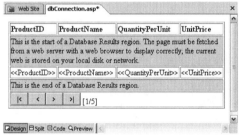

Figure 13.16 Once you've finished using the Database Results Wizard, FrontPage returns you to the now-formatted page.

Figure 13.17 When you save a page containing a database connection, FrontPage automatically assigns it an .asp suffix.

9. When the fifth screen of the Database Results Wizard appears (**Figure 13.15**), choose whether to *Display all records together* or *Split records into groups*. If you decide to split them, enter a number into the *records per group* text box.

10. Click *Finish* and you'll be returned to your page where placeholders for the database results (marked by << >>) will be displayed (**Figure 13.16**). The yellow areas mark the beginning and end of the database results and the explanatory text will not appear when the page is posted to the Web.

11. Save the page ([Ctrl][S]) and when the Save As dialog box appears, FrontPage will have automatically given the file an .asp file suffix (**Figure 13.17**). ASP (Active Server Pages) files contain scripts linked to the server where the database resides. Click *Save* and the page will be saved as a database region.

(continued)

CREATING DATABASE CONNECTIONS

12. Click the Preview in Browser button in FrontPage's Standard toolbar (**Figure 13.18**) to get a more accurate sense of how the results will look to site visitors (**Figure 13.19**). To modify the results, see *To create a database connection* on page 348.

✔ Tips

- If you have only a handful of records to display, the *Split records into groups* choice will be dimmed in the wizard's fifth screen.

- When naming your database connection (step 4), it's helpful to include Conn in the name so it's always clear that this is the connection, rather than the database itself.

- If you want to display another set of records from this same database (or a different database), you'll need to create a second database connection by repeating steps 1–11.

- If you make a mistake in setting up the database connection, you can return to the Database Results Wizard by right-clicking any placeholder and choosing Database Results Properties from the shortcut menu (top, **Figure 13.20**). When the alert dialog box appears (bottom, **Figure 13.20**), click *OK* and the wizard will reappear.

Figure 13.18 To see how the database connection will appear, click the Preview in Browser button in the Standard toolbar.

Figure 13.19 The database connection as it appears from within a Web browser.

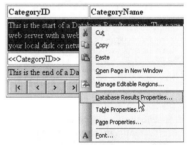

Figure 13.20 To jump back to the Database Results Wizard, right-click any cell and choose Database Results Properties from the shortcut menu (top), then click *OK* to close the alert dialog box (bottom).

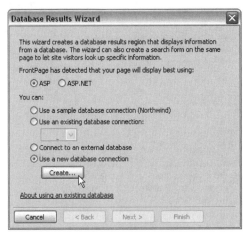

Figure 13.21 To establish a new connection, choose *Use a new database connection* and click *Create*.

Figure 13.22 When the Site Settings dialog box appears, click the *Database* tab, then click *Add*.

Figure 13.23 When the New Database Connection dialog box appears, name the connection, choose a type, and click *Browse* to find the database.

To create a new database connection

1. Click in the page where you want the database to appear and choose Insert > Database > Results (**Figure 13.6**).

2. When the Database Results Wizard appears (**Figure 13.21**), choose *Use a new database connection* and click *Create*.

3. When the Site Settings dialog box appears, click the *Database* tab, then click *Add* (**Figure 13.22**).

4. When the New Database Connection dialog box appears, type in a distinctive *Name* (**Figure 13.23**).

5. Use the *Type of connection* section to make a choice based on where the database you'll be using resides: a file-based database already on your Web site, data on a Web server, or data on a database server. For details on the choices, see *New Database Connection options* on page 355.

6. Click *Browse* to navigate your way to the database you want to use.

7. Once you find the database you're looking for, click *OK* to return to the New Database Connection dialog box, where the pathname for the database will be pasted into the text box.

(continued)

8. Click *OK* and the database connection will be listed in the Site Settings dialog box's *Database* tab (**Figure 13.24**). Click *OK* one more time, and you'll be returned to the first screen of the Database Results Wizard.

9. Click *Next* and, after a moment, the second screen of the Database Results Wizard will appear (**Figure 13.8**). To continue, see step 5 in *To create a database connection* on page 349.

Figure 13.24 Established database connections are listed under the *Database* tab of the Site Settings dialog box.

Figure 13.25 Use the New Database Connection dialog box to set up a new connection to a database.

New Database Connection options

To reach the New Database Connection dialog box (**Figure 13.25**), choose Tools > Site Settings. When the Site Settings dialog box appears, click the *Database* tab, then click *Add* (**Figure 13.22**).

❶ **Name:** By default, FrontPage will have assigned the field a generic name, such as *Database1*. When you type in a distinctive name, it's helpful to put conn at the beginning so it's clear this is a database *connection*, not the database itself.

❷ **Type of connection:** Make your choice based on the kind of database you're connecting to and where it resides.

File or folder in current Web site: Use this choice to connect to a database stored within your Web site. FrontPage will automatically create a connection for Microsoft Access databases placed on your site. For other database formats, make sure you import them in a format FrontPage supports. For details, see *Importing Databases* on page 346.

System data source on web server: Use this choice to connect to a System Data Source Name on a Web server. The data can be a file-based database or a database management system.

Network connection to database server: Use this choice to connect to a server dedicated to handling a large database, such as a Microsoft SQL Server.

Custom definition: Use this choice to connect to a custom file or query designed to retrieve the necessary data. Use this option to edit the connection string when, for example, you're using a database that requires parameters that FrontPage can't set directly.

❸ **Advanced:** Click to set up user names, and set up passwords if Web users will be connecting to a password-protected database.

Filtering and sorting options

Use FrontPage's filtering options to limit the data that Web visitors see. Use the sorting options to fine-tune how the results are displayed.

To filter or sort the database results

1. To filter or sort the database more precisely, click *More Options* in the third screen of the Database Results Wizard (**Figure 13.10**).

2. When the More Options dialog box appears (**Figure 13.26**), click *Criteria* to filter the database records or *Ordering* to sort the results.

3. When the Criteria dialog box appears (**Figure 13.27**), click *Add* to set up the filtering criteria.

4. When the Add Criteria dialog box appears (**Figure 13.28**), use the drop-down menus to select a *Field Name* and create a *Comparison* with the *Value*, then make a choice in the *And/Or* drop-down menu. Once you've set up the relationship, click *OK* and it will be added to the Criteria dialog box. Repeat until you've set up all your filtering criteria, then click *OK* (**Figure 13.29**).

Figure 13.26 To filter records, click *Criteria* in the More Options dialog box. To sort the results, click *Ordering*.

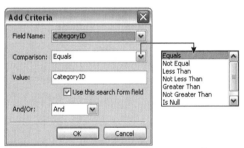

Figure 13.27 When the Criteria dialog box appears, click *Add* to set up the criteria for filtering records.

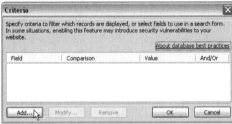

Figure 13.28 Use the drop-down menus to select a *Field Name*, set up a *Comparison* with the *Value*, and choose *And/Or*.

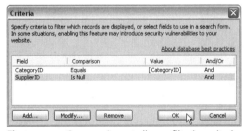

Figure 13.29 Once you've set all your filtering criteria using the *Add* button, click *OK*.

Figure 13.30 Use the Ordering dialog box to set which fields to sort and their sort order.

5. When the More Options dialog box reappears, click *Ordering* if you want to sort the database results.

6. When the Ordering dialog box appears, click listings in *Available fields* that you want to *Add* to the *Sort order* (**Figure 13.30**). To reverse the sort of any field, select it in the *Sort order* list and click *Change Sort*. Use the *Move Up* and *Move Down* buttons to rearrange the order in which the sorted fields will be displayed on your Web page. When you're done, click *OK* and you'll be returned to the More Options dialog box.

7. Click *OK* one more time, and you'll be returned to the third screen of the Database Results Wizard (**Figure 13.10**).

8. Click *Next* and, after a moment, the fourth screen of the Database Results Wizard will appear (**Figure 13.12**). To continue, see step 8 in *To create a database connection* on page 350.

Verifying a database connection

Make sure your database connection will work by first verifying it. If FrontPage verifies that the connection is correct, you're all set to publish your Web pages containing database connections. If FrontPage cannot verify the connection, probably because the database has been moved, you'll need to modify the connection. For details, see *To change a database connection* on page 359.

To verify a database connection

1. Choose Tools > Site Settings (**Figure 13.31**).

2. When the Site Settings dialog box appears, click the *Database* tab, choose an unverified connection (marked by a question mark in the *Status* column), and click *Verify* (top, **Figure 13.32**).

3. If FrontPage verifies the connection, the question mark will become a checkmark. If there's a problem, such as the database has been moved, the question mark will become a broken chain link (bottom, **Figure 13.32**). To fix a broken link, see *To change a database connection* on the next page.

Figure 13.31 To check or change your database settings, choose Tools > Site Settings.

Figure 13.32 Top: To check an unverified connection—marked by a question mark—click *Verify*. Bottom: Verified connections are marked by a checkmark, connections with problems by a broken chain.

Figure 13.33 To change a database connection, select it in the Site Settings dialog box's *Database* tab and click *Modify*.

Figure 13.34 Use the Database Connection Properties dialog box to change the connection or to find a database's new location.

Changing a database connection

If you move a database to another location, the connection to it will stop working. Fortunately, FrontPage makes it easy to change any database connection.

To change a database connection

1. Choose Tools > Site Settings (**Figure 13.31**).

2. When the Site Settings dialog box appears, click the *Database* tab, choose one of the database connections listed, and then click *Modify* (**Figure 13.33**).

3. When the Database Connection Properties dialog box appears (**Figure 13.34**), change the *Type of connection* or click *Browse* to find a database's new location.

4. Click *OK* and the changes will be applied to the database connection.

✔ Tip

■ The Database Connection Properties dialog box works identically to the New Database Connection dialog box (**Figure 13.25**). For details, see page 355.

CHANGING CONNECTIONS

To remove a database connection

1. Choose Tools > Site Settings (**Figure 13.31**).

2. When the Site Settings dialog box appears, click the *Database* tab, choose from the database connections listed, and then click *Remove*. The connection will be deleted.

3. Find any Web pages containing regions linked to the previously connected database and either delete the regions or connect them to another database by changing the connection. For details, see *To change a database connection* on the previous page.

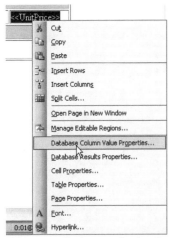

Figure 13.35 To change a database's column values, right-click the database field and choose *Database Column Value Properties*.

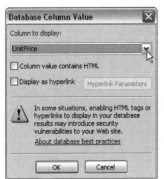

Changing column values

If you want to change the columns displayed in a database connection, FrontPage offers a quick way to do it without running the Database Results Wizard again.

To change column values in a database

1. While in Page view, right-click the database field and choose *Database Column Value Properties* from the shortcut menu ([Alt][Enter]) (**Figure 13.35**).

2. When the Database Column Value dialog box appears, use the *Column to display* drop-down menu to choose another column (**Figure 13.36**).

3. Click *OK* and the new column value will be pasted into the Web page.

Figure 13.36 Use the *Column to display* drop-down menu to choose another column.

CHANGING COLUMN VALUES

BUILDING STYLE SHEETS AND DYNAMIC EFFECTS

14

Cascading Style Sheets, known as CSS, represent a leap forward for Web designers. Before CSS came along, you had much less control over the appearance and positioning of text in your Web pages. Now that version 4 and later Web browsers support CSS, it's much easier to lay out a Web page without constantly worrying about how it looks on different computer platforms.

CSS lets you apply a set of styles across your entire Web site, which means your pages will look more consistent. It also means a whole lot less work. Want to revise a headline style? Just make the change in your external style sheet, and it's applied to the whole site. CSS is not without problems. The type formatting controls in CSS (known as CSS1) work fairly consistently in version 4 or later of Internet Explorer and Netscape Navigator. The positioning controls (CSS2) are applied less consistently. However, this is not a major problem since a browser simply ignores—rather than mangles—any CSS2 code it can't interpret.

Using Dynamic HTML, which depends in part on CSS2, you can make text and graphics fly onto your page. If used judiciously, it can give a page a bit of dramatic snap. Sometimes mistakenly called text "animation," DHTML uses a completely different process than animated graphics, which are explained in *Adding Videos or Animations* on page 237.

Since FrontPage is designed to shield you, as much as possible, from coding by hand, this chapter just focuses on what you need to get rolling. Explaining all the ins and outs of style sheets and DHTML would take another whole book or two. If you want to get down to the nitty-gritty of both, check out Elizabeth Castro's *HTML for the World Wide Web with XHTML and CSS, Fifth Edition: Visual QuickStart Guide* (Peachpit Press) and Jason Cranford Teague's *DHTML and CSS for the World Wide Web, Third Edition: Visual QuickStart Guide* (Peachpit Press).

BUILDING STYLE SHEETS AND DYNAMIC EFFECTS

Using Cascading Style Sheets

Style sheets come in three varieties: *external style sheets* control styles across multiple pages or an entire Web site, *embedded style sheets* control styles for individual pages, and *inline styles* control individual page elements. Put them all together and you have the coding rules that create Cascading Style Sheets.

With CSS you can define in one place exactly how you want all of your headings to appear on every page, right down to the size and color. At the same time, if you like, you can create a special heading style for a particular page—without disturbing your site-wide styles. That's the *cascading* part of CSS, which contains a set of definitions dictating which style takes precedence. In FrontPage, for example, if a single page contains inline styles, embedded styles, and a link to an external style sheet, the inline style comes first and the external style sheet last.

Inline styles are the least powerful of the three since their effect is confined to a single HTML element on a single page. For that reason, this chapter focuses on embedded and external style sheets.

Compared with embedded style sheets, external style sheets take a bit more work to set up. But because external style sheets can be applied site wide, they will save you hours of work in the long run. External style sheets offer another welcome bonus—faster downloads, since each page doesn't have to contain all the HTML formatting data.

To activate Cascading Style Sheets

1. Choose Tools > Page Options
(**Figure 14.1**).

2. When the Page Options dialog box
appears, click the *Authoring* tab
(**Figure 14.2**).

3. Within the *Browsers* section of the tab,
use the *Schema version* drop-down menu
to set the compatibility of your pages for
the Web browsers used by your site's visitors (**Figure 14.3**). If you want to use
Cascading Style Sheets, you need to
choose *Internet Explorer 4.0/Navigator 4.0*
or *Internet Explorer 5.0*.

4. In the *Browsers* section, also make sure
that *CSS 1.0 (formatting)* and *CSS 2.0
(positioning)* are checked (**Figure 14.4**).
Click *OK* to close the Page Options dialog
box and activate the CSS feature.

Figure 14.1 To activate CSS
or DHTML, choose Tools >
Page Options.

Figure 14.2 Click the Page Options dialog box's
Authoring tab to set which browser technologies
your pages will use.

Figure 14.3 Use the
Schema version drop-
down menu to set the Web
browser compatibility of
your pages.

Figure 14.4 To activate CSS, make sure
that *CSS 1.0 (formatting)* and *CSS 2.0
(positioning)* are checked in the lower
right of the *Authoring* tab.

Figure 14.5 To reach the Style dialog box, choose Format > Style (top) or click the Style toolbar (bottom).

Figure 14.6 To create a new style, click *New* in the Style dialog box.

Figure 14.7 When the New Style dialog box appears, type a distinctive name into the *Name (selector)* text box and pick one of the *Format* drop-down menu items—*Font*, *Paragraph*, *Border*, *Numbering*, or *Position*.

Figure 14.8 The Font dialog box is one of five available for defining a style.

Creating and Editing Embedded Style Sheets

An embedded style sheet can only be used for the single page in which it was created. To apply styles across multiple pages or an entire Web site, see *To create an external style sheet* on page 372. By the way, just in case you come across the term, embedded style sheets are sometimes called *internal* style sheets.

To create and apply an embedded style sheet

1. Make sure you're in Page view and choose Format > Style or click the Style toolbar if it is active (**Figure 14.5**).

2. When the Style dialog box appears (**Figure 14.6**), click *New*.

3. When the New Style dialog box appears, type a distinctive name into the *Name (selector)* text box and click *Format* (**Figure 14.7**).

4. Pick one of the *Format* drop-down menu items—*Font*, *Paragraph*, *Border*, *Numbering*, or *Position*—and use the dialog box that appears to choose properties for your new style (**Figure 14.8**). Once you've made one set of choices for, say, *Font*, you can use the *Format* drop-down menu to add *Border* properties.

(continued)

CREATING EMBEDDED STYLE SHEETS

5. Once you're done, inspect the results in the *Preview* area, and click *OK* (**Figure 14.9**). The new style—and any other HTML styles that you change—will be listed as a *User-defined style* in the Style dialog box (**Figure 14.10**). Click *OK* to close the Style dialog box.

6. Select the page element to which you want to apply your new style, then click the *Class* drop-down menu in the Style toolbar and select the new style (top, **Figure 14.11**). Release your cursor and the new style will be applied to the page element immediately (bottom, **Figure 14.11**).

7. To create another new style, repeat steps 1–6.

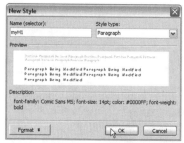

Figure 14.9 Once you've defined your new style, inspect it in the *Preview* area, and then click *OK*.

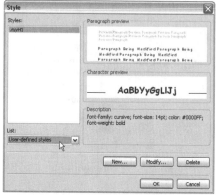

Figure 14.10 A new or modified style will be listed as a *User-defined style* in the Style dialog box.

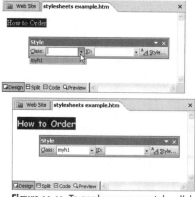

Figure 14.11 To apply your new style, click the *Class* drop-down menu in the Style toolbar and select the new style (top). Release your cursor and the new style will be applied to the page element (bottom).

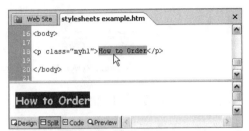

Figure 14.12 To see the CSS coding, select the page element in *Design* view, then click the *Split* tab.

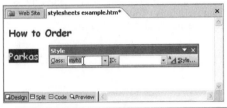

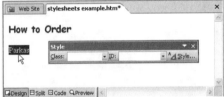

Figure 14.13 To detach a style from an element, select it, and when the style's name appears press Delete .

✔ Tips

- Use the Style dialog box's *List* drop-down menu (**Figure 14.6**) to toggle between views of *HTML tags* and *User-defined styles*. The *HTML tags* list shows all the HTML tags that also act as CSS rules. The *User-defined styles* list shows just the CSS rules you've created for the particular page.

- If you want to see the CSS coding, select the affected page element in *Design* view, then click the *Split* tab (**Figure 14.12**).

- To detach a style from an element, select it and the style's name will appear in the *Class* window of the Style toolbar (top, **Figure 14.13**). Press Delete and the style will be removed from the selected element (bottom, **Figure 14.13**).

To edit an embedded style sheet

1. Make sure you're in Page view and choose Format > Style or click the Style toolbar if it is active (**Figure 14.5**).

2. When the Style dialog box appears, use the *List* drop-down menu to find a standard HTML tag (*HTML tags*) or a style you've already created (*User-defined styles*) (**Figure 14.14**). After making your selection with the *List* drop-down menu, choose a style you want to change in the *Styles* list, and click *Modify* (**Figure 14.15**).

3. When the Modify Style dialog box appears, the selected style will be listed in the *Name (selector)* text box. Click *Format* and choose the option you want to modify from the drop-down menu (**Figure 14.16**).

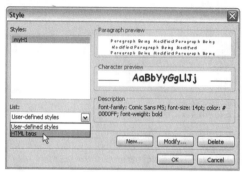

Figure 14.14 Use the *List* drop-down menu to find a standard HTML tag (*HTML tags*) or a style you've already created (*User-defined styles*).

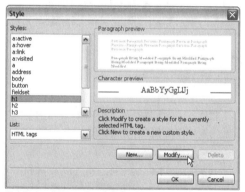

Figure 14.15 To edit an embedded style, select it in the *Styles* list and click *Modify*.

Figure 14.16 The Modify Style dialog box works just like the New Style dialog box.

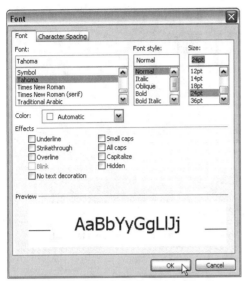

Figure 14.17 When the dialog box related to your option appears, make your changes, and click *OK*.

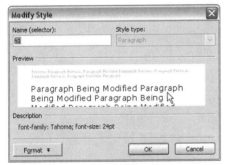

Figure 14.18 Once you modify a style, you can inspect the changes in the Modify Style dialog box's *Preview* and *Description* areas.

4. When the dialog box related to your option appears, make your changes, and click *OK* (**Figure 14.17**). The Modify Style dialog box will reappear, with the changes reflected in the *Preview* and *Description* areas (**Figure 14.18**).

5. If you want to change other aspects of the style as well, use the Modify Style dialog box's *Format* drop-down menu to make additional choices. Once you're done, click *OK* in the Modify Style dialog box and you'll be returned to the Style dialog box (**Figure 14.10**).

6. If you want to change another style, select it in the *Styles* list and click *Modify*.

7. When you're done changing styles, click *OK* in the Style dialog box and the changes will be made within the page's HTML code.

Building External Style Sheets

Using external style sheets is a three-step process: First you create the sheet, then you build it or edit it by defining its styles, and finally you link your Web site or individual pages to the sheet.

Parts of the process are similar to working with embedded style sheets, but there are some key differences. For that reason, the entire process of creating, building, editing, and linking external style sheets is laid out here in detail.

To create an external style sheet

1. Choose File > New (Ctrl N) and when the *New* task pane appears, click *More page templates* in the *New Page* section.

2. When the Page Templates dialog box appears, click the *Style Sheets* tab (**Figure 14.19**).

3. If you want to start from scratch with a blank style sheet, choose the *Normal Style Sheet*. Otherwise, choose one of the style sheet templates listed, which you can easily edit later to suit your purposes.

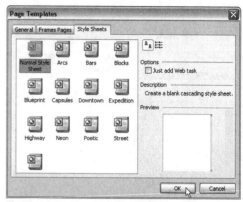

Figure 14.19 When the Page Templates dialog box appears, click the *Style Sheets* tab and choose *Normal Style Sheet* or one of the style sheet templates.

Figure 14.20 Until you add to it by defining styles, there's not much to see in a new external style sheet.

Figure 14.21 A template-based external style sheet gives you a head start by including definitions of a variety of HTML elements.

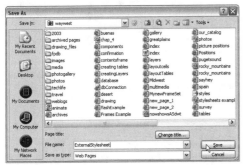

Figure 14.22 When saving and naming an external style sheet, the .css suffix will be applied automatically.

Figure 14.23 You can preview some of the template-based style sheets in the Theme dialog box.

4. Click *OK* and FrontPage will create a page, give it a .css suffix, and display the page in the main window. If it's a new style sheet, there's not much to see-even the tabs at the bottom of the main window no longer appear (**Figure 14.20**). If it's based on a template, it already will include definitions for a variety of HTML elements (**Figure 14.21**). In either case, save the page (Ctrl S). When the Save As dialog box appears, give the page a distinctive name (the .css suffix will be applied automatically) (**Figure 14.22**). You're now ready to build your new style sheet by defining styles for it. Or, if you've used a template for your style sheet, you're ready to modify the styles that already exist within it. For details, see *To build an external style sheet* on page 374 or *To edit an external style sheet* on page 376.

✔ Tips

- When creating a new style sheet, do not press Ctrl N or you'll bypass the New dialog box and wind up with a new HTML page, when what you want is a CSS page.

- While the Page Templates dialog box includes a text description of the various style sheet templates, the *Preview* area isn't available. Many of the templates, however, are based on FrontPage themes, which you can take a peek at by choosing Format > Theme to reach the Theme dialog box (**Figure 14.23**).

To build an external style sheet

1. Open the external style sheet, which will be completely blank (**Figure 14.24**).

2. Choose Format > Style or click the Style toolbar if it is active (**Figure 14.5**).

3. When the Style dialog box appears (**Figure 14.25**), select from the *Styles* list an HTML tag for which you want to create a style, and click *Modify*.

4. When the Modify Style dialog box appears, the HTML tag you selected will be listed in the *Name (selector)* text box (**Figure 14.16**). Click *Format*, then choose *Font*, *Paragraph*, *Border*, *Numbering*, or *Position* and use the related dialog box to modify the HTML tag. Your style changes will appear in the Modify Style dialog box's *Preview* and *Description* areas.

5. If you want to change other aspects of the HTML tag, use the *Format* drop-down menu to make additional choices. Once you're done, click *OK* in the Modify Style dialog box and you'll be returned to the Style dialog box where your new style will be listed in the *User-defined styles* (**Figure 14.26**).

6. To create styles for other HTML tags in your style sheet, use the Style dialog box's *List* drop-down menu to switch back to *HTML tags*. Repeat steps 3–5 until you've created styles for all the HTML tags you want.

Figure 14.24 If you're starting from scratch, a new external style sheet will be completely blank.

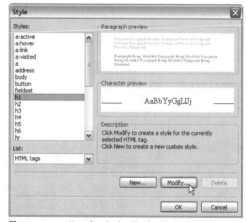

Figure 14.25 Use the *Styles* list in the Style dialog box to select an HTML tag you want to modify.

Figure 14.26 After you've defined a style, the Style dialog box will include it in the *User-defined styles* list and offer a preview.

Figure 14.27 To create a custom style in the Style dialog box, switch to *User-defined styles* and click *New*.

Figure 14.28 When creating a new style, give it a distinctive name and use the *Format* button's choices to define it.

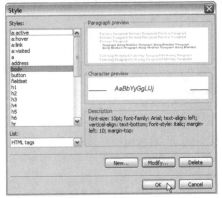

Figure 14.29 The Style dialog box will list all your new styles as you define them in your external style sheet.

Figure 14.30 After you have defined your styles, the once-blank external style sheet will list all the additions that will be applied.

7. If you want to create some new custom styles, use the Style dialog box's *List* drop-down menu to switch to *User-defined styles* and then click *New* (**Figure 14.27**).

8. When the New Style dialog box appears, type a distinctive name for your custom style into the *Name (selector)* text box and click *Format* (**Figure 14.28**).

9. Choose *Font, Paragraph, Border, Numbering,* or *Position,* and use the related dialog boxes to define your new custom style. As you proceed, the style changes will appear in the New Style dialog box's *Preview* and *Description* areas.

10. Once you're done, click *OK* in the New Style dialog box and you'll be returned to the Style dialog box where your custom styles—along with the HTML tags you modified—will be listed in the *User-defined styles* (**Figure 14.29**).

11. Once you're satisfied with your custom styles, click *OK* and the changes will be added to your external style sheet (**Figure 14.30**). Save the page ([Ctrl][S]) and you're ready to apply it to your Web site's pages. See *To link to external style sheets* on page 379.

To edit an external style sheet

1. Open the style sheet, and choose Format > Style or click the Style toolbar if it is active.

2. When the Style dialog box appears (**Figure 14.31**), select an item in the left-hand *Styles* list that you want to edit, and then click *Modify*.

3. When the Modify Style dialog box appears, the style you selected will be listed in the *Name (selector)* text box (**Figure 14.32**). Click *Format* and choose an option from the drop-down menu.

4. When the dialog box related to that option appears, make your changes, and then click *OK*. Continue clicking *Format* and choosing options from the drop-down menu until you've made all your changes.

5. Click *OK* and the changes will appear in the Style dialog box's preview windows, along with a *Description* listing the style's attributes (**Figure 14.33**).

6. If you want to change the style of another item, select it in the *Styles* list, click *Modify*, and repeat steps 3–5.

7. Once you've made all the style changes you want, click *OK* in the Style dialog box and the style sheet will list all your style changes.

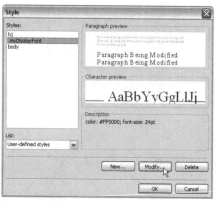

Figure 14.31 When the Style dialog box appears, select an item in the left-hand *Styles* list that you want to edit and click *Modify*.

Figure 14.32 Use the *Format* drop-down menu options to change aspects of the selected style.

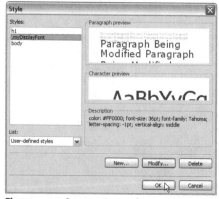

Figure 14.33 Once you've made your changes, the Style dialog box will present a preview of the edited style.

Table 14.1

Most Common Font Families		
SERIF	WINDOWS	MACINTOSH
	Times	Times
	Times New Roman	Palatino
SANS SERIF	WINDOWS	MACINTOSH
	Arial	Geneva
		Helvetica

Table 14.2

CSS Generic Font Values	
CSS VALUE	SOME EXAMPLES
serif	Times, Garamond, Bodoni
sans serif	Arial, Helvetica, Geneva, Futura
monospace	Courier, Monaco, Letter Gothic
cursive (script)	Mistral, Park Avenue
fantasy (decorative)	Copperplate Gothic, VAG Round

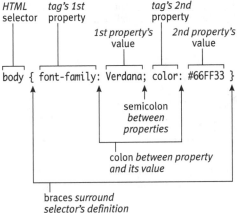

Figure 14.34 Each CSS style contains a *selector*, and at least one *property* and one *value*, which are set off by *braces*, *colons*, or *semicolons*.

Specifying Multiple Fonts in External Style Sheets

Being able to specify multiple fonts in your styles is one of the best reasons for using external style sheets. In effect, you're telling the visitor's Web browser to use Font A and, if that's not on the visitor's computer, then use Font B, and if Font B's not present, then use Font C, and so on. That way, if your Web visitor doesn't have the oh-so-cool font you've specified, at least they can see it in a font that is roughly similar.

For example, if your first-choice font family for H1 headings is a classic Oldstyle face, such as Bembo, then you'll want to specify similar looking but perhaps more common serif faces, such as Garamond and Caslon, as the second- and third-choice font families. As a backup plan for site visitors who have very few fonts on their computers, you also can include *generic* font family specifications so that their Web browsers will at least use a serif face. For a list of the most common font families found on computers, see **Table 14.1**. For a list of CSS's generic font specifications, see **Table 14.2**.

Unfortunately, FrontPage includes no way to specify multiple fonts without coding directly in the external style sheet. Fortunately, however, if you've already created an external style sheet it's pretty easy to add the multiple font specs.

Still, it's helpful to understand a little about how CSS styles are constructed (**Figure 14.34**). Each HTML element (known as a *selector* in CSS jargon) has at least one *property* and a *value* for that property. It's also possible for a selector to have several properties, and each property to have several values, such as multiple fonts.

To specify multiple fonts

1. First create a style sheet following *To build an external style sheet* on page 374, then open it.

2. When the external style sheet opens, find the font definition to which you want to add multiple fonts (**Figure 14.35**).

3. Click your cursor at the end of the first font family listed (**Figure 14.36**), immediately in front of the semicolon.

4. Type a comma, a space, and the name of a second font family you want included in the definition. Continue adding font families, preceding each with a comma and space until you've added all the font families you want specified (**Figure 14.37**). Be sure to add a generic font specification as well.

5. Save the page ((Ctrl)(S)) and you're ready to apply it to your Web site's pages. See *To link to external style sheets* on the next page.

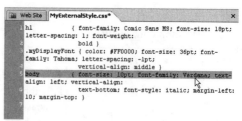

Figure 14.35 Find within the external style sheet the font definition to which you want to add multiple fonts. This example uses the *font* selector, but you also could specify multiple fonts for *h1*, *h2*, or any selector that accepts fonts.

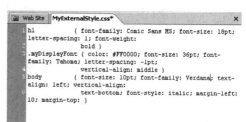

Figure 14.36 To list additional fonts, click between the font name and the semicolon.

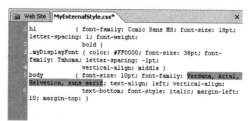

Figure 14.37 Separate each font you add with a comma and a blank space, then save the page (Ctrl)(S).

Figure 14.38 Open the page to which you want the external style sheet applied.

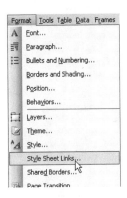

Figure 14.39 To link the page to the external style sheet, choose Format > Style Sheet Links.

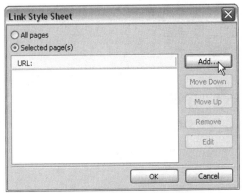

Figure 14.40 Choose *Selected page(s)* if you want to apply the style sheet to only the current page. Choose *All pages* if you want to apply the external style sheet to your entire Web site. Click *Add* to find the style sheet.

Linking to External Style Sheets

You can define an external style sheet to your heart's content, but you must link pages to that style sheet for its styles to be applied.

To link to external style sheets

1. Make sure you're in Page view and open the page you want linked to the external style sheet (**Figure 14.38**).

2. Choose Format > Style Sheet Links (**Figure 14.39**).

3. When the Link Style Sheet dialog box appears (**Figure 14.40**), choose *Selected page(s)* if you want to apply the style sheet to only the current page. Choose *All pages* if you want to apply the external style sheet to your entire Web site. Click *Add*.

(continued)

4. When the Select Style Sheet dialog box appears, navigate to the style sheet you want to use, select it, and its URL or path-name will be pasted into the *URL* text box (**Figure 14.41**). Click *OK*.

5. The external style sheet will be listed in the Link Style Sheet dialog box (**Figure 14.42**). Click *OK* and the style sheet will be applied to the page(s) you selected (**Figure 14.43**).

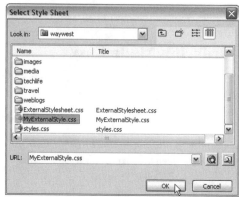

Figure 14.41 Use the Select Style Sheet dialog box to navigate to the style sheet you want to use.

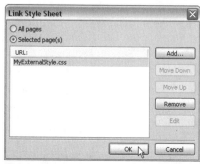

Figure 14.42 Once you've added the style sheet, click *OK* to apply it to the selected page(s).

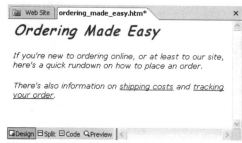

Figure 14.43 Click *OK* and the style sheet will be applied to the page(s) you selected.

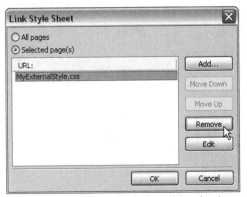

Figure 14.44 To remove a style sheet link, select it and click *Remove*.

To remove links to external style sheets

1. Open the page that's linked to the external style sheet.

2. Choose Format > Style Sheet Links (**Figure 14.39**).

3. When the Link Style Sheet dialog box appears, choose *Selected page(s)* if you want to remove the link only for the current page. Choose *All pages* if you want to remove all the Web site's links to the external style sheet. Select the style sheet in the *URL* window, and click *Remove* (**Figure 14.44**).

4. Click *OK* and the selected pages will lose the styles previously applied by the external style sheet.

Deleting Styles

Whether you're working with embedded styles or external style sheets, you can get rid of individual custom styles at any time. And if you've customized an HTML tag, such as H1, the same process will return the tag to its standard definition.

To delete custom styles

1. Make sure you're in Page view and choose Format > Style or click the Style toolbar if it is active (**Figure 14.5**).

2. When the Style dialog box appears (**Figure 14.45**), select in the *Styles* list the user-defined style you want to delete and click *Delete*. The custom style will be removed from the *Styles* list (**Figure 14.46**).

✔ Tips

■ Despite that word Delete, when it comes to standard HTML tags, this procedure is more like Undo. For example, in step 2 if you delete a custom version of a standard HTML tag, such as H1, it will disappear from the *User-defined styles* list. But it will still appear in the *HTML tags* list—just without the custom style it had previously (**Figure 14.47**).

■ When you delete a custom style, it will be removed from the *Styles* list without any warning, so check the *Preview* area to make sure you've selected the style you really want to delete.

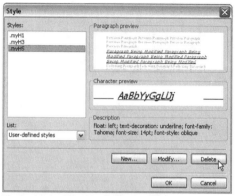

Figure 14.45 Select in the *Styles* list the user-defined style you want to remove and click *Delete*.

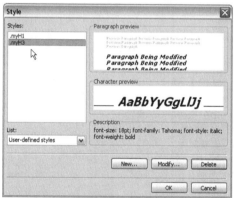

Figure 14.46 Once deleted, the customized *myH5* disappears from the *User-defined styles* list.

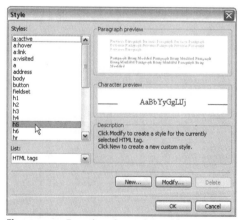

Figure 14.47 Even though you deleted its *custom* style definition, a *generic* h1 tag remains part of your list of *HTML tags*.

Figure 14.48
To apply DHTML, make sure the DHTML Effects toolbar is visible by choosing View > Toolbars > DHTML Effects.

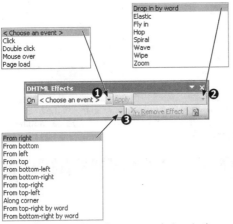

Figure 14.49 The drop-down menu choices in the DHTML Effects toolbar vary depending on which page element you select.

Figure 14.50 To apply an effect, first select a page element.

Using Dynamic HTML Effects

DHTML can be used to zip text around your pages, send graphics spiraling, and trigger events as visitors mouse around your site. The exact DHTML options available vary, depending on which elements you select on a page. In general, there are more DHTML options for text than there are for graphics. DHTML tags work with version 4 or later Microsoft Internet Explorer or Netscape Navigator browsers. Earlier browsers will simply show static—but correct—versions of your pages, which means browser compatibility is one less thing to worry about.

To apply dynamic effects

1. Make sure the DHTML Effects toolbar is visible by choosing View > Toolbars > DHTML Effects (**Figure 14.48**). The toolbar will appear (**Figure 14.49**), and you can move it to a convenient spot on your screen.

2. Select the page element to which you want to apply DHTML (**Figure 14.50**).

3. Use the toolbar's *On* drop-down menu ➊ (**Figure 14.49**) to select *when* the effect will be applied.

4. Use the toolbar's *Apply* drop-down menu ➋ (**Figure 14.49**) to select *which* effect will be applied.

5. Depending on your choice in step 4, use the *<Choose Settings>* drop-down menu ➌ (**Figure 14.49**) to further define the effect.

(continued)

6. If you want, select another page element and apply DHTML effects to it by repeating steps 3–5.

7. Once you're done setting the effects, click the *Preview* tab in FrontPage's main window to see how the effects look (**Figure 14.51**).

✔ Tip

■ If you need to adjust the effect, click the *Design* tab in FrontPage's main window, then click the toolbar and use the toolbar drop-down menus to change the settings. When you want to check the effect, be sure to click the *Preview* tab again.

To remove a dynamic effect

1. Select the page element whose effect you want to cancel.

2. Click on the DHTML Effects toolbar, then click *Remove Effect* (**Figure 14.52**). The effect will be canceled.

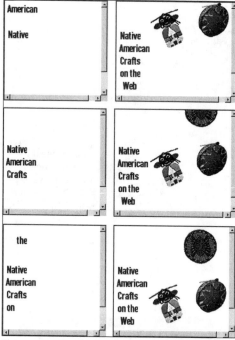

Figure 14.51 Use the *Preview* tab to see the final effect. In this example, *Drop in by word* was applied to the headline and *Fly in* to the graphic.

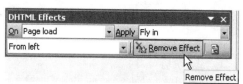

Figure 14.52 To cancel an effect, select the page element and click *Remove Effect* in the DHTML Effects toolbar.

USING DYNAMIC HTML EFFECTS

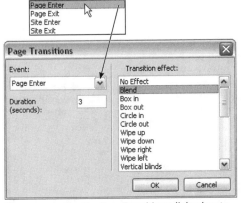

Figure 14.53 To add page transitions, choose Format > Page Transition.

Figure 14.54 Use the Page Transitions dialog box to select an *Event*, a *Transition effect*, and a *Duration*.

Using Page Transitions

This particular DHTML feature lets you create video-like transitions when a site visitor enters or leaves a page or your site. FrontPage includes more than 20 transition effects.

To add page transitions

1. Make sure you're in Page view and the *Design* tab is selected. Click anywhere in the page and choose Format > Page Transition (**Figure 14.53**).

2. When the Page Transitions dialog box appears (**Figure 14.54**), use the *Event* drop-down menu to select *when* the effect will be applied.

3. Use the *Transition effect* scrolling menu box to select *which* effect will be applied.

4. Enter a number in the *Duration (seconds)* text box to set *how long* the transition will take to complete.

5. Once you've made your selections, click *OK*. Click the *Preview* tab in FrontPage's main window to see how the transition looks.

To remove page transitions

1. Make sure you're in Page view and the *Design* tab is selected. Click anywhere in the page and choose Format > Page Transition (**Figure 14.53**).

2. When the Page Transitions dialog box appears (**Figure 14.54**), use the *Transition effect* scrolling menu box to select *No Effect*, which is the first item in the list.

3. Click *OK* and the transition will be removed.

Using Behaviors

By adding script-based behaviors to different elements of your Web pages, a wide range of actions can be triggered by a visitor's cursor movements. Examples include pop-up messages, displaying another page, showing or hiding items, and adding messages to the status bar. The best thing about FrontPage's behaviors is that you don't have to create these scripts yourself. Instead, FrontPage does it automatically based on your choices in simple point-and-click dialog boxes. In the example below, a cursor-triggered behavior is used to change the visibility of different layers, creating an interactive set of drop-down navigation menus. You'll find further exploration of the Behaviors task pane well worth the time.

To add behaviors to layers

1. Make sure you're in Page view and that the *Design* tab is selected. Now choose Tools > Page Options. When the Page Options dialog box appears, click the *Authoring* tab and make sure that the *Schema version* at the bottom is set to *Internet Explorer 5.0* (**Figure 14.55**). Click *OK* to close the dialog box when you're done.

2. Open the page with the page element you want to control and choose Format > Behaviors (**Figure 14.56**).

3. When the *Behaviors* task pane appears, select the page element to which you want to add a behavior (in this case *layer 1*) and click the *Insert* button in the *Behaviors* task pane (**Figure 14.57**). In the *Insert* drop-down menu choose Change Property (**Figure 14.58**).

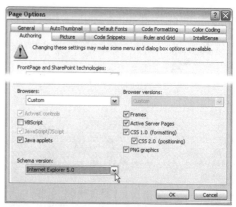

Figure 14.55 In the Page Options dialog box, click the *Authoring* tab and make sure that the *Schema version* at the bottom is set to *Internet Explorer 5.0*.

Figure 14.56 Open the page with the page element you want to control and choose Format > Behaviors.

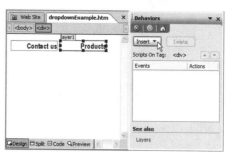

Figure 14.57 Select the page element to which you want to add a behavior (in this case *layer 1*) and click the *Insert* button in the *Behaviors* task pane.

Figure 14.58 In the *Insert* drop-down menu choose Change Property.

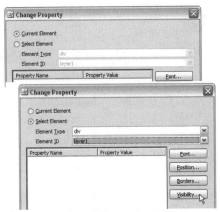

Figure 14.59 *Current Element* is selected by default (top), but choose *Select Element* instead, then choose *layer 1* in the *Element ID* drop-down menu, and click the *Visibility* button (bottom).

4. When the Change Property dialog box appears, *Current Element* will be selected by default (top, **Figure 14.59**). Choose *Select Element*, then choose *layer 1* in the *Element ID* drop-down menu, and click the *Visibility* button (bottom, **Figure 14.59**).

5. When the Visibility dialog box appears, choose *Hidden* and click *OK* to close the dialog box (**Figure 14.60**). When the Change Property dialog box reappears, the layer's *Property Value* will be listed as *hidden* (**Figure 14.61**). At the bottom left of the dialog box, select the *Restore on mouseout event* checkbox and click *OK* to close the dialog box.

(continued)

Figure 14.60 When the Visibility dialog box appears, choose *Hidden* and click *OK* to close the dialog box.

Figure 14.61 When the Change Property dialog box reappears, the layer's *Property Value* will be listed as *hidden*. Be sure also to select the *Restore on mouseout event* checkbox.

6. When the *Behaviors* task pane reappears, it will list two *Events*: *onclick* and *onmouseout* (left, **Figure 14.62**). Click the *onclick* drop-down menu and choose onmouseover (right, **Figure 14.62**). The *Behaviors* task pane will now show a pair of *Events* matched with a pair of *Actions*. In this example, *layer 1* will change its property (become hidden) onmouseover and restore its original property (become visible) onmouseout (**Figure 14.63**).

7. Save the page, select the *Preview* tab, and roll the cursor over the visible *Products* layer to see how the behavior kicks in to hide the layer (**Figure 14.64**).

Figure 14.62 The *Behaviors* task pane now lists two *Events*: *onclick* and *onmouseout* (left). Change the first by clicking the *onclick* drop-down menu and choosing onmouseover (right).

Figure 14.63 The *Behaviors* task pane now shows a pair of *Events* matched with a pair of *Actions*.

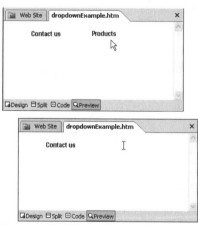

Figure 14.64 Using the *Preview* tab, you can see how the *Products* layer (top) becomes hidden when the cursor rolls over it (bottom).

USING BEHAVIORS

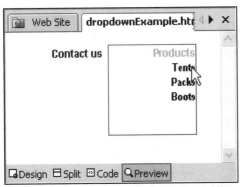

Figure 14.65 Using behaviors to change the visibility of overlapping layers, you can create a set of interactive drop-down menus.

Figure 14.66 To change the details of the action for a particular event, double-click it in the *Actions* column.

8. By repeating steps 3-7 with *layer 2* and setting its visibility so that it's normally hidden but becomes visible with an onmouseover behavior, you can create a set of interactive drop-down menus (**Figure 14.65**).

✔ Tip

■ You can change the details of the action for a particular event by double-clicking it in the *Actions* column (**Figure 14.66**) and then making your changes in the Change Properties dialog box when it appears.

PART 4

MANAGING AND PUBLISHING WEB SITES

Chapter 15:   Managing Web Site Workflow   393

Chapter 16:   Checking and Publishing
              Web Sites   417

MANAGING
WEB SITE
WORKFLOW

Like most publishing, Web publishing is usually a team sport. Writers create stories, editors proof copy and add headlines, artists produce graphics and illustrations, and designers lay it all out. Keeping track of who's doing what on a Web site can be a challenge. Sometimes even if you're doing it all yourself, it's easy to forget key tasks. FrontPage's tasks and reports views can be a big help in managing the workflow on the typical Web site with a zillion-and-one details.

You can use most of FrontPage's workflow features no matter how you're set up. Others, such as the system of checking Web files in and out (explained on page 411), will work only if your Web server has the FrontPage Server Extensions installed. For more on the extensions, see pages 417 and 437.

Creating Tasks

Essentially you have two choices in using FrontPage to create tasks: a close-focus, from-the-ground-up approach or a broader, top-down approach. Each has its place in the publishing process.

In the close-focus method, you would begin by linking specific files to a specific task, such as "create home page image maps." This works well when you already have a firm sense of exactly what work needs to be done. This is the process explained in *To link files to a task* on the next page, *To link a file to a review* on page 402, *To assign a file* on page 407, and *To start a task* on page 416.

This files-based approach, however, may not be the best in every circumstance. Sometimes you may find it more helpful to begin by broadly defining the tasks and not associating them with any particular files. Only later would you create detailed tasks linked to specific files. In those cases, the broader, top-down approach works better, especially if you want to leave it to others to figure out the actual steps needed to accomplish the broader task. This more general approach is explained in *To create a task not linked to a file* on page 397, *To assign a task* on page 405, and *To mark a task completed* on page 415.

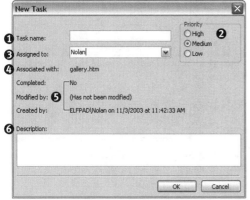

Figure 15.1 To link an open page to a task, click the New icon in the Standard toolbar and choose Task.

Figure 15.2 Use the New Task dialog box to create and assign tasks.

To link files to a task

1. Open the page to which you want to assign a task and click the New icon in the Standard toolbar and choose Task (**Figure 15.1**).

2. When the New Task dialog box appears (**Figure 15.2**), you'll notice that the current Web page will appear listed next to *Associated with* ❹.

3. Type a short description of the task or give it a name in the *Task name* text box ❶.

4. Use the option buttons to give the task a *Priority* ❷, though you can do that later if you prefer.

5. Type a name into the *Assigned to* text box or use the drop-down menu ❸ to pick from a list of previously used names. For details, see *To create a names master list* on page 404.

6. FrontPage will automatically supply the information in the middle of the dialog box ❺, so skip down to the *Description* area ❻ if you want to add any details about the task.

(continued)

CREATING TASKS

7. When you've finished (**Figure 15.3**), click *OK*. Repeat steps 2–6 to link other files with tasks if you wish.

8. Switch to the Tasks view by clicking the Tasks icon in the Views Bar and the new task will appear in the Tasks list (**Figure 15.4**).

✔ Tips

■ To launch the files you've linked to a particular task, see *To start a task* on page 416.

■ If you want to link certain files to a category instead of a task, see *To categorize files* on page 401.

■ You don't have to assign a task when you create it. Instead, you can do it any time. See *To assign a task* on page 405.

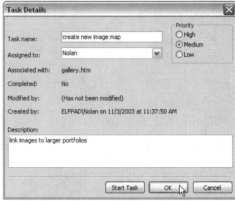

Figure 15.3 Once you've filled in the New Task dialog box, click *OK*.

Figure 15.4 Switch to the Tasks view to see a list of tasks for building your Web site.

Figure 15.5 To create a task not linked to a particular file, choose Edit > Tasks > Add Task.

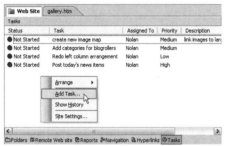

Figure 15.6 You also can create a task *not* linked to a file by right-clicking and choosing *Add Task* from the shortcut menu.

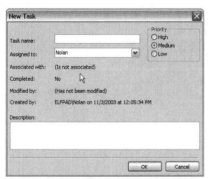

Figure 15.7 When the New Task dialog box appears, give it a name, priority, and, if you want, a description.

Figure 15.8 The new task will be added to the *Tasks* list.

To create a task not linked to a file

1. In any view, choose Edit > Tasks > Add Task (**Figure 15.5**). You also can switch to the Tasks view (View > Task or click the Web Site tab), right-click in the main window, and choose *Add Task* from the shortcut menu (**Figure 15.6**).

2. When the New Task dialog box appears (**Figure 15.7**), describe the task or give it a shorthand name in the *Task name* text box.

3. Use the option buttons to give the task a *Priority*.

4. Type a name into the *Assigned to* text box or use the drop-down menu to pick from a list of previously used names. For details, see *To create a names master list* on page 404.

5. FrontPage will automatically provide the information in the middle of the dialog box, so skip down to the *Description* area if you want to add any details about the task.

6. When you've finished, click *OK*. The new task will be added to the *Tasks* list (**Figure 15.8**). Repeat the steps to add as many tasks as you need.

✔ Tips

- Unlike in **Figure 15.2**, you'll notice that in step 2 (**Figure 15.7**) the *Associated with* line says *(Is not associated)*. That tells you that the task you're creating or editing is a freestanding one that's not linked with any file.

- You don't have to assign a task when you create it. Instead, you can do it any time. See *To assign a task* on page 405.

Organizing Files

FrontPage helps you organize your Web files with several labeling options. By labeling files by category, for example, you could create a Redesign category for all the files related to the upcoming redesign of your Web site. You can use whatever categories make sense: organizational categories, such as Production; product categories, such as New Widgets. The categories do not appear on the Web site itself, just in FrontPage's reports view.

FrontPage also includes another labeling choice, which it calls *review status*, for marking files that should be checked before they're published. By building your own master list of review procedures or mileposts, you can use the reports view to quickly see whether files and pages have been checked over by others on your Web site team. Before you begin labeling files by category or review status, it will speed your work if you first create a master list for each.

Figure 15.9
To create any master list for a file, right-click the file and choose *Page Properties* from the shortcut menu.

Figure 15.10 Use the buttons in the *Workgroup* tab to create master lists.

Figure 15.11
Use the Master Category List dialog box to add or remove file categories.

Figure 15.12 The new categories you create will be added to the *Available categories* list.

To create a categories master list

1. Right-click any open page and choose *Page Properties* from the shortcut menu (**Figure 15.9**).

2. Click the *Workgroup* tab in the dialog box that appears (**Figure 15.10**).

3. Click the *Categories* button to reach the Master Category List dialog box (**Figure 15.11**).

4. Type a category into the *New category* text box and click *Add*. The name will be added to the dialog box's existing list.

5. Repeat step 4 until you've added all the categories you want to the list.

6. Click *OK* and the categories will be added to the *Available categories* scrolling text box under the *Workgroup* tab (**Figure 15.12**). To label files by category, see *To categorize files* on page 401.

✔ Tips

- To remove a category from the master list, select one in the dialog box's list, and click *Remove* (**Figure 15.11**). The category will be removed.

- If you change your mind while changing categories in the master list, click *Reset* and the list will return to how it was before you opened it.

CREATING MASTER LISTS

399

To create a review status master list

1. Right-click any file in the Folder List or under the *Web Site* tab and choose *Properties* from the shortcut menu (**Figure 15.13**).

2. Click the *Workgroup* tab in the dialog box that appears, then click the *Statuses* button (**Figure 15.14**).

3. When the Review Status Master List dialog box appears, type a category into the *New review status* text box and click *Add* (**Figure 15.15**). The new review procedure will be added to the dialog box's existing list.

4. Repeat step 3 until you've added all the review procedures you want to the list. Click *OK* and they will be available in any of FrontPage's review status drop-down menus. For details, see *To link a file to a review* on page 402.

✔ Tips

- To remove a review procedure from the master list, select one in the dialog box's list, and click *Remove* (**Figure 15.15**). The review procedure will be removed.

- If you change your mind while adding or deleting review procedures, click *Reset* and the list will return to how it was before you opened it.

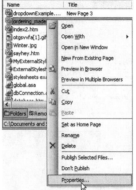

Figure 15.13
To create a review status master list, right-click any file in the Folder List or under the *Web Site* tab and choose *Properties*.

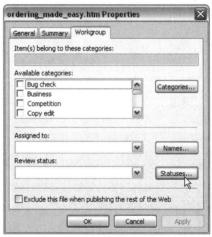

Figure 15.14 Click the *Statuses* button to build a review status master list.

Figure 15.15 Use the Review Status Master List dialog box to add or remove review procedures for files.

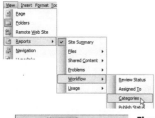

Figure 15.16 To categorize files, choose View > Reports > Workflow > Categories (top), or if the Reports view is active, click the *Site Summary* tab and choose Workflow > Categories (bottom).

Figure 15.17 To categorize multiple files at once, Ctrl-click them and then right-click and choose Properties from the shortcut menu.

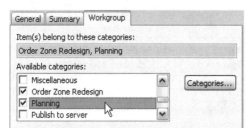

Figure 15.18 Check the categories you want applied to the file(s) within the *Available categories* scrolling text box.

To categorize files

1. Choose View > Reports > Workflow > Categories or, if the Reports view is active, click the *Site Summary* tab and choose Workflow > Categories (**Figure 15.16**).

2. When the Categories report appears, right-click the file you want categorized and choose Properties from the shortcut menu. To categorize multiple files at once, Ctrl-click them and then right-click and choose Properties from the shortcut menu (**Figure 15.17**).

3. Click the *Workgroup* tab in the dialog box that appears, then, in the *Available categories* scrolling text box, check off the category boxes you want applied to the file(s) (**Figure 15.18**). As you check boxes, the categories will be added to the *Item(s) belong to these categories* text box.

4. Click *OK* and the chosen categories will be applied to the file(s) (**Figure 15.19**).

✔ Tip

- You can apply *multiple* categories to a *single* file.

Figure 15.19 Multiple categories can be applied to a single file or multiple files.

CATEGORIZING FILES

To link a file to a review

1. Choose View > Reports > Workflow > Review Status (**Figure 15.20**).

2. When the Review Status report appears, click in the *Review Status* column of any file you want linked to a review, and a drop-down menu, with the first line blank, will appear (**Figure 15.21**).

3. Use the drop-down menu to link an existing review procedure to the file or type a new procedure into the text box (**Figure 15.22**).

4. Release the cursor and press [Enter] to link the file and the review step (**Figure 15.23**). Repeat until you've linked reviews to all the files you need (**Figure 15.24**).

✔ Tips

- Once a file has been reviewed, use the Review Status drop-down menu in step 3 to select the next necessary review. Or press [←Backspace] to clear the menu if all the necessary reviews of the file have been completed.

- Speed up the process by creating a master list of review procedures ahead of time. See page 400 for details.

- A file can only have one review status linked to it at a time, which makes sense if you think of the file as needing to clear a sequence of review hurdles: first this, then that, then the final OK.

Figure 15.20 Choose View > Reports > Workflow > Review Status.

Figure 15.21 Click in the *Review Status* column of any file you want linked to a review, and a drop-down menu, with the first line blank, will appear.

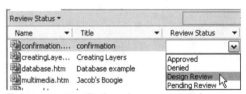

Figure 15.22 Use the drop-down menu to link a review procedure to a file or type a new procedure into the text box.

Figure 15.23 Once a file's linked to a review procedure, the procedure will be listed in the Review Status report.

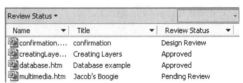

Figure 15.24 By creating a series of review procedures, you can quickly see the progress of work.

LINKING FILES

Figure 15.25 Use the *Review status* drop-down menu to apply a procedure to multiple files.

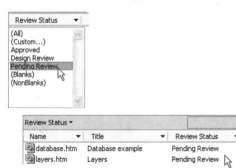

Figure 15.26 Make a choice in the Review Status drop-down menu (top) to find all items with the same status (bottom).

To simultaneously link multiple files to a review

1. Choose View > Reports > Workflow > Review Status (**Figure 15.20**).

2. When the Review Status report appears, select multiple files by pressing Ctrl as you click each file in the list.

3. Right-click the selected files and choose *Properties* from the shortcut menu.

4. Click the *Workgroup* tab in the dialog box that appears and type a status name into the *Review status* text box or use the drop-down menu (**Figure 15.25**).

5. Click *OK* and the review status procedure will be assigned to all the selected files.

✔ Tip

- You can find all items with the same status by making a choice in the Review Status drop-down menu (**Figure 15.26**). Since every column in the Reports view has the same sort of drop-down menu, you can quickly find almost anything.

Assigning Tasks

FrontPage lets you assign tasks to a specific person or workgroup. It also lets you assign particular files to a person or workgroup. For example, you can assign all the image files to the art department. While it's common to assign a task as you create it, you also can assign it—or reassign it—later.

While FrontPage lets you create names for assignments one at a time, sometimes it's faster to go ahead and create a master list of people involved in a project. That way, any time you click an assignment drop-down menu, every name you need will appear.

To create a names master list

1. Right-click any file in the main window or in the Folder List and choose *Page Properties* from the shortcut menu (**Figure 15.9**).

2. Click the *Workgroup* tab in the dialog box that appears, then click the *Names* button (**Figure 15.27**).

3. When the Usernames Master List dialog box appears, type a name into the *New username* text box and click *Add* (**Figure 15.28**). The name will be added to the dialog box's existing list.

4. Repeat step 3 until you've added all the names you want to the list. Click *OK* and the added names will be available in any of FrontPage's name drop-down menus.

✔ Tips

■ To remove a name from the master list, click a name in the dialog box, then click *Remove* (**Figure 15.29**). The name will be removed from the name drop-down menus.

■ If you change your mind while changing names in the master list, click *Reset* and the list will return to how it was before.

Figure 15.27 To create a names master list, click the *Names* button in the dialog box's *Workgroup* tab.

Figure 15.28 The Usernames Master List dialog box lets you add the names of people working on your site.

Figure 15.29 To remove a name from the master list, select it and click *Remove*.

ASSIGNING TASKS

Figure 15.30 To assign a task, click in the *Assigned To* column and a drop-down menu will appear.

Figure 15.31 Choose a name from the drop-down menu and press Enter to assign a task.

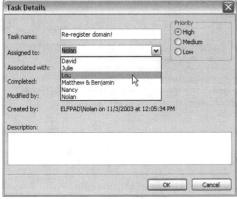

Figure 15.32 If you're in Tasks view and want to change an assignment, double-click a task to jump straight to the Task Details dialog box.

To assign a task

1. Switch to the Reports view and click in the *Assigned To* column of the task you want to assign. A drop-down menu, with the first line blank, will appear (**Figure 15.30**).

2. Use the drop-down menu to assign a name or type a new name into the text box.

3. Release the cursor and press Enter to apply the assignment (**Figure 15.31**).

✔ Tip

- If you're in Tasks view, you also can double-click the task and make your assignment changes in the Task Details dialog box (**Figure 15.32**).

ASSIGNING TASKS

To reassign a task

1. Switch to the Tasks view and click in the *Assigned To* column of the task you want to reassign (**Figure 15.33**). A drop-down menu will appear, listing everyone who has been assigned tasks so far.

2. Use the drop-down menu to assign another name to the task or type a new name into the text box (**Figure 15.34**).

3. Release the cursor and press Enter to apply the reassignment (**Figure 15.35**).

Figure 15.33 To reassign a task, click in the *Assigned To* column of the task you want to reassign.

Figure 15.34 Use the drop-down menu to assign another name to the task or type a new name into the text box.

Figure 15.35 Press Enter to apply a reassignment in the *Review Status* view of the Tasks list.

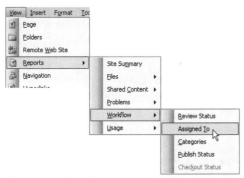

Figure 15.36 To assign a task, choose View > Reports > Workflow > Assigned To.

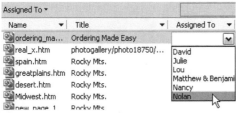

Figure 15.37 Click in the *Assigned To* column and use the drop-down menu to assign a name or type a new name into the text box.

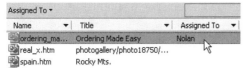

Figure 15.38 Press Enter to apply the assignment to the file.

To assign a file

1. Choose View > Reports > Workflow > Assigned To (**Figure 15.36**).

2. When the Assigned To list appears, click in the *Assigned To* column of any file you want assigned, and a drop-down menu, with the first line blank, will appear (**Figure 15.37**).

3. Use the drop-down menu to assign a name or type a new name into the text box.

4. Release the cursor and press Enter to apply the file assignment (**Figure 15.38**). Repeat until you've assigned all the files you need.

✔ Tip

■ By creating a master list of names, you can speed up the assignment process. See page 404 for details.

Editing Tasks

As noted earlier, FrontPage lets you change many aspects of a task after you've created it. You can make multiple changes within the Task Details dialog box or change individual aspects directly within the Tasks list.

To make multiple changes to a task

1. Switch to Tasks view, right-click the task you want to change, and choose *Edit Task* from the shortcut menu (**Figure 15.39**).

2. When the Task Details dialog box appears (**Figure 15.32**), use the *Task name* text box to rename the task.

3. Use the option buttons to give the task a new *Priority*.

4. Type a new name into the *Assigned to* text box or use the drop-down menu to pick from the other names listed.

5. Use the *Description* area to change any details about the task.

6. Click *OK* and the changes will be applied to the task.

✔ Tip

■ To quickly reach the Task Details dialog box (**Figure 15.32**), just double-click the task in the Tasks List.

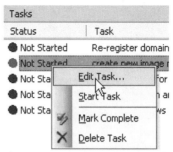

Figure 15.39 To edit a task, right-click it and choose *Edit Task* from the shortcut menu.

Tasks
Status
Task
Assigned To
Not Started
Re-register domain!
Lou
Not Started
create new image map
Nolan
Not Started
Add categories for blogrollers
Nolan
Not Started
Redo left column arrangement
Nolan
Not Started
Post today's news items
Nolan

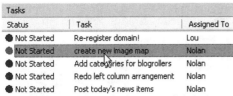

Figure 15.40 To change a task's name, click the item and when it becomes highlighted, type in a new name.

Tasks
Status
Task
Assigned To
Not Started
Re-register domain!
Lou
Not Started
create new image map
Nolan
Not Started
Add categories for blogrollers
Nolan
Not Started
Redo left column arrangement
Nolan
Not Started
Post today's news items
Nolan

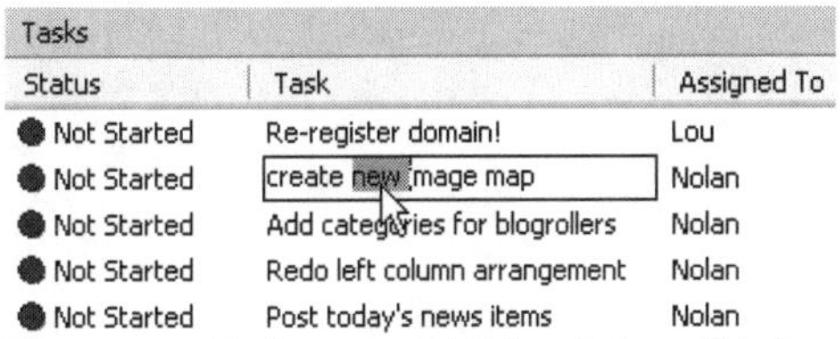

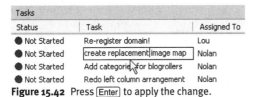

Figure 15.41 To change a task's description, click the item and when it becomes highlighted, type in a new description.

Tasks
Status
Task
Assigned To
Not Started
Re-register domain!
Lou
Not Started
create replacement image map
Nolan
Not Started
Add categories for blogrollers
Nolan
Not Started
Redo left column arrangement
Nolan

Figure 15.42 Press Enter to apply the change.

To change a task's name or description

1. Switch to the Tasks view and click the task name or description you want to change.
2. When the item becomes highlighted, type in a new name (**Figure 15.40**) or description (**Figure 15.41**).
3. Press Enter and the change will be applied (**Figure 15.42**).

✔ Tip

- If a task is listed in the *Status* column as *Completed*, you cannot change its name. However, you can change its description.

To change a task's priority

1. Switch to the Tasks view and click *once* in the *Priority* column on the task you want to change.

2. When the task becomes highlighted, click the item's priority once more. A drop-down menu will appear.

3. Use the drop-down menu to change the item's priority (**Figure 15.43**). Press ⏎Enter and the new priority will be applied.

To sort tasks

1. Switch to the Tasks view by choosing View > Tasks or, if the *Web Site* tab is visible, click *Tasks* in the status bar (**Figure 15.44**).

2. Click any column label to sort the Tasks list by that column's value (**Figure 15.45**).

✔ Tip

- To reverse the sort order of any column, click the column label a second time (**Figure 15.46**).

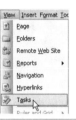

Figure 15.43 To change a task's priority, use the *Priority* column's drop-down menu.

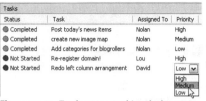

Figure 15.44 Switch to the Tasks view by choosing View > Tasks (top) or, if the *Web Site* tab is visible, click *Tasks* in the status bar (bottom).

Figure 15.45 Click the column labels to sort the Tasks list by, for example, *Status* (top) or *Assigned To* (bottom).

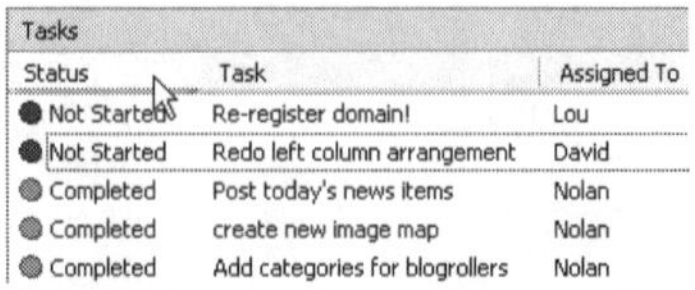

Figure 15.46 To reverse the sort order of any column, click the column label a second time.

Figure 15.47 To activate the checkout system, choose Tools > Site Settings.

Figure 15.48 Click the Site Settings dialog box's *General* tab and check *Use document check-in and check-out*.

Figure 15.49 When the alert dialog box appears, click *Yes*. The recalculating only takes a few seconds.

Using the Checkout System

FrontPage's checkout system offers a handy way to coordinate all the work being done on different files for your Web site. While a file is checked out, it cannot be changed by anyone else—a process known as source control. Others can read the last version of the file but cannot make any changes until the file is checked back in. When a file is checked back in, FrontPage saves any changes made to the file. New to FrontPage 2003 is the ability to check out files from your local Web site or from the Web server running your published site.

To activate the checkout system

1. Choose Tools > Site Settings (**Figure 15.47**).

2. When the Site Settings dialog box appears, click the *General* tab and check *Use document check-in and check-out* (**Figure 15.48**). You then need to decide whether to control the check out of the files from your *Remote Web Site*, where the site is published, or from your *Local Web Site*, before the files are actually published to your Web server.

3. Click *OK* and when the alert dialog box appears, click *Yes* (**Figure 15.49**). Checkout control will be applied to the Web site.

✔ Tip

- When activating the checkout system, be sure to check *Prompt to check out file when opening a page* (**Figure 15.48**). Otherwise, group members can check out a file without others realizing it.

To check out a file

1. While in Folders or Reports view (or with the Folder List visible), right-click the file you want to use, and choose *Check Out* from the shortcut menu (**Figure 15.50**).

2. A red checkmark will be placed next to the file, preventing anyone else from making changes to the file while it's checked out (**Figure 15.51**).

✔ Tip

■ If you try to check out a file that's already been checked out, a dialog box will remind you and give you the choice of opening the file in read-only mode (*Yes*) or canceling your request (*No* or *Cancel*) (**Figure 15.52**).

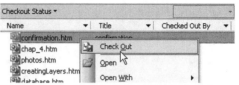

Figure 15.50 To check out a file, right-click it and choose *Check Out* from the shortcut menu.

Figure 15.51 Files in use are marked with a checkmark.

Figure 15.52 If you try to open a file that's in use, an alert box reminds you and asks what you want to do.

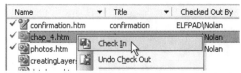

Figure 15.53 Right-click on the file you want to check back in and choose *Check In* from the shortcut menu.

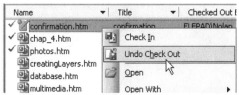

Figure 15.54 If you check out a file and want to check it back in without making any changes, right-click the file and choose *Undo Check Out*.

To check in a file

1. Make sure to first save your changes to the file you've checked out (Ctrl S).

2. While in Folders or Reports view (or with the Folder List visible), right-click on the file you want to check back in and choose *Check In* from the shortcut menu (**Figure 15.53**). The file will now be available for others to check out and change, as denoted by the disappearance of the red checkmark.

✔ Tip

■ Suppose you check out a file, make some changes, and then decide you don't want to make those changes after all. To check the file back in *without* saving those changes, right-click the file you've checked out and choose *Undo Check Out* from the shortcut menu (**Figure 15.54**). The file will be checked back in without being changed.

To see a list of checked-out files

1. To quickly see which files are checked out and by whom, choose View > Reports > Workflow > Checkout Status (**Figure 15.55**).

2. When the Checkout Status report appears, files *you* have checked out will be marked by a checkmark, while those checked out by others will be marked with a lock (**Figure 15.56**).

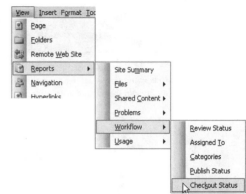

Figure 15.55 To see which files are checked out, choose View > Reports > Workflow > Checkout Status.

Figure 15.56 In the Checkout Status report, files you're using show a checkmark. Files in use by others show a lock.

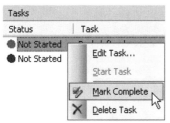

Figure 15.57 Once a task is finished, switch to Tasks view, right-click the task, and choose *Mark Complete*.

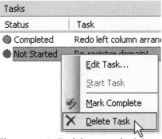

Figure 15.58 To delete a task, right-click the task, and choose *Delete Task*.

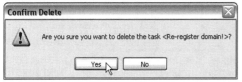

Figure 15.59 When you try to delete a task, a Confirm Delete dialog box will ask you to confirm your decision.

Completing Tasks

It's fine to assign, sort, and categorize tasks, but at some point you want to get them done. For general tasks not associated with any file, you can mark the task completed or delete it. For tasks with files linked to them, FrontPage offers another choice—Start Task—which launches the files tied to the task, even if they use another application. Once a file's ready to be published, see *To check or change a page's publishing status* on page 420.

To mark a task completed

◆ While in Tasks view, right-click a task that's been finished and choose *Mark Complete* from the shortcut menu (**Figure 15.57**). The task's status will change to *Completed* and the task's bullet will turn green.

To delete a task

1. While in Tasks view, right-click the task you want to delete and choose *Delete Task* from the shortcut menu (**Figure 15.58**).

2. When the Confirm Delete dialog box appears, click *Yes* (**Figure 15.59**). The task will be deleted, although any *files* associated with it will remain on your Web site.

COMPLETING TASKS

To start a task

◆ While in Tasks view, right-click a task whose linked files you want to work on and choose *Start Task* from the shortcut menu (**Figure 15.60**). The files associated with the task will open and, if they use another application, that program also will be launched.

✔ Tip

■ You also can start a task by double-clicking it and, when the Task Details dialog box appears, clicking the *Start Task* button (**Figure 15.61**).

Figure 15.60 If files are linked to a task, right-click the task, choose *Start Task*, and the files will open.

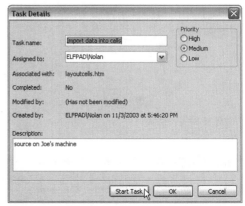

Figure 15.61 You also can open a file linked to a task by double-clicking the task and clicking *Start Task* in the Task Details dialog box.

CHECKING AND PUBLISHING WEB SITES

16

Two crucial steps remain before you actually copy your local files over to a Web server. First, use FrontPage to analyze if any pages have problems, such as broken hyperlinks or slow-to-download files. Second, look at every page with a Web browser to check its general appearance.

When you're ready to publish, you'll need to have an Internet Service Provider (ISP) lined up to host your site, unless you're copying the files to an inhouse intranet. Your ISP's Web server does not need the FrontPage Server Extensions for your Web site's essential features to work properly. However, some of FrontPage's advanced bells and whistles will not be available unless the extensions are installed on the server. The FrontPage features that require the extensions to work include most of the custom form handlers and many of the components found in the Insert menu. The extensions, which act as translators between your Web site and the Web server, are on your FrontPage installation disc. They also can be downloaded for free from www.microsoft.com/frontpage/

To take full advantage of all FrontPage's features, your Web server should be running Microsoft Windows Server 2003 with Microsoft Windows SharePoint Services. Check with your ISP to see what server services they offer.

Checking Your Site

FrontPage's reporting tools make it much easier and faster to get your site ready to publish. Instead of depending on your Web browser to find every problem, FrontPage provides a site summary of possible problems. The reports feature also lets you mark any pages on the site that you do not want published yet, avoiding the all-too-common problem of accidentally publishing pages prematurely.

To check and fix your site

1. Choose View > Reports > Site Summary (left, **Figure 16.1**). Or if the Reports view is already visible, click the drop-down menu below the *Web Site* tab and choose Site Summary (right, **Figure 16.1**).

2. When the Site Summary appears in FrontPage's main window, it will list general site information and any problems (**Figure 16.2**).

3. If the summary lists problems, such as *Broken hyperlinks*, double-click that line in the report to see a list of the problem pages.

4. To fix an individual page in the list, double-click it and the appropriate dialog box will appear, allowing you to fix the problem (**Figure 16.3**).

5. Repeat steps 2–4 until you've fixed all the problems.

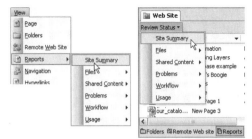

Figure 16.1 To check your Web site for problems, choose View > Reports > Site Summary (left) or, if the Reports view is already visible, click the drop-down menu below the *Web Site* tab and choose Site Summary (right).

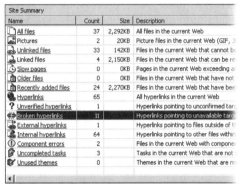

Figure 16.2 The Site Summary provides a detailed overview of your site's problems. Double-click any line for details.

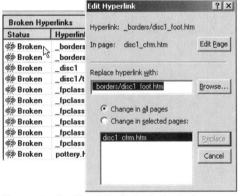

Figure 16.3 Double-click a listing in the Broken Hyperlinks report and the Edit Hyperlink dialog box will appear, enabling you to fix the link.

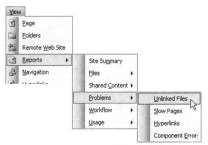

Figure 16.4 To examine a particular problem, choose View > Reports > Problems and pick the relevant command in the submenu.

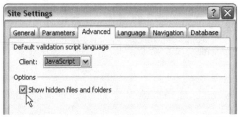

Figure 16.5 To see hidden folders, check *Show hidden files and folders* under the *Advanced* tab.

✔ Tips

■ To return to the Site Summary after you've double-clicked to an individual problem report, click the drop-down menu below the *Web Site* tab and choose Site Summary.

■ If you want to check for a particular problem, such as broken links, choose View > Reports > Problems and pick the relevant command in the submenu (**Figure 16.4**).

■ By default, any files placed inside hidden folders (those preceded by an underscore, such as the *_private* folder) will not appear in the Site Summary or problem reports. To have those files show up in reports, choose Tools > Site Settings, then click the *Advanced* tab, and check *Show hidden files and folders* (**Figure 16.5**).

Marking pages to publish

Running a quick check of the publishing status of your site's pages gives you a chance to mark pages that are not yet ready for public viewing. It also enables you to switch pages you previously marked *Don't Publish* to *Publish* if you have finished working on them. Running the review doesn't do anything to actually prepare the pages for publication. It's just meant to help keep you from accidentally publishing pages prematurely by highlighting which pages are set to be published.

To check or change a page's publishing status

1. Choose View > Reports > Workflow > Publish Status, or if the Reports view is already visible, click the drop-down menu below the *Web Site* tab and choose Workflow > Publish Status (**Figure 16.6**).

2. FrontPage's main window will switch to the Reports view and show the publishing status of all your site's files (**Figure 16.7**). If you spot pages whose status you want to switch, click in the page's *Publish* column and use the drop-down menu to change its status (**Figure 16.8**).

✔ Tip

■ To change more than one page at a time, press Ctrl as you click pages in the Publish Status report, then right-click the selected pages, and choose *Properties* from the shortcut menu (**Figure 16.9**). When the Properties dialog box appears for the page(s), click the *Workgroup* tab and check (or uncheck) *Exclude this file when publishing the rest of the Web* at the bottom of the dialog box (**Figure 16.10**). Click *OK* and the status changes will be applied.

Figure 16.6 If the Reports view is already visible, click the drop-down menu below the *Web Site* tab and choose Workflow > Publish Status.

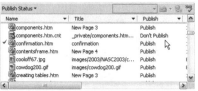

Figure 16.7 The *Publish Status* report shows which Web pages are and aren't marked for publishing.

Figure 16.8 Use the *Publish* column's drop-down menu to change a page's status.

Figure 16.9 To change the publishing status of several pages, right-click them in the *Publish Status* report and choose *Properties* from the shortcut menu.

Figure 16.10 Check (or uncheck) the *Exclude this file* box to change the publishing status of the selected pages.

Figure 16.11 To add meta tags to a page, first choose File > Properties.

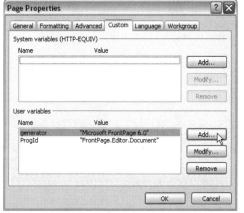

Figure 16.12 Click *Add* under the *User variables* section of the *Custom* tab to create a new meta tag.

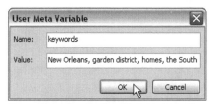

Figure 16.13 Use the User Meta Variable dialog box to add keywords to your meta tags.

Adding Meta Tags for Search Engines

Meta tags are bits of HTML coding which, among many uses, help search engines such as Google or Yahoo! create directories to the World Wide Web. FrontPage makes it easy to add meta tags to attract the attention of search engines or keep them out of your site. Adding keyword meta tags makes it easier for search engines to categorize your site. The robot meta tags used on page 423 keep the same engines from indexing your site or following all its links, something you may want to do for a site intended just for friends and family or to keep spam generators from harvesting email addresses listed on the site. The robot tags won't block every robot, but they will help.

To help search engines index your site

1. With your Web site open, choose File > Properties (**Figure 16.11**).

2. When the Page Properties dialog box appears, click the *Custom* tab, then click *Add* in the *User variables* section (**Figure 16.12**).

3. When the User Meta Variable dialog box appears, type keywords into the *Name* text box, then type the actual keywords that summarize your site's topics—each separated by a comma and a single space—into the *Value* text box (**Figure 16.13**).

(continued)

Name = keywords
Value = GPS, ␣ PDA,␣ Sat␣Nav,␣
    Training,␣ navigation ????

4. Click *OK* to close the User Meta Variable dialog box and the keywords will be listed in the *User variables* section of the Page Properties dialog box (**Figure 16.14**).

5. If you want to change the keywords, select that line in the *User variables* list and click *Modify*. To delete the keywords entirely, click *Remove*.

6. Once you're satisfied with the keyword changes, click *OK*. The keywords will be added to your site's meta tags.

✔ Tips

■ If you want to inspect the normally invisible meta tag keywords, click the *Code* tab at the bottom of the main window and you'll find the keywords in the section above <title> (**Figure 16.15**).

■ Always use multiple keywords to create broad *and* narrow descriptions of your site. That way, people using a search engine will pick up your site in a general category search but also find it when looking for a particular product or service.

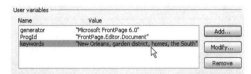

Figure 16.14 New meta tags are added to the *User variables* section of the Page Properties dialog box.

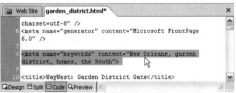

Figure 16.15 To see the normally invisible meta tag keywords, click the *Code* tab.

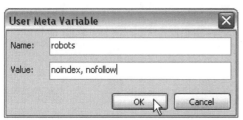

Figure 16.16 To block search engines from indexing your site, type robots into the *Name* text box, and noindex, nofollow into the *Value* text box.

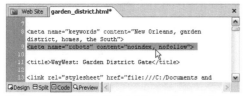

Figure 16.17 Click the *Code* tab to see the robot-blocking meta tags.

To keep out search engines

1. With your Web site open, choose File > Properties (**Figure 16.11**).

2. When the Page Properties dialog box appears, click the *Custom* tab, then click *Add* in the *User variables* section (**Figure 16.12**).

3. When the User Meta Variable dialog box appears, type robots into the *Name* text box, then type noindex, nofollow into the *Value* text box (**Figure 16.16**).

4. Click *OK* to close the User Meta Variable dialog box and return to the Page Properties dialog box. Click *OK* and the meta tags will be added to your site's coding (**Figure 16.17**).

Publishing to the Web

After you've fixed your Web pages, marked which ones should be published, and (just as importantly) which ones should *not* be published, you should preview them in several Web browsers. Use Internet Explorer *and* Netscape Navigator (in several versions of each) to check each page's appearance and links, since each browser interprets code a bit differently. Make a point of also checking your pages on a Macintosh, particularly since PC-created images can look a bit washed out on Mac-driven monitors, which run a tad brighter than PC-driven monitors. Depending on how the pages look and behave, you may need to readjust some of your pages to avoid cross-platform problems. For details on which Web technologies work with various browsers, see *Setting Web Browser Compatibility* on page 444.

Once you've fixed any problems found in the browsers, you're finally ready to copy your Web site files from your local hard drive to the Web server you'll be using. Before you start, you'll need to know the server address that you'll be copying your files to, plus a user name and password to gain access to the server. Check with your ISP or the Web server's administrator if you need help.

URL ?

By the way, the publishing process also can be used to create a backup of your local site. In fact, making a backup site should be the first thing you do before actually publishing to the remote Web server. The steps are nearly the same, so consider it a practice run. Given how easy it can be to accidentally overwrite your local Web site files with the remote Web site's files, making a backup site first is always a smart move.

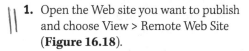

Figure 16.18 Open the Web site you want to publish and choose View > Remote Web Site.

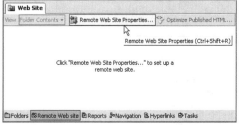

Figure 16.19 Within the Web Site window, click the *Remote Web Site Properties* button to set the publishing destination.

Figure 16.20 The first tab in the Remote Web Site Properties dialog box offers four choices for where to publish your site.

To set the publishing destination and options

1. Open the Web site you want to publish and choose View > Remote Web Site (**Figure 16.18**).

2. Within the Web Site window, click the *Remote Web Site Properties* button (**Figure 16.19**).

3. When the Remote Web Site Properties dialog box appears (**Figure 16.20**), you have four choices for where to publish your site:

   ◆ Choose *FrontPage or SharePoint Services* if your remote Web server includes FrontPage extensions or runs SharePoint Services. In most cases, this will be your first choice.

   or

   ◆ Choose *WebDAV* if your remote Web server supports Distributed Authoring and Versioning, which offers an alternate to FrontPage's own file checkout system. To use this choice, your Web server must have WebDAV already installed.

   or

   ◆ Choose *FTP* if you are running a plain vanilla Web server and want to move files to it using the long-standing File Transfer Protocol.

   or

   ◆ Choose *File System* if you want to make a backup copy of your local Web site instead of actually publishing it. The backup copy can reside on your own computer or another computer anywhere on the Internet.

   (continued)

SETTING THE PUBLISHING DESTINATION

4. Once you make your choice, type a URL or local file path into the *Remote Web site location* text window or click *Browse* to navigate to a folder on the Web or an internal server. Unless you want to change the default settings in the other two tabs, *Optimize HTML* and *Publishing*, skip to step 7.

5. Click the dialog box's *Optimize HTML* tab and, if you like, select the first checkbox (**Figure 16.21**). Then select any of the other checkboxes to remove various coding items from your Web pages before they are published. For more information, see the *Tip*.

6. Click the dialog box's *Publishing* tab and, if you like, change the defaults for whether all or just changed local pages are published to the remote site (**Figure 16.22**). Use the *Changes* section to set how FrontPage determines which pages have changed.

Figure 16.21 Use the *Optimize HTML* tab in the Remote Web Site Properties dialog box to remove extraneous coding from pages before they are published.

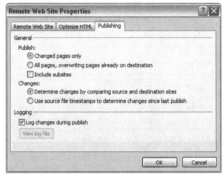

Figure 16.22 Use the *Publishing* tab in the Remote Web Site Properties dialog box to set whether all or just changed local pages are published to the remote site.

Figure 16.23 An alert dialog box will appear if the destination does not already contain a FrontPage Web site. Click *Yes* and the site will be created.

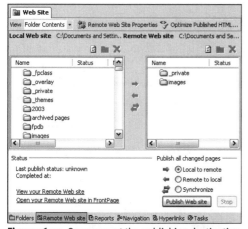

Figure 16.24 Once you set the publishing destination and options, the *Web Site* window will reappear with the files for the *Local Web site* on the left and the nearly empty *Remote Web site* pane on the right.

7. Once you've made your choices, click *OK* to close the dialog box. An alert dialog box will appear if the destination does not already contain a FrontPage Web site (**Figure 16.23**). Click *Yes* and the site will be created. Depending on where the remote site resides, you also may need to enter a user name and password.

8. The Web Site window will reappear with the files for the *Local Web site* on the left and the nearly empty *Remote Web site* pane on the right (**Figure 16.24**). To mark which local files should not be published, see *To keep local files from being published* on the next page. To publish the site, see page 429.

✔ Tip

■ In step 5, you have the choice of optimizing the coding in the pages published to your remote Web site by removing unnecessary HTML (**Figure 16.21**). An example of such extraneous code would be the comments in your page coding that you add as an explanatory note to yourself or others helping create the site. There also may be whitespace in your local pages to make it easier to read the coding. While you may need the comments or whitespace on the local site, you do not need them included in the pages you publish to the remote site. By removing this code from the remote pages, you ensure that they download more quickly to a visitor's computer.

To keep local files from being published

1. If the Web Site window is not already visible, choose View > Remote Web Site (**Figure 16.18**).

2. Scroll through the left-hand list of files to find which local files you do not want published. Right-click the file and choose Don't Publish from the shortcut menu (**Figure 16.25**). The *Status* column will update to display *Don't publish* for the file (top, **Figure 16.26**).

✔ Tips

■ In step 2, you can change the publishing status of multiple files simultaneously by Ctrl-clicking them before you right-click to use the shortcut menu.

■ To quickly spot which files have already been marked as *Don't publish*, click the top of the *Status* column, which will sort the files by status (bottom, **Figure 16.26**).

Figure 16.25 Scroll through the list of files to find ones you do not want published, then right-click each file and choose Don't Publish from the shortcut menu.

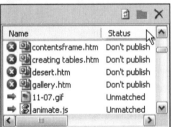

Figure 16.26 The *Status* column will update to display *Don't publish* and a red X will appear next to the selected file (top). To spot files marked as *Don't publish*, click the top of the *Status* column to sort the files by status (bottom).

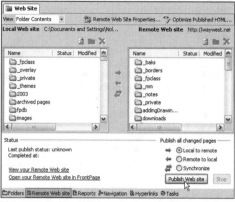

Figure 16.27 To publish your site, select the *Local to remote* button and click *Publish Web site*.

Figure 16.28 Type in your *User name* and *Password* when the Connect to dialog box appears.

Figure 16.29 If a series of alert dialog boxes appear, either click *Ignore and Continue* to resume the publishing process or *Cancel* to double-check your settings.

To publish your site

1. Once you have set the destination and options for your remote Web site, open the Web site (View > Remote Web Site).

2. When the Web Site window appears, check *Local to remote* in the lower-right corner (**Figure 16.27**). Now click *Publish Web site* and FrontPage will use your default Internet access connection to connect to your Web server. For more information on the Web Site window, see *Publishing options* on page 432.

3. When the Connect to dialog box appears, type in the user name and password that your ISP or Web server administrator assigned you (**Figure 16.28**).

4. Depending on your site setup, a series of alert dialog boxes may appear (**Figure 16.29**). The alerts may include security reminders or note pages that may not work on your Web server. Either click *Ignore and Continue* to resume the publishing process or *Cancel* to double-check or change your settings.

(continued)

5. There will be a brief pause as FrontPage compiles a list of the pages that need to be uploaded to the Web server (**Figure 16.30**). After another pause (the length will depend on how many new pages you're uploading and your connection speed), FrontPage will begin copying your Web pages to the Web server.

6. Once FrontPage publishes the site, the newly transferred files will be listed in the right-hand *Remote Web site* pane (**Figure 16.31**). The *Status* pane in the lower-left corner offers you the choice of three links to see a log file of what's been published, view your remote Web site within a Web browser, or open the remote site within FrontPage. Since you can already see the remote site's files in the right-hand pane, click *View your Remote Web site* and it will appear in your default Web browser (**Figure 16.32**). For more information, see *Publishing options* on page 432.

Figure 16.30 There will be a brief pause as FrontPage compiles a list of pages to upload to the Web server.

Figure 16.31 Once FrontPage publishes the site, the newly transferred files will be listed in the right-hand *Remote Web site* pane.

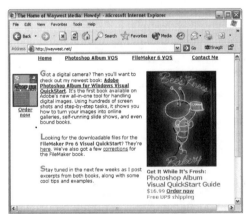

Figure 16.32 By clicking the *View your Remote Web site* button in the *Status* pane, your Web browser will launch and display your now-published site.

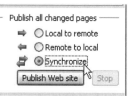

Figure 16.33 After the first time you publish your Web site, you can choose File > Publish Site to publish later updates.

Figure 16.34 You also can use the publishing process to move files from the *Remote to local* site or *Synchronize* the files by putting the most current version of each file on both sites.

✔ Tips

- Depending on how your Internet connection is configured, you may need to connect to your Web server before clicking the *Publish Web site* button in the Web Site window. Once you're done uploading your site to the server, disconnect from the Internet if you're using a dial-up connection.

- If you choose to overwrite pages already on the Web site, FrontPage will alert you if that will change the site's navigation structure. You'll have the choice of leaving the structure as is, replacing it with your changes, or merging both versions by using only the newest pages.

- After the first time you publish your Web site, and assuming your remote Web site settings remain the same, you can save yourself some steps whenever you update your remote Web site. Just choose File > Publish Site (**Figure 16.33**) or click the *Publish Web site* button in the Web Site window and the remote site will be updated. The site will be published without opening any dialog boxes. If you need to change any publishing settings, use the Web Site window instead.

- You also can use the publishing process to move files from the *Remote to local* site or *Synchronize* the files by putting the most current version of each file on both sites (**Figure 16.34**).

Publishing options

To reach the Web Site window (**Figure 16.35**), choose View > Remote Web Site.

❶ **Local Web site:** This is the file path name for your local Web site on your computer.

❷ **Local Web site's folders/files:** Beneath the path name for your local site are listed all the local site's folders and files. By clicking the column labels (*Name, Status, Modified,* etc.), you can sort the files based on that column. Click the chosen column again to reverse the sort order.

❸ **Status pane:** Besides telling you when the site was last published, the pane also includes links to a log listing every file moved, a Web-browser view of your remote site, and the view you now see within FrontPage of your remote site.

❹ **View drop-down menu:** Click the arrow on the drop-down menu to filter the list of files and folders. This can help you quickly find particular files without scrolling through the entire file list.

❺ **Remote Web Site Properties:** Click this button to set or change the destination and other properties of your remote Web site. For more information, see *To set the publishing destination and options* on page 425.

❻ **Optimize Published HTML:** Click this button to set what parts, if any, of the HTML coding in your local files will be kept when they are published to your remote Web site. For more information, see the *Tip* on page 427.

❼ **Remote Web site:** This is the URL or file path name for your remote Web site. The remote site can be the Web server containing your Web site, but it also can be a backup copy of your local site stored on your computer or anywhere on the Internet. See *To set the publishing destination and options* on page 425.

❽ **Buttons to control Local Web site file list:** Click the first button to update the folder/file list. Click the second button to move up one level in the hierarchy of the folder/file list. To use the third button, select a file or folder and click the X to delete the selected file.

❾ **Buttons to control Remote Web site file list:** Click the first button to update the folder/file list. Click the second button to move up one level in the hierarchy of the folder/file list. To use the third button, select a file or folder and click the X to delete the selected file.

❿ **Remote Web site's folders/files:** Beneath the path name for your remote site are listed all the remote site's folders and files. By clicking the column labels (*Name, Status, Modified,* etc.), you can sort the files based on that column. Click the chosen column again to reverse the sort order.

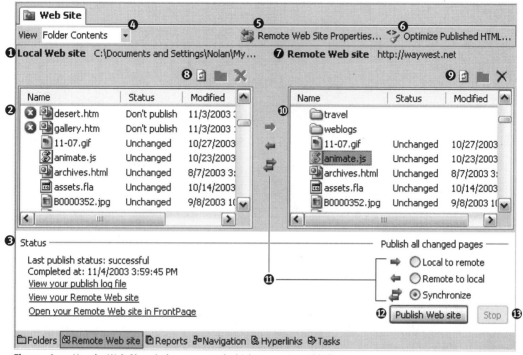

Figure 16.35 Use the Web Site window to control which pages are published.

⓫ **Buttons to control direction of file movement:** Two sets of arrow buttons— one set in the middle between the folder/file lists, the other set in the lower-right of the window—control which way folders/files move between your local and remote Web sites. Use the middle set of arrows to move only the folders/files you have selected in the adjacent list panes. Use the lower-right set of buttons to control all the files in the local or remote sites. The button with a pair of arrows synchronizes the local and remote folders/files by comparing the modification times of each and placing the most current versions on *both* sites.

⓬ **Publish Web site:** After setting the lower-right set of arrow buttons to your preference, click the *Publish Web site* button to move the folders/files. If you do not have an always-on Internet connection, you may need to connect to your Web server before clicking the *Publish Web site* button.

⓭ **Stop:** Click to immediately stop the process of moving files between the sites. Files that have already been moved to the other site, however, will not be moved back.

Part 5

Appendix
& Index

Appendix A: **Installing & Configuring**
FrontPage   **437**

Index   **447**

INSTALLING & CONFIGURING FRONTPAGE

It's tempting to install FrontPage and immediately start building your Web site. But take a minute to configure how FrontPage handles HTML codes, and you'll be assured that your Web site will be compatible with the Web browsers people use when they visit your site. If you just want to build Web pages and don't need to run a Web server on your local machine, then FrontPage 2003 works fine with Windows 2000 or later. If you plan on installing a FrontPage-enabled Web server on your local computer, you will need to be running Microsoft Windows Server 2003 with either the FrontPage server extension or Windows SharePoint Services. Installing a local Web server, by the way, falls beyond the scope of this book.

What you'll need before starting

◆ A PC equipped with the equivalent of an Intel Pentium 233 MHz or higher chip, with a Pentium III recommended.

◆ At least 128 MB of RAM (memory) with an operating system of Microsoft Windows 2000 with Service Pack 3 or later, or Windows XP.

◆ At least 180 MB of free space on your hard drive (more to install some of the clip art included on the CD).

◆ A 56Kbps modem for dial-up Internet connections. Office networks typically have much faster, hardwired Internet connections, so you'll have plenty of speed there.

◆ A color monitor capable of displaying at least 256 colors.

◆ A CD-ROM drive for installing FrontPage.

Installing FrontPage

If you need to save hard drive space and do not have enough room for FrontPage's standard version, see *To install a custom version of FrontPage* on page 442.

To install the standard version of FrontPage

1. Turn off all programs, including any anti-virus program you have running in the background.

2. Put the FrontPage 2003 CD in your disc drive. Once the CD launches, enter the 25-character *Product Key*, which you'll find inside the CD's case, and then click *Next* (**Figure A.1**).

3. When the *User information* screen appears, enter your *User name*, *Initials*, and *Organization*, and click *Next* (**Figure A.2**).

4. When the *End-User License Agreement* screen appears, read the agreement, check *I accept the terms in the License Agreement*, and click *Next* (**Figure A.3**).

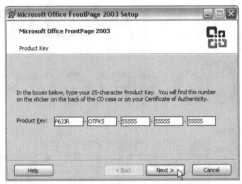

Figure A.1 Begin by entering the 25-character *Product Key* found inside the CD case.

Figure A.2 When the *User information* screen appears, enter your *User name*, *Initials*, and *Organization*, and click *Next*.

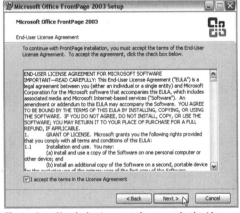

Figure A.3 Check the *I accept the terms in the License Agreement* box and click *Next*.

INSTALLING FRONTPAGE

Figure A.4 By default, the *Typical Install* is selected, but you can choose one of three other configurations: *Complete Install, Minimal Install,* or *Custom Install.*

Figure A.5 The *Summary* screen lists what will be installed and how much hard drive space it will require.

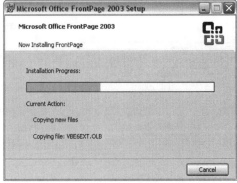

Figure A.6 Once the installation begins, a progress bar appears.

5. By default, the next screen will have *Typical Install* already selected (**Figure A.4**). In most cases, you should just click *Next* and the standard version of FrontPage will be installed. Or you can select one of three other installation configurations: *Complete Install, Minimal Install,* or *Custom Install.* For more information on these options, see *To install a custom version of FrontPage* on page 442. If you want to change the installation location, click *Browse* and navigate to where you want the program installed. Once you make all your choices, click *Next.*

6. The next screen will list what will be installed (**Figure A.5**). Click *Install* and the standard version of FrontPage will be installed (**Figure A.6**).

(continued)

7. Once FrontPage is installed, you'll be asked whether you want to check Microsoft's Web site for any updates to the program. In a constant battle to stay ahead of malicious coders, Microsoft regularly posts security updates for most programs. For that reason, leave the box selected and click *Finish* (**Figure A.7**).

8. If your Web browser is not already running, it will launch and take you directly to where Microsoft posts updates for FrontPage (**Figure A.8**). If there is an update, download it and FrontPage will automatically install it.

9. At this point, FrontPage's Activation Wizard will launch and give you the choice of exchanging information with Microsoft over the Internet or telephoning them for an activation code that you'll have to enter manually (**Figure A.9**). Unless you like being on hold on the phone, leave the default Internet choice selected and click *Next*. The Internet activation occurs fairly quickly. By the way, if it's not activated, FrontPage will only launch 49 more times before it locks you out of many program features.

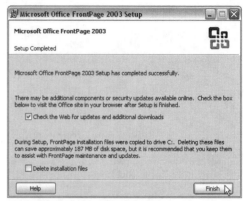

Figure A.7 Once FrontPage is installed, make sure to check for any security updates by clicking *Finish*, which will send your Web browser to Microsoft's Web site.

Figure A.8 Check for and download any FrontPage updates at the Microsoft Web site.

Figure A.9 When FrontPage asks whether you want to activate it, click *Next*.

Figure A.10 The Activation Wizard will ask if you want to register your software, but it's not necessary.

Figure A.11 If you decide to register FrontPage, you'll need to have a Microsoft Passport or create one by following the onscreen prompts.

Figure A.12 Remember after registering to use the *Manage Your Profile* link on Microsoft's Web site to prevent being inundated by junk mail or calls from Microsoft partners.

10. At this point, you can click *Close* to quit the Activation Wizard and restart your computer to begin using FrontPage. The wizard will ask you if you want to register your software, but it's not necessary (**Figure A.10**). If you do decide to register, you'll need to have a Microsoft Passport or create one by following the onscreen prompts (**Figure A.11**). Just remember when you're done registering to use the *Manage Your Profile* link on Microsoft's Web site to prevent being inundated by junk mail or calls from Microsoft partners (**Figure A.12**).

To install a custom version of FrontPage

1. If you want to install a custom version, follow steps 1–4 in *To install the standard version of FrontPage* on page 438. When the installer asks you to *choose another type*, select *Complete Install, Minimal Install,* or *Custom Install* then click *Browse* and navigate to where you want the program installed (**Figure A.13**). Finally, click *Next*.

2. When the *Advanced Customization* screen appears (**Figure A.14**), you'll need to decide which parts of FrontPage to install—and which to leave out. To reach any subitems, click on the + to expand items in the list. To collapse the list, click the –.

3. Click the drop-down menu of any item to select your installation option for that item (**Figure A.15**). For details on your choices, see **Table A.1**.

4. Once you've made all your choices, click *Next* and then *Install*. FrontPage will be installed based on your choices (**Figure A.6**). To finish the process, see steps 7–10 on pages 440–441.

Table A.1

ICON	TEXT	EXPLANATION
	Run from My Computer	Installs item & default subitems
	Run all from My Computer	Installs item & all subitems
	Run from CD	Runs item if CD in player
	Run all from CD	Runs item & all subitems if CD in player
✕	Not Available	Will not be installed
	Installed on First Use	If item ever used, asks for CD & installs

Figure A.13 To install a custom version of FrontPage, select *Complete Install, Minimal Install,* or *Custom Install,* then click *Browse* and navigate to where you want the program installed.

Figure A.14 When the *Advanced Customization* screen appears, you'll need to decide which parts of FrontPage to install.

Figure A.15 Use the drop-down menu of any item to select an installation option for that item.

Figure A.16 Use the *Space Required* and *Space Available* figures at the bottom of the installation screen to gauge if you'll have enough hard drive space for all your choices.

Figure A.17 Click to expand an item if you want to see which subitems will be installed.

✔ Tips

■ It can seem a bit confusing but the + and – in step 2 simply expand or collapse your *view* and have nothing to do with which items will or won't be installed. Instead, you must use each item's drop-down menu (as described in step 3) to set which items are installed.

■ As you select items to install in step 3, use the *Space Required* and *Space Available* figures at the bottom of the *Advanced Customization* screen to gauge if you'll have enough hard drive space for all your choices (**Figure A.16**).

■ The standard (default) installation does not install all the subitems under each item. Click to expand an item if you want to see which subitems will be installed (**Figure A.17**).

Setting Web Browser Compatibility

If every Web browser rendered HTML, Cascading Style Sheets, and various scripts the same way, creating Web pages would be so simple. In that perfect world, you wouldn't need to remember how different coding tags look in Internet Explorer vs. Netscape Navigator or which tags work in old or new browsers. Still, FrontPage offers a decent compromise. You decide which browsers you want to code for and FrontPage automatically generates the proper HTML. As more users have switched to newer computers, it's become much easier to strike an acceptable balance in creating Web pages that run properly for most users without having to forego newer interactive features. By the end of 2003, surveys showed that 97 percent of all Web browsers are version 4 or later, which means most computers have no problem displaying pages that use CSS 1 (style sheets) and CSS 2 (absolute positioning).

To set browser compatibility

1. Choose Tools > Page Options (**Figure A.18**).

2. When the Page Options dialog box appears, click the *Authoring* tab (**Figure A.19**).

3. Use the *Browsers* drop-down menu to choose which Web browsers you'll be coding for (**Figure A.20**). Your choice will check or uncheck boxes in the section below the drop-down menu, indicating which scripting technologies you'll be able to use with that choice.

Figure A.18 To set browser compatibility and how FrontPage handles code, choose Tools > Page Options.

Figure A.19 Use the *Authoring* tab to set which browsers you want to code for, and FrontPage will automatically generate the proper coding.

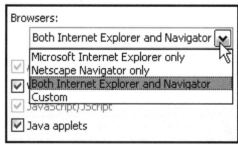

Figure A.20 Use the *Browsers* drop-down menu to choose which Web browsers you'll be coding for.

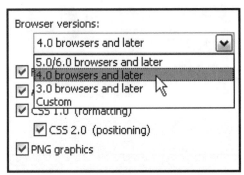

Figure A.21 Use the *Browser versions* drop-down menu to choose which versions you'll be coding for.

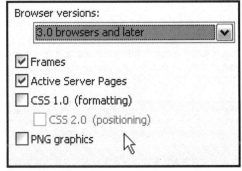

Figure A.22 If you choose *3.0 browsers and later*, you won't be able to use CSS coding.

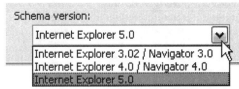

Figure A.23 The *Schema version* drop-down menu controls the syntax FrontPage uses in coding pages.

4. Use the *Browser versions* drop-down menu to choose which versions you'll be coding for (**Figure A.21**). This choice also will check or uncheck the browser features that your pages will support.

5. Once you're done making your choices, click *OK*, and FrontPage will base its page coding on those choices. If you change your mind, you can change the settings any time, though only pages coded after that point will reflect your new choices.

✔ Tips

■ In deciding what version of browsers to support, you'll see that if you choose *3.0 browsers and later* in step 4 you won't be able to use *CSS 1.0 (formatting)* or *CSS 2.0 (positioning)* (**Figure A.22**).

■ The *Schema version* drop-down menu controls the syntax FrontPage uses in coding your pages. In general, leave it as it is, though you'll need to change it to *Internet Explorer 5.0* if you want to use script-based behaviors (**Figure A.23**). For more information, see *Using Behaviors* on page 386.

SETTING WEB BROWSER COMPATIBILITY

Setting Coding Preferences

You don't need to mess with this unless you intend to tweak FrontPage's coding directly.

To set code preferences

1. If you have a Web page with the coding set how you want it, open it ([Ctrl][O]). Otherwise, skip to step 2.

2. Choose Tools > Page Options (**Figure A.18**).

3. When the Page Options dialog box appears, click the *Code Formatting* tab (**Figure A.24**).

4. If you opened a page in step 1, click *Base on current page* ❶. Otherwise, set the code's appearance with the three checkboxes ❷, and the text boxes/arrows for *Indent* ❸ and *Right margin* ❹.

5. Now, click the *Color Coding* tab within the Page Options dialog box to set the colors used in all your coding.

6. When the *Color Coding* tab appears (**Figure A.25**), use the drop-down menus to change any of the default colors. For details on using the color drop-down menus, see step 4 on page 158.

7. Once you're done setting the *Code Formatting* and *Color Coding* tabs, click *OK*. The changes will be applied to your HTML coding.

✔ Tip

■ If you change your mind while making changes under either the *Code Formatting* or *Color Coding* tabs, click *Reset* or *Reset Colors* to return to the original settings.

Figure A.24 Use the *Code Formatting* tab to set how you want the coding to appear when you switch to FrontPage's *Code or Split* views.

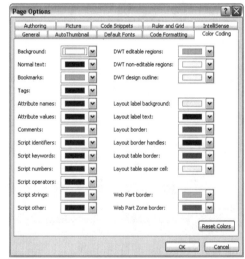

Figure A.25 Use the *Color Coding* tab to set the colors used in your coding and script tags.

INDEX

A

Absolute button (Position dialog box), 202
absolute links, 144
absolute positioning, images, 201–205
Activation Wizards, 440
Active graphics option (Theme dialog box), 90
Add Choice dialog box, 331
Add Criteria dialog box, 356
Add link button, 70
Add Link button (Add to Link Bar dialog box), 75
Add or Remove Buttons (toolbars), 29
Add to Link Bar dialog box, 71
advanced controls, author-time component, 244
Advanced Customization screen, 442
Align Left icon (Formatting toolbar), 122
Align or Distribute command (Drawing toolbar), 223
Align Right icon (Formatting toolbar), 122
alignment
    drawings, 223
    images, 182–183
    paragraphs, 128
    text, 122
Alignment option (Horizontal Line Properties dialog box), 185
All pages radio button (Shared Borders dialog box), 77
Alternative representations section (Picture Properties dialog box), 178
anchor links. *See* bookmarks
animation
    inserting in pages, 238–240
    loop setting, 241

Application menu, 16–17
Apply Changes command, 55
Apply using CSS option (Theme dialog box), 90
Attach Dynamic Web Template command, 87
Attach Dynamic Web Template dialog box, 87
author, contacting, 10
author-time components, 244
Authoring settings (status bar), 16–17
Authoring tab (Page Options dialog box), 245
Auto Thumbnail command (Tools menu), 191
Auto Thumbnail tab (Page Options dialog box), 192
AutoShapes command (Insert menu), 210
AutoShapes dialog box, 222
AutoShapes icon (Drawing toolbar), 210
Autostretch tables, 6, 287

B

back/next link bars, creating, 69–72
Background picture option (Theme dialog box), 90
Banner Ad Manager Properties dialog box, 251
banner ads, 251–252
Bar based on navigation structure option (Insert Web Component dialog box), 64
Bar with back and next links option (Insert Web Component dialog box), 69
Bar with custom links option (Insert Web Component dialog box), 73

behaviors, style sheets, 386–389
Behaviors command (Format menu), 386
Behaviors task pane, 386
Bevel button (Pictures toolbar), 200
beveled images, 200
bit depths, 171
Blank Page command (New icon), 37
BMPs, 170
Bold icon (Formatting toolbar), 120
Bookmark button (Insert Hyperlink dialog box), 147
Bookmark command (Insert menu), 153
Bookmark dialog box, 153
Bookmark Properties command, 156
bookmarks. *See also* hyperlinks
   clearing, 157
   creating, 153
   finding, 156
   linking current page, 154
   linking other than current page, 155
Border Properties dialog box, 77
borders
   images, 183
   tables, 275
Break command (Insert menu), 103
Break dialog box, 103
brightness, images, 198
Bring Forward button (Positioning toolbar), 204, 299
browse-time components, 244
Browsed Pages button (Insert Hyperlink dialog box), 147
bulleted lists, 133
Bullets and Numbering command (Format menu), 136
Bullets and Numbering dialog box, 136
Bullets button (Formatting toolbar), 133
Button Properties command, 166

C

Captions Properties dialog box, 261
cascading style sheets. *See* CSS
Castro, Elizabeth, 364
Cell Formatting command (Table menu), 288
Cell Properties dialog box, 276

cells
   adding to layout table, 284
   layout tables
      adding, 284
      formatting, 288–289
   tables, 264
      adding, 266
      colors, 278
      formatting, 276
      headers, 277
      merging, 271
      splitting, 270
Center icon (Formatting toolbar), 122
Change Property dialog box, 387
Change title button (Save As dialog box), 40
Character spacing tab (Font dialog box), 123–124
Check Box icon (Form toolbar), 327
Check Box Properties dialog box, 328
check boxes, forms, 327–328
Checkout Status report, 414
child layers, 301
Choose an orientation pane, 65, 70
Choose Editable Regions for Content dialog box, 87
Circular Hotspot icon (Pictures toolbar), 161
Clip Art command (Insert menu), 174
Clip Art task pane, 172
   options, 174–175
Clip Board view, 22
Clip Organizer, 175
Close application button, 17
Close command (File menu), 41
close-focus method, creating tasks, 394
Close Web Site command (File menu), 46
Code Coding tab (Page Options dialog box), 446
Code tab, 16
Code view, 6, 19
Code View toolbar, 25
codes, snippets, 5
collaborative controls, 7
Color button (Pictures toolbar), 200
Color option (Horizontal Line Properties dialog box), 185
Color Schemes tab (Modify Theme dialog box), 93
Color Wheel tab (Modify Theme dialog box), 93

colors
    hyperlinks, 158–159
    images
        removing, 200
        transparency, 199
    table cells, 278
    themes, modifying, 93
Column Properties dialog box, 286
columns, tables, 265
    distributing evenly, 273
Command and Options dialog box, 263
commands
    Edit menu
        Cut, 101
        Find, 105–112
        Paste, 101
        Redo, 102
        Replace, 109–112
        Tasks, 397
        Undo, 102
    File menu
        Close, 41
        Close Web Site, 46
        Exit, 18
        New, 37, 304
        Open, 39
        Open Site, 46
        Page Setup, 42
        Preview in Browser, 19, 242
        Print, 42
        Print Preview, 42
        Properties, 421
        Publish Site, 431
        Save, 40
        Save All, 72
        Save As, 41
    Format menu
        Behaviors, 386
        Bullets and Numbering, 136
        Dynamic Web Template, 87
        Layers, 292
        Paragraph, 131
        Position, 202
        Remove Formatting, 125
        Shared Borders, 77
        Style, 367
        Style Sheet Links, 379
        Theme, 89

commands (continued)
    Frames menu
        Delete Frame, 313
        Split Frame, 315
    Help menu, Microsoft Office FrontPage
        Help, 36, 204
    Insert menu
        Bookmark, 153
        Break, 103
        Database, 348
        File, 262
        Form, 321
        Horizontal Line, 184
        Hyperlink, 144
        Interactive Button, 164
        Layer, 293
        Navigation, 64
        Picture, 172
        Web Component, 193, 263
    Table menu
        Cell Formatting, 288
        Delete Cells, 269
        Distribute Columns Evenly, 272–273
        Distribute Rows Evenly, 272
        Draw Table, 258
        Insert, 259, 266
        Layout Tables and Cells, 280
        Merge Cells, 271
        Select, 264–265
        Split Cells, 270
    Tools menu
        Auto Thumbnail, 191
        Customize, 31
        Internet Options, 179
        Options, 23
        Page Options, 116, 192
        Site Settings, 358
        Spelling, 113–114
    View menu
        Folder List, 21
        Hyperlinks, 167
        Navigation, 50
        Page, 98
        Recalculate Hyperlinks, 152
        Remote Web Site, 425, 432–433
        Reports, 401, 414
        Reveal Tags, 129

commands, View menu *(continued)*
  Task, 397
  Task Pane, 22, 23
  Toolbars, 27, 160, 209
Commands tab (Customize dialog box), 30
conditional behaviors, 5
Confirm Delete dialog box, 415
Confirmation Field Properties dialog box,
  336, 337
confirmation pages, forms, 336–337
Connect to dialog box, 429
contrasting, images, 198
Copy icon, 101
Create New Document button (Insert
  Hyperlink dialog box), 146
Create New Link Bar dialog box, 70
Create New Web Site dialog box, 44
Criteria dialog box, 356
Crop button (Pictures toolbar), 199
CSS (cascading style sheets), 7, 363–364
  adding behaviors to layers, 386–389
  basics, 365–366
  deleting styles, 382
  DHTML effects, 383–384
    page transitions, 385
  embedded style sheets
    creating, 367–369
    editing, 370–371
  external style sheets
    building, 374–375
    creating, 372–373
    editing, 376
    links, 379–381
    specifying multiple fonts, 377–378
  image absolute positioning, 201–205
Current Folder button (Insert Hyperlink
  dialog box), 147
Current page radio button (Shared Borders
  dialog box), 77–78
cursor, moving, 99
curved lines, 211
custom installation choices, 442
Custom tab (Modify Theme dialog box), 93
Customize command (Tools menu), 31
Customize dialog box, 30
Cut command (Edit menu), 101
Cut icon, 101

D

Data menu commands, 35
Database Column Value dialog box, 361
Database command (Insert menu), 348
Database Connection Properties dialog box, 359
Database Results Wizard, 348–352
databases
  compatible formats, 346
  connections, 345–346
    changing, 358
    column value changes, 361
    creating, 348–354
    options, 355
    removing, 360
    verification, 358
  filtering and sorting results, 356–357
  importing into Web site, 346–347
  saving form results, 343
DeBabelizer, Web graphics, 170
Decrease Indent button (Formatting toolbar), 129
default labels, link bars, 67–68
Defined Term command, 134
definition lists, 134
Delete Cells command (Table menu), 269
Delete Frame command (Frames menu), 313
Delete option (Customize dialog box), 32
Delete Page dialog box, 58
Delete this page from the Web site option
  (Delete Page dialog box), 58
design, Web site
  structure, 14
  visual organization, 13–14
Design tab, 16
Design view, 6, 17, 19
Detach Dynamic Web Template command, 88
DHTML and CSS for the World Wide Web, 364
DHTML (Dynamic Hypertext Markup
  Language)
  CSS
    application, 383–384
    page transitions, 385
  image absolute positioning, 201–205
DHTML Effects toolbar, 25, 383
dictionaries, changing language, 116
Displayed Fields dialog box, 349
Distribute Columns Evenly command
  (Table menu), 272–273
Distribute Rows Evenly command
  (Table menu), 272

docking toolbars, 28
download time (status bar), 16–17
Draw Layer tool, 293
Draw Layout Cell tool, 284
Draw Layout Table tool, 281
Draw Table button (Tables toolbar), 258
Draw Table command (Table menu), 258
Drawing Canvas toolbar, 25, 226, 229
Drawing toolbar, 208
    accessing, 209
drawings
    accessing Drawing toolbar, 209
    alignment, 223
    arrangement, 224
    AutoShapes, 210
    canvas
        creating, 226–227
        formatting, 233
        moving, 228
        rescaling, 231–232
        resizing, 229–230
    changing appearance, 219–222
    curved lines, 211
    freeform shapes, 212
    grouping, 225
    scribble tool, 213–215
    WordArt, 216–218
Drop-Down Box icon (Form toolbar), 331–334
Drop-Down Box Properties dialog box, 331–334
Drop-Down Box Validation dialog box, 334
drop-down boxes, forms, 331–334
Dynamic Hypertext Markup Language. See DHTML
dynamic templates, 4
Dynamic Web Template command (Format menu), 83, 87
Dynamic Web toolbar, 85

E

e-mail
    contacting author, 10
    hyperlinks, 149
    saving form results, 341–342
E-mail Address button (Insert Hyperlink dialog box), 146, 149
Edit Hyperlink dialog box, 151–152, 163, 418

Edit menu commands, 33
    Cut, 101
    Find, 105–112
    Paste, 101
    Redo, 102
    Replace, 109–112
    Tasks, 397
    Undo, 102
Edit Picture dialog box, 196
Edit WordArt Text dialog box, 216–217
editable regions, templates, 84–85
Editable Regions dialog box, 84
embedded style sheets
    creating, 367–369
    editing, 370–371
Empty Web Site icon (Web Site Templates dialog box), 43
End-User License Agreement, 438
EPSs, 170
Excel spreadsheets, 262–263
Existing File or Web Page button (Insert Hyperlink dialog box), 146
Exit command (File menu), 18
Expand icon (Drawing Canvas toolbar), 229
Expedia, author-time component, 244
external style sheets
    building, 374–375
    creating, 372–373
    editing, 376
    links, 379–381
    specifying multiple fonts, 377–378

F

fields, forms, 321
    adding, 322–323
File command (Insert menu), 262
File menu commands, 33
    Close, 41
    Close Web Site, 46
    Exit, 18
    New, 37, 304
    Open, 39
    Open Site, 46
    Page Setup, 42
    Preview in Browser, 19, 242
    Print, 42

File menu commands *(continued)*
   Print Preview, 42
   Properties, 421
   Publish Site, 431
   Save, 40
   Save All, 72
   Save As, 41
File name text box (Save As dialog box), 40
File Open dialog box, 194
files
   categorizing, 401
   naming, 52
   organizing, 398–403
Find and Replace dialog box, 105–112
Find command (Edit menu), 105–112
Find in Navigation command, 53
Fireworks, Web graphics, 170
Fit icon (Drawing Canvas toolbar), 230
Flip Horizontal button (Pictures toolbar), 197
Flip Vertical button (Pictures toolbar), 197
flipping
   drawings, 220
   images, 197
Folder List command (View menu), 21
Folder List icon (Standard toolbar), 21
Folder List pane
   creating Web site, 50–51
   renaming Web page, 53
Folder List tab, 21
Folder Options dialog box, 242
Folders icon, 20–21
Font Color icon (Formatting toolbar), 121
Font dialog box, 118, 123–124, 367
Font tab (Font dialog box), 123–124
fonts
   external style sheets, 377–378
   formatting
      changing face, 118
      color, 121
      options, 123–124
      size, 119
      style, 120
Form command (Insert menu), 321
Form Page Wizard, 80
Form Properties dialog box, 338–340
Format Drawing Canvas dialog box, 233
Format menu commands, 34
   Behaviors, 386
   Bullets and Numbering, 136

Format menu commands *(continued)*
   Dynamic Web Template, 87
   Layers, 292
   Paragraph, 131
   Position, 202
   Remove Formatting, 125
   Shared Borders, 77
   Style, 367
   Style Sheet Links, 379
   Theme, 89
Format WordArt dialog box, 218
Formatted style, paragraphs, 132
Formatting toolbar, 16–17, 24, 117, 127
forms
   check boxes, 327–328
   confirmation pages, 336–337
   creating, 320–321
   drop-down box, 331–334
   fields, 321
      adding, 322–323
   option buttons, 329–330
   push buttons, 335
   saving results
      to database, 343
      to e-mail, 341–342
      to file, 338–339
      options, 340
   text
      adding, 324–325
      validation options, 326
Frame Properties dialog box, 316–317
frames
   creating, 303–306
   formatting, 313
   options, 317
   page, 303, 306
      setting as home page, 312
      spacing change, 316
   resizing, 314
   splitting, 315
   targets
      defaults, 310
      options, 311
      setting, 308–309
Frames menu commands, 35
   Delete Frame, 313
   Split Frame, 315
framesets, 303

freeform shapes, drawings, 212
freestanding toolbars, 28
FrontPage
  installation
    code preference setting, 446
    custom version, 442–443
    standard version, 438–441
    system requirements, 437
    Web browser compatibility, 444–445
  launching, 18
  main window, 16–17
  new features, 4–5
  purpose of, 3
  quitting, 18
  updates, 439
  updates and patches, 10

G

Getting Started view, 22
GIFs (Graphical Interchange Format), *versus*
  JPEGs, 170
graphics, 7. *See also* images
  adding, 172–173
  alignment, 182–183
  alternates
    low-resolution images, 180–181
    text, 178–179
  converting formats, 176–177
  editing
    bevels, 200
    colors, 199–200
    contrast and brightness change, 198
    cropping, 199
    resampling, 188–190
    resizing, 187
    rotating and flipping, 197
    thumbnails, 191–196
    undo, 186
  horizontal lines, 184–185
  hyperlinks
    hotspots, 161–163
    linking to file, 160
  positioning absolutely, 201–203
    moving, 204–205
  tables, 260
  themes, modifying, 93
  Web formats, 170–171

Group command (Drawing toolbar), 225
grouping drawings, 225

H

handles, scribble tool, 214–215
headings
  adding, 141
  changing size, 142
  table cells, 277
Help, searching, 16–17
Help menu commands, 35–36
  Microsoft Office FrontPage Help, 36, 204
Highlight Hotspots button (Pictures
    toolbar), 163
Hit Counter Properties dialog box, 253–254
hit counters, 253–254
  browser-time component, 244
Horizontal Line command (Insert menu), 184
Horizontal Line Properties command, 184
Horizontal Line Properties dialog box, 185
horizontal lines, images, 184–185
Horton, Sarah, 11
hotspots, hyperlinks, 161–163
*HTML for the World Wide Web with XHTML
    and CSS,* 364
HTML (HyperText Markup Language)
  codes, find and replace, 108–112
  tags
    meta tags, 421–423
    viewing, 129
  XML integration, 5
HTML Tags tab (Find and Replace dialog
    box), 112
Hyperlink button (Standard toolbar), 144
Hyperlink command (Insert menu), 144
Hyperlink Properties command, 151–152
hyperlinks
  absolute versus relative links, 144
  bookmarks
    clearing, 157
    creating, 153
    finding, 156
    linking current page, 154
    linking other than current page, 155
  deleting, 152
  e-mail links, 149
  editing, 151–152

hyperlinks *(continued)*
  external Web page link, 145
  images
    hotspots, 161–163
    linking to file, 160
  interactive buttons
    adding, 164–165
    editing, 166
  options, 146–147
  pages not created, 150
  setting colors, 158–159
  target frames, 303
    defaults, 310
    options, 311
    setting, 308–309
  viewing, 167
  Web site link, 148
Hyperlinks command (View menu), 167
Hyperlinks icon (View bar), 167
Hyperlinks to add to page option (Link Bar
  Properties dialog box), 66
Hyperlinks view, 20–21
HyperText Markup Language. *See* HTML

I

images. *See also* graphics
  adding, 172–173
  alignment, 182–183
  alternates
    low-resolution images, 180–181
    text, 178–179
  converting formats, 176–177
  editing
    bevels, 200
    colors, 199–200
    contrast and brightness change, 198
    cropping, 199
    resampling, 188–190
    resizing, 187
    rotating and flipping, 197
    thumbnails, 191–196
    undo, 186
  horizontal lines, 184–185
  hyperlinks
    hotspots, 161–163
    linking to file, 160

images *(continued)*
  positioning absolutely, 201–203
    moving, 204–205
  tables, 260
  themes, modifying, 93
  Web formats, 170–171
Included in Link Bars command, 68
Increase Indent button (Formatting toolbar), 129
indenting, paragraphs, 129–130
indexing images, 171
Insert command (Table menu), 259, 266
Insert Hyperlink dialog box, 145–150, 161–162,
  305, 308
Insert menu commands, 34
  Bookmark, 153
  Break, 103
  Database, 348
  File, 262
  Form, 321
  Horizontal Line, 184
  Hyperlink, 144
  Interactive Button, 164
  Layer, 293
  Navigation, 64
  Picture, 172
  Web Component, 193, 263
Insert Picture From File button (Standard
  toolbar), 260
Insert Rows or Columns dialog box, 267–268
Insert Table button (Standard toolbar), 259
Insert Table dialog box, 259
Insert Web Component dialog box, 64, 246, 337
Insert WordArt icon, 216–218
installation, FrontPage
  code preference setting, 446
  custom version, 442–443
  standard version, 438–441
  system requirements, 437
  Web browser compatibility, 444–445
Interactive Button command (Insert menu), 164
Interactive Button dialog box, 164–166
interactive buttons
  author-time Web component, 244
  hyperlinks
    adding, 164–165
    editing, 166
Internet Options command (Tools menu), 179
Internet Options dialog box, 179

INDEX

Internet Service Provider (ISP), 417
ISP (Internet Service Provider), 417
Italic icon (Formatting toolbar), 120

J-K

JavaScript-based buttons, 5
Joint Photographic Experts Group (JPGs), 170
JPEGs (Joint Photographic Experts Group),
    versus GIFs, 170
Justify icon (Formatting toolbar), 122

keyboard shortcuts, 9
    text selection and deleting, 100

L

languages, dictionary, 116
Layer command (Insert menu), 293
layers, 4
    adding new, 296–297
    creating, 292–293
    images
        absolute positioning, 201–203
        moving, 204–205
    moving, 294
    nested layer creation, 300–301
    resizing, 295
    setting visibility, 302
    stack order, 298–299
Layers command (Format menu), 292
Layers task pane, 292
layout tables, 280–281
    cells
        adding, 284
        formatting, 288–289
    converting existing table to, 290
    deleting, 282–283
    formatting, 288–289
    resizing, 285–287
Layout Tables and Cells command (Table
    menu), 280
Layout Tables and Cells task pane, 280
Less Brightness button (Pictures toolbar), 198
Less Contrast button (Pictures toolbar), 198

line breaks
    showing hidden marks, 104
    text, 103
Line command (AutoShapes toolbar), 211
Link Bar Properties dialog box, 65, 70, 75–76
link bars
    appearance, 66
    author-time Web component, 244
    changing default labels, 67–68
    changing properties, 75–78
    creating, 64–65
        back/next, 69–72
        custom, 73–74
    purpose of, 62–63
Link Style Sheet dialog box, 379
Link to column (Add to Link Bar dialog box), 72
Link to File dialog box, 148
links. *See* hyperlinks
List Item Properties dialog box, 139
List Properties dialog box, 136
lists
    customizing, 136–138
    definition, 134
    nested, 139–140
    ordered, 135
    unordered, 133
Look in column (Add to Link Bar dialog box), 72
loops, videos, 241
low-resolution images, 180–181
Lynch, Patrick J., 11

M

Macromedia Flash, 7
    inserting Flash movies in Web pages, 240
Manage Editable Regions command, 84, 86
Manage Editable Regions icon (Dynamic Web
    toolbar), 86
Manage Your Profile link, 441
mapping images, 171
Marquee Properties dialog box, 246–248
marquees
    adding, 246
    author-time component, 244
    changing, 248
    options, 247
Master Category List dialog box, 399

Maximize window button, 17
Menu bar, 16–17
menus, 33–36
Merge Cells button (Tables toolbar), 270
Merge Cells command (Table menu), 271
meta tags, Web publishing, 421–423
Microsoft
    online clips, 175
    Web site, 10
Microsoft Excel Worksheet, 262
Microsoft Office FrontPage Help command
        (Help menu), 36, 204
Microsoft Passport, 441
Minimize window button, 17
Modify Link dialog box, 76
Modify Style dialog box, 370, 374
Modify Theme dialog box, 92–94
More Brightness button (Pictures toolbar), 198
More Contrast button (Pictures toolbar), 198
More Options dialog box, 356
More page templates option (New task
        pane), 38
More Web site templates option (New task
        pane), 45
Move Backward button (Positioning
        Toolbar), 299
Movie in Flash Format command
        (Insert menu), 240
MSN, author-time component, 244
MSNBC, author-time component, 244
multilevel lists. *See* nested lists
multimedia
    animation
        inserting in pages, 238–240
        loop setting, 241
    sounds, adding to page background, 243
    videos
        inserting in pages, 238–240
        loop setting, 241
        previewing problems, 242
    Web components
        banner ad, 251–252
        hit counters, 253–254
        marquees, 246–248
        table of contents, 249–250
        Top Ten list, 255
        turning on or off, 244–245
multiple cells, tables, 264

N

Navigate folders on local machine/network icon
        (Insert Hyperlink dialog box), 147
Navigate Web browser icon (Insert Hyperlink
        dialog box), 147
Navigation command
    Insert menu, 64
    View menu, 50
Navigation tab, 21
Navigation toolbar, 26
Navigation view, 20–21
nested layers
    creating, 300–301
    parent-child relationship, 301
nested lists, 139–140
New command (File menu), 37, 304
New Database Connection dialog box, 353–355
new features, 4–5
New icon, 37
New Page command (Navigation view), 50–51
New Style dialog box, 367, 375
New Task dialog box, 395
New Toolbar dialog box, 31
<No ID> tag, 202
Normal style, paragraphs, 131
numbered lists, 135
Numbering button (Formatting toolbar), 135
Numbers tab (List Properties dialog box), 137

O

Open command (File menu), 39
Open File dialog box, 39
Open icon, 39, 46
Open last Web site automatically option
        (Options dialog box), 23
Open Site command (File menu), 46
Open Site dialog box, 46
Open with dialog box, 242
Option Button Properties dialog box, 329
option buttons, forms, 329–330
Options Button icon (Form toolbar), 329
Options command (Tools menu), 23
Options dialog box, 23
Order command (Drawing toolbar), 224
ordered lists, 135

Ordering dialog box, 357
organization, workflow, 398–403
Other tab (List Properties dialog box), 137

P

Page command, 80
  File menu, 304
  New icon, 38
  View menu, 98
Page Options command (Tools menu), 116, 192
Page Options dialog box, 116, 192, 245, 366, 444–446
Page Properties dialog box, 158–159, 243, 421
page selection tabs, 16–17
Page Setup command (File menu), 42
page size setting (status bar), 16–17
Page Templates dialog box, 80, 304, 336, 372
page transitions, 385
Page Transitions dialog box, 385
Page views, 6
  tabs, 16–17
Pages Templates dialog box, 38
Paragraph command (Format menu), 131
Paragraph dialog box, 130–131
paragraphs
  adding to text, 104
  formatting
    alignment, 128
    custom indention, 130
    indention, 129
  showing hidden marks, 104
  style
    Formatted, 132
    Normal, 131
parent layers, 301
Paste command (Edit menu), 101
Paste icon, 101
patches, 10
photo galleries
  author-time Web component, 244
  image thumbnails
    changing, 196
    creating, 193–195
Photo Gallery Properties dialog box, 193–196
Photoshop, Web graphics, 170

Picture Bullets tab (List Properties dialog box), 137
Picture command (Insert menu), 172
Picture dialog box, 172–173
Picture File Type button (Picture Properties dialog box), 176
Picture File Type dialog box, 176
Picture Hotspot Properties command, 163
Picture Options dialog box, 173
Picture Properties dialog box, 176–177, 241
pictures. *See* images
Pictures command (View menu), 160
Pictures dialog box, 260
Pictures toolbar, 160–162, 169
Place in This Document button (Insert Hyperlink dialog box), 146
Plain Bullets tab (List Properties dialog box), 137
PNGs (Portable Network Graphics), 170
Polygonal Hotspot icon (Pictures toolbar), 161
Portable Network Graphics (PNGs), 170
Portrait/Landscape command, 61
Position command (Format menu), 202
Position dialog box, 202
positioning, text, 124
Positioning toolbar, 26
Preview in Browser command (File menu), 19, 242
Preview tab, 16
Preview view, 19
Print command (File menu), 42
Print Preview command (File menu), 42
printing, Web pages, 42
Product Key, 438
Properties command (File menu), 421
Publish Site command (File menu), 431
Publish Status report, 420
publishing. *See* Web publishing
Push Button icon (Form toolbar), 335
Push Button Properties dialog box, 335
push buttons, forms, 335

Q-R

RASs, 170
realignment, table cells, 279

INDEX

Recalculate Hyperlinks command (View menu), 152

Recent Files button (Insert Hyperlink dialog box), 147

Recently used templates option (New task pane), 38, 45

Rectangular Hotspot icon (Pictures toolbar), 161

Redo command (Edit menu), 102

Redo icon, 102

relative links, 144

Remote Web Site command (View menu), 425, 432–433

Remote Web Site Properties dialog box, 425–427

Remote Web site view, 20–21

Remove Formatting command (Format menu), 125

Remove Link button (Add to Link Bar dialog box), 75

Remove page from the navigation structure option (Delete Page dialog box), 58

Rename command, 52

Replace command (Edit menu), 109–112

Reports command (View menu), 401, 414

Reports view, 20–21

Resample button (Pictures toolbar), 188

resampling, images, 188–190

Reset Toolbar command, 29

resizing
    drawings, 219
    frames, 314
    images, 187
    layers, 295
    layout tables, 285–287
    toolbars, 28

Restore button (Pictures toolbar), 186

Reveal Tags command (View menu), 129

Review Master List dialog box, 400

review status reports, 402

Rotate Left button (Pictures toolbar), 197

Rotate or Flip command (Drawing toolbar), 220

Rotate Right button (Pictures toolbar), 197

rotating
    drawings, 220
    images, 197

Row Properties dialog box, 286

rows, tables, 265
    distributing evenly, 272

S

Save All command (File menu), 72

Save As command (File menu), 41

Save As dialog box, 40

Save command (File menu), 40

Save Embedded Files dialog box, 172, 177, 239

Saving Results dialog box, 341–342

Scale Drawing icon (Drawing Canvas toolbar), 231–232

Screentip button (Insert Hyperlink dialog box), 147

scribble tool, drawings, 213–215

Scribble Tool icon, 213

script-based behaviors, 386–389

search engines, meta tags, 421–423

Search for text window, 36

Select command (Table menu), 264–265

Select File dialog box, 262

Select Place in Document dialog box, 155

Select Style Sheet dialog box, 380

Send Backward button (Positioning toolbar), 204

server types, 425

Set Page Title dialog box, 40

Set Transparent Color button (Pictures toolbar), 199

shared borders
    adding, 77–78
    purpose of, 63

Shared Borders command (Format menu), 77

Shared Borders dialog box, 77

Show All icon (Standard toolbar), 104, 202

Show status bar option (Options dialog box), 27

Site Settings command (Tools menu), 358

Site Settings dialog box, 67, 353, 411

Site Summary report, 418

Size option (Horizontal Line Properties dialog box), 185

Size To Fit command, 61

sounds, adding to page background, 243

spacing
    images, 183
    text, 124

spell checking, text, 113–116

Spelling command (Tools menu), 113–114

Spelling dialog box, 113

Spelling icon (Standard toolbar), 113

Split Cells button (Tables toolbar), 270
Split Cells command (Table menu), 270
Split Cells dialog box, 270
Split Frame command (Frames menu), 315
Split Frame dialog box, 315
Split tab, 16
Split view, 19
splitting
    frames, 315
    table cells, 270
spreadsheets, author-time Web component, 244
Standard toolbar, 16–17, 24
Start button, 18
Startup Task Pane option (Options dialog
        box), 23
status bar, 16–17
structure, Web sites
    adding pages, 57
    controlling views, 59–61
    deleting page, 58
    rearranging, 54–56
Style command (Format menu), 367
Style dialog box, 94, 367, 374
Style option
    Horizontal Line Properties dialog box, 185
    Link Bar Properties dialog box, 66
Style Sheet Links command (Format menu), 379
Style toolbar, 26
subtrees
    rearranging Web sites, 56
    viewing, 60
Summary screen, 439
synchronizing files, Web publishing, 431
system requirements, 437

T

Table AutoFormat icon, 275
Table menu commands, 35
    Cell Formatting, 288
    Delete Cells, 269
    Distribute Columns Evenly, 272–273
    Distribute Rows Evenly, 272
    Draw Table, 258
    Insert, 259, 266
    Layout Tables and Cells, 280
    Merge Cells, 271

Table menu commands *(continued)*
    Select, 264–265
    Split Cells, 270
table of contents, 249–250
    author-time Web component, 244
Table of Contents link (Help), 36
Table of Contents Properties dialog box, 249
Table Properties dialog box, 274, 290
tables
    Autostretch, 6
    captions, 261
    cells, 264
        adding, 266
        colors, 278
        formatting, 276
        headers, 277
        merging, 271
        realignment, 279
        splitting, 270
    columns, 265
        distributing evenly, 273
    creating, 258
    deleting, 269
    Excel spreadsheets, 262–263
    formatting, 274–275
    images, 260
    inserting, 259
    layout table, 280–281
        adding cells, 284
        converting existing table to, 290
        deleting, 282–283
        formatting, 288–289
        formatting cells, 288–289
        resizing, 285–287
    rows, 265
        distributing evenly, 272
    text, 260
Tables toolbar, 26, 257, 258
tags (HTML), viewing, 129
Target Frame button (Insert Hyperlink dialog
        box), 147
Target Frame dialog box, 308, 311
target frames
    defaults, 310
    hyperlinks, 303
    options, 311
    setting, 308–309
Task command (View menu), 397

Task Details dialog box, 405, 416
Task Pane command (View menu), 22, 23
task panes, 22–23
    Clip Art, 172
tasks
    assigning, 404–407
    completing, 415–416
    creating, 394–397
    editing, 408–410
Tasks command (Edit menu), 397
Tasks view, 20–21
Teague, Jason Cranford, 364
templates
    attaching to pages, 87–88
    creating page, 80
    dynamic, 4
    dynamic Web site page, 83
    editable regions
        adding to dynamic template, 84–85
        removing from dynamic template, 86
    Web page creation, 38
    Web site creation, 45, 81–82
text
    adding paragraphs, 104
    adding to images, 189
    alignment, 122
    deleting, 100
    entering, 98–99
    finding
        across Web site, 106–107
        HTML code search, 108
        single page, 105
    formatting
        font, 118–121, 123–124
        removing, 125
    forms, 324–325
        validation options, 326
    images alternates, 178–179
    line break, 103
    moving, 101
    replacing
        across Web site, 111–112
        single page, 109–110
    selection shortcuts, 100
    spell checking, 113–116
    tables, 260
    themes, modifying, 94
    undo/redo actions, 102

Text Box Properties dialog box, 322
Text Box Validation dialog box, 326
text boxes, adding to forms, 322–323
Text button (Standard toolbar), 189
Text to display window (Insert Hyperlink dialog
        box), 147
TextArea Box Properties dialog box, 325
TGAs, 170
The Art and Science of Web Design, 11
The Non-Designer's Web Book, 11
Theme command (Format menu), 89
Theme dialog box, 89, 373
themes, 7, 89–90
    modifying, 91–92
    options, 93–94
3-D settings (Drawing toolbar), 221
thumbnails, images
    creating, 191
    photo gallery, 193–196
    properties, 192
TIFFs, 170
titles, Web pages, 52
Tollett, John, 11
toolbars, 24–27
    creating, 31
    customizing, 29–32
    deleting, 32
    rearranging, 27–28
Toolbars command (View menu), 27, 160, 209
Tools menu commands, 34
    Auto Thumbnail, 191
    Customize, 31
    Internet Options, 179
    Options, 23
    Page Options, 116, 192
    Site Settings, 358
    Spelling, 113–114
Top 10 List Properties dialog box, 255
top-down method, creating tasks, 394
Top Ten lists, browser-time component, 244

U

Underline icon (Formatting toolbar), 120
Undo command (Edit menu), 102
undo editing, images, 186
Undo icon, 102

Ungroup command (Drawing toolbar), 225
unordered lists, 133
User information screen, 438
User Meta Variable dialog box, 421
Usernames Master List dialog box, 404

V

validation, forms, 326
vector-based drawings, 207–208
Veen, Jeffrey, 11
Video dialog box, 238
videos
  inserting in pages, 238–240
  loop setting, 241
  previewing problems, 242
View menu commands, 20–21, 33
  Folder List, 21
  Hyperlinks, 167
  Navigation, 50
  Page, 98
  Recalculate Hyperlinks, 152
  Remote Web Site, 425, 432–433
  Reports, 401, 414
  Reveal Tags, 129
  Task, 397
  Task Pane, 22, 23
  Toolbars, 27, 160, 209
View Subtree Only command, 60
Viewing settings (status bar), 16–17
views
  hyperlinks, 166
  options, 19–21
  Page, 6
  Web site structure, 59–61
Visibility dialog box, 387
Vivid colors option (Theme dialog box), 90

W

Wash Out command (Color button), 190
washing out images, 190
Web browser, Viewing settings, 16–17
Web Component command (Insert menu),
    193, 263

Web components
  banner ad, 251–252
  hit counters, 253–254
  marquees, 246–248
  table of contents, 249–250
  Top Ten list, 255
  turning on or off, 244–245
Web pages. *See also* Web sites
  closing, 41
  creating, 37
    renaming, 53
    titling, 52
    within Web site structure, 50–51
  name, 16–17
  open existing, 39
  printing, 42
  rearranging Web site structure, 54–56
  saving, 40–41
  template, 38
  themes, 89–90
    modifying, 91–92
Web publishing
  adding meta tags, 421–423
  checking for errors, 418–419
  marking pages to publish, 420
  options, 432–433
  setting destination and options, 425–427
    files not to publish, 428
    publishing site, 429–431
Web site command (File menu), 43
Web Site tab, 21
Web Site Templates dialog box, 43–45, 81–82
Web site window options, 432–433
Web sites. *See also* Web pages
  closing, 46
  creating, 43–44, 49
  deleting, 47
  design considerations, 11–14
  dynamic template page, 83
  hyperlinks, 148
  link bars
    appearance, 66
    changing default labels, 67–68
    changing properties, 75–78
    creating, 64–65, 69–74
    purpose of, 62–63
  main window, 16–17
  open existing, 46

Web sites *(continued)*
  shared borders
    adding, 77–78
    purpose of, 63
  structure
    adding pages, 57
    controlling view, 59–61
    deleting page, 58
    rearranging, 54–56
  templates, 45, 81–82
    attaching to pages, 87–88
    creating page, 80
    dynamic, 4
    dynamic Web site page, 83
    editable regions, 84–86
  themes, 89–90
    modifying, 91–92
  wizard, 45
Web Style Guide: Basic Design Principles
    for Creating Web Sites, 11
Williams, Robin, 11
Window control buttons, 16–17
Window menu commands, 35
wizards
  Activation, 440
  Database Results, 348–352
  Form Page, 80
  Web sites, 45

WordArt, drawings, 216–218
WordArt Gallery dialog box, 216–218
WordArt toolbar, 25, 208, 216–218
workflow
  assigning tasks
    file assignments, 407
    names master list, 404
    reassignments, 406
    task assignment, 405
  checkout system
    activating, 411
    check in file, 413
    file checkout, 412
    listing checked-out files, 414
  completing tasks, 415–416
  creating tasks, 394–397
  editing tasks, 408–410
  organizing files, 398–403

X-Y-Z

XML, integration, 5
XML View toolbar, 26

Zoom command, 61